Washington DC

THE ROUGH G

There are more than one hundred and fifty Rough Guide titles
covering destinations from Amsterdam to Zimbabwe

Forthcoming titles include
Cuba • Dominican Republic • Las Vegas • Sardinia • Switzerland

Rough Guide Reference Series
Classical Music • Drum 'n' Bass • English Football • European Football
House • The Internet • Jazz • Music USA • Opera • Reggae
Rock Music • World Music

Rough Guide Phrasebooks
Czech • Dutch • European • Egyptian Arabic • French • German • Greek
Hindi & Urdu • Hungarian • Indonesian • Italian • Japanese
Mandarin Chinese • Mexican Spanish • Polish • Portuguese • Russian
Spanish • Swahili • Thai • Turkish • Vietnamese

Rough Guides on the Internet
www.roughguides.com

Rough Guide Credits

Text Editor:	Gavin Thomas
Series Editor:	Mark Ellingham
Editorial:	Martin Dunford, Jonathan Buckley, Jo Mead, Kate Berens, Amanda Tomlin, Ann-Marie Shaw, Paul Gray, Helena Smith, Kieran Falconer, Judith Bamber, Olivia Eccleshall, Orla Duane, Ruth Blackmore, Sophie Martin, Geoff Howard, Claire Saunders, Alexander Mark Rogers, Polly Thomas, Joe Staines, Lisa Nellis, Andrew Tomičíc (UK); Andrew Rosenberg, Mary Beth Maioli (US)
Online Editors:	Alan Spicer (UK); Kelly Cross (US)
Production:	Susanne Hillen, Andy Hilliard, Link Hall, Helen Ostick, Julia Bovis, Michelle Draycott, Anna Wray, Katie Pringle, Robert Evers
Picture Research:	Louise Boulton
Cartography:	Melissa Baker, Maxine Burke, Nichola Goodliffe, Ed Wright
Finance:	John Fisher, Gary Singh, Ed Downey
Marketing & Publicity:	Richard Trillo, Niki Smith, David Wearn, Jemima Broadbridge (UK); Jean-Marie Kelly, Myra Campolo, Simon Carloss (US)
Administration:	Tania Hummel, Charlotte Marriott, Demelza Dallow

Acknowledgements

Thanks to Gavin and all at Rough Guides for another excellent production. Special thanks to Katie who used her initiative: I couldn't write books – or do much else – without her. Also, thanks for ongoing support from friends and family – above all Sam and Greg, Ian and Linda, Jo, Mum and Dad, and Christine. Sadly, Capt. I. Little's brave underwater swim up the Potomac was, as ever, a glorious failure.

Thanks also to Helen Ostick and Judy Pang for typesetting, Silke Kerwick and Jason Clampet for research in Australia and North America, Margaret Doyle for proofreading and help with American-English usage, and cartographers Ed Wright and Melissa Baker for her huge efforts on the new colour maps.

The publishers and authors have done their best to ensure the accuracy and currency of all information in *The Rough Guide to Washington DC*; however, they can accept no responsibility for any loss, injury or inconvenience sustained by any traveller as a result of information or advice contained in the guide.

This second edition published November 1999 by Rough Guides Ltd, 62–70 Shorts Gardens, London WC2H 9AB. Previous edition published March 1997.

Distributed by the Penguin Group:
Penguin Books Ltd, 27 Wrights Lane, London W8 5TZ, UK.
Penguin Books USA Inc, 375 Hudson Street, New York 10014, USA.
Penguin Books Australia Ltd, 487 Maroondah Highway, PO Box 257, Ringwood, Victoria 3134, Australia.
Penguin Books Canada Ltd, 10 Alcorn Avenue, Toronto, Ontario, Canada M4V 1E4.
Penguin Books (NZ) Ltd, 182–190 Wairau Road, Auckland 10, New Zealand.

Printed in England by Clays Ltd, St Ives PLC
Typography and original design by Jonathan Dear and The Crowd Roars.
Illustrations throughout by Edward Briant.

© Jules Brown 1999

368pp. Includes index.

A catalogue record for this book is available from the British Library.

ISBN 1-85828-465-1

Washington DC

THE ROUGH GUIDE

Written and researched by
Jules Brown

THE ROUGH GUIDES

Help us update

We've gone to a lot of trouble to ensure that this second edition of *The Rough Guide to Washington DC* is completely up to date and accurate. However, things do change: hotels and restaurants come and go, opening hours are notoriously fickle, and prices are extremely volatile. We'd appreciate any suggestions, amendments or contributions for future editions of the guide. We'll credit all letters and send a copy of the next edition (or any other Rough Guide) for the best.

Please mark all letters "Rough Guide to Washington DC Update" and send to:
Rough Guides, 62–70 Shorts Gardens, London WC2H 9AB or
Rough Guides, 375 Hudson St, 3rd floor, New York NY 10014.

Email should be sent to:
mail@roughguides.co.uk

Online updates about Rough Guide titles can be found on our Web site at *www.roughguides.com*

The Author

Jules Brown first visited the United States in 1988. Apart from this book he has also written and researched Rough Guides to Scandinavia, Barcelona, England and Hong Kong, and contributed to guides on Portugal, Spain, the Pyrenees, Italy, and Malaysia and Singapore. He is a regular contributor to the *Daily Mail* travel pages and to various Fodor's publications.

Readers' letters

Rebeca Amboaje, John Paul Anderson, Philip Hearty, Heidy Huber, Rosalind M. Jarvis, Margaret Kelly, B.C. Plaister, N. Powell, Jason Rix, Margaret Roberts, Claire Tait.

Rough Guides

Travel Guides • Phrasebooks • Music and Reference Guides

We set out to do something different when the first Rough Guide was published in 1982. Mark Ellingham, just out of University, was traveling in Greece. He brought along the popular guides of the day, but found they were all lacking in some way. They were either strong on ruins and museums but went on for pages without mentioning a beach or taverna. Or they were so conscious of the need to save money that they lost sight of Greece's cultural and historical significance. Also, none of the books told him anything about Greece's contemporary life – its politics, its culture, its people, and how they lived.

So with no job in prospect, Mark decided to write his own guidebook, one which aimed to provide practical information that was second to none, detailing the best beaches and the hottest clubs and restaurants, while also giving hard-hitting accounts of every sight, both famous and obscure, and providing up-to-the-minute information on contemporary culture. It was a guide that encouraged independent travelers to find the best of Greece, and was a great success, getting shortlisted for the Thomas Cook travel guide award, and encouraging Mark, along with three friends, to expand the series.

The Rough Guide list grew rapidly and the letters flooded in, indicating a much broader readership than had been anticipated, but one which uniformly appreciated the Rough Guides' mix of practical detail and humor, irreverence and enthusiasm. Things haven't changed. The same four friends who began the series are still the caretakers of the Rough Guide mission today: to provide the most reliable, up-to-date and entertaining information to independent-minded travelers of all ages, on all budgets.

We now publish 150 titles and have offices in London and New York. The travel guides are written and researched by a dedicated team of more than 100 authors, based in Britain, Europe, the USA and Australia. We have also created a unique series of phrasebooks to accompany the travel series, along with the acclaimed series of music guides, and a best-selling pocket guide to the Internet and World Wide Web. We also publish comprehensive travel information on our Web site: *www.roughguides.com*

Contents

Part Four Contexts 329

List of Maps

MAP SYMBOLS

Symbol		Symbol	
(95)	Interstate	(i)	Tourist office
(1)	US Highway	🏛	Memorial
= = = =	Tunnel	⊙	Statue
———	Minor road	O	Hospital
■—■—	Railway	♰	Grave
———	Waterway	■	Building
– – –	Chapter division boundary	⊞	Church
✕	Airport	†₊†	Cemetery
M	Metro station	▨	Park

Introduction

s a nation's capital, **Washington DC** – showtown USA – takes some beating. Along its triumphant avenues stand historic buildings that define a world-view, while on either side of the central Mall sit the various museum buildings of the planet's greatest cultural collection, the Smithsonian Institution. For an introduction to America or a crash course in politics, portraiture or paleontology look no further than the spacious, well-ordered, Neoclassical sweep that is downtown DC.

Just don't expect Washington to fulfill any reasonable expectations of a living, breathing, warts-and-all American city. Born of compromise, it was built as an experiment, and in many ways continues as one – careering along in political turmoil, without repre-sentation, bankrupt, neglected, socially psychotic: a federal basket case. These attributes don't necessarily preclude a city from great-ness – look at New York – but in Washington's case, history and pol-

---

One of these days this will be a very great city if nothing happens to it.
Henry Adams, 1877

I went to Washington as everybody goes there, prepared to see every-thing done with some furtive intention, but I was disappointed – pleasantly disappointed.

Walt Whitman, 1888

Past a certain hour of the night, when all the good people have gone – or been chased – indoors, the nation's capital turns into a lifestyle sep-tic tank.

P.J. O'Rourke, *Parliament of Whores*, 1991

My home city of Washington has become a vast memorial to those dead in wars that have glorified the odd president [and] enriched the military industrial complex.

Gore Vidal, 1996

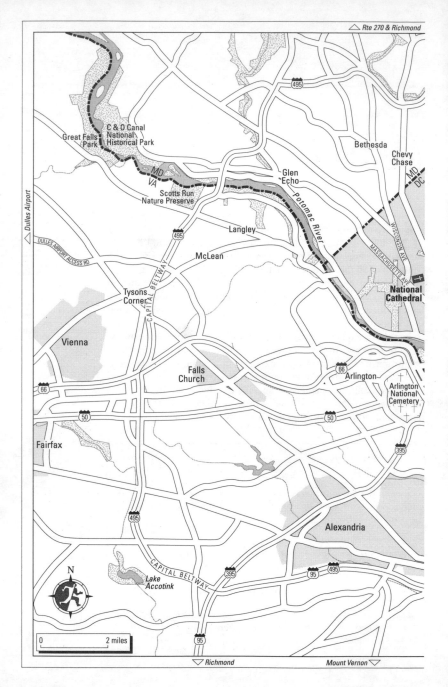

495

C & O Canal
National
Historical Park

Great Falls
Park

Bethesda

Chevy
Chase

MD
VA

Glen
Echo

MD
DC

Scotts Run
Nature Preserve

Dulles Airport

WISCONSIN AVE

Potomac River

DULLES AIRPORT ACCESS RD

495

Langley

MASSACHUSETTS AVE

McLean

CAPITAL BELTWAY

Tysons
Corner

National
Cathedral

Vienna

Falls
Church

66

Arlington

66

Arlington
National
Cemetery

50

50

Fairfax

395

495

Alexandria

N

CAPITAL BELTWAY

395

95

495

Lake
Accotink

0   2 miles

95

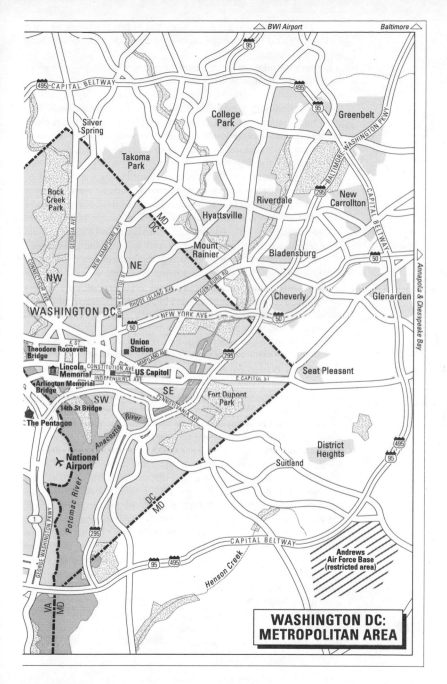

WASHINGTON DC:
METROPOLITAN AREA

itics have combined to produce a city full of fine buildings, soaring monuments and improving experiences but short on soul and long on contradictions.

Its very foundation – the result of political wrangle – proved a harbinger of what was to come. In the late eighteenth century, Congress acceded to the demands of the Northern states to assume their Revolutionary War debts, but squeezed a key concession for the South: rather than being sited in one of the big Northern cities the new federal capital would be built from scratch on the banks of the Potomac River, midway along the eastern seaboard. And while not actually *in* the Deep South, Washington – named for the republic's first president – in the Territory (later District) of Columbia, was very definitely *of* the South. French architect Pierre L'Enfant planned the city on a diamond-shaped piece of land donated by the tobacco-rich states of Virginia and Maryland; slave-labor drained the floodlands and erected the public buildings, and Virginian high society frequented the townhouses and salons which flourished after the government moved in during 1800. Capital of all America it may have been, but in its early years Washington rejoiced in its southern proclivities – bolstered by the fact that during the first fifty years of its existence, eight out of eleven presidents (and their entourage), between the administrations of John Adams and Zachary Taylor, were from the South.

But to paint DC as a Southern city is to miss the point. John F. Kennedy, a resident before he was president, famously pointed out its contradictions in his waspish comment that Washington was "a city of southern efficiency and northern charm". Even more important than its geographical character or location was its unique experimental nature – a modern, planned capital built for a disparate collection of states seeking security in unity. As a symbol of union, its finest hour came within a generation of its foundation when the city that was built largely by slaves became the frontline headquarters of the fight against slavery, as Abraham Lincoln directed the Union troops from the capital's halls and offices. With Virginia and the Confederate states only a river crossing away, DC was secure only when peace was at hand: relief was palpable in the unconfined joy of the victorious Union Army parade down Pennsylvania Avenue in May 1865. After the Civil War, thousands of Southern blacks arrived in search of a sanctuary from racist oppression: to some extent they found one. Racial segregation was banned in public places and Howard University, the only US institution of higher learning that enrolled black people, was set up in 1867. By the 1870s African-Americans made up over a third of the population, but economic resources were soon stretched to breaking point. As poverty and squalor worsened, official segregation was reintroduced in 1920, banning blacks from government buildings and the jobs they had come to find.

For much of this century, DC has been both a predominantly black city and a federal fortress. Shunned by the white political aristocracy, the city is run as a virtual colony of Congress, where residents have only non-voting representation and couldn't even participate in presidential elections until the 1970s. Suffering an endless cycle of boom and bust, the city has one of the country's highest crime rates, and appalling levels of unemployment, illiteracy and drug abuse – much bandied-about statistics usually dub it the nation's "murder and crack cocaine capital". Federal government money props up the city, pays its administrators and affects virtually every aspect of local commerce and industry – galling in the extreme to the majority of American citizens to whom Washington is a dirty word, inhabited only by self-seeking politicians isolated within the fabled Beltway, the ring road which circles the city and is used as a metaphor for all that's different about DC.

Meanwhile, twenty million visitors come to Washington each year for fun, making it one of the most visited destinations in the country. Kept away from the city's peripheral dead zones, they tour a scrubbed, policed and largely safe downtown swathe where famous landmark follows world-class museum with unending and uplifting regularity. Politics and power are the daily spectacle in the **White House, US Capitol** and **Supreme Court**, as well as the **FBI** and Arlington's military **Pentagon** building – all open to the general public. Overpowering **memorials and monuments** to George Washington, Abraham Lincoln, Thomas Jefferson, Franklin Delano Roosevelt and the Vietnam and Korean War veterans punctuate the magnificent showpiece Mall; the **National Gallery of Art** or any of the thirteen **Smithsonian** museums (and its zoo) hold collections unrivaled in their field; while just outside the city, **Arlington National Cemetery** – most famously, burial place of the Civil War dead and the Kennedys – and **Mount Vernon**, George Washington's birthplace, elevate DC to pilgrimage center. Even better, most of what you see in Washington is free, and getting around (on a subsidized transport system that has few equals in the United States) is easy.

True, a sense of community, or even neighborhood, is rare – especially downtown, where like in so many American cities the entire place falls strangely silent after 6pm and on weekends. But pockets of vitality do stand out, in historic Georgetown, arty Dupont Circle or trendy Adams-Morgan, where what nightlife there is shakes its fist at the otherwise conservative surroundings. You wouldn't necessarily choose to come shopping or clubbing in DC, but you'll eat well, from a bounty of different cuisines, and nowhere will you be better informed about what's happening in America. Pick up the paper, switch on the TV or radio, and tune in to the thousands of broadcasters, lobbyists, journalists and politicians who shape the views of the world from a medium-sized east coast city of glorious compromise and dubious future.

Climate

Before air conditioning Washington was deserted from mid-June to September . . . But [now] Congress sits and sits while the presidents – or at least their staffs – never stop making mischief.
Gore Vidal, *Armageddon: Essays 1983–1987*

The local climate isn't great, it has to be said – often unbearably hot and humid in summer and bitterly cold in winter. It's claimed, with some measure of truth, that such an inauspicious spot was picked precisely to discourage early elected leaders from making government a full-time job. The advent of widespread air-conditioning during the 1950s alleviated matters, though, and as long as you're suitably kitted out for venturing outdoors you'll encounter few periods when sightseeing becomes unpleasant. **Best times to visit** are spring, early summer and fall, when the weather is at its most benign; there's usually snow (occasionally severe) in January and February, while late summer (July and August) is too hot and humid. Whenever you come, bring suitable, comfortable shoes – there's a lot of walking to be done.

Washington DC Climate

	Jan	Feb	Mar	Apr	May	Jun	July	Aug	Sept	Oct	Nov	Dec
Average daily max temp (°F)	42	44	53	64	75	83	87	84	78	67	55	45
Average daily min temp (°F)	27	28	35	44	54	63	68	66	59	48	38	29
Average rainfall (in)	3.4	3	3.6	3.3	3.7	3.9	4.4	4.3	3.7	2.9	2.6	3.1

This book is dedicated to my parents, who, happily, show no signs of slowing down.

Basics

Getting there from North America

The easiest way to get to Washington DC from most parts of the US and Canada is to fly – competition on major routes keeps fares down, while advance-purchase tickets, discount fares and special deals offer further savings. Alternatively, Amtrak rail services allow a more leisurely – if scarcely less expensive – approach, while Greyhound and other bus companies cater to travelers on a budget.

By plane

Three **airports** serve the DC area – Reagan National, Dulles and Baltimore-Washington (BWI) – and competition is such that you'll find little difference between the major airlines' basic fares at any one time. Though there are no official **seasonal variations** for domestic flights, airfares do vary depending on the time, seat availability, and whether there's a price war going on. Traveling during the week tends to be cheaper than on the weekend, and you should book well in advance during the major holidays (Fourth of July, Christmas, Thanksgiving, and college spring break).

The cheapest option when dealing with the airlines direct is usually to buy an **advance-purchase** – sometimes known as **Apex** – ticket. These can come with a variety of restrictions, including having to travel at a certain time of day or on certain days of the week, or having to stay for a fixed length of time (usually including a Saturday night), tickets must be booked between 7 and 21 days in advance. Fares operate on a sliding scale, usually based on how far ahead you book.

Airlines

Air Canada	☎ 1-800/776-3000
www.aircanada.com	
AirTran	☎ 1-800/825-8538
www.airtran.com	
American Airlines	☎ 1-800/433-7300
www.aa.com	
Canadian Airlines	
	Canada ☎ 1-800/665-1177
	US ☎ 1-800/426-7000
www.cdnair.ca	
Continental	☎ 1-800/525-0280
www.continental.com	
Delta	☎ 1-800/221-1212
www.delta-air.com	
Northwest	US ☎ 1-800/374-7747
	Canada ☎ 1-800/361-5073
www.northwest-airlines.com	
Southwest	☎ 1-800/435-9792
www.southwest.com	
TWA	☎ 1-800/221-2000
www.twa.com	
United	☎ 1-800/241-6522
www.united-airlines.com	
US Airways	☎ 1-800/428-4322
www.usairways.com	

Discount Travel Companies

Council Travel
New York   ☎ 1-800/226-8624
www.counciltravel.com
plus branches in other US cities

New Frontiers/Nouvelles Frontières
New York   ☎ 1-800/366-6387
Montréal   ☎ 514/526-8444
www.new-frontiers.com
plus branches in Los Angeles, San Francisco
and Québec City

STA Travel
New York   ☎ 1-800/777-0112
www.sta-travel.com
plus branches in Los Angeles, San Francisco
and Boston

Travac Tours
New York   ☎ 1-800/872-8800
www.thetravelsite.com

Travel CUTS
Toronto   ☎ 1-416/979-2407
www.travelcuts.com
plus other branches all over Canada

Worldtek Travel
New Haven   ☎ 1-800/243-1723

Typical advance-purchase **fares** for flights to DC, booked fourteen days ahead, traveling midweek and staying one Saturday night, are around $140 from New York, $240 from Chicago, and $250 from Miami. Flights from the west coast are more liable to fluctuate – fares from LA, San Francisco or Seattle may occasionally fall as low as $360–400, but are more likely to be between $450 and $500. If you don't mind flying into Baltimore, check out Southwest's excellent deals: $118 from Chicago, $128 from Fort Lauderdale, and $310 from San Francisco. Although these fares are non-refundable, most airlines will allow you to change your plans for a fee of $50–75.

If you're traveling **from New York**, Delta and US Airways both offer an unreserved weekend fare from New York La Guardia to Washington Reagan National of $85 one-way, valid all day Saturday and on Sunday until 2.30pm, and an advance ticket (must be booked three days ahead) costing $55 one-way, valid all day Saturday and on Sunday until 11.30am. Both airlines also run hourly shuttles (7am–9pm) from La Guardia to Reagan National during the week at a one-way fare of $174 (US Airways) or $202 (Delta). Delta also has flights from New York JFK to Reagan National.

Look out for other **special deals** offered by the major airlines: these tend to be advertised in newspapers, often last only a few days, and may require booking months in advance. Many airlines now send weekly email bulletins featuring last-minute discounts of over fifty percent off their published fourteen-day advance-purchase fares. Bulletins usually go out at the beginning of the week and apply to the following weekend only. You can sign up for the service directly through the airlines' Web sites. If you're under 26 and have flexible travel plans, you might find that air-

---

Internet Discount Sellers

Magazines, virtual stores, news sites and most Web portals offer reservation systems either in-house or via links to other sites. The locations listed below are just a few of the Internet's many travel sites.

Airlines of the Web
www.flyaow.com
Online air travel info and reservation site with links to airlines' own pages.

Priceline
www.priceline.com (also ☎ 1-800/774-2354)
Finds unused seats based on general location and dates of your choosing. Enter a price and your credit card number and you'll be issued a non-refundable ticket.

TheTrip
www.thetrip.com
Caters to the business traveler's hotel, air and car needs.

Travelocity
www.travelocity.com
Ticket consolidator owned and operated by American Airlines' SABRE reservation system

lines can quote you an even cheaper **standby** rate. For overseas visitors traveling to DC from within the US, an **air pass** may offer considerable savings – see p.11 for details.

You'll save yourself a lot of time, stress, and maybe money, too, by checking out the **discount agents** listed opposite first. Some, like STA and Council Travel, specialize in youth/student fares, but even if you don't fit into that category, they'll do their best to find you the cheapest available flight – though this may not be by the most direct route, it will often offer considerable savings.

For details of flights **from Canada**, see p.7.

By train

Buoyed by business and government commuter traffic, the sprawling metropolitan area between Boston and Washington has of recent years had the most dependable **Amtrak** service in the country (☎1-800/872-7245, www.amtrak.com). Amtrak's new high-speed system, Acela features a new all-electric line which will reduce the travel time between New York and Washington to just two and a half hours. If you're traveling from downtown New York City or points south this is probably the most convenient way of reaching Washington, not least because it will drop you right in the middle of town.

Fares on Amtrak services to Washington from cities **outside the northeast** are comparable to or higher than the equivalent airfare, and if you want any extras (like a sleeping compartment) you'll have to pay a good deal more than the prices quoted in the box on this page. To make the three day rail journey from Los Angeles in relative comfort, for instance, will cost you over $1000 round-trip with an economy sleeper bed. In general, rail travel is not really a budget option, although some of the journeys are pleasant enough – the Silver Star, which travels from Miami through Georgia, the Carolinas and Virginia to DC, in particular, makes for a rewarding 22-hour trip.

If you plan on using Amtrak one-way only, they have an arrangement with United Airlines that allows you to fly one leg and travel the other by rail (**AirRail** ☎1-800/437-3441). You could also bring your own car with you using the **Auto Train Superliner**, which runs from Sanford, FL (near Orlando) to Lorton, VA, just an hour south of Washington. The price of transporting the car each way is $185, plus an additional $173 per person.

> **Sample Rail Fares to DC**
>
> The following round-trip fares are based on ticket purchase two weeks in advance of travel. Prices in the northeast corridor are often twice as high for the all-reserved Metroliner service than the fares given below.
>
> **From Boston** (9hr): $63 each way
>
> **From Chicago** (17hr 20min): $113 each way
>
> **From Miami** (22hr): $147 each way
>
> **From New York** (3hr–3hr 30min): $60 each way
>
> **From Los Angeles** (3 days): $242 each way

If Washington is part of a longer itinerary, Amtrak and VIA's (Canada's national rail company) **North American Rail Pass** allows thirty days' unlimited travel for $645/CND$895 high season (June to mid-Oct) and $450/CND$625 low season (mid-Oct to May).

Seasonal special offers for two or more people traveling together turn up quite often. It's easiest to check these through the Amtrak Web site – which also offers a booking service – or by phone. Amtrak also organizes packages to DC; see p.7.

By bus

Buses are cheaper and more frequent than the train, but they do take forever and, in a worst-case scenario, you may need to use one of those toilets. The chief operator to DC is **Greyhound** (☎1-800/231-2222, www.greyhound.com); in addition, the **Peter Pan** company (☎1-800/343-

> **Sample Greyhound Fares to DC**
>
> The following are standard weekday fares: you'll pay a bit more if you travel between Friday and Sunday. Regular tickets allow three stopovers, and some have a fifteen percent cancellation fee.
>
> **From Chicago** (18hr): $78 one-way, $152 round-trip
>
> **From Dallas** (22hr): $108 one-way, $209 round-trip
>
> **From Boston** (9hr 20min): $52 one-way, $98 round-trip
>
> **From Los Angeles** (3 days): $125 one-way, $209 round-trip

9999, *www.peterpan-bus.com*) runs services to Washington from New York, Philadelphia and Boston.

The **Greyhound Ameripass** gives unlimited travel on the Greyhound network for $199 (7 days), $299 (15 days), $409 (30 days) and $599 (60 days), half that for accompanying children. All passes are non-refundable and are only really worthwhile for domestic travelers including DC as part of a longer itinerary, or for those coming from the West Coast. For details of bus pass deals available to overseas travelers, see the box on p.11.

By car

Renting a car to get to DC gives you freedom and flexibility, but will be of little use in the city itself (see p.45). Rates vary wildly, though in general you'll get better deals over the weekend than during the week. The **lowest rates** are usually available at airports, where an economy class car usually costs around $200 per week. When booking, check any discounts from airlines, credit cards and the like that you might qualify for, be sure to get free unlimited mileage, and be aware that prices can go up by as much as $200 if you want to pick the car up in one location and leave it at another. Always read the small print carefully for details on Collision Damage Waiver (sometimes called Liability Damage Waiver), a form of insurance which often isn't included in the initial rental charge but is well worth having. This specifically covers the car you are driving (you are in any case insured for damage to other vehicles). At $10–15 a day, Collision Damage Waiver

---

Driving to DC

From Chicago: 16hr (710 miles)

From Miami: 24hr (1057 miles)

From Montréal: 14hr (610 miles)

From New York: 5hr 30min (240 miles)

From San Francisco: 3 days (2845 miles)

From Toronto: 12hr (570 miles)

---

can add substantially to the total cost, but without it you're liable for every scratch to the car – even those that aren't your fault. Then again, don't be suckered into insurance you already have – call your credit card company to see if they offer free insurance if you use your card to pay. If you are **under 25** be prepared for hefty surcharges of as much as $20–40 a day, depending on the company.

One option worth considering is a **driveaway**, whereby you drive a car from one place to another on behalf of the owner, paying only for the gas you use – look in the Yellow Pages under "Automobile Transporters" and "Drive-Away Companies". You must be 21 or older and may be asked to prove you have a "good" driving record (US citizens can obtain one from their state police). The deposit, refundable on delivery, can vary from $200 to $500 and may depend on the age of the driver. Some companies will only accept cash or travelers checks. Note that you might be expected to average as much as 400 miles a day.

Car Rental Companies

Alamo *www.freeways.com*	☎ 1-800/354-2322	**Hertz** *www.hertz.com*	☎ 1-800/654-3131
Avis *www.avis.com*	☎ 1-800/331-1212	**Holiday Autos**	☎ 1-800/422-7737
Budget *www.budgetrentacar.com*	☎ 1-800/527-0700	**National** *www.nationalcar.com*	☎ 1-800/227-7368
Dollar *www.dollar.com*	☎ 1-800/421-6868	**Rent-A-Wreck** *www.rentawreck.com*	☎ 1-800/535-1391
Enterprise *www.enterprise.com*	☎ 1-800/566-9249	**Thrifty** *www.thrifty.com*	☎ 1-800/367-2277

Most agencies in DC have offices at Reagan National, Dulles and BWI airports and at Union Station. For associated car rental companies in foreign countries, see p.10 (Britain), p.10 (Ireland), and p.14 (Australia and New Zealand).

Specialist Operators

American Adventures
☎ 1-800/864-0335
Camping and youth hostel trips featuring DC as part of longer tours swinging south from Cape Cod.

Amtrak Great American Vacations
☎ 1-800/250-4989; *www.amtrak.com*
Train trips through the northeast.

Collette Tours
☎ 1-800/832-4656
All-inclusive packages from the west coast and midwest including three- or four-night tours staying in four-star hotels.

Contiki Tours
☎ 1-800/266-8454; *www.contiki.com*
Trips for the 18–35 crowd; their seven-day Eastern Discovery tour includes DC.

Continental Vacations
☎ 1-800/634-5555
Packages including hotel, flight and guided tours.

Delta Dream Vacations
☎ 1-800/872-7786
Packages including five-star hotel, flight and guided tours.

Globus/Cosmos
☎ 1-800/221-0090
Seven-day tour of New York, Pennsylvania Dutch Country, Niagara Falls and Washington.

Saga Holidays
☎ 1-800/343-0273
Catering mostly to the over-50s, with stays in four-star hotels and evenings at the Kennedy Center. Regional tours available too.

Trek America
☎ 1-800/221-0596
Youth-oriented tours including DC as part of larger tours of the region.

Tours

Package deals with airlines and hotels offer excellent **weekend get-away packages**, with deep discounts at some of DC's pricier hotels. For **specialist tours**, prices depend on when you go and what you want to do. For contact details, **see** the box above.

From Canada

Of the major airlines, only US Airways and Air Canada have **direct flights** to DC (from Toronto and Montréal). Although US Airways has the edge on special deals, Air Canada offers better standard fares, with four daily direct flights from Toronto (CDN$600) and Montréal (CDN$650). Their cheapest fare from Vancouver (via Toronto) is CDN$1370. (Fares quoted are fourteen-day advance round-trip including one Saturday night.)

You can also get to DC from Canada by **bus**: Greyhound's Montréal–DC fare is CDN$94 one way/CDN$135 round-trip, with a travel time of between thirteen and sixteen hours. From Toronto it's CDN$73/CDN$125 and takes nineteen to twenty hours. For a more leisurely trip, **Amtrak** has services from Toronto (via Niagara Falls, upstate New York and New York City), and Montréal (via New England). For more details on Amtrak, see box above and p.5.

Getting there from Britain and Ireland

It's not quite as cheap yet to fly to DC as it is to New York, so whatever kind of travel deal you're looking for – flight-only, fly-drive or package – it pays to shop around for the best offers. Calling a specialist flight agent or tour operator can give you an overview of the available options, while competition is such that it's always worth phoning the airlines direct to check on current deals. Other useful resources include the travel ads in the weekend papers and, in London, *Time Out* and the *Evening Standard*.

AIRLINES

Air Canada	☎ 0990/247 226	KLM	☎ 0990/750 9000
Air France	☎ 0181/742 6600	Lufthansa	☎ 0345/737 747
American Airlines	☎ 0345/789 789	Northwest	☎ 0990/561 000
British Airways	☎ 0345/222 111	TWA	☎ 0345/333 333
Continental	☎ 0800/776 464	United Airlines	☎ 0845/844 4777
Delta	☎ 0800/414 767	US Airways	☎ 0800/783 5556
Icelandair	☎ 0171/388 5599	Virgin Atlantic	☎ 01293/747 747

DISCOUNT FLIGHT AGENTS

Alpha Flights	☎ 0171/209 2819	Trailfinders	
APA Travel	☎ 0171/387 5337	London	☎ 0171/938 3366
Council Travel	☎ 0171/437 7767	Birmingham	☎ 0121/236 1234
		Bristol	☎ 0117/929 9000
Destination Group	☎ 0171/400 7000	Glasgow	☎ 0141/353 2224
Flightbookers	☎ 0171/757 2000	Manchester	☎ 0161/839 6969
North South Travel	☎ 01245/492 882	Travel Bug	☎ 0161/721 4000
Nouvelles Frontières	☎ 0171/629 7772	Union Travel	☎ 0171/493 4343
STA Travel		Usit Campus	
		London	☎ 0171/730 2101
Bristol	☎ 0117/929 4399	Birmingham	☎ 0121/414 1848
Cambridge	☎ 01223/366 966	Brighton	☎ 01273/570 226
Manchester	☎ 0161/834 0668	Bristol	☎ 0117/929 2494
Leeds	☎ 0113/244 9212	Cambridge	☎ 01223/324 283
London	☎ 0171/361 6262	Edinburgh	☎ 0131/668 3303
Newcastle	☎ 0191/233 2111	Manchester	☎ 0161/273 1721
Oxford	☎ 01865/792 800	Oxford	☎ 01865/242 067

Overseas visitors can buy **train, bus and air passes** for travel throughout the United States. These usually have to be bought in advance of your trip; for more details, see p.11.

Flights from London

There are **non-stop flights** to Washington DC from London Heathrow with United Airlines, British Airways and Virgin Atlantic; these take around seven hours, though following winds ensure that return flights are always an hour or so shorter than outward journeys. Flights out usually leave Britain mid-morning, while flights back from the US tend to arrive in Britain early in the morning. All other airlines serving DC fly via their respective American or European hubs, taking an extra two to three hours each way. The only direct services are from London – coming from UK regional airports, you'll need to allow for the extra cost of the connection to London, typically under £100 round-trip.

Fares vary widely according to whether the flight is direct or not, as well as according to season, availability and the current level of inter-airline competition. They're most expensive during high season, which runs roughly between June and August and around Easter and Christmas; May and September/October are slightly less pricey (shoulder season), and the rest of the year is considered low season and is cheaper still. **Weekend rates** for all round-trip flights tend to be around £30 more expensive than those in the week, and remember to add £25–35 **airport tax**, whenever you travel.

Conditions and restrictions on the cheapest **economy fares** (given different names by different airlines) are fairly standard. Seats must usually be purchased between 7 and 28 days in advance, depending on the airline, and you must stay at least one Saturday night. Tickets are normally valid for between one and six months and are not usually refundable or changeable. The cheapest round-trip fares to Washington DC (booking at least 21–28 days in advance, staying minimum one week, maximum one month) currently cost around £420 (high season), dropping to £320 (shoulder) and as little as £200 in low season. More flexible tickets requiring less advance booking time cost around £100 more whenever you buy. If you're under 26 or a student, an **agent** specializing in low-cost flights (like Usit Campus or STA; see opposite) may be able to undercut the regular fares, bringing low-season prices to DC down to around £180 round-trip.

International flights to DC use Dulles airport, though if availability is tight or Dulles flights are inconvenient for any reason, it's also worth checking fares to **Baltimore** (BWI), which is just an hour from downtown DC. With an **open-jaw** ticket you can fly into one city (DC) and out of another (say New York). Fares are calculated by halving the round-trip fares to each destination and adding the two figures together. This is a convenient option for those who want a fly-drive holiday (see "Package and fly-drive holidays" below).

For details on how to reach downtown DC from the various airports, see "Introducing the City", p.31.

Package and fly-drive holidays

Typically, a summer **city break** – round-trip flight plus three-star (room-only) accommodation for three nights in Washington DC – costs from around £399–489 per person, perhaps £100 more in a five-star hotel; prices drop between £50

Specialist Holiday Operators in the UK

AmeriCan Adventures	☎01892/511 894	**Northwest Flydrive**	☎01424/224 400
Bon Voyage	☎01703/330 332	**Premier Holidays**	☎01223/516 516
British Airways Holidays	☎0870/242 4243	**Trans Atlantic Vacations**	☎01293/774 441
Destination USA	☎0171/400 7000	**Travel 4**	☎0541/550 066
First Choice	☎0161/745 7000	**Travelscene**	☎0181/427 4445
Key to America	☎01784/248 777	**TrekAmerica**	☎01295/256 777
North America Travel Service		**Unijet**	☎0990/336 336
	☎0113/243 2525	**Virgin Holidays**	☎01293/617 181

Car Rental Companies in the UK	
Alamo	☎ 0990/994 000
Avis	☎ 0990/900 500
Budget	☎ 0800/181 181
Direct Car Hire	☎ 0800/328 5634
National Car Rental	☎ 0990/365 365
Hertz	☎ 0990/996 699
Holiday Autos	☎ 0990/300 400

and £100 in low season. Good first contacts for city breaks are companies like First Choice, Key to America, North America Travel Service, Premier Holidays, Travel 4, and Travelscene. Most of the specialist operators listed on p.9 can arrange tailor-made holidays of a week or more, using DC as a base to visit nearby Civil and Revolutionary War sites; others include two or three days in DC as part of a longer American tour, camping holiday or adventure trip. Obviously, these are considerably more expensive (and prices vary wildly according to what's being offered), but the DC element of

USEFUL ADDRESSES AND CONTACTS IN IRELAND

Airlines

Aer Lingus		**Delta**	
Belfast	☎ 0645/737 747	Belfast	☎ 01232/480 526
Cork	☎ 021/327 155	Dublin	☎ 1-800/414 767
Dublin	☎ 01/844 4777	**United Airlines**	
Limerick	☎ 061/474 239	Dublin	☎ 1-800/535 300
British Airways			
Belfast	☎ 0345/222 111	**Virgin Atlantic**	
Dublin	☎ 0141/222 2345	Dublin	☎ 01/873 3388

Car Rental Agencies

Avis		**Hertz**	
Eire	☎ 01/874 5844	Eire	☎ 01/676 7476
Northern Ireland	☎ 0990/900 500	Northern Ireland	☎ 0990/996 699
Budget		**Holiday Autos**	
Eire	☎ 0800/973 159	Eire	☎ 01/872 9366
Northern Ireland	☎ 0800/181 181	Northern Ireland	☎ 0990/300 400

Discount Flight Agents and Tour Operators

American Holidays		**Trailfinders**	
Belfast	☎ 01232/238 762	Dublin	☎ 01/677 7888
Dublin	☎ 01/679 8800	**Twohigs**	
Apex Travel		Dublin	☎ 01/677 2666
Dublin	☎ 01/671 5933	**Usit Campus**	
Flight Finders International		Belfast	☎ 01232/324 073
Dublin	☎ 01/676 8326	Cork	☎ 021/270 900
Joe Walsh Tours		Derry	☎ 01504/371 888
Cork	☎ 021/277 959	Dublin	☎ 01/602 1700
Dublin	☎ 01/676 3053	Galway	☎ 091/565 177
Student & Group Travel		Limerick	☎ 061/415 064
Dublin	☎ 01/677 7834	Waterford	☎ 051/872 601
Thomas Cook		**World Travel Centre**	
Belfast	☎ 01232/550 232	Dublin	☎ 01/671 7155
Dublin	☎ 01/677 0469		

TRAVEL PASSES FOR OVERSEAS VISITORS

Overseas visitors traveling around the US have a choice of **train, bus and air passes**, which must usually be bought in advance of their trip.

They're of little use if you plan simply to visit Washington DC, but if the city forms part of a longer trip you may find them worthwhile.

Amtrak Rail Passes

The most useful Amtrak/VIA rail pass for Washington is the **15-Day Northeastern North America Rail Pass**. For this pass, "northeast" is defined as the areas east from Chicago to Halifax and north from Newport News, VA, to Jonquiere in Canada, but your trip must include travel in both countries. During July and August, a pass valid for fifteen days costs $400/CDN$555; the rest of the year, $300/CDN$416. In the UK, pass-es are available from specialist holiday operators (see p.9) or Destination Marketing (☎0171/978 5212); in Ireland, contact Usit Campus (see p.10). In Australia, contact Canada & America Travel Specialists, Sydney (☎02/9922 4600) or Rail Plus, Melbourne (☎03/9642 8644 or 1300/555003). In New Zealand, contact Walshes World, Auckland (☎09/379 3708) or Thomas Cook (☎09/379 3902).

Greyhound Ameripasses

The **Greyhound Ameripass** offers unlimited bus travel within a set time limit (4–60 days; £70–930). It is only available before leaving home: most travel agents can oblige. In the UK, Greyhound's office is at Sussex House, London Rd, East Grinstead, West Sussex RH19 1LD (☎01342/317317). In Australia, the pass is available from Canada & America Travel Specialists, Sydney (☎02/9922 4600); in New Zealand from Greyhound International, Auckland (☎09/479-6555). Your pass will be dated by the ticket clerk the first time you use it; this becomes the starting date of the ticket.

Air Passes

All the main American airlines offer **air passes** for travel within the US: these have to be bought in advance, and are usually sold with the proviso that you reach the US with the same airline. All the deals are broadly similar, involving the purchase of at least three coupons (costing around US$300–350 for the first three coupons, US$50–75 for each additional one), each valid for a flight of any duration within the US.

---

the trip makes a suitably monumental start or finish to an American holiday. As tour and holiday details change from time to time, it's worth calling the operators listed to request brochures to see exactly what's on offer.

You won't need a car in Washington DC, but if you plan to see more of the country, **fly-drive** deals – which give cut-rate (sometimes free) car rental when buying a transatlantic ticket from an airline or tour operator – are always cheaper than renting on the spot. Most of the companies listed in the "Specialist holiday operators" box on p.9 offer fly-drive packages, though watch out for hidden extras, such as local taxes, "drop-off" charges and extra insurance, and note that you'll probably have to pay more for the flight than if you booked it through a discount agent.

You can also save up to sixty percent by booking **car rental** in advance with a major firm which has representation in Washington DC (see the list of rental companies opposite). If you choose not to pay until you arrive, take a written confirmation of the price with you. If you need to arrange car rental once you're **in Washington**, see p.6, while for the hideous intricacies of driving in DC itself, see p.45.

Flights from Ireland

There are no non-stop flights from Ireland to Washington DC, though Delta and Aer Lingus offer services from **Dublin via New York**, which take between nine and eleven hours. Other airlines (like BA, Virgin Atlantic and United) will **route** you through London. Prices are similar on either route. Alternatively, you could arrange your own discount Dublin/Belfast–London flight and pick up an onward service from there – see "Flights from London" p.9. Fares from Dublin to DC are around IR£420 (low season), IR£500–700 (high season); a tax of IR£25 is added to all flights. You can call the airlines direct, but it's best to deal with a **discount agent** specializing in low-cost flights – see the list on p.10. If you're **under 26**

or a **student**, contact Usit Campus or Student & Group Travel for the most competitive fares.

For information about **package holidays** and city breaks, call any of the high-street travel agents. These (as well as the discount agents listed on p.10) can also advise about **fly-drive** deals; to compare prices, call one of the car rental agencies in Ireland with representation in DC (also listed on p.10). For more details, see "Fly-drive holidays" on p.9, and also p.11.

Getting there from Australia and New Zealand

There are no direct scheduled flights to Washington DC from either Australia or New Zealand. The quickest way to reach DC is by flying via Los Angeles with Qantas or United Airlines. Alternatively, there are indirect flights on a number of carriers to the west coast of the US, from where onward travel to DC is easily arranged. Specialist agents can help sort out all the routes; several of the best are listed on p.13. Flight Centres and STA Travel generally have the best discounts.

Flights

Qantas and United Airlines have **daily flights** to DC via Los Angeles from Sydney, Melbourne and

Auckland (United also has services via San Francisco), while Korean Airlines flies several times a week to Washington from Sydney, Brisbane and Auckland via Seoul. Alternatively, you can pick up a cheaper flight to the west coast (usually LA) and then either buy an add-on fare to Washington (around A$470/NZ$550; it's cheaper using an air pass – see p.11), or by traveling overland.

The high season for air **fares** to the US runs from mid-December to mid-January; low season is February to March, June, and mid-October to the end of November; shoulder season is at all other times. Fares to DC on major airlines like United Airlines and Qantas run from A$2230/NZ$2750 (low season) to A$2930/NZ$3200 (high), roughly the same as a "Round-the-World" ticket (see p.13). Korean Airlines' flight to DC with an overnight stopover in Seoul is the cheapest available, costing around A$1790/NZ$2100 (low season), A$1990/NZ$2300 (high). The cheapest fares to the west coast are with Air New Zealand (A$1600/NZ$1800 low season, A$1950/NZ$2100 high), with one or two stops at various Pacific islands, or you can travel via Asia with Malaysia Airlines, Cathay Pacific, Thai Airways and Japan Airlines, although these fares are more expensive (A$1800–2060/NZ$2100–2350). Canadian Airlines flies to LA via Vancouver from Sydney (A$2000–$2100/

AIRLINES

Air New Zealand
Sydney ☎ 02/9223 4666 or 13/2476
Auckland ☎ 09/366 2803

American Airlines
Sydney ☎ 1300/650 747
Auckland ☎ 09/309 9159 or 0800/887997

Cathay Pacific
Sydney ☎ 02/9931 5500 or 13/1747
Auckland ☎ 09/379 0861

Delta
Sydney ☎ 02/9251 3211 or 1800/128 510
Auckland ☎ 09/379 3370

Japan Airlines
Sydney ☎ 02/9272 1111
Auckland ☎ 09/379 9906

Korean Airlines
Sydney ☎ 02/9262 6000
Auckland ☎ 09/307 3687

Malaysia Airlines
Sydney ☎ 13/2627
Auckland ☎ 09/373 2741

Qantas
Sydney ☎ 13/1313
Auckland ☎ 09/357 8900 or 0800/808 767

Thai Airways
Sydney ☎ 02/9844 0999 or 1300/651 960
Auckland ☎ 09/377 3886

United Airlines
Sydney ☎ 02/9237 8888 or 13/1777
Auckland ☎ 09/379 3800

DISCOUNT TRAVEL AGENTS

Anywhere Travel
Sydney ☎ 02/0663 0411

Budget Travel
Auckland ☎ 09/366 0061 or 0800/808040

Destinations Unlimited
Auckland ☎ 09/373 4033

Flight Centres
Sydney ☎ 02/9241 2422
Melbourne ☎ 03/9650 2899
Brisbane ☎ 07/3229 9211
Auckland ☎ 09/209 6171
Christchurch ☎ 03/379 7145
Wellington ☎ 04/472 8101
Australia-wide ☎ 13/1600 or 13/3133 (after hours), plus other branches countrywide
Web site: *www.flightcentre.com*

Passport Travel
Malvern ☎ 03/9867 3888

STA Travel
Sydney ☎ 02/9212 1255
Melbourne ☎ 03/9654 7266
Auckland ☎ 09/309 0458
Christchurch ☎ 03/379 9098

Wellington ☎ 04/385 0561
Australia: telesales ☎ 1300/360 960
Australia: nearest branch ☎ 13/1776
plus other branches countrywide
Web site: *www.statravelaus.com.au*

Status Travel
Darwin ☎ 08/8941 1843

Student Uni Travel
Sydney ☎ 02/9232 8444
plus branches in state capitals

Thomas Cook
Sydney ☎ 02/9248 6100
Melbourne ☎ 03/9650 2442
Auckland ☎ 09/849 2071
Australia: telesales ☎ 1800/063 913
Australia: nearest branch ☎ 13/1771

Topdeck Travel
Adelaide ☎ 08/8232 7222

Trailfinders
Sydney ☎ 02/9247 7666

Travel.com (The Travel Specialists)
Sydney ☎ 02/9290 1500
Web site: *www.travel.com.au*

NZ$2300–2400). Departures vary, but all carriers have several flights each week.

Round-the-World fares, with four to six stopovers worldwide (including DC) cost around A$2000–3000/NZ$2700–3300 depending on the season, mileage and zones covered. The best deals are with the One World consortium (book-able through Qantas); routings are offered on a zoned (A$2000–3100/NZ$2700–3700) or mileage (A$2500–$3000/NZ$3090–3550) basis. The Star Alliance (bookable through Ansett or Air New Zealand) has mileage-based fares (A$2699–3209/NZ$3000–3500). Call any of the agents or airlines in box above for more information.

Packages, passes and car rental

Several agencies organize **package holiday tours** which include DC, from city breaks and tours of historical and Civil War sites to longer overland camping trips; some of the best operators are listed in the box below. If you're planning a longer

Package Tour Operators	
Adventure World	
Sydney	☎ 02/9956 7766
Brisbane	☎ 07/3229 0599
Perth	☎ 08/9221 2300
Auckland	☎ 09/524 5118
Creative Holidays	
Sydney	☎ 02/9386 2111
Drive-A-Rama	
Hurstville NSW	☎ 02/9580 6555
	or 1800/251 354
Wiltrans/Maupintour	
Sydney	☎ 02/9255 0899

Car Rental Agencies	
Australia	
Avis	☎ 1800/225 533
Budget	☎ 13/2848 or 1300/ 362 848
Hertz	☎ 13/3039 or 1800/550 067
New Zealand	
Avis	☎ 09/526 2847
Budget	☎ 09/256 8690 or 09/367 6350
Hertz	☎ 09/309 0989

trip in the US, you may also want to check prices for **rail and bus passes** (see p.11), which are available in Australia and New Zealand before you leave. **Car rental** can also be arranged in advance, either by calling one of the major rental companies with representatives in DC (listed above) or by buying a fly-drive holiday from one of the specialist operators listed opposite. For more on driving in the US and DC, see p.6, p.25, and p.45.

Insurance

Insurance in the US and Canada

Before purchasing **travel insurance**, US residents should check that they are not already covered by their existing insurance – some home-owners'

policies are valid on vacation, and credit cards such as American Express often include some medical or other insurance if you use them to buy your ticket, while most Canadians are covered for medical mishaps overseas by their provincial healthcare plans. If you aren't already covered, consider taking out specialist travel insurance. Reasonably priced deals include those offered by Access America (☎ 1-800/284-8300), whose policy, valid up to thirty days, covers trip cancellation, life, emergency medical and dental, medical evacuation, lost or stolen baggage, baggage and travel delay and default protection (in case your airline or travel agent goes broke). For a trip up to thirty days and costing under $500, the policy is $42; for a trip costing up to $1000, $58. Extensions over thirty days are available at $2.50 a day. Travel Guard's (☎ 1-800/826-1300) similar package for a trip up to thirty days costing up to $500 is $45, up to $1000 it's $75, with extra days for both available at $5 a day. Children under sixteen traveling with an insured adult are covered at no extra charge.

Insurance in Britain and Ireland

Though not compulsory, **travel insurance** including medical cover is *essential* in view of the high costs of health care in the US. Policies are fairly standard, and generally include around £1m medical insturance. Credit cards (particularly American Express) often have certain levels of medical or other insurance included, especially if you use them to pay for your trip. In addition, if you have a good "all risks" home insurance policy it may well cover your possessions against loss or theft even when overseas, and many private medical schemes also cover you while abroad. Note that if you're visiting Washington DC as part of a wider American trip and are also planning to do some watersports or skiing, you'll almost certainly have to pay an extra premium. Check carefully that your policy will cover you in case of an accident. Most travel agents and tour operators will offer you travel insurance – those policies offered by Usit Campus or STA in the UK and Usit Campus in Ireland are usually reasonable value. If you feel the cover is inadequate, or you want to compare prices, any insurance broker, bank or specialist travel insurance company should be able to help: try Columbus Travel Insurance (☎0171/375 0011); Worldwide (☎01892/833 338) or Endsleigh Insurance (☎0171/436 4451). Cover for a two-week trip to the US should cost around £45, a month around £54.

Insurance in Australia and New Zealand

Travel insurance in **Australia and New Zealand** is put together by the airlines and travel agent groups such as United Travel Agents Group (UTAG; ☎1800/809 462), Australian Federation of Travel Agents (AFTA; ☎02/9264 3299), Cover-More (☎02/9202 8000 or 1800/251 881) and Ready Plan (☎1300/555 017) in conjunction with insurance companies. All have similar premiums and coverage. A typical policy for the US costs from A$160–190/NZ$200–220 for one month, A$320/NZ$400 for three months. Contact STA or any Flight Centres (see p.13) for details.

Visas, work and study

Under the **Visa Waiver Scheme**, if you're a citizen of the UK, Ireland, Australia, New Zealand or most western European countries (check with your nearest US embassy or consulate) and visiting the United States for a period of less than ninety days, you only need an onward or return ticket, a full passport and a visa waiver form. The latter (an I-94W) will be provided either by your travel agency, or by the airline during check-in or on the plane, and must be presented to immigration on arrival. The same form covers entry across the land borders with Canada and Mexico.

Prospective visitors from other parts of the world not mentioned above require a valid passport and a **non-immigrant visitor's visa** for a maximum ninety-day stay. For a brief excursion into the US, **Canadian citizens** do not necessarily need even a passport, just some form of ID, though for a longer trip you should carry a passport, and if you plan to stay for more than ninety days you need a visa too. If you cross into the

US Embassies and Consulates

Australia
Moonah Place, Yarralumla,
Canberra, ACT 2600 ☎ 02/6214 5600

Britain
24 Grosvenor Square,
London W1A 1AE ☎ 0171/499 9000

24hr visa hotline ☎ 09068/200 290

3 Regent Terrace,
Edinburgh EH7 5BW ☎ 0131/556 8315

Canada
100 Wellington St,
Ottawa, ON K1P 5T1 ☎ 613/238 5335

Ireland
Queens House, 14 Queen St,
Belfast BT1 6EQ ☎ 01232/328 239

42 Elgin Rd,
Ballsbridge, Dublin ☎ 01/668 7122

New Zealand
29 Fitzherbert Terrace,
Thorndon, Wellington ☎ 04/472 2068

For details of foreign embassies and consulates in Washington DC, see p.326.

States by car, your vehicle is subject to spot searches by US Customs personnel. Remember, too, that Canadians are legally barred from seeking gainful employment in the US.

How you **obtain a visa** depends on what country you're in and your status on application, so telephone your nearest US embassy or consulate, listed in the box above.

Extensions

The date stamped on your passport is the latest you're legally allowed to stay. Leaving a few days later may not matter, especially if you're heading home, but more than a week or so can result in a protracted, rather unpleasant, interrogation from officials, which may cause you to miss your flight. Overstaying may also cause you to be turned away next time you try to enter the US.

To get an extension before your time is up, apply at the nearest **US Immigration and Naturalization Service** (INS) office, whose address will be under the Federal Government Offices listings at the front of the phone book. In DC they're at 425 I St NW (☎514-4316). They will assume that you're working illegally and it's up to you to convince them otherwise, by providing evidence of ample finances. If you can, bring along an upstanding American citizen to vouch for you. You'll also have to explain why you didn't plan for the extra time initially.

Work and study

Anyone planning an extended stay in the United States should apply for a special **working visa** at any American embassy before setting off.

Different types of visas are issued, depending on your skills and length of stay, but unless you've got parents or children over 21 in the US or a prospective employer to sponsor you, your chances are at best slim.

Illegal work is nothing like as easy to find as it used to be, and the government has introduced hefty fines for companies caught employing anyone without the legal right to work in the US. Even in the traditionally more casual establishments, like restaurants and bars, things have really tightened up, and if you do find work it's likely to be of the less visible, poorly paid kind – dishwasher instead of waiter.

Foreign students wishing to **study** at an American university should apply to that institution directly; if they accept you, you're more or less entitled to unlimited visas so long as you remain enrolled in full-time education.

Another option for work, peculiar to DC, is to acquire a place as an **intern**, basically a general administrative dogsbody serving someone connected, however tenuously, to the nation's political system. Senators, representatives, White House staff, federal agencies and lobbyists all hire interns over the summer, and applications should be made early in the New Year to anyone you can think of who might be interested in your skills and experience. Large city bookstores carry guides to applying for internships. Most posts are unpaid and filled by college students keen to get on in American politics, though foreign visitors with a special interest can try writing in the first instance to their local parliament members, who often have contacts or reciprocal arrangements with members of Congress.

Information and maps

There's a wealth of information available about Washington DC, but you'll have to be specific about your inquiries to get anything more than a map and a list of museums. If contacting the relevant offices, write well in advance of your visit,

and be as focused as possible about your interests. Otherwise, trawling the various Web sites (detailed below) is likely to be just as rewarding.

Information

The main city information sources for tourists are the **DC Chamber of Commerce** and the **Washington DC Convention and Visitors Association** – see the box below for details. You can contact these and other organizations in Washington DC in advance of your trip for brochures, information leaflets, visitor guides, events calendars and maps. Although you can call all of them while in the city for specific help, only the Chamber of Commerce Visitor Center is set up for walk-in visits. However, other **information offices in DC** can be visited in person, particularly those staffed by rangers of the National Park Service, which oversees most of the city's monuments and memorials. For more on city offices and information line numbers, see p.41,

---

Tourist Information Offices

Washington DC

DC Chamber of Commerce, 1301 Pennsylvania Ave NW, Suite 309, Washington DC 20004 ☎ 202/347-7201, fax 347-3538; Visitor Center, Ronald Reagan Building, 1300 Pennsylvania Ave NW, Washington DC 20004 ☎ 202/328-4748; Web site: *www.dcchamber.org*

DC Committee to Promote Washington, 1212 New York Ave NW, Suite 200, Washington DC 20005 ☎ 202/724-5644, fax 724-2445, free brochures on ☎ 1-800/422-8644

National Park Service, National Capital Region, 1100 Ohio Drive SW, Washington DC 20242 ☎ 202/619-7222, fax 619-7302; Web site: *www.nps.gov*

Washington DC Convention and Visitors Association, 1212 New York Ave NW, Suite 600, Washington DC 20005 ☎ 202/789-7000, fax 789-7037; Web site: *www.washington.org*

Delaware

Delaware Travel Office, 99 Kings Highway, Dover, DE 19903 ☎ 1-800/441-8846

Maryland

Maryland Office of Tourism, 217 E Redwood St, Baltimore, MD 21202 ☎ 1-800/543-1036

Virginia

Virginia Division of Tourism, 901 E Byrd St, Richmond, VA 23219 ☎ 804/786-2051 or 1-800/847-4882

West Virginia

West Virginia Travel Office, 2101 Washington St, East Charleston, WV 25305 ☎ 304/558-2286 or 1-800/225-5982

UK

Washington DC Convention and Visitors Association ☎ 0181/877 4521

---

and for details of city newspapers and listings magazines see p.327.

Also note the addresses and numbers of tourist offices and visitor bureaux in **the surrounding states** (see box on p.17) – useful if you're planning to travel on from Washington.

Maps

The maps in this guide, together with the untold number of free city plans you'll pick up from tourist offices, hotels and museums, will be sufficient to help you find your way around. For something more comprehensive, best is the small, shiny, foldout *Streetwise Washington DC* map ($5.95), available from book, travel and map stores (see p.319 for store locations in DC). For details of how to **orientate** yourself in the city, see p.39.

Moving on from DC, the **free road maps** issued by each state are usually fine for general driving and route planning. To get hold of one, either write to the state tourist office directly or stop by any state welcome center or visitor center. Rand McNally (in the US call ☎1-800/333-0136 for the location of their nearest store) produce good commercial state maps, while for something more detailed, say for **hiking**, camping shops generally have a good selection, and ranger stations in national parks, state parks and wilderness areas sell good-quality local hiking maps for $1–3.

The American Automobile Association (☎1-800/222-4357) provides free maps and assistance to its members, and to British members of the AA and RAC.

Costs, money and banks

DC may be the nation's capital, but it's a lot more affordable to vacation here than in most American cities: nearly all the major museums, monuments and sights are free, public transit is cheap and efficient, and the presence of so many students, interns and public service officials means that many establishments have great deals on drinks and food. That's not to say that you can't spend money in Washington – the city has some of the nation's finest and most expensive hotels and restaurants. But if you're sticking to any kind of budget, you're unlikely to have too hard a time.

Average costs

Accommodation will be your biggest single expense: the cheapest, reasonable double hotel rooms go for $70–110 a night, though a few spartan hostels, dingy budget hotels and rather nicer B&Bs undercut this. However, within that price range you'll be able to cut some good deals on weekends and in the less popular summer months – see p.274. After you've paid for your room, count on a **minimum** of $35 a day, which will buy you breakfast, fast-food lunch, a budget dinner and a beer, but not much else. Eating fancier meals, taxi-taking and drinking and socializing (especially drinking and socializing) will mean allowing for more like $60–70 a day. If you want to go regularly to the theater or major concerts, rent a car or take a tour, then double that figure.

What's good about DC is how much is **free**. Visiting the major national museums and art col-

Currency Exchange in DC

Banks		**Thomas Cook**	
Crestar Bank	☎ 202/879-6000	1800 K St NW	☎ 202/872-1233
Riggs National Bank	☎ 202/835-6000	Georgetown Park Shopping Mall, 3222 M St NW	
American Express		Union Station,	
1150 Connecticut Ave NW	☎ 202/457-1300	Massachusetts Ave NE	☎ 202/371-9219
1776 Pennsylvania Ave NW	☎ 202/289-8800		
Pentagon City Mall, Arlington, VA	☎ 703/415-5400		

Most banks in Washington DC are open Monday to Friday 9am–3pm; some stay open until 5pm or 6pm on Friday, a few open on Saturday 9am–noon. For currency exchange **outside normal business hours** and **on weekends** try major hotels, Thomas Cook at Georgetown Park or Union Station, or National (7am–9pm) or Dulles (7am–11pm) airports.

---

lections (and taking specialist guided tours around them); tours of the White House, US Capitol, FBI Building and Pentagon; spring and summer concerts, festivals, parades, gatherings, children's events – none costs a cent. The Metro and bus system gets you everywhere you want to go for a dollar or two at a time (or five bucks a day with a special ticket), taxis are inexpensive, and bars and restaurants routinely offer happy-hour drinks and food.

However, note that **sales tax** in Washington DC is 5.75 percent (and isn't part of the marked price on goods); **hotel tax** is 14.5 percent on top of the room rate.

Taking, changing and accessing money

US dollar travelers' checks are the safest way to carry money, for both American and foreign visitors, and are universally accepted as cash in stores and restaurants. Many banks will **change foreign travelers' checks and currency**. Airport exchange bureaux tend to charge less commission.

For many services, however, it's simply taken for granted that you'll be paying with plastic.

To find the location of your nearest **ATM**, call:

Amex	☎ 1-800/CASH-NOW
Plus	☎ 1-800/843-7587
Cirrus	☎ 1-800/424-7787

When renting a car or checking into a hotel, you will be asked to show a **credit card** – even if you intend to settle the bill in cash. Most major credit cards issued by foreign banks are honored in the US. Visa, Mastercard, Diners Club, American Express and Discover are the most widely used. With Mastercard or Visa it is also possible to **withdraw cash** at any bank displaying relevant stickers, or from appropriate automatic 24-hour teller machines (**ATMs**). Diners Club cards can be used to cash personal checks at Citibank branches. American Express cards can only get cash, or buy travelers' checks, at American Express offices or from the travelers' check dispensers at most major airports. American holders of ATM cards from out of state are likely to discover that their cards work in the machines of certain banks in DC (check with your bank before you leave home). Foreign cash-dispensing cards linked to international networks such as Cirrus and Plus are also widely accepted in the US – check with your home bank before you set off which branches you can use, as otherwise the machine may simply gobble up your plastic friend.

Emergencies

Emergency phone numbers to call if your checks and/or credit cards are stolen are on p.25. Assuming you know someone who is prepared to send you money in a crisis, the quickest way is to have them take the cash to the nearest **American Express Moneygram** (☎ 1-800/543-4080) office and have it instantaneously **wired** to the office nearest you, subject

Money: A Note for Foreign Travelers

Generally speaking, one **pound sterling** will buy $1.60–1.70; one **Canadian dollar** is worth 70–90¢; one **Australian dollar** is worth 60–80¢; and one **New Zealand dollar** is worth 50–65¢.

US currency comes in **bills** of $1, $5, $10, $20, $50 and $100. All are the same size and same green colour, so check bills carefully. The dollar is made up of 100 cents in **coins** of 1 cent (known as a **penny**), 5 cents (a **nickel**), 10 cents (a **dime**) and 25 cents (a **quarter**). Change (quarters are the most useful) is needed for buses, vending machines and telephones, though automatic machines are increasingly fitted with slots for dollar bills.

When working out your daily budget, allow for **tipping**, which is universally expected. You really shouldn't depart a bar or restaurant without leaving a tip of *at least* fifteen percent (unless the service is utterly disgusting), twenty percent in more upmarket places. About the same amount should be added to taxi fares – and round them up to the nearest 50¢ or dollar. A hotel porter should get $1 a bag, $3–5 for lots of baggage; chambermaids $1–2 a day, valet parking attendants $1.

to the deduction of ten percent commission. In the US this process should take no longer than ten minutes. See the box on p.19 for addresses of the main Amex offices in DC. **Western Union** (☎1-800/325-6000 in the US; ☎0800/833 833 in the UK; 1-800/649565 in Australia; and ☎09/3020143 in New Zealand) offers a similar service, at slightly higher rates; if credit cards are involved they charge an extra $10. In the UK, **Thomas Cook** (☎01733/318 922) can arrange to send money via its Telegraphic Transfer service (for £15 plus one percent of the amount to be sent), though it takes 1–2 days to arrive. They can also credit foreign bank accounts for the same fee.

If you have a few days' leeway, sending a postal money order, which is exchangeable at any post office, through the mail is cheaper. The equivalent for foreign travelers is the **international money order**, for which you need to allow up to seven days in the mail before arrival. An ordinary check sent from overseas takes two to three weeks to clear.

As a last resort, foreign visitors can have money wired directly from a bank in their home country to a bank in the US: the person wiring the funds to you will need to know the telex number of the bank the funds are being wired to. Foreign travelers in real difficulties also have the final option of throwing themselves on the mercy of their nearest national **consulate** (see p.326), who will – in worst cases only – repatriate you, but will *never*, under any circumstances, lend money.

Telecommunications and mail

essary, a voice comes on the line telling you to pay more. Such calls are much less expensive if made between 6pm and 8am – the **cheapest rates** are from 11pm to 8am. In general telephoning from your **hotel room** is considerably more expensive than using a payphone, costing up to $1 for a local call; that said, some budget hotels offer free local calls. An increasing number of public phones accept **credit cards**, while all the major US phone companies issue their own charge cards. Detailed information about calls, codes and rates is listed at the front of the **telephone directory** in the *White Pages*.

International telephone calls

International calls can be dialed direct from public phones. Alternatively, you can get assistance from the **international operator** (☎00). The **lowest rates** for international calls to Europe are usually between 11pm and 8am (plus all day Sat and all day Sun except 5–11pm), when a direct-dialed three-minute call will cost roughly $5.

In **Britain**, it's possible to obtain free charge-cards from **British Telecom** (☎0800/345 600), **AT&T** (☎0500/626262) and **Mercury** (☎0500/100505). Using access codes for the particular country you are in, and personal PIN numbers, you can make calls from most hotel, public and private phones which are then charged to your own domestic account. The benefit of calling cards is mainly one of convenience, as rates aren't necessarily cheaper than calling from a public phone, but as they're free you may as well apply for one to use in emergencies. In the same way, Australia's **Telstra Telecard** (☎1-800/626 008) or the **Optus Calling Card** (☎1-300/300 300) and **New Zealand Telecom's Calling Card** (☎04/382-5818) can be used to make calls charged to a domestic account or credit card.

To make an international call **to Washington DC**, dial your country's international access code, then 1 for the US, followed by 202 for DC. To call **from DC to the rest of the world**, dial 011, then the country code (Britain is 44, Ireland 353, Canada 1, Australia 61 and New Zealand 64), and finally the number (minus the initial 0 of the area code).

Telephones

All telephone numbers in this guide have a ☎202 area code (for Washington DC), unless otherwise stated. You do not need to dial the area code within the District. Outside DC, dial 1 before the area code and number. Calls within the greater DC metropolitan area are counted as local even if they require a different code (☎703 for northern Virginia, or ☎301 for parts of Maryland, for example).

Making **long-distance calls** to a different area code you'll need plenty of change – when nec-

---

Service Numbers

Emergencies
☎911 for fire, police or ambulance

Local directory information
☎411

Long-distance directory information
☎1 + area code + 555-1212

Operator
☎0

Directory inquiries for toll-free numbers
☎1-800/555-1212

For other information line and emergency numbers in DC, see the City Directory (p.326) and Introducing the City (p.41).

For details of **time differences** between the US and the rest of the world, see "Time", p.28.

US mail

Air mail between the US and Europe generally takes about a week. Letters that don't carry the **zip code** are liable to get lost or at least delayed; phone books carry a list for their service area, and post offices – even abroad – have directories. In this guide the zip code for addresses is given where it may be necessary to write in advance.

Letters sent to you c/o **General Delivery** (known elsewhere as **poste restante**) *must* include the post office zip code and will only be held for thirty days before being returned to sender – so make sure there's a return address on the envelope. In DC, the post office which handles General Delivery mail is miles out of the centre at 900 Brentwood Rd NE, 20090 (Mon–Fri 8am–8pm, Sat 10am–6pm, Sun noon–6pm; ☎635-5300). Try and have mail held at a hotel, American Express office or some other address.

DC's main **downtown post office** is across from Union Station at 2 Massachusetts Ave NE, 20002 (Mon–Fri 7am–midnight, Sat & Sun 7am–8pm; ☎523-2628); there are also useful counters in the Old Post Office building on Pennsylvania Ave NW (see p.181), in the National Museum of American History (p.98) and in the US Capitol (p.112). Downtown **mail boxes** can be found on Constitution Ave NW at 11th, 14th and 21st; on Independence at 14th; and on 15th outside the Bureau of Engraving and Printing.

Telegrams, faxes and email

To send a **telegram**, go to a Western Union office (listed in the *Yellow Pages*; and see p.20); credit card holders can dictate messages over the phone. **International telegrams** sent in the morning from the US should arrive at their overseas destination the following day. For domestic telegrams ask for a **mailgram**, which will be delivered to any address in the country the next morning. Public **fax** machines, which may require your credit card to be swiped through an attached device, are found at city photocopy centres and, occasionally, bookstores. You can receive and send **email** from PCs at an increasing number of places: there's Internet access from the PCs in the Martin Luther King Memorial Library (see p.203), while several DC coffee shops are starting to provide PCs for customers.

Opening hours, public holidays and festivals

Museums generally open daily 10am–5.30pm, though some have extended summer opening hours; a few art galleries stay open until 9pm or so one night a week. Smaller, private museums close for one day a week, usually Monday or Tuesday. **Federal office buildings** (some of which incorporate museums) open Monday to Friday 9am to 5.30pm. Most of the national **monuments** in the city are open daily 24 hours, though they tend to be staffed only between 8am and midnight. Finally, **stores** are usually open Monday to Saturday 10am to 7pm, while some have extended Thursday night hours. In neighborhoods like Georgetown, Adams-Morgan and Dupont Circle many stores

National Holidays

January
1: New Year's Day
3rd Monday: Dr Martin Luther King Jr's Birthday

February
3rd Monday: President's Day

March/April
Easter Monday

May
Last Monday: Memorial Day

July
4: Independence Day

September
1st Monday: Labor Day

October
2nd Monday: Columbus Day

November
11: Veterans' Day
Last Thursday: Thanksgiving Day

December
25: Christmas Day

open on Sunday, too (usually noon–5pm); **malls** tend to be open Monday to Saturday 10am to 7pm or later and Sunday noon–6pm.

For the opening hours of specific attractions, see the relevant accounts in the Guide. Telephone numbers are provided throughout so that you can check current information with the places themselves.

On the national **public holidays** listed above, stores, banks and public and federal offices are liable to be closed all day. The Smithsonian museums and galleries, on the other hand, close only on Christmas Day. The traditional **summer season** for tourism, when many attractions have extended opening hours, runs from **Memorial Day to Labor Day**.

Washington has a huge variety of **annual festivals and events**, many of them national in scope: America's Christmas Tree is lit each year on the Ellipse in front of the White House; the grandest Fourth of July Parade in the country takes place along and around the Mall; while every four years the new President takes part in a triumphal Inaugural Parade up Pennsylvania Avenue. Many of the national holidays listed above also feature special events and celebrations in the city. Such is the range of festivals throughout the year, it's hard to turn up without coinciding with at least one; DC's full **festival calendar** is detailed in Chapter 18. Note, however, that at all major festival periods – Cherry Blossom Festival and Easter, Memorial Day and Fourth of July particularly – it can be very difficult to find accommodation in the city: book well in advance.

Crime and personal safety

For many years Washington has had a poor reputation in terms of crime and personal safety. You'll be confidently told that it's the "Murder Capital" of the United States (even though, statistically, that's no longer true), and stories of drug dealers in business just blocks from the White House are in routine circulation amongst visitors and locals alike.

It's true, DC ain't Kansas: scan any copy of the *Washington Post* for a rundown of the latest daily drive-by shootings and crack-war escapades. However, to get things in perspective, almost all the crime that makes the newspaper headlines takes place in **neighborhoods** (most of NE, SE and distinct parts of upper NW) that tourists have no business venturing into – there's nothing there to see and certainly no "real" Washington that you'd want to experience. Where neighborhoods are borderline in terms of personal security, this guide makes it clear where you should and shouldn't go; if there's a sight or museum you really want to see, get a cab there and back. However, in the places you will be spending most of your time – downtown, along the Mall, in Georgetown – all the

Emergency numbers

See City Directory, pp.326–28, for **emergency numbers** for the police, Travelers Aid and the hospital.

major tourist sights, the Metro system and the main nightlife zones are invariably well lit and well policed. Indeed, the Mall between the US Capitol, White House and Lincoln Memorial is probably the most heavily policed district in America, brimming with regular police officers, Secret Service operatives and park rangers.

Mugging and theft

Most people will have few problems, and if things do go wrong, foreign visitors tend to report that the **police** are helpful and obliging, although they'll be less sympathetic if they think you brought the trouble on yourself through carelessness.

You shouldn't be complacent. The fact that DC attracts so many tourists means that it has more than its share of **petty crime**, simply because there are plenty of unsuspecting holidaymakers to prey on. Keep your wits about you in crowds; know where your wallet or purse is; and, of course, avoid parks, parking lots and dark streets at night. Be careful when using ATMs in untourist-ed areas: try to use machines near downtown hotels, shops or offices, and during daylight. After the Metro has closed down, take taxis back from bars, restaurants and clubs. And if you have to ask directions, choose carefully who you ask (go into a store, if possible).

Should the worst happen, hand over your money, and afterwards find a phone and dial ☎**911**, or hail a cab and ask the driver to take you to the nearest police station. Here, report the theft and get a reference number on the report to claim insurance and travelers' check refunds. Ring the local Travelers Aid (see City Directory, p.327) for practical advice about hospitals and emergency services.

Another potential source of trouble is having your **hotel room burgled**. Always store valuables in the hotel safe when you go out. When inside, keep your door locked and don't open it to anyone you are suspicious of. If they claim to be hotel staff and you don't believe them, call reception to check. In hostels and budget hotels, you may want to keep your valuables on your person, unless you know the security measures to be reliable.

Emergency Numbers for Lost Cards and Checks

American Express Cards	☎ 1-800/528-4800
American Express Checks	☎ 1-800/221-7282
Citicorp	☎ 1-800/645-6556
Diners Club	☎ 1-800/234-6377
Mastercard/Access	☎ 1-800/826-2181
Thomas Cook/Mastercard	☎ 1-800/223-9920
Visa Checks	☎ 1-800/227-6811
Visa Cards	☎ 1-800/336-8472

Needless to say, having bags that contain travel documents snatched can be a big headache, none more so for foreign travelers than **losing your passport**. Make photocopies of everything important before you go (including the business page of your passport) and keep them separate from the originals. If the worst happens, go to the nearest consulate and get them to issue you a **temporary passport**, basically a sheet of paper saying you've reported the loss, which will get you back home.

Keep a record of the numbers of your **travelers' checks** separately from the actual checks; if you lose them, call the issuing company on the toll-free number above. They'll ask you for the check numbers, the place you bought them, when and how you lost them and whether it's been reported to the police. All being well, you should get the missing checks reissued within a couple of days – and perhaps an emergency advance to tide you over.

Finally, it goes without saying that you should *never* **hitch** anywhere in DC, or indeed the entire US.

Car crime

Crimes committed against tourists driving **rented cars** have garnered headlines around the world in recent years, but there are certain precautions you can take to keep yourself safe. Not driving in DC itself would be a good first step: it's not necessary, since public transportation and cheap taxis can get you most places you'd want to go. On longer trips, pick up your rental car on the day you leave the city. Any car you do rent should have nothing on it – such as a particular license plate – that makes it easy to identify as a rental car. When driving, under no circumstances stop in any unlit or seemingly deserted urban area – and especially not if someone is waving you down and suggesting that there is something wrong with your car. Similarly, if you are "accidentally" rammed by the driver behind, do not stop but drive on to the nearest well-lit, busy area and phone the police at ☎911. Keep your doors locked and windows never more than slightly open. Do not open your door or window if someone approaches your car on the pretext of asking directions. Hide any valuables out of sight, preferably locked in the trunk or in the glove compartment (any valuables you don't need for your journey should be left in your hotel safe).

Outside the city, if your **vehicle breaks down** on an interstate or heavily traveled road, wait in the car for a patrol car to arrive. One option is to rent a mobile phone with your car, for a small additional charge – a potential lifesaver.

Travelers with disabilities

Washington DC is one of the most accessible cities in the world for travelers with special needs. All public buildings, including hotels and restaurants, have to be wheelchair accessible and provide suitable toilet facilities. Almost all street corners have dropped curbs, and the public transit system has facilities such as subways with elevators, and buses that "kneel" to let people board.

Planning your trip

It's always a good idea for people with special needs to alert their travel agents when booking: things are far simpler when the various travel operators or carriers are expecting you. A **medical certificate** of your fitness to travel, provided by your doctor, is also useful; some airlines or insurance companies may insist on it. Most **airlines** do whatever they can to ease your journey, and

---

Contacts for Travelers with Disabilities

Australia

ACROD (Australian Council for Rehabilitation of the Disabled)
Curtin, ACT ☎ 02/6282 4333
Cabarita, NSW ☎ 02/9743 2699

NICAN
Curtin, ACT ☎ 1800/806 769

Ireland

Disability Action Group
Belfast ☎ 01232/491 011
A good source of general advice.

Irish Wheelchair Association
Dublin ☎ 01/833 8241
National voluntary organization with services for holidaymakers.

New Zealand

Disabled Persons Assembly
Wellington ☎ 04/811 9100

North America

Directions Unlimited
Bedford Hills, NY ☎ 914/241-1700
Tour operator specializing in custom tours for people with disabilities.

Mobility International USA
Eugene, OR (voice and TDD) ☎ 541/343-1284; *www.minsa.org*
Information and referral services, access guides, tours and exchange programs. Annual

membership $35 (includes quarterly newsletter).

National Tour Association
Lexington, KY ☎ 606/226-4444
Can recommend organizations facilitating travel for the disabled.

Society for the Advancement of Travel for the Handicapped (SATH)
New York ☎ 212/447-7284
Non-profit travel industry grouping including travel agents, tour operators, hotel and airline management, and people with disabilities. It will pass on any inquiry to the appropriate number, but allow plenty of time for a response.

Twin Peaks Press
Vancouver ☎ 360/694-2462 or 1-800/637-2256
Publishes *Directory of Travel Agencies for the Disabled* ($19.95, $6 p/h) and *Travel for the Disabled* ($14.95, $6 p/h).

UK

Holiday Care Service
Horley, Surrey ☎ 01293/774 535
Information on all as pects of travel.

RADAR,
London ☎ 0171/250 3222
Minicom ☎ 0171/250 4119
A good source of advice on holidays and travel abroad.

---

will usually let attendants of more seriously disabled people accompany them at no extra charge. The *Americans with Disabilities* Act 1990 obliged all air carriers to make the majority of their services accessible to travelers with disabilities within five to nine years. Almost every **Amtrak train** includes one or more coaches with accommodation for passengers with disabilities. Guide dogs travel free and may accompany blind, deaf or disabled passengers in the carriage. Be sure to give 24 hours' notice. Hearing-impaired passengers can get TDD information on ☎ 1-800/523-6590. **Greyhound buses** are not equipped with lifts for wheelchairs, though staff will assist with boarding, and the "Helping Hand" scheme offers two-for-the-price-of-one tickets to passengers unable to travel alone (make sure to carry a doctor's certificate).

The American Automobile Association produces the Handicapped Driver's Mobility Guide for **disabled drivers** (available from Quantum-Precision Inc, 225 Broadway, Suite 3404, New York, NY 10007). The larger car rental companies provide cars with hand-controls at no extra charge, though only on their full-size (which is to say most expensive) models; reserve well in advance.

Disabled access in the city

The **Washington DC CVA** (see p.17) produces a free handout on accessibility in the city: call ☎ 202/789-7064. You can also contact Washington Ear, Inc (☎ 301/681-6636) for large-print and tactile atlases of the DC area; Columbia Lighthouse for the Blind (☎ 202/462-2900) has free tactile maps of the Metro system and pamphlets on how best to get around the city. Other helpful information is available from the Center for

Independent Living (☎ 202/388-0033) and from the Information, Protection and Advocacy Center for People with Disabilities (☎ 202/966-8081).

The American Public Transit Association, 1201 New York Ave, Suite 400, Washington DC 20005 (☎ 202/898-4000), provides information about the accessibility of **public transit** in American cities, including, of course, DC. Each station on the **Metro** (subway) system has an elevator (with braille controls) to the platforms; the wide train aisles can accommodate wheelchairs; there are reduced fares and priority seating available, and some Metro buses have wheelchair lifts. For a free guide offering complete information on Metro access for the disabled, call ☎ 202/635-6434.

Most of the **monuments and memorials** in DC have elevators to viewing platforms and special parking facilities, and at some sites large-print brochures and sign-language interpreters are available. The White House has a special entrance reserved for visitors in wheelchairs, who don't need to wait in line for a ticket. For more information on any site operated by the National Park Service call ☎ 202/619-7222. All **Smithsonian museum** buildings are wheelchair accessible and with notice staff can serve as sign-language interpreters or produce large-print, braille or cassette material. The free *Smithsonian Access* is available in large print, braille or audio cassette. by calling ☎ 202/357-2700.

In addition, most new downtown **shopping malls** have wheelchair ramps and elevators. **Union Station** (shops, trains and cinema) is fully accessible, as are the **Kennedy Center** (p.314) and **National Theater** (p.314), both of which also have good facilities for visually and hearing impaired visitors.

Directory

CLIMATE For details of DC's climate, see the Introduction, p.xiv.

DATES Dates are written in the following order: month, day, year. The date 4-1-98 is the first of April.

ELECTRICITY The US electricity supply is 110 volts AC. Plugs are standard two-pins – foreign visitors will need an adaptor and voltage converter for their own electrical appliances.

FLOORS The first floor in the US is what would be the ground floor in Britain; the second floor would be the first floor and so on. However, the design of some DC buildings and institutions (including various Mall museums and galleries) incorporates underground and mezzanine levels, so on occasion buildings do have a "ground floor" on the level at which you enter. This is never as confusing as it sounds.

HEALTH MATTERS Most travelers do not require inoculations to enter the US, though you may need certificates of vaccination if you're en route from cholera- or typhoid-infected areas in Asia or Africa – check with your doctor before you leave. For an ambulance, dial ☎ **911** (or whatever variant may be on the information plate of the payphone you're at). To find a doctor or pharmacy in DC, see the City Directory, p.326.

ID Carry ID all times. Two pieces should suffice, one of which should have a photo: a passport or driving license and credit card(s) are best. Not having your license with you while driving is an arrestable offense.

MEASUREMENTS AND SIZES American pints and gallons are about four-fifths the quantity of Imperial ones. Clothing sizes are two figures less than in the UK – a British women's size 12 is a US size 10 – while British shoe sizes are a half size below American ones for women, and one size below for men.

SENIOR TRAVELERS Anyone over the age of 62, who can produce suitable ID, can enjoy certain discounts. Amtrak and Greyhound, for example, offer (smallish) percentage reductions on fares to older passengers. US residents aged over fifty can join the American Association of Retired Persons, 601 E St NW, Washington DC 20049 (☎ 202/434-2277), which organizes group travel for senior citizens and can provide discounts on accommodation and vehicle rental.

TAXES For a rundown of local taxes, see p.19.

TEMPERATURES Always given in Fahrenheit.

TIME Washington DC is in the Eastern zone, which covers the area inland to the Great Lakes and the Appalachian Mountains; this is five hours behind Greenwich Mean Time (-5 GMT), so 10am London time is 5am in Washington DC. Daylight saving time operates between April and October (check newspapers for specific dates), when the clocks go back an hour.

The City

Chapter 1

Introducing the City

Washington isn't a city, it's an abstraction.

Dylan Thomas, 1956

I t comes as some surprise to find that **Washington DC**, capital of a thriving nation of 250 million people and self-professed political arbiter of the Free World, is a small-fry in city terms. With a population of just 600,000 it comes way down the list of American cities and is outnumbered by just about every foreign capital you could think of. Sparsely populated it may be, but it's certainly not small in scale. Everywhere, Washington boasts the sweeping expanses, generous sightlines and monumental architecture of a carefully planned city which, originally, at least, was destined to fill a hundred square-mile diamond of land between Virginia and Maryland – Virginia later demanded its chunk of land back, which is why there's a bite out of the diamond shape across the Potomac River. So while locals (and boozy Welsh poets) talk about DC as being more a collection of disparate neighborhoods than a coherent whole, and critics sneer that it can't hold a candle to a "real" city like New York, visitors get on with familiarizing themselves with the bus and Metro systems – essential if they're to get around every nook and cranny of the United States' capital.

This isn't to say that DC is not a city for walking around. There's no better way to get to grips with the "magnificent distances" trumpeted by nineteenth-century boosters than a two-mile stroll along the grassy reach of the **Mall** (Chapter 2) – the city's principal thoroughfare – where the views unfold from the US Capitol through the Washington Monument to the Lincoln Memorial. The majority of the peerless Smithsonian museums and galleries reside here, as do the overwhelming art collection of the National Gallery of Art and the major memorials to Thomas Jefferson, Franklin Delano Roosevelt, and the Vietnam and Korean vets.

The US Capitol, at the Mall's eastern end, marks the geographical center of the city, since all neighborhoods and quadrants radiate out from its familiar white dome. **Capitol Hill** (Chapter 3) is one of

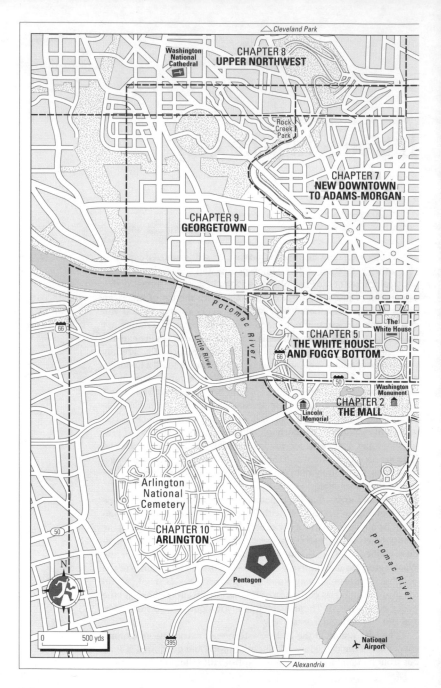

△ Cleveland Park

CHAPTER 8
UPPER NORTHWEST

Washington
National
Cathedral

Rock
Creek
Park

CHAPTER 7
**NEW DOWNTOWN
TO ADAMS-MORGAN**

CHAPTER 9
GEORGETOWN

Potomac River

Little River

66

66

The
White House

CHAPTER 5
**THE WHITE HOUSE
AND FOGGY BOTTOM**

50

Washington
Monument

Lincoln
Memorial

CHAPTER 2
THE MALL

Arlington
National
Cemetery

CHAPTER 10
ARLINGTON

Pentagon

Potomac River

N

0   500 yds

50

395

National
Airport

▽ Alexandria

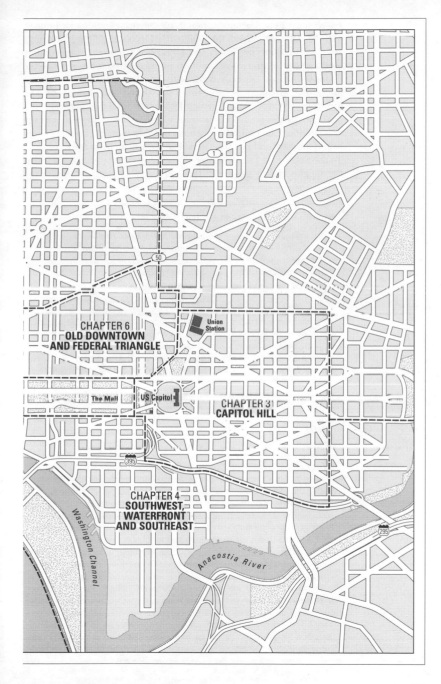

CHAPTER 6
OLD DOWNTOWN
AND FEDERAL TRIANGLE

Union
Station

The Mall   US Capitol

CHAPTER 3
CAPITOL HILL

CHAPTER 4
SOUTHWEST,
WATERFRONT
AND SOUTHEAST

Washington Channel

Anacostia River

DC's oldest neighborhoods, rich in nineteenth-century row houses, and ripe for a stroll from the Capitol itself to other defining buildings such as the Supreme Court and Library of Congress. Immediately **south of the Mall**, two of the most popular attractions in DC – the Federal Bureau of Engraving and Printing and the Holocaust Memorial Museum – are the undisputed highlights of the **Southwest/Waterfront** (Chapter 4). Monolithic federal office buildings occupy the rest of the no-man's-land between the Mall and the Washington Channel, though a thriving fish market and several waterfront seafood restaurants pull visitors away from the museums. To the **Southeast** (also Chapter 4), hard against the Anacostia River, the neighborhood toughens: there are sporadic attractions at the

---

The Planning of a Capital City

It is sometimes called the City of Magnificent Distances, but it might with greater propriety be termed the City of Magnificent Intentions; for it is only on taking a bird's-eye view of it from the top of the Capitol that one can at all comprehend the vast designs of its projector, an aspiring Frenchman.

Charles Dickens, *American Notes*, 1842

In 1790, the year after George Washington was inaugurated as first President of the United States, it fell to Congress to decide upon a permanent site for the country's capital. Since Independence, Congress had met in half a dozen different cities – the President was inaugurated in New York – and a dozen others, in North and South, had competing claims and loud promoters. Ultimately the decision came down to political wrangling: in return for Congress assuming the states' debts from the Revolutionary War (a key Northern demand), the new federal capital would be sited in the South, somewhere on the sparsely populated banks of the Potomac River.

With the help of Major Andrew Ellicott, a surveyor from Maryland, and the black mathematician and scientist Benjamin Banneker, Washington – no mean surveyor himself – suggested a diamond-shaped, hundred-square-mile site at the confluence of the Potomac and Anacostia rivers. It seemed a canny choice – centering on the confluence, and thus ripe for trade, the site incorporated the ports of Alexandria in Virginia and Georgetown in Maryland; it would have its own port in Anacostia, and, no small matter for Washington, it was only eighteen miles upriver from his home at Mount Vernon. Maryland ceded roughly seventy square miles of land, Virginia thirty; all Washington had to do was find someone to plan his city, which Congress – in honor of the President – decreed would be named **Washington**, in the Territory (later District) of Columbia (a reference to Christopher Columbus).

Washington found his "aspiring Frenchman", **Major Pierre Charles L'Enfant**, who had been a member of Washington's Continental Army staff. His reputation as an engineer stemmed from his successful redesign of New York's Federal Hall for the presidential inauguration; now the President gave him the chance to create an entire city. Within a year L'Enfant had come up with an ambitious plan to transform a wilderness into gridded

---

Navy Yard and, across the river, in Anacostia itself, but these areas do not lend themselves to casual exploration – certainly not by tourists on foot. There are no such caveats about the heavily visited area around the **White House and Foggy Bottom** (Chapter 5), a neighborhood which stretches off to the northwest of the Mall. Quite apart from the President's house, this compact block of streets holds heavyweight attractions like the Corcoran Gallery of Art, the renowned Kennedy Center and the infamous Watergate building.

See everything along and around the Mall and you've seen the greater part of monumental Washington, but you still won't have much impression of a living, working city. What's known as **Old Downtown** (Chapter 6) – north of the Mall between the White

---

streets and diagonal avenues, radiating from ceremonial squares and elegant circles. A "Grand Avenue" (later known as the Mall) formed the centerpiece; government buildings were assigned their own plots; a central canal linked the city's ports; sculptures, fountains and parks punctuated the design. Its initial inspiration was the city of Paris and the seventeenth-century palace of Versailles, though L'Enfant did adopt suggestions made by others – not least Secretary of State Thomas Jefferson, who proposed the sites of the US Capitol and the President's Mansion (later called the White House). The plan named avenues after the fifteen states that existed in 1791, placing avenues named after Northern states north of the Capitol, Southern ones to the south – the most populous states, Virginia, Pennsylvania and Massachusetts, were represented by the longest avenues.

Washington was delighted with the scheme, though the existing landowners were less than pleased with the injunction to donate any land needed for public thoroughfares. L'Enfant was planning avenues 100ft wide – whether he knew it or not, clearly following the Parisian model of making streets too broad for the public to barricade and big enough for troops to maneuver in during times of unrest. Disagreements with the landowners aside, L'Enfant found himself in constant dispute with the District Commissioners who had been appointed by Washington to oversee the construction. His obstinacy cost him his job in 1792, and the design of the Capitol and White House were both later thrown open to public competition. L'Enfant turned down the $2500 he was offered as payment for his services, sued Congress (unsuccessfully) for $100,000, harried the legislature with his grievances for the rest of his life and died in penury in 1825.

For decades L'Enfant's plan seemed full of empty pretensions as Washington DC struggled to make its mark. Any number of nineteenth-century observers commented upon the hilarious contrast between such "vast designs" and the less-than-impressive reality. But for all that, this unique attempt to create a capital city that could define a nation was a remarkable enterprise. Perhaps the last word should be with nineteenth-century abolitionist and orator Frederick Douglass, who said: "It is our national center. It belongs to us, and whether it is mean or majestic, whether arranged in glory or covered with shame, we cannot but share its character and its destiny."

House and Union Station – was where nineteenth-century Washington first set out its shops and services along the spine of Pennsylvania Avenue, the country's most prominent parade route. After years of neglect, it's today undergoing spirited restoration and can count revitalized streets, plazas, galleries and restaurants alongside its traditional attractions: the FBI Building, Old Post Office and the buildings associated with President Lincoln's assassination. North of Pennsylvania Avenue, another development zone centers on the MCI Center, a sports-and-entertainment arena which sits between Chinatown and the fast-emerging 7th Street corridor. Wedged against the Mall, **Federal Triangle** (also Chapter 6) siphons off downtown sightseers to the National Archives; fewer make the effort to tour the district's other splendid Neoclassical buildings.

It's in the business district of **New Downtown**, along and around K Street, that Washington most resembles any other modern American city. From here, long diagonal avenues march off through a number of neighborhoods that mark the end of the line for most tourists. The historic townhouses and mansions of chic **Dupont Circle** hide a gaggle of low-key museums and an expanding enclave of art galleries; the bar-and-restaurant zone of **Adams-Morgan** to the north gets trendier by the day at the same time as it squeezes out its Latino heritage; while, to the east, the historic black neighborhood of **Shaw** boasts the thriving nightlife corridor of U Street. All these neighborhoods, from New Downtown to Adams-Morgan, are covered in Chapter 7.

The first *bona fide* city suburbs were in the **Upper Northwest** (Chapter 8), where the nineteenth-century wealthy created picket-fence paradise in areas like Woodley Park and Cleveland Park. The Metro brings visitors out here today for the hugely enjoyable National Zoological Park and the landmark National Cathedral; with more time and your own transportation, you can get to the glades, dales and riverbanks of Rock Creek Park. West of downtown, across Rock Creek, the historic neighborhood of **Georgetown** (Chapter 9) pre-dates DC and was once a thriving town in its own right. It's now the quintessential hangout of the chattering classes and the students of Georgetown University, who make the shops, galleries, bars and restaurants very much their own.

As a cursory glance at the map will tell you, that still leaves a lot of Washington to cover. Seventy percent of the city's population, predominantly black, lives outside the environs of the Mall and the affluent Northwest – what P.J. O'Rourke calls the "white pipeline" of the city. But there's little that tourists are encouraged to see in the disparate neighborhoods of Northeast and Southeast Washington – with just a few exceptions, these contain some of the poorest, most run-down areas in the city. Instead visitors are steered south and west across the Potomac into Virginia, to **Arlington** (Chapter 10), easily accessible by Metro and holding the city's major military sights: Arlington National Cemetery, the Marine Corps (Iwo Jima) Memorial and the Pentagon. Further **out from the city** (Chapter 11), most people make day-trips to the historic town of Alexandria (fifty years older than Washington DC) and to Mount Vernon, the family estate and burial place of George Washington.

Arrival

The most central points of arrival are for those reaching the city by **train** (at Union Station), or **bus** (downtown Greyhound terminal). From the **airports**, you can't count on being downtown much within the hour, though the various bus, train and Metro transfers are smooth enough; free shuttle buses run from National and BWI airports to the relevant stations. Taking a **taxi** from the airport won't save much time, especially if you arrive during rush hour, though filling a cab with three or four people may save a few dollars.

Telephone area codes for organizations and services listed in this chapter are ☎202, for Washington DC, unless otherwise stated.

By air

Most domestic arrivals land at **National Airport** (☎703/417-8000) – officially the Ronald Reagan Washington National Airport   four miles south of downtown. Driving or by bus it takes thirty minutes to an hour to reach the center, depending on traffic; National Airport Metro station is linked directly to Metro Center, L'Enfant Plaza and Gallery Place-Chinatown (for more on the Metro, see p.41). A taxi downtown costs around $12–15 (including $1.25 airport surcharge), or take the SuperShuttle bus (continuous service 24hr; one-way $8, round-trip $16), which drops you at your requested hotel or the city terminal at 1517 K St NW (see "Leaving DC" on p.38).

The area's major airport, **Dulles International** (☎703/572-2700), 26 miles west in northern Virginia, handles most international and some domestic services. The drive in or out can take between forty minutes and an hour; taxis downtown run to around $45–50. It's cheaper to take the Washington Flyer Express bus (every 20–30min, Mon–Fri 6am–10.30pm, Sat & Sun 7.30am–10.30pm; one-way $8, round-trip $14) to the **West Falls Church Metro** station, a twenty-minute ride; from here, trains run into Metro Center (20min) and on to downtown. There's also a **direct bus** from Dulles to the Washington Flyer Express downtown terminal at 1517 K St NW (every 30–60min, daily 5.20am–10.20pm; one-way $16, round-trip $26), where you can link up with courtesy shuttles to various hotels (see "Accommodation", p.274).

There's a Washington Flyer Express bus service between National and Dulles airports (every 1–2hr, 5am–11pm; one-way $16, round-trip

Arrival

Leaving DC: Getting to the Airports

Give yourself plenty of time to get to the airport, especially if you're driving: in rush hour, it can take up to thirty minutes to reach National, more like an hour to Dulles or BWI. For a list of **taxi** companies, see p.44.

Two companies – Washington Flyer Express and SuperShuttle – run **buses** to the airports from the same downtown bus terminal at 1517 K St NW, three blocks north of the White House; nearest Metro is Farragut North. Note that the terminal has a check-in service for all United flights (Mon–Fri 10am–5pm).

Washington Flyer Express ☎1-888/927-4359

To Dulles from the terminal: every 30–60min, 6.15am–9.15pm; $16, round-trip $26.

To Dulles from West Falls Church Metro: every 20–30min, Mon–Fri 6.30am–11pm, Sat & Sun 7.30am–10pm; $8, round-trip $14.

Between National and Dulles: every 1–2hr, 5am–11pm; $16 one-way, round-trip $26.

SuperShuttle ☎1-800/258-3826

To National on request, from your hotel: $8, round-trip $16.

To BWI from the terminal (reservations essential): every 30min, 5am–8pm; $21, round-trip $34.

There are information counters and car-rental desks at each airport.

Other international and domestic arrivals land at **Baltimore-Washington International (BWI) Airport** (☎301/261-1000), 25 miles northeast of DC (and ten miles south of Baltimore). This too is up to an hour's drive from downtown DC, with taxis costing $50–55 – agree on the price before setting off. SuperShuttle buses into Washington (every 30min, daily 6am–11.30pm; one-way $21, round-trip $34) drop off at the 1517 K St NW terminal an hour later. It's cheaper to take the train from BWI Airport: either the frequent peak-hour departures of the MARC commuter line (Mon–Fri only, 5.30am–6.40pm; one-way $5, round-trip $7.25) or the quicker, daily Amtrak trains (hourly; one-way $14, round-trip $28) – services take 35–55 minutes and terminate at Washington's Union Station (see "By train and bus", see below).

By train and bus

See p.127 for an account of Union Station. Train and bus inquiry numbers and departures are detailed on p.327 and p.326 respectively.

The gleaming malls of **Union Station**, 50 Massachusetts Ave NE, three blocks north of the Capitol, see arrivals from all over the country, including local **trains** from Baltimore, Richmond, Williamsburg and Virginia Beach, and major east coast connections from Philadelphia, New York and Boston. .Trains are operated either by Amtrak (☎1-800/872-7245) – which has regular and Metroliner (quicker, more expensive) services to most destinations – or the Maryland Rail Commuter Service (MARC; ☎1-800/325-7245), which connects DC to Baltimore, BWI Airport and suburban Maryland. Union Station has a connecting Metro station, and taxis line up outside. There are car-rental desks here, too.

Greyhound (☎1-800/231-2222, in DC ☎289-5155) and Peter Pan Trailways (☎1-800/343-9999) **buses** – from Baltimore, Philadelphia, New York, Boston, Richmond and other cities – stop at the modern terminal at 1005 1st St NE at L St, in a fairly unsavory part of town, five long blocks north of Union Station; take a cab, especially at night, at least as far as Union Station Metro (around $6).

By car

Driving into DC is a sure way to experience some of the worst traffic on the east coast. The six- to eight-lane freeway known as the **Capital Beltway** (due to be twelve-lane in parts within five years) circles the city at a ten-mile radius from the center and is busy eighteen hours a day. It's made up of two separate highways: I-495 on the western half and I-95/I-495 in the east. If it's the Beltway you want, follow signs for either.

Approaching the city **from the northeast** (New York/Philadelphia) you need I-95 (south), before turning west on Route 50, which will take you to New York Avenue, which heads directly to the White House; **from Baltimore** there's the direct Baltimore–Washington Parkway, which also joins Route 50. Route 50 itself is the main way in **from the east** (Annapolis, MD, and Chesapeake Bay). **From the south**, take I-95 to I-395, which crosses the river via the 14th Street (George Mason Memorial) Bridge to reach 14th Street. **From the northwest** (Frederick, MD, and beyond), come in on I-270 until you hit the Beltway, then follow I-495 (east) for Connecticut Avenue south. **From the west** (Virginia) use I-66, which runs across the Theodore Roosevelt Bridge for Constitution Avenue. At peak periods inside the Beltway, high-occupancy vehicle restrictions apply on I-66 eastbound (6.30–9am) and westbound (4–6.30pm); at these times cars with fewer than three people face a small surcharge at the toll booths.

Road routes into Washington DC are shown on the map on p.x–xi.

Orientation

Washington is divided into four **quadrants** – northeast (NE), northwest (NW), southeast (SE), southwest (SW) – whose axes center on the US Capitol. Separating the quadrants, a central cross is formed by North Capitol Street (stretching north of the Capitol), East Capitol Street, South Capitol Street and – in the first of many exceptions – the grassy expanse of the Mall (West Capitol Street doesn't exist). The few sights in the NE, SE and SW quadrants cluster around the Capitol and south of the Mall; almost all other sights and neighborhoods of note (including Georgetown) are in the NW quadrant.

Within the city, there's a simple right-angled grid plan in which, progressing away from the Capitol, **north–south streets are num-**

bered (in numerical order, from 1), **east–west ones are lettered** (in alphabetical order, from A). After W (there are no X, Y or Z streets), two-syllable names, still in alphabetical order, are used for east–west streets (Adams, Bryant, College), changing to three-syllable names further out. In addition, broad **avenues**, all named for states, run diagonally across the grid of streets, meeting up at monumental **traffic circles** like Dupont Circle and Washington Circle. The system only breaks down in **Georgetown**, which predates the city – here quite a few streets retain their older names. Other **oddities** to note are that the Mall has swallowed up A and B streets NW and SW (what would be B St NW is now Constitution Ave NW, and so forth); I Street is often written Eye Street; and there's no J Street in any quadrant (probably because the eighteenth-century city plan used the Latin alphabet, which has no J).

It's crucial to note the relevant two-letter **quadrant code** (NW, NE, SW, SE) in any address or direction. Each grid address (say 1200 G St) could be in one of four quadrants and is impossible to find without the code; 1200 G St NW is a long way from 1200 G St SE. As in other grid plans, **addresses** of avenues and lettered streets relate to the numbered cross-streets – thus, the White House, 1600 Pennsylvania Ave NW, is at 16th St, while 1220 E St NW is between 12th and 13th. On numbered streets, the address is keyed to the numeric equivalent of the letter of the street at the intersection, so 800 9th St NW is at H St (H being the eighth letter of the alphabet); remember that there's no J St, so 1000 9th St is at K St, and so on.

Information

To acquire information on DC before you arrive, see "Information and Maps" (p.17).

On arrival, maps and information are available at desks in the airports, Union Station and in most hotels. Most useful is the free *Washington DC Visitors Guide*, with listings, reviews and contact numbers. For **accommodation services**, contact one of the agencies listed on p.271.

Once in the city, first stop should be at the **DC Chamber of Commerce Visitor Center**, Ronald Reagan Building (Wilson Plaza entrance), 1300 Pennsylvania Ave NW (Mon–Sat 8am–6pm, Sun noon–5pm; ☎328-4748), which can help with maps, tours, bookings and citywide information. Other useful information sources include the **White House Visitor Information Center**, 1450 Pennsylvania Ave NW (see p.150), which has details on National Park sights all over DC; and the **Smithsonian Institution Building** (see p.108) on the Mall, which is the best stop for Smithsonian museum information. Out and about in Washington, you'll come across National Park Service **rangers** – in kiosks on the Mall, at the major memorials, etc – who should also be able to answer general queries. One of the most usefully located sites is the **Ellipse Visitor Pavilion** (daily 8am–4pm), on the east side of the Ellipse (in front of the White

Useful Information Numbers

**DC Chamber of Commerce
Visitor Center** ☎328-4748
Main city information source.

**DC Committee to Promote
Washington** ☎724-5644
*DC-government-sponsored
information on festivals, current events, transportation and
accommodation services.*

Dial-A-Museum ☎357-2020
*Smithsonian Institution exhibits
and special events.*

Dial-A-Park ☎619-7275
*Events at National Park Service
attractions.*

Post-Haste ☎334-9000
*Washington Post information
line for news, weather, sports,
restaurants, events and festivals.*

**Washington DC Convention and
Visitors Association** ☎789-7000
City-wide information source.

**White House Visitor Information
Center** ☎208-1631 or 1-800/717-1450
Maps, brochures and information about major city sights.

House) near the bleacher seats. The **National Park Service
Information Office** (Mon–Fri 9am–5pm; ☎619-7275), inside the
Department of the Interior on C St NW, between 18th and 19th, has
information about all the city's national monuments and memorials.

For details of the various **local newspapers and listings magazines** see chapters 13, 14 and 15. Basically, though, armed with a
free copy of the weekly *CityPaper* (available in stores, bars and
restaurants), the free monthly *Where: Washington* magazine (from
major hotels and terminals) and Friday's *Washington Post*, you
can't go far wrong. Many neighborhoods (Georgetown in particular)
and all the universities also issue free weekly or monthly papers, full
of news, reviews and listings peculiar to their area.

City transit

Most places downtown – including the Mall museums, the major
monuments and the White House – are within walking distance of
each other, while an excellent public transportation system connects
downtown to outlying sites and neighborhoods. The **Washington
Metropolitan Area Transit Authority** (WMATA) operates a subway
system (Metrorail) and a bus network (Metrobus); other options
include using taxis or even renting a bike. Car rental (at least within
the city) is less appealing. For details of city tours, see p.46.

The Metro

Washington's subway – the **Metrorail**, or simply the **Metro** – is
quick, cheap and easy to use. It currently runs on five lines which
cover most of the downtown areas and suburbs (with the notable

*The transit
system and
sights in DC
are – for the
most part –
fully accessible
for travelers
with disabilities; see
pp.26–27 for
details.*

City Transit

exception of Georgetown), while a number of new stations are due to open over the next decade, particularly on the Green Line, which by 2001 should be linked between U Street-Cardozo and Fort Totten and extended southeast beyond Anacostia.

Each line is **color-coded** and studded with various **interchange stations**: Metro Center, L'Enfant Plaza and Gallery Place-Chinatown are the most important downtown. Stations are identifiable outside only by the letter "M" on top of a brown pylon; inside, the well-lit, uncluttered, vaulted halls make the Washington Metro one of the safest in the world. Nevertheless, you should **take the usual precautions** – the system itself may be substantially safe but a few of its stations are in fearsome neighborhoods.

Operating hours are Monday to Friday 5.30am to midnight, Saturday, Sunday and most public holidays 8am to midnight. During rush hour, services run every five minutes on most lines, and every ten to twelve minutes at other times.

Fares and passes

Each passenger needs a **farecard**, bought from machines before passing through the turnstiles. Fares are based on when and how far you travel; maps and ticket prices are posted by the machines. **One-way fares** range from $1.10 (base rate, off-peak) to $3.50; the higher, **peak-rate** fares are charged Mon–Fri 5.30–9.30am and 3–8pm. If you're going to use the Metro several times, it's worth putting in more money – cards with a value of over $20 get you ten percent extra free. Then feed the card through the turnstile and retrieve it; when you do the same thing at the end of your journey, the machine prints out on the card how much fare remains. If you've paid the exact amount, the turnstile keeps the card; if you don't have enough money remaining on the card for the journey, insert it into one of the special exit-fare machines, deposit more money and try the turnstile again. If you're catching a bus after your Metro ride, get a **rail-to-bus transfer** pass from the machine on the platform.

The **Metrorail One Day Pass** ($5) gives unlimited travel after 9.30am on weekdays or all day on the weekend. There's also a **Fast Pass** ($50), for fourteen consecutive days' unlimited travel, and the **28-Day Pass** ($100) for 28 consecutive days. If you're also going to use buses (see below), you might consider the **Bus/Rail Super Pass** ($65), valid for fourteen days' unlimited bus and Metro travel. All passes are available at Metro Center station; at Metro Headquarters (see opposite); at most Safeway, Giant and SuperFresh stores; or through TicketMaster (☎432-7328).

Buses

WMATA is also responsible for DC's **buses**, which operate largely the same hours as the Metro (though some run until 2am). We've listed the most useful services below. The entire system is shown on two

---

Useful Bus Routes

• **Foggy Bottom to Woodley Park**: #L1
via Virginia Ave, C St, 23rd St, Washington Circle, New Hampshire Ave, Dupont Circle, Connecticut Ave (National Zoological Park).

• **L'Enfant Plaza to McPherson Square**: #52
via 6th St, Independence Ave, 14th St.

• **McPherson Square to Woodley Park**: #L2
via K St, 20th St, Dupont Circle, 18th St (Adams-Morgan), Calvert St, Connecticut Ave (National Zoological Park).

• **Metro Center to Adams-Morgan**: #42
via Metro Center (10th and F), H St, Connecticut Ave, Dupont Circle, Columbia Rd (Adams-Morgan).

• **Pennsylvania Ave to Georgetown**: #30, #32, #34, #35, #36
via Eastern Market, US Capitol, Independence Ave, 7th St, Pennsylvania Ave, 15th St, Pennsylvania Ave, Wisconsin Ave (Georgetown).

• **Pentagon–Mall Loop**: #13A, #13B
via 14th St Bridge (Jefferson Memorial), Bureau of Engraving & Printing/Holocaust Museum, Independence Ave, 7th St, Constitution Ave, Lincoln Memorial, Arlington.

• **Union Station to Georgetown**: #D2, #D4
via E St, 13th St, K St, Dupont Circle, Q St (Georgetown).

• **Union Station to Kennedy Center**: #80, #81
via North Capitol St, Massachusetts Ave, H St, New York Ave, Pennsylvania Ave, Foggy Bottom, Watergate Complex.

Metro System Route Maps (one for DC/Virginia, one for DC/Maryland; $2 each), which also mark the Metrorail interchanges. They're available from Metro sales offices (see p.42).

Fares and passes

The **base fare** for most bus journeys is $1.10, payable to the driver, though surcharges and zone crossings can increase this; the same peak-hour rates apply as on the Metro. If you're transferring from the Metro, give your pass to the driver, who'll give you a small discount on the fare. Tourists are unlikely to get full value out of a bus pass – the two most relevant are the Bus/Rail Super Pass (see p.43) and the **DC Base Flash Pass** ($20), which gives fourteen days' unlimited base-fare trips in DC only. **Outside DC**, Maryland and Virginia have their own local bus systems. The only time you're likely to need these is in Alexandria (whose system is called DASH) and en route to Mount Vernon, which you can reach on a Fairfax Connector bus. Both systems link with the Metro: for timetable information call DASH on ☎ 703/370-3274, or Fairfax Connector on ☎ 703/339-7200.

Taxis

Taxis are a useful adjunct to the public transportation system, especially in outposts like Georgetown and Adams-Morgan, which aren't on the Metro. If you know you're going to be out late in these neighborhoods, it's a good idea to book a taxi in advance.

For more information on DC cabs, zones and fares, call the Taxicab Commission at ☎ 645-6005.

There are plans to install meters in all taxis, but for now **fares** are charged on a concentric zoned basis. Standard rates are posted in each cab; a ride at the basic rate within one zone costs $4. Most crosstown fares run from $4 to $12.50 (the maximum for any ride in the city limits) – Georgetown to Dupont Circle, say, costs around $5.50. During rush hours (Mon–Fri 7–9.30am & 4–7pm) there's a $1 surcharge, and if travelling in a group you may be asked to pay $1.50 for each extra person. Don't be surprised if the driver pulls over to pick up another passenger: this is perfectly legal, provided they don't have to go more than five blocks out of the way to reach your destination – everybody pays the set amount for their journey. Once you get out of DC, into Maryland or Virginia, you'll be charged as normal on the meter, which can prove expensive.

Either flag cabs down on the street or use the ranks at hotels and transport terminals; there are always cabs available at Union Station. To **call a taxi in advance** ($1.50 surcharge), try Yellow Cab (☎ 544-1212), Diamond Cab (☎ 332-6200) or Capitol Cab (☎ 546-2400). Washington Flyer Taxi (☎ 703/661-8230) offers a 24-hour metered service to Dulles airport, and most of its cars accept credit cards.

Driving

It's not worth **driving** in the capital unless you have to. If you're heading out of the city by car, either pick up your vehicle at the end of your stay (there are rental desks at Union Station; you don't have to go back to the airports) or leave your own car at your hotel for the duration. For lists of **car rental agencies**, see p.6, p.10 and p.14.

One-way streets can play havoc with the best-formulated driving routes, while the city's **rush hour** (Mon–Fri 6.30–9.30am & 4–7pm, plus lunchtime) traffic-control system means that many lanes, or even whole streets, **change direction** at particular times of the day, and left turns are often periodically forbidden; read the signs carefully. To top it all, the roads are diabolical – even on major thoroughfares you'll want to keep a wary eye out for potholes and ridges.

Most mid- and upper-range hotels have secure parking (from around $10 per night); **parking lots and garages** cost from $5 per hour to $15 a day. Looking for free **on-street parking** is not likely to pay for itself in terms of time and energy expended: there are free, limited-wait (2–3hr) parking spots around the Mall (Jefferson and Madison Drives, Independence Ave SW) and in West Potomac Park, but they're heavily subscribed. **Parking meters** tend to operate between 9.30am and 6.30pm, usually giving a maximum stay of two hours; stay longer and you'll get a $15 ticket. At other times, just when you think you've found the perfect spot, it will almost certainly be reserved for local workers, or on a street that becomes one-way during rush hour, or temporarily illegal to park because it *is* rush hour, or in a clearway reserved for snow plows, or rendered useless for a million and one other reasons. Naturally, the places you might want to drive to for an evening out, like Georgetown, Dupont Circle or Adams-Morgan, are, again, heavily cruised for parking space.

If your car gets towed away, call the Brentwood Impoundment Lot at ☎576-7217; expect to pay up to $100 to get it back. Vehicles towed away after 7pm on a Friday won't be returned until after 9am the following Monday.

Bikes and boats

Given the traffic, few visitors will want to brave the streets on a **bicycle**, though several outfits can fix you up and provide maps and advice on local trails: Big Wheel Bikes (Georgetown ☎337-0254, Eastern Market ☎543-1600, or Old Town Alexandria ☎703/739-2300), City Bikes (Adams-Morgan ☎265-1564) and Better Bikes (☎293-2080 – will deliver anywhere in DC) all rent bikes for around $25 a day, $100 a week (slightly more for mountain bikes); you'll need to leave a deposit and/or a credit card or passport. Alternatively, you can always join a **cycling tour** – see p.47

The nicest option is to rent a bike for short **rides along the Potomac River** or the **C&O Canal towpath**, something you can do at Big Wheel Bikes' Georgetown branch, Thompson's Boat Center, near the Watergate Complex (2900 Virginia Ave NW at Rock Creek Parkway ☎333-4861; March–Oct only), and Fletcher's Boat House (4940 Canal Rd NW ☎244-0461; March–Oct only), two miles further up the canal towpath. This costs around $25 a day and is infinitely safer than careering around the city. Long-distance **cycle paths** include one in Rock Creek Park (see p.238), the 18.5-mile Mount Vernon Trail (see p.260), and the entire 184-mile length of the C&O towpath (see p.242). The eleven-mile Capital Crescent Trail, starting at Thompson's, branches off the C&O towpath after three miles and follows the course of an old railway line up into Bethesda, MD and on to Silver Spring.

Thompson's and Fletcher's also rent out **rowboats and canoes**, as do Jack's Boats (under the Key Bridge at 3500 K St NW, Georgetown ☎337-9642) and Swain's Lock Boat House (☎301/299-9006), twenty miles up the canal: reckon on $6–8 per hour, $20–25 per day for either.

City tours

There are any number of operators prepared to show you the sights, though even with just a couple of days it's easy to see most things on your own. However, some of the more popular tour-bus services, like the Tourmobile, are useful, since they allow you to get on and off the bus at will and shuttle you out to the more far-flung sights. **River cruises**, too, can be worth considering, especially in high summer when the offshore breeze comes as a welcome relief. **Specialist tours** show you a side of Washington you may not otherwise see; some of the best are picked out below.

Walking tours

All telephone numbers are area code ☎202 unless otherwise stated.

DC Heritage Tours ☎639-0908. Ninety-minute walking tours of downtown DC, run in conjunction with Discovery Channel and starting from their flagship store at 601 F St NW. Tours daily throughout the year; tickets ($7.50) available at the store.

Anthony S. Pitch ☎301/294-9514. Highly recommended historical walking tours of Adams-Morgan, Lafayette Square and Georgetown, led by the amiable Mr Pitch (call for schedules). They last 2hr and cost $10.

Bus and trolley tours

Gray Line ☎289-1995. City bus tours ($25–40), trolley tour ($19) and black heritage tour (groups only), from the Gray Line terminal in Union Station.

Old Town Trolley Tours ☎832-9800. Motorized, board-at-will trolleys covering downtown, Georgetown and National Cathedral. Tickets cost $24 a day, available at trolley stops and downtown hotels.

Tourmobile ☎554-5100. Narrated, open-sided Tourmobile buses allow unlimited stops at numerous city locations. A $14 day ticket covers downtown and Arlington Cemetery; an extra $22 gets you to Mount Vernon and back, and $7 to the Frederick Douglass Home; two-day tickets for unlimited travel on both routes cost $37 (DC and Mount Vernon) or $28 (DC and Frederick Douglass). Bought after 1pm (after 3pm, mid-June to Labor Day), a $16

Building Tours

For special, extended tours of the following buildings you must make reservations; see the relevant accounts for details. American citizens should contact their Congressional representatives well in advance for special tours of government buildings. Tours arranged like this will be on a specific day, usually outside opening hours; most last longer than the normal walk-in tours and show you areas or rooms not normally open to the public.

Bureau of Engraving and Printing, see p.139.

Department of State, see p.166.

Federal Bureau of Investigation, see p.180.

Federal Reserve Building, see p.166.

National Archives, see p.185.

Old Executive Office Building, see p.157.

Treasury Building, see p.158.

US Capitol, see p.112.

Washington Post, see p.215.

White House, see p.147.

advance ticket is also valid for all the next day. Tickets from the office on the Ellipse, kiosks on the Mall (there's one at the Washington Monument) or on the bus itself.

Bicycle tours

Bike the Sites Inc ☎966-8662. Three-hour guided bike tours of the city's major sights ($35, includes bike and helmet), plus tours of Mount Vernon and customized tours throughout the district. No fixed schedule; call for details. Advance reservations required.

Cruises

Capitol River Cruises ☎301/460-7447. Regular 50-minute sightseeing cruises leaving hourly throughout the day from Georgetown's Washington Harbor (end of 31st St NW); April–Oct; $10 per person, reservations not necessary.

DC Ducks ☎832-9800. Converted amphibious carriers which cruise the Mall and then splash into the Potomac on a cruise (90min). Hourly departures from Union Station (10am–4pm) in July & Aug; weekends only March–June and Sept–Nov ($24).

Spirit Cruises ☎554-8000. Swish two-hour river cruises with bar and showbands, $26–30; three-hour dinner cruises for $60. Tickets and departures from Pier 4, 6th and Water streets SW (Waterfront Metro).

Specialist tours and activities

Air Pegasus ☎484-8484. Fifteen-minute helicopter tours ($80 per person) above the sights of central DC; daily departures April–Sept (reservations required) from the airfield at 1724 S Capitol St SE.

Goodwill Embassy Tour ☎636-4225. Every May, some of DC's finest embassy buildings throw open their doors for one day; reserve well in advance (advance bookings $25; $30 on the day). Many embassies also offer free guided tours provided you reserve in advance; for numbers see p.326.

Kalorama House and Embassy Tour ☎387-4062. Various ambassadors' residences and private homes open to the public for one day every September; reserve in advance ($20).

Smithsonian Associates, 1100 Jefferson Drive SW ☎357-3030 (Mon–Fri 9am–5pm). Full program of after-hours tours, performances, lectures and films in the museums and galleries. *The Associate* magazine (from Smithsonian museum shops) carries a monthly list of activities.

Museums, galleries, monuments and memorials

Full details are given for each **museum, gallery, monument, memorial and public building** reviewed in this guide – address, telephone number (all area code ☎202 unless otherwise stated), public transit links, opening hours and adult admission price (where applicable). The majority of DC's museums and sights are **free**; where there is an admission charge, **children** and, usually, **senior citizens** get in for half-price. For details of specific exhibits and events call in advance. Note that all the Smithsonian museums and galleries have the same information line (☎357-2700). Most museums and attractions are **closed** on December 25 and over New Year; many are closed on public holidays, too (for a list of which, see p.23).

Chapter 2

The Mall

S crubbed, manicured and heavily policed, the showpiece greensward of **THE MALL** is quite unlike the center of any other American city, though European visitors, used to triumphal structures, royal parks and boulevards, will feel right at home. Laid out along two carefully tended miles between the US Capitol and the Potomac River are nine Smithsonian **museums**, unrivaled in their field; the two buildings of the National Gallery of Art; and the city's four most famous **monuments and memorials** – to George Washington, Abraham Lincoln, Franklin Delano Roosevelt and the Vietnam veterans. A fifth, to Thomas Jefferson, and the White House itself, stand perfectly aligned on either side.

The Mall is also where Washington comes to relax – Albert Camus talked fondly of "placid evenings on the vast lawns" during his visit in 1946 – and to party, not least at the annual Festival of American Folklife and on the Fourth of July. Yet its central role in a planned capital city also places it at the very heart of the country's **political** life. When there's a protest to be made, the National Mall – to give it its full title – is the place to make it. The 1963 March on Washington brought Dr Martin Luther King Jr to the steps of the Lincoln Memorial to deliver his "I have a dream" speech; in 1967, at the height of the anti-war protests, the notorious March on the Pentagon started from the same place; three decades later, in 1995, the controversial minister, Louis Farrakhan of the Nation of Islam, brought hundreds of thousands of black men here on the Million Men March. The sheer expanse of the Mall inspires grand gestures: on several occasions the AIDS Memorial Quilt – a patchwork of 40,000 individual squares remembering America's AIDS victims – has been laid in commemoration the full mile from the Capitol to the Washington Monument.

As a visitor, you'd have to concoct a fairly perverse **itinerary** to avoid setting foot on the Mall. Given a normal appetite for museums, galleries and monuments, and a fair constitution, you could get around most things in three days or so. But it's better to return at various times during your stay, if only to avoid complete cultural

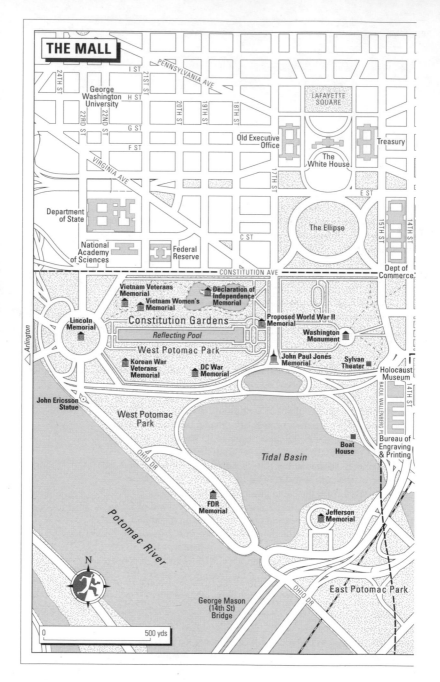

THE MALL

George Washington University

24TH ST
22ND ST
22ND ST
23RD ST
21ST ST
20TH ST
19TH ST
18TH ST
17TH ST
15TH ST
14TH ST

I ST
H ST
G ST
F ST

PENNSYLVANIA AVE

LAFAYETTE SQUARE

Old Executive Office

Treasury

The White House

E ST

VIRGINIA AVE

Department of State

The Ellipse

National Academy of Sciences

Federal Reserve

C ST

Dept of Commerce

CONSTITUTION AVE

Vietnam Veterans Memorial

Declaration of Independence Memorial

Vietnam Women's Memorial

Proposed World War II Memorial

Constitution Gardens

Washington Monument

Lincoln Memorial

Reflecting Pool

West Potomac Park

John Paul Jones Memorial

Sylvan Theater

Holocaust Museum

Korean War Veterans Memorial

DC War Memorial

Arlington

John Ericsson Statue

West Potomac Park

RAOUL WALLENBERG PL

14TH ST

Bureau of Engraving & Printing

Boat House

Tidal Basin

Potomac River

FDR Memorial

Jefferson Memorial

N

East Potomac Park

OHIO DR

George Mason (14th St) Bridge

OHIO DR

0   500 yds

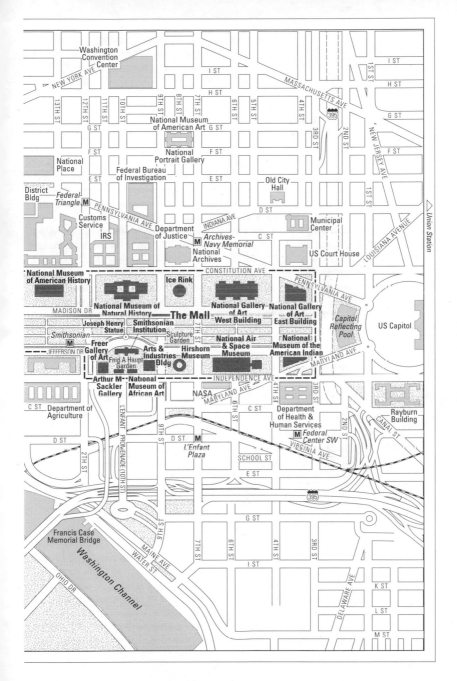

overload. Many of the attractions lend themselves to being seen with a combination of other city sights: the western monuments with the White House (Chapter 5); the Jefferson and Roosevelt memorials with the Holocaust Museum or Bureau of Engraving and Printing (Chapter 4); the museums on the Mall's north side interspersed with a stroll around Old Downtown (Chapter 6).

Some history

French military engineer **Pierre Charles L'Enfant**'s plan for the new capital city had at its heart a 400-foot-wide Grand Avenue, leading west from the site of the Capitol. Along it he envisaged gardens and mansions for the political elite and, where a line drawn west from the Capitol met one drawn south from the President's Mansion (today's White House), was to stand a commemorative monument to George Washington – ambitious schemes indeed for a piece of land that was, at the time, little more than a muddy, bug-infested swamp. Due to lack of funds work didn't start on the Washington Monument until 1848, by which time any prospect of what had become known as "The Mall" transforming itself into a splendid avenue was laughable: cows, pigs and goats grazed on the open land, while along the north side ran the malodorous city canal (linking the C&O Canal in Georgetown with the Anacostia River), stinking with rotting refuse, spoiling fish, entrails and dead animals from Washington's 7th Street Center Market.

Following the building of the **Smithsonian Institution** "Castle" between 1849 and 1855, eminent landscape gardener **Andrew Jackson Downing** was employed to design an elegant green space in keeping with L'Enfant's original plan, but the money only stretched to one tree-planted park by the Smithsonian. Even here, people dared not venture at night since it soon became the haunt of footpads and ne'er-do-wells. What's more, by 1855 work had been halted on the nearby Washington Monument, which stood incomplete for the next twenty years. The Mall continued to deteriorate and, as the city grew, its south side became home to meat-markets and warehouses, while the avenue itself was crisscrossed by the ungainly tracks of the Baltimore and Potomac Railroad.

For more on L'Enfant's plan for the city, see pp.34–35.

During the **Civil War**, President Lincoln had been determined to continue building as "a sign we intend the Union shall go on", and postwar Reconstruction saved the Mall from further decline. The city canal was filled in (it's now Constitution Ave) and Center Market was closed; a Board of Public Works was established to build sewers, sidewalks and streets; mature trees were planted; and in 1884 the Washington Monument was finally completed. Several of Downing's other schemes were resurrected, extending beyond the Mall to incorporate the Ellipse and the gardens on either side of the White House – finally placing the Mall at the ornamental heart of the city.

With the addition of the **Arts and Industries Building** in 1881
– America's first national museum – the Mall became seen as the
natural site for grand public institutions (following L'Enfant's hope
that it would be "attractive to the learned and afford diversion to the
idle"). The Botanic Gardens followed in 1902, the Museum of
Natural History in 1911 and, eventually, the Smithsonian's first art
gallery, the Freer, in 1923. Meanwhile, members of the **McMillan
Commission** of 1901, under Senator James McMillan, charged with
improving the Mall and the city's park system, returned from
Europe fired up with plans to link the Mall with a series of gardens
and memorials and to demolish the unsightly railroad station (later
replaced by Union Station). Not everyone concurred: House
Speaker Joseph Cannon railed that he "would rather see the Mall
sown in oats than treated as an artistic composition". However,
McMillan's proposals prevailed and, following the completion of the
Lincoln Memorial in 1922, the Mall was extended west of the
Washington Monument for the first time, reaching to the banks of
the Potomac River and incorporating the grounds known today as
West Potomac Park. More improvements came in the 1930s, under
the auspices of Roosevelt's New Deal-era Works Progress
Administration (WPA), including the planting of the now-famous
elms. Meanwhile, the **National Park Service** was granted stewardship of the Mall and its monuments.

The erection of the Jefferson Memorial in 1943 completed the
Mall's initial triumvirate of Presidential monuments. The same archi-
tect, John Russell Pope, designed the contemporaneous National
Gallery of Art; the 1960s and 1970s contributed museums of
American History and Air and Space, the Hirshorn art gallery and an
East Building for the National Gallery; the 1980s, the Sackler Gallery
and African Art museum. The dedication of the Vietnam Veterans
Memorial (1982) and the Korean War Veterans Memorial (1995)
proved that there's still space, too, for further **additions**, the most
popular of recent times being the FDR Memorial (1997). Meanwhile
a National World War II Memorial is in the design stage, and the last
free block in the eastern Mall, next to the Air and Space Museum, is
reserved for the National Museum of the American Indian, scheduled
to open in 2003.

Monuments and memorials

On the face of it, the Mall presents the easiest of choices to visitors:
monuments and memorials to the west and **museums** to the east,
with the Washington Monument standing sentinel between the two.
Most people make a beeline for the Washington Monument, which is
no bad thing. But there's an argument, too, for approaching the
Monument **on foot from the east**, keeping to the central paths and
resisting the temptation to dive into the museums. This way you get

Mall Transportation

The nearest **Metro stations** for the eastern Mall are Smithsonian (south side) and Federal Triangle or Archives-Navy Memorial (both north side); L'Enfant Plaza and Federal Center SW are both two blocks, or a ten-minute walk, from the south side. For **west** of the Washington Monument, the best bet is to take **bus #13A/13B** (Pentagon–Mall Loop; see p.43), or the Tourmobile (see p.46), which both run along Constitution Avenue, though Foggy Bottom-GWU Metro puts you within six blocks of the Mall.

a flavor of the piecemeal development of the Mall, the landscaped grounds and buildings reflecting 150 years of architectural styles, while at the same time coming to a fuller appreciation of the sheer scale of the Washington Monument itself.

Approaching the Washington Monument: the eastern Mall

From the eastern end of the Mall it's just under a mile to the Washington Monument, walking past the museums which lie on either side. Starting in the northeastern corner of the Mall lie the two buildings of the **National Gallery of Art** (p.81). Built in 1941 by John Russell Pope, what is now known as the **West Building** (at 7th and Constitution) was DC's last great Neoclassical construction. With its domed rotunda and sweeping front steps, it's a veritable palace of pink Tennessee marble, though one that was not to every-one's taste; one critic complained it was "hollow and pompous . . . an outdated extravaganza". This is not a charge that could fairly be leveled at I.M. Pei's **East Building** of 1978, which lies across 4th Street, connected to the main building by underground tunnel. Using the same pink marble as the original building, Pei fashioned a thoroughly modern interlocking triangular design – his hand part-ly forced by the shape of the block of land on which the building stands. A similar curtailment of space faced Douglas Cardinal, Canadian architect of the future **National Museum of the American Indian**, which will face the East Building on a site bounded by Independence Avenue, Maryland Avenue and Jefferson Drive. Initial designs indicate that it will differ greatly from the Mall norm of lines and angles: influenced by Western landscapes (and by Cardinal's Native American ancestry), from the awkward plot will rise a curv-ing, multi-layered stone-and-glass building with terraced facade and forest and wetland landscapes.

There are no such space restraints immediately to the west, where the 700-foot-long **National Air and Space Museum** (p.76) fills the land between 4th and 7th. All the adventure here is inside; the building itself, designed by Gyo Obata, is a rather dull spread of squat marble boxes split by glass frames. Further along the south

The Mall's museums and galleries are covered on pp.67–109.

Work on the National Museum of the American Indian is due to be complet-ed by 2003.

side of Independence Avenue is Gordon Bunshaft's cylindrical **Hirshorn Museum** (p.74) of 1974, a neat counterweight to the angular gymnastics employed by Pei. Here, you're at possibly the single most rewarding stretch of the Mall, with a further five museums and galleries imaginatively sited in the blocks between 9th and 12th streets. Most prominent of all is the **Smithsonian Institution Building** (p.108), the original home of the Smithsonian and known more widely as the "**Castle**". Completed in 1855 by James Renwick, its Gothic towers and battlements jut out into the Mall, halfway between the Capitol and the Washington Monument. It was mocked at the time by architect and sculptor Horatio Greenhough as a "medieval confusion*", though today it's considered a triumph in red brick – one to which you're steadily drawn as you make your way down the Mall, since its central tower is the only structure other than the Washington Monument to rise above the trees. Between the Castle and the Hirshorn Museum, the **Arts and Industries Building** (p.70) was the Mall's second public construction, built in 1881 to house exhibits from Philadelphia's 1876 Centennial Exhibition. Architects Cluss and Schulze clearly warmed to their brief, and it's positively jaunty in comparison with the Castle, featuring playful polychromatic brick-and-tile patterns.

There's a century beween the Arts and Industries Building and its two near neighbors, the adjacent **National Museum of African Art** (p.96) and **Arthur M. Sackler Gallery** (p.68). Both designed by the same Boston architectural firm and opened in 1987, the twin embellished, granite-and-limestone cubes complement each other in their interior and exterior thematic use of shapes (circles for the African Art, triangles for the Sackler). They're also connected by underground passage; indeed, all the gallery space at both museums is underground, a reflection of the shortage of room along this part of the Mall. Outside, between the two, sits the flower-filled **Enid A. Haupt Garden** (daily: June–Sept 7am–8pm; Oct–May 7am–5.45pm), where you'll find several topiary bison – live animals were once kept here in pens so that nineteenth-century Smithsonian boffins could study their expressions and posture before stuffing the beasts destined for their natural history collection. The museum grouping on this side is completed by Charles A. Platt's **Freer Gallery of Art**

---

*Greenhough was singularly ill-placed to criticize the work of others, having been on the end of a public lashing from Congress after he'd delivered his commissioned statue of George Washington in 1841, destined to be placed in the Capitol. It was too big to get through the door into the Rotunda, which had to be dismantled, and too heavy for the floor, into which it sank. When finally on display, according to Washington historian E.J. Applewhite, "The seated, half-naked figure . . . with a toga draped over his knees and right shoulder, provoked only derision and embarrassment". The statue was eventually donated "in a gesture more desperate than generous" to the National Museum of American History, where it remains today.

(p.71), a granite-and-marble Italianate palazzo added to the corner plot at 12th and Independence in 1923. You can also reach this by underground passage, from the Sackler Gallery.

Across the Mall from the Castle, the north side buildings finish in some style with Hornblower and Marshall's domed, Neoclassical **National Museum of Natural History** (p.106), built in 1911 (though with two further wings added in the 1960s), and the symmetrical, Beaux-Arts **National Museum of American History** (p.98) of 1964. The two are divided by 12th Street as it tunnels under the Mall and by fifty years of architectural tradition, but both in their lofty, virtuous way find their echoes in the splendid Federal Triangle buildings of the Great Depression, located across Constitution Avenue. Indeed, like the Federal Triangle buildings, the American History Museum comes laden with exterior inscriptions, with the sheer Mall-facing facade etched with improving quotations by such luminaries as Smithsonian founder James Smithson and John Quincy Adams. The **ice rink** on the east side of the Museum of Natural History (between 7th and 9th) is a nice spot, with skates for rent in winter and shade, snacks and drinks in summer.

The Washington Monument

15th St NW at Constitution Ave ☎426-6841; Smithsonian Metro. Daily: April–Aug 8am–midnight; Sept–March 8am–5pm. Admission free.

If there's one structure that symbolizes Washington, it is surely the **Washington Monument**, an unadorned marble obelisk built in memory of the first US president. Simple, elegant, majestic and, above all, huge, it's immediately recognizable from all over the city (and from a fair distance beyond), providing the Mall and the capital with a striking central ornament.

There had been much early talk about honoring the achievements of George Washington with a commemorative monument. L'Enfant's original city plan proposed an equestrian statue at the intersection of the south axis of the White House with the west axis of the Capitol, an idea of which Washington himself approved. Yet even after Washington's death in 1799 virtually no progress was made save the placing of a small **stone marker** on the proposed spot by Thomas Jefferson in 1804; the "Jefferson Pier" is still visible today. Impatient at Congress's apparent lack of enthusiasm for the work, the **National Monument Sociey** was established in 1833 and fostered a design competition and subscription drive, from which emerged **Robert Mills**' hugely ambitious scheme to top a colonnaded base containing the tombs of Revolutionary heroes with a massive obelisk: L'Enfant's original idea received a nod by the addition of a statue of Washington driving a horse-drawn chariot.

The Society took one look at the meager collected subscriptions and settled for the obelisk on its own. In retrospect – given the trouble in getting even this built – it proved to be a wise decision. Early excavations revealed that L'Enfant's chosen spot was too marshy to build on and when the cornerstone was finally laid on July 4, 1848, it was on a bare knoll 360ft east and 120ft south of the true intersection – which explains why the monument looks off-center on the map. By 1853, when funds ran out, the monument was just 152ft high, and stayed that way for almost 25 years – grievously truncated, bordered by the fetid Washington Canal, the site roamed by cattle awaiting slaughter at a nearby abattoir. Mark Twain likened it to a "factory chimney with the top broken off", while the *New York Tribune*, in a fairly universally held opinion, condemned it as a "wretched design, a wretched location".

After the Civil War, Congress finally authorized government funds to complete the monument and appointed **Lt Colonel Thomas Casey** of the Army Corps of Engineers to the work. He suffered his own tribulations, not least the discovery that the original marble source in Maryland had dried up; you can still see the transition line at the 150-foot level where work resumed with marble of a slightly different tone. At long last, by December 1884, the Monument was finally ready and, at a shade over 555ft, stood unchallenged as the tallest building in the world; it's still the tallest all-masonry structure on the planet. Fifty-five feet wide at the base, tapering to 34ft at the top, where it's capped by a small aluminum pyramid, it was originally accessible by a steam-powered elevator, which took twenty minutes to reach the top. Women and children were forced to toil up the 897 steps because the elevator was considered too dangerous.

Today, the **elevator** up takes seventy seconds and deposits you at the 500-foot level from where the views, naturally, are tremendous, glimpsed through surprisingly narrow windows on all four sides. The view aside, the only other diversion is provided by the bronze **statue of Washington** at ground level, which faces east towards the Capitol. Almost 7ft high, this is a faithful copy of the renowned statue by eighteenth-century French master sculptor Jean-Antoine Houdon,* which was commissioned for the Virginia State Capitol in Richmond and placed there in 1796. Washington, wearing the uniform of Commander-in-Chief of the Continental Army, holds a cane in one hand and is flanked on the other by a bundle of bound rods and a plowshare, signifying authority and peace respectively.

The views of the city are, arguably, even better from the Old Post Office on Pennsylvania Avenue; see p.181.

---

*Houdon was the first major European artist to visit America, traveling to George Washington's home at Mount Vernon in 1785, where he stayed long enough to make a life mask and other studies. Washington had to lie flat on his back, his face covered with grease and then slapped with plaster of Paris, breathing through tubes while the facemask set – at which point, so the story goes, his step-granddaughter, Eleanor, came into the room and fled in tears, thinking him dead.

George Washington

The Washington family, originally from the north of England, emigrated to America in 1656 after the English Civil War, during which they had been fierce loyalists. On February 22, 1732, George Washington was born on the wealthy family plantation in Westmoreland County, Virginia. Though most of what is known about his early life is almost entirely the product of various fawning and fictitious nineteenth-century biographies, it is clear that he received intermittent schooling, learned to ride and excelled in most outdoor pursuits. He also displayed a talent for surveying, and in 1748 assisted in the surveying of the new town of Alexandria (see p.258).

At the age of 21, he was appointed by Virginia's governor to travel into the Ohio Valley to ascertain the strength of the French forces, which had been steadily encroaching on Crown British land. This experience led him to be appointed lieutenant-colonel in the Virginia Regiment and, later, aide-de-camp in the French and Indian War, in which he gained his first battle experience – a bad defeat, though Washington gained local respect for his leadership qualities. Finishing the war as regimental commander he was subsequently elected to the Virginia House of Burgesses in Williamsburg. Giving up his commission, in January 1759 he married the equally wealthy Martha Dandridge Custis – who came with two children from a previous marriage – and settled at Mount Vernon (see p.264) into the agreeable life of a gentleman plantation owner, a lifestyle buttressed by the endeavor of a large number of slaves. George and Martha never had any children of their own, but later became guardians to the youngest two of Martha's grandchildren by her first marriage.

Washington continued to serve in the House of Burgesses throughout the 1760s, during the growing confrontation with Britain. Acquiring a reputation for honesty and judgment, Washington was one of the Virginian delegates at the Continental Congress in 1774; the following year, when British soldiers clashed with American volunteers at Lexington and Concord, confrontation turned into revolution. At a second meeting of the Continental Congress in June 1775, the 43-year-old Washington was appointed commander-in-chief of the nascent American forces – as much for the fact that he was from Virginia (Congress wanted to combine the existing New England army with a general who would also attract southern volunteers) as for his military experience, which was fairly modest.

Washington's achievements in the field during the Revolutionary War have been subsequently overplayed. He wasn't a great general: making early mistakes, his under-equipped Continental Army lost more battles than it won and it took seven years to defeat a largely incompetently led British force fighting far from home. There was often insufficient money to pay, clothe or supply the American militiamen, who regularly deserted;

To visit the monument, you must pick up a free **ticket** from the 15th Street kiosk (on the Mall, south of Constitution Ave), which allows you to turn up at a fixed time later in the day, or you can reserve with TicketMaster (☎ 1-800/505-5040; $1.50 per person). It's also worth calling the monument to ask about ranger-led **walk-down tours** of the interior steps – these were discontinued a couple of years ago but may have restarted.

the locals and often Congress, too, proved unsupportive, and to top it all he was ill-served by traitors in his camp. But Washington was a dogged figure, determined to impose order and hierarchy onto the fledgling army. He also retained the respect of his forces during trying times, not least by sharing their hardships – throughout the war years, he stayed away from his Mount Vernon estate, Martha spending the winters encamped with George in his northern redoubts.

After Yorktown in 1781 and the winning of independence, Washington resisted military demands to assume an American "kingship", resigned his commission in 1783 and returned to Mount Vernon. However, four years later, at the Constitutional Convention in Philadelphia, Washington was back in the political frame. Called to safeguard the Revolution by devising a permanent system of government for the nation, the Convention unanimously elected Washington its presiding officer, as the only man to command universal respect. Once the Constitution had been drawn up and ratified, there was only one realistic choice for the post of first President of the United States – indeed, there's evidence that the powers outlined in the Constitution concerning the presidency were specifically tailored with Washington's character and probity in mind. In February 1789, George Washington was unanimously elected president for the first time.

Washington defined the uncharted role of president, bestowing upon it an hauteur that became almost monarchical, while developing the relationship between the executive and the other branches of government. It's doubtful anyone else could have contained the subtle machinations of various members of his cabinet as the Federalists and Republicans skirmished for influence. Luckily, he presided over an early economic boom; skillfully, and despite severe provocation by both sides, he kept America out of the war between England and France. During his first term, he even negotiated the political minefield that was deciding upon the site of the new federal capital (see p.34). The city was promptly named after him, and the president laid the cornerstone of the US Capitol in 1793 (though he never lived in Washington or the White House – which wasn't finished until 1800 – shuttling instead between New York, Philadelphia and other northeastern cities).

Washington was elected to a second term in 1793 and would undoubtedly have been granted a third, but in 1797 he was 65 and wanted nothing more than to retire to his farm. Delivering a farewell address to both houses of Congress, he went home to Mount Vernon, where he died two and a half years later on December 14, 1799, from a fever induced by being caught out in a snowstorm on his estate. Congress adjourned for the day, and even the British and French fleets lowered their flags in respect. Martha lived on until May 1802 (and on her death, Washington's will freed all their slaves); they're buried together in the grounds at Mount Vernon.

The Lincoln Memorial

West Potomac Park at 23rd St NW ☎426-6841 or 426-6895; Foggy Bottom-GWU Metro or #13A/B bus from Constitution Ave. Daily 24hr; staffed 8am–midnight. Admission free.

Proposals to erect a monument to the revered sixteenth President were raised as early as 1865, the year of his assassination (see p.204):

*The Lincoln
Memorial is
pictured on
the back of
every $5 bill
and penny
coin.*

*An earlier
statue of
Lincoln
(1909), jointly
undertaken by
Daniel Chester
French and the
memorial
architect
Henry Bacon,
stands in front
of a wall
inscribed with
the Gettysburg
Address in the
Capitol
grounds, in
Lincoln,
Nebraska.*

the problem was always to pinpoint a suitable structure and appropriate site. There was certainly no shortage of ideas: one early plan suggested building a Lincoln Highway between Washington and Gettysburg, while arch Neoclassicist John Russell Pope submitted four designs (including a vast pyramid and a stone funeral pyre), all of which were rejected. In 1901 the McMillan Commission grasped the nettle and finally approved the construction of a Greek temple in the marshlands of the newly created West Potomac Park. This, the **Lincoln Memorial**, has stood the test of time to become the best-loved of all DC's commemorative structures: solemn, inspirational, and providing a proportioned Classical counterpoint to the grandeur of both the Washington Monument and, beyond, of the US Capitol.

Work began on the memorial in February 1914 under the aegis of New York architect **Henry Bacon**, who erected a bastardized Doric temple on a small rise in the park. Its 36 columns symbolize the number of states that made up the Union at the time of Lincoln's death, while bas-relief plaques on the attic parapet commemorate the 48 states of the Union that existed when the memorial was completed in 1922 (Alaska and Hawaii get a mere inscription on the terrace). But for all its restrained beauty, the temple is upstaged by what lies inside, the seated **statue of Lincoln** by Daniel Chester French (1850–1931), which faces out through the colonnade – one of America's most enduring images. French certainly succeeded in his intention to "convey the mental and physical strength of the great war President": full of resolve, a steely Lincoln clasps the armrests of a thronelike chair with determined hands, his unbuttoned coat falling to either side; the American flag is draped over the back of the chair. It's a phenomenal work, one which took French thirteen years to complete, fashioning the nineteen-foot-tall statue from 28 blocks of white Georgia marble.

Climbing the steps to the memorial is one of DC's more profound moments, as first you meet Lincoln's gaze and then turn to look out over the Reflecting Pool (see opposite) and down the length of the Mall. Turn back and you'll notice **murals** on the north and south walls, painted by Jules Guerin, representing Fraternity, Unity of North and South, and Charity (north wall) and Emancipation and Immortality (south wall), directly under which are carved inscriptions of Lincoln's two most celebrated **speeches**. On the north wall is the Gettysburg Address of November 19, 1863 – the speech that Lincoln himself thought a "flat failure" – while on the south is the measured eloquence of Lincoln's Second Inaugural Address of March 4, 1865, in which he strove "to bind up the nation's wounds" caused by the Civil War.

The Memorial wields an emotional influence far beyond its commemorative function. In many ways, it's as much a memorial to the preservation of the Union as to Lincoln himself, as the inscription behind the statue makes clear: "In this temple as in the hearts of the people for whom he saved the Union the memory of Abraham Lincoln is enshrined forever." Ironic, then, that on its dedication day

---

Lincoln and the Gettysburg Address

*Four score and seven years ago our fathers brought forth on this con-
tinent, a new nation, conceived in Liberty, and dedicated to the
proposition that all men are created equal . . .*

Abraham Lincoln's Gettysburg Address astonished observers with its brevi-
ty – the official photographer hadn't even got his equipment ready before
the President sat down again. At events such as the dedication of the war
cemetery of Gettysburg, orators were expected to expound lengthily, as
indeed did Edward Everett (former senator and one-time Secretary of
State), who was first to speak at the ceremony. Everett later claimed he
wished he had even come close in two and a half hours to what Lincoln had
managed to encapsulate in two and a half minutes. Yet the president's
speech was poorly received: Lincoln himself was convinced that the audience had failed to appreciate its fine nuances, while the *Chicago Times*
lambasted it as "silly, flat, and dish-watery utterances". Other newspapers
had a keener sense of history – *Harper's Weekly* thought it "as simple and
felicitous and earnest a word as was ever spoken".

---

in May 1922, while President Warren G. Harding and Lincoln's surviving son Robert could watch proceedings from the comfort of the
speakers' platform, Dr Robert Moton, president of the Tuskegee
Institute who was to make the principal address – was forced to
watch from a roped-off area since the crowds were segregated by
color. From this point on, the memorial became a focus for demonstrations in the name of **civil rights**: Spanish Civil War veterans from
the Abraham Lincoln Brigade marched here in 1938; a year later, on
Easter Sunday 1939, black opera singer Marian Anderson performed
from the steps to a crowd of 75,000, having been refused permission
to appear at the nearby Constitution Hall – pointedly dedicating the
event to "the ideals of freedom for which President Lincoln died".
Groups from the American Nazi Party to the Black Panthers have
exercised their First Amendment rights at the memorial (as anyone
can, provided they don't climb on the statue or hang banners from
the building); but its brightest day saw the appearance of **Dr Martin
Luther King Jr**, who chose the memorial to the Great Emancipator
from which to make his "I have a dream" speech to the 200,000 people who gathered here on August 28, 1963, during the March on
Washington for Jobs and Freedom. Five years later, in June 1968,
after King's assassination, his successors brought the ill-fated Poor
People's March to the memorial (see the "Resurrection City" box on
p.62); while Jesse Jackson addressed a 50,000-strong crowd here in
1988 on the twenty-fifth anniversary of King's celebrated speech.

*The memori-
al's lower
lobby exhibit
fleshes out its
history; there
are also
restrooms
here.*

The Reflecting Pool and Constitution Gardens
The view from the memorial would lose a significant part of its attraction were it not for the 2000-foot-long, 160-foot-wide **Reflecting Pool**
which reaches out from the steps toward the Washington Monument.

Every
September on
Constitution
Day, the sign-
ing of the
Constitution is
celebrated in
the gardens
by, among
other things,
an outdoor
naturalization
service for for-
eign-born DC
residents.

Resurrection City

At the time of Dr Martin Luther King Jr's assassination, the Civil Rights leader was planning a second march on the capital, an idea which his successors saw to fruition. Under the auspices of the Southern Christian Leadership Conference, the **Poor People's March** of May 1968 converged on Washington from Mississippi, its organizers determined to force Congress to take a serious stand against poverty and unemployment. The 3000 marchers set up camp around the Reflecting Pool, in view of the US Capitol, and called their shantytown structures **Resurrection City**. Water and electricity were supplied, and churches and charities brought in food, but rain was heavy that June and the mud-caked camp soon lost its momentum. Many residents left early; those that stayed were joined at the Lincoln Memorial by a crowd of 50,000 on June 19, Solidarity Day, to listen to a Peter, Paul and Mary concert and hear various fiery speeches. However, the turnout was much lower than expected and, with an ebbing of public support, the dispirited camp was dissolved a week later as city police cleared away the tents.

Supposedly inspired by the pools and canals at Versailles and by the landscaping at the Taj Mahal, the mirror images of memorial and monument captured in the water have the capacity to bring strollers up short with a gasp. It's particularly affecting at night, when both pool and memorial are lit. A National World War II Memorial has been allocated a site at the eastern end of the Reflecting Pool, though no completion date has yet been announced.

The pool was established at the same time as the Lincoln Memorial, in 1922. Though it was envisaged that the surrounding area – **West Potomac Park** – would be landscaped, "temporary" cement-board munitions and office buildings erected around the Reflecting Pool during both world wars proved hard to shift. Reconstruction was only considered seriously when President Nixon suggested the grounds might benefit from being turned into a Tivoli Gardens-style park in time for the Bicentennial. Money worries and aesthetic considerations produced the less flamboyant **Constitution Gardens** in 1976, a fifty-acre area of trees and dells surrounding a kidney-shaped lake. A plaque on the island in the center commemorates the 56 signatories of the Declaration of Independence.

The Vietnam Veterans Memorial

Constitution Gardens, Henry Bacon Drive and Constitution Ave at 21st St NW
☎634-1568; Foggy Bottom-GWU Metro or #13A/B bus from Constitution Ave. Daily 24hr, staffed 8am–midnight. Admission free.

The polished, black, V-shaped granite walls of the **Vietnam Veterans Memorial** cut straight into the green lawns of Constitution Gardens and straight into the psyche of a country scarred by a war it tried to forget. Here, the names of the 58,191 American casualties of the war in Vietnam are recorded in chronological order (1959–75), etched into an east and west wall which each run for 250ft, slicing deeper into the ground, until meeting at a vertex 10ft high. It's a sobering experience to walk past the ranks of names and the untold experiences they represent, not least for the friends and relatives who come here to take rubbings of the names and leave memorial tokens at the foot of the walls. Many of these artifacts – dog tags to teddy bears – end up at the National Museum of American History (see p.98). Directories list the names and their locations for anyone trying to find a particular person, and a ranger is on hand until midnight to answer questions. The annual Veterans Day ceremony held at the memorial on November 11 is one of the most emotional in the city, with the memorial walls decked in wreaths and overseen by military color-guards.

In so much as it commemorates human life rather than US involvement in the war, this extraordinary memorial serves its purpose with distinction. Indeed it coincides perfectly with the wishes of the Vietnam vets who first conceived the idea of a contemplative memorial in Washington: their sole intention was to record the sacrifice of every person killed or missing in action without making a political statement.

Once the grounds had been earmarked, a national competition was held in 1980, open to all US citizens, to determine the memorial's design; it was won by Maya Ying Lin, a 21-year-old Yale student from Ohio (whose original design is now held, and sometimes displayed by, the Library of Congress in its Jefferson Building). Determining that the names would become the memorial, she chose to record them on walls of reflective black granite which point to the city's lodestones, the Lincoln Memorial and Washington Monument, and which gradually draw visitors into a rift in the earth. Each **name** has appended the date of casualty and either a diamond (a confirmed death) or cross (missing in action and still unaccounted for – around 1100 names).

In the end, the memorial's non-political stance came to be seen as a political act itself by some ex-soldiers. Concerned that these somber, dignified walls made no overt reference to military (as opposed to personal) sacrifice, successful lobbying led to the commissioning of a separate martial statue to be added to the site. This, the **sculpture** of three servicemen by Frederick Hart, stands at the west end, heralded by a sixty-foot flagpole flying the Stars and Stripes. These three young men, despite bulging with weaponry and ammunition, have an air of vulnerability all too easy to understand in the bewildering maelstrom that was Vietnam.

More lobbying – in particular by Diane Evans, a former army nurse – led to the establishment of the **Vietnam Women's Memorial** in 1993, which stands in a grove of trees at the eastern end of the main site. Few realize that 11,000 American women served in Vietnam (eight were killed), while almost a quarter of a million provided support services throughout the world during the conflict. The bronze sculpture, by Glenna Goodacre, shows one nurse on her knees, exhausted; one tending a wounded soldier; and a third raising

The movie To Heal a Nation *tells the story of Vietnam vet Jan Scruggs (Eric Roberts), prime mover in collecting donations to build the memorial.*

her eyes to the sky in trepidation – none of the servicewomen bears insignia, emphasizing the universal intent of the sculpture.

The Korean War Veterans Memorial

West Potomac Park, south of Lincoln Memorial Reflecting Pool ☎619-7222; Smithsonian Metro or #13A/B bus from Constitution Ave to Lincoln Memorial. Daily 24hr, staffed 8am–midnight. Admission free.

The **Korean War Veterans Memorial** lies south of the Reflecting Pool, just a few minutes' walk from the Lincoln Memorial. Dedicated in July 1995 (and, again, largely funded by private contributions), its main component is a Field of Remembrance in which nineteen life-sized, heavily armed combat troops sculpted from stainless steel advance across an open field toward the Stars and Stripes. It's a moving ensemble, which rather overshadows the flanking, reflecting black granite wall, inscribed "Freedom is not free" and etched with a mural depicting military support crew and medical staff. A plaque at the flagstand proclaims "Our nation honors her sons and daughters who answered the call to defend a country they never knew and a people they never met".

And what a call it was: between 1950 and 1953, when the war ended, almost 55,000 Americans were killed in Korea (with another 8000 missing in action and over 103,000 wounded), a harbinger of the slaughter to begin in Vietnam a decade later. Unlike Vietnam, however, the American soldiers sent into battle by President Truman on behalf of the South Korean government went, however tenuously, in the name of the United Nations; the memorial lists the fifteen other countries who volunteered forces, with Britain, France, Greece and Turkey in particular suffering significant casualties. Perhaps it's not the place, but the statistic the memorial signally fails to record is that of the Korean civilian casualties. It's difficult to be certain but best estimates are that around three million (North and South) Koreans died – quite apart from half a million North Korean, 50,000 South Korean and possibly one million Chinese soldiers.

The memorial has a CD-ROM database; relatives and friends can type in the name of a veteran and call up and print out their rank, serial number, unit, casualty date and a photograph.

The Franklin Delano Roosevelt Memorial

West Potomac Park, Basin Drive, south bank of the Tidal Basin ☎376-6704; Smithsonian Metro or #13A/B bus from Constitution or Independence avenues. Daily 24hr, staffed 8am–midnight. Admission free.

DC's most recent presidential memorial – that to **Franklin Delano Roosevelt**, president from 1933 to 1945 – would never have seen the light of day had it been up to FDR himself. Accepting that he would one day be so honored, he favored only a small stone memorial on Pennsylvania Avenue (see p.179) but, after his death, others insisted on a far more impressive memorial. Designed by Lawrence Halprin, and dedicated in 1997, it spreads across a seven-acre site on the banks of the Tidal Basin, and is made up of a series of interlinking granite outdoor galleries punctuated by waterfalls, statuary, sculpted reliefs, groves of trees and shaded alcoves and plazas. In its way it's among the most successful of DC's memorials – and certainly one of the most popular – with an almost Athenian quality to its open spaces, resting-places and benches, and improving texts. On a bright spring or fall day, with the glistening basin waters and emerging views of the Washington Monument and Jefferson Memorial, it's one of the finest places in the city for a contemplative stroll.

As architect of the New Deal and wartime leader, Roosevelt's underlying political spirit is captured in a series of carved quotations which defined his presidency, perhaps most famously "The only thing we have to fear is fear itself". The four galleries of rustic stone (one for each of his terms of office) turn upon seminal periods: in the second gallery stand the sculpted figures of a city breadline and a man listening to one of Roosevelt's famous radio fireside chats; in the third room a tangle of broken granite blocks represents the war years, alongside a seated statue of FDR, his dog Fala and the heartfelt message "I have seen war . . . I hate war". The memorial ends in the fourth gallery with a timeline of dates and events inscribed in the steps and, perhaps more importantly, a recognition of Roosevelt's greatest ally in the shape of a statue of his wife, the redoubtable Eleanor.

There's great significance, too, in something most visitors don't notice about the memorial, namely that it is fully accessible to people in wheelchairs. At the age of 39, FDR contracted polio, which left him paralyzed from the waist down – a fact largely kept from the American people during his run for the governorship of New York and, later, the presidency. Believing, possibly correctly, that public knowledge of his disability would count against his political ambitions, he was almost always pictured standing while making speeches and only used his wheelchair when out of public view, a state of affairs with which reporters and photographers connived throughout his life. This led to a problem when it came to deciding how FDR should be portrayed in his statue at the memorial, the matter neatly sidestepped by having him seated, his wasted legs largely covered by the flowing cape he wore at the 1945 Yalta conference with Churchill and Stalin.

The Jefferson Memorial and the Tidal Basin

West Potomac Park, south bank of the Tidal Basin near 15th St SW and Ohio Drive ☎426-6821; Smithsonian Metro or #13A/B bus from Constitution or Independence avenues. Daily 8am–midnight. Admission free.

The last of the McMillan Commission's specific proposals was for a memorial to be erected to Thomas Jefferson, third President of the United States, prime drafter of the Declaration of Independence (see p.186) and the closest thing to Reniassance Man yet produced in America. When the **Jefferson Memorial** was finally completed in 1943 it was long overdue: Jefferson had died in 1826, yet was well

The Jefferson Memorial is undergoing long-term restoration to combat the effects of fifty years of pollution. Scaffolding will be in place for several years, though the memorial remains open for visits.

beaten to national memorials by both Washington and Lincoln. It was-n't for the want of inspiration, for with Jefferson there was more than enough to honor. A speaker of six languages, he practiced law, stud-ied science, mathematics and archeology, was an accomplished musi-cian and keen botanist, a lucid writer and self-taught architect of con-siderable prowess – the only surprise is that he didn't build the memo-rial himself.* With the US Capitol, Washington Monument, White House and Lincoln Memorial already in place, the obvious site lay on the southern axis, south of the Washington Monument, but it proved contentious. Many bemoaned the destruction of some of the city's famous cherry trees when the ground around the Tidal Basin was cleared (a few protesters even chained themselves to the trunks), while others argued that the memorial would block the view of the river from the White House. More practically, the site proved difficult to reach, since the basin blocked direct access from the north. This, in fact, provides much of its charm today, as the sinuous walk around the tree-lined basin makes for a fine approach.

If the site had its critics then so did the memorial, when John Russell Pope – architect of the National Gallery of Art – revealed his plans for a Neoclassical, circular, colonnaded structure with a shal-low dome housing a nineteen-foot-high bronze statue. However, while for some it was too similar to the Lincoln Memorial, it was at least a design in keeping with Jefferson's own tastes. Not only was it influenced by the Neoclassical styles which he had helped popularize in the United States after his stint as ambassador to France in the 1780s, but also it echoes closely the style of Jefferson's own (self-designed) country home at Monticello, in Charlottesville, Virginia.

It's one of the most harmonious structures in the city: a white marble temple, reminiscent of the Pantheon, with steps down to the water's edge and framed by the cherry trees of the Tidal Basin. The standing bronze **statue of Jefferson** (by Rudolph Evans) gazes determinedly out of the memorial, while the inscription around the frieze sets the high moral tone, trumpeting "I have sworn upon the altar of God eternal hostility against every form of tyranny over the mind of man". Inside, on the walls, four more texts flank the statue, most notably the seminal words from the 1776 Declaration of Independence (for Jefferson's role in which, see p.186).

---

*The genius Jefferson suffered a number of prejudices that put his achieve-ments into perspective. The man who publicly strove to abolish slavery did nothing to free his own slaves, whose labor kept him in the luxurious style to which he was accustomed (DNA testing has also confirmed longstanding alle-gations that Jefferson fathered at least one child by his house slave, Sally Hemings). He was permanently in debt (spending $3000 on wine alone during his first year in the White House), fondly asserted that women should be kept in the home, and enjoyed a severely isolationist view in which immigrants were feared since they would dilute the virtues of the hardworking, independent farmers who formed his American Arcadia.

Around the Tidal Basin

The **Tidal Basin** fills most of the space between the Lincoln and Jefferson memorials. This large inlet, formerly part of the Potomac River, was created in 1882, primarily to prevent flooding, while the famous **cherry trees** – a gift from Japan – were planted around the edge in 1912; the annual Cherry Blossom Festival each spring (usually early April) celebrates their blooming with concerts, parades and displays of Japanese lanterns.

South of the Jefferson Memorial, the long spit of East Potomac Park has more cherry trees, while if you walk around the western side of the basin, following Ohio Drive, you pass the site of the FDR Memorial (see p.64) before reaching the **statue of John Ericsson**, south of the Korean War Veterans and Lincoln memorials. Ericsson, the Swedish-born inventor of the screw-propellor, also designed the ironclad warship *Monitor* – known in its day as a "tin can on a raft" – which in 1862 held its own in battle against the Confederate vessel *Virginia* – the first naval conflict between iron ships. Nearby memorials on the north side of the basin include one to **John Paul Jones**, marooned on a traffic island at the foot of 17th Street, and a colonnaded marble bandstand hidden in the trees to the west which doubles as the **DC War Memorial**, honoring the city's World War I dead.

Monuments and memorials

Paddle boats can be rented from the Boat House on the Tidal Basin (daily 10am–8pm; 2-seaters $7/hr, 4-seaters $14/hr).

Museums and galleries

There are nine **museums and galleries** along the Mall, most of them national in name and scope and all but one (the National Gallery of Art) coming under the umbrella of the Smithsonian Institution. Quite

---

The Smithsonian Institution: Practicalities

There are eight **museums** of the **Smithsonian Institution** on the Mall; the original building – known as the **Smithsonian Castle** – serves as the main information center (see p.108). Four more museums lie north of the Mall – the National Museum of American Art (p.197), National Portrait Gallery (p.192), Renwick Gallery (p.158) and National Postal Museum (p.129); one to the south, the Anacostia Museum (p.146); the National Zoological Park (p.235), a few miles north beyond Rock Creek, is also part of the Smithsonian. The Cooper-Hewitt National Design Museum and the National Museum of the American Indian are in New York City; a Washington branch of the latter is due to open in 2003.

All Smithsonian museums and galleries are **open daily all year** (except Christmas Day) from 10am until 5.30pm; some have **extended spring and summer hours** – details are given in the text. **Admission** is free, though charges are levied for some special exhibitions. For details on **current exhibitions and events**, or a copy of the *Smithsonian Access* brochure for disabled visitors, call ☎357-2700 (Mon–Fri 9am–5pm, Sat & Sun 10am–4pm); there's a 24-hour recorded announcement on ☎357-2020; or access the Smithsonian's homepage at *www.si.edu*.

For a history of the Smithsonian Institution, see p.108.

apart from anything else, they're all free so there's little excuse not to look around at least one. Top of many lists are the **National Air and Space Museum** and the two buildings of the **National Gallery of Art**; followed by the **National Museum of American History** and the **Hirshorn Museum** of modern art and sculpture. Lesser-known standouts include the **Arthur M. Sackler Gallery** of Asian art, and the **Freer Gallery of Arts**' peerless matching of Asian and American art, specifically the finest single display of the works of James McNeill Whistler.

The museums and galleries are reviewed below in **alphabetical order**.

Arthur M. Sackler Gallery

1050 Independence Ave SW ☎357-4880 or 357-2700; Smithsonian Metro. Daily 10am–5.30pm. Admission free.

Underground galleries connect the Sackler to the Freer Gallery of Art (p.71) and the National Museum of African Art (p.96).

The angular, pyramidal **Arthur M. Sackler Gallery** conceals its artworks and devotional objects from Asia in comfortable, well-lit, underground galleries. Around a thousand pieces were originally donated to the Smithsonian by research physician, publisher and art collector Dr Sackler, who also coughed up $4 million toward the museum's construction (the governments of Japan and Korea weighed in with $1 million apiece too). We've covered the most permanent of the exhibitions below. However, **temporary exhibitions** taken from the gallery's collection might cover themes such as South Asian textiles and village arts; contemporary Japanese ceramics; early Islamic texts from Iran, gorgeously colored in gilt, silver, lapis lazuli and crushed stone pigments; or splendid fifteenth- to seventeenth-century illuminated Indian manuscripts. Of particular note is the Vever Collection, an unrivaled group of works related to the art of the Islamic book from the eleventh to the nineteenth centuries.

The **information desk** (daily 10am–4pm) at ground level should be your first stop. Ask about the highly informative free daily (except Wed) **guided tours**. The gallery also has a **shop**, with a fine range of prints, fabrics, ceramics and artistic gewgaws (see p.321), and an Asian art research **library**, shared with the Freer and open to the public (Mon–Fri 10am–5pm).

The permanent exhibitions

The **permanent exhibitions** are located on the first level, most prominently "**The Arts of China**", which highlights the Sackler's noted group of three-thousand-year-old **Chinese bronzes**. As early as the fifteenth century BC, ritual wine containers were being fashioned from bronze and were showing decoration, such as the faces and tails of dragons, that would become ever more refined. By the time of the late Shang Dynasty (twelfth and eleventh centuries BC) the decorative motifs are outstanding, the artisans producing elegant bronze vessels with bold designs – all the decorated detail was pro-

duced using intricate clay molds: there was no carving of the surface
after casting. The subsequent Western and Eastern Zhou dynasties
(1050–221 BC) refined the vessels further, with the bird now
appearing as the major motif – many of the pieces on display feature
bird-shaped handles, or show wispy reliefs of plumage and feathers.
Jade pendants also depicted birds and, more commonly, intricate
dragon shapes, with the technique here just as impressive – since
jade is too hard to be carved, the lapidaries would rub an abrasive
paste across the surface with wood or bamboo to shape and polish
the stone. The Sackler's collection of later Chinese art reveals other
skills, notably of the ceramicists of the Tang Dynasty (618–907) who
produced technicolored temple guard figures, designed to ward off
evil spirits. The last Chinese dynasty, the Qing (1644–1911), witnessed the flourishing era of the imperial scholars, who would place
so-called "scholar's rocks" (natural pieces of stone resembling
mountains) on their desks to encourage lofty thoughts. From this
period, too, date the Sackler's remarkably well-preserved carved
wooden cabinets and book stands, showing a simple, understated
decoration that English and Scandinavian craftsmen would later
adopt as their own. By way of contrast, Qing imperial porcelain was
richly embellished with symbolic figures and motifs – a plate depicting a young boy holding a pomegranate (full of seeds), a cockerel
and ladies holding fans with painted butterflies, for instance, is an
evocation of fertility.

"**Luxury Arts of the Silk Route Empires**" – taking up part of the
underground walkway to the Freer – is designed to show the historic
free-flow of artistic ideas between central, west and east Asia and the
Mediterranean world. The decorative forms seen in medieval
Western metalwork and ceramics are echoed in silver Syrian bowls,
Persian plates and Central Asian swords and buckles. Dr Sackler's
favorite piece from his entire collection shows these influences – a
beautifully worked, fourth century Iranian silver drinking vessel
(called a *rhyton*) shaped in the form of a gazelle. Here, too, you'll
find more Tang Dynasty ceramics, utilizing either simple white
porcelain or vibrant tricolored glazes, as well as contemporaneous
silverware – from everyday items like a ladle and stem cup to a fine
mirror, inlaid with a winged horse and dragon motif. From the same
period come the "Buddhist Heavenly Beings", floating angelic figurines of gold that once formed part of an altar set.

"**Sculpture of South and Southeast Asia**" traces the spread of
devotional sculpture across the continent. The earliest piece here is
from ancient Gandhara (now part of Pakistan and Afghanistan), a
third-century carved head of the Buddha whose features were directly influenced by images from Greece and Rome, with which
Gandhara traded. Later Hindu temple sculpture from India shows
more pronounced Eastern traits: among the bronze, brass and granite representations of Brahma, Vishnu and Shiva, you'll find a superb

thirteenth-century stone carving of the elephant-headed Ganesha (the remover of obstacles) – his trunk burnished by years of illicit, furtive touching by museum visitors. From India, Hinduism and Buddhism spread to the Khmer kingdom (Cambodia), which as well as adopting classical Indian styles also developed its own naturalistic artistic style – on a thirteenth-century temple lintel, male figures are shown entwined with vines, alongside an unidentified female goddess with conical crown and sarong.

Also on the first level, "**Metalwork and Ceramics from Ancient Iran**" displays a collection of vessels, weapons and ornaments made between 2300 and 100 BC. Many of the ceramic vessels here are animal-shaped, or painted with animal motifs, while a trio from northern Persia resemble metal, such was the craftsman's skill in firing. There's great dexterity, too, displayed in the metalwork, particularly the bronze and copper finials (ornamental pole tops) depicting demons (denoting magical powers) or vegetation (fertility).

The Arts and Industries Building

900 Jefferson Drive SW ☎357-2700; Smithsonian Metro. Daily 10am–5.30pm. Admission free.

America celebrated its centenary in 1876 by inviting its constituent states and forty foreign nations to display a panoply of inventions and exhibits that would celebrate contemporary human genius. The subsequent **Centennial Exhibition** in Philadelphia was a roaring success, though at its close the federal government was presented with an unforeseen problem when most of the exhibits were abandoned by their owners, who couldn't afford to take or ship them home. Congress made the Smithsonian responsible for the objects and voted funds for a new "National Museum" – now the **Arts and Industries Building** – to house them.

The Arts and Industries Building hosts a regular children's program at its Discovery Theater (see p.314) – the popular Carousel is right outside.

Opened in 1881 in time to host President Garfield's inaugural ball, the building soon became rooted in people's consciousness as the "nation's attic", since quite apart from the Centennial exhibits – which included an entire American steam locomotive and Samuel Morse's original telegraph – the Smithsonian came to acquire ever more bequests and purchases, not all of a strictly educational nature. Over the years, as the National Museum filled to bursting point, most of the Smithsonian holdings were farmed out to new, specialized museums, which rather diminished the quirky appeal of the Arts and Industries Building: as Bill Bryson laments, with tongue only slightly in cheek, "At the old Smithsonian it could have been absolutely anything – a petrified dog, Custer's scalp, human heads adrift in bottles."

The building was restored completely for the Bicentennial celebrations of 1976. Only the central rotunda and four of the original exhibit halls remain as first envisaged, but these show off the **Victorian interior** to splendid effect – the colorful tiled floor, high windows and abundant use of natural light signal the involvement of Montgomery C. Meigs, who went on to design the equally adventurous Pension Building (see p.190).

For twenty years after the Bicentennial, the Arts and Industries Building continued to house many of the items from the Philadelphia exhibition. Assorted bits and bobs of American Victoriana will probably remain on display for some time, but these days the building is used for **temporary exhibitions** sponsored by the African-American History Center (which may eventually make the building its permanent home), by the Anacostia Museum, and by the nascent Museum of the American Indian.

Freer Gallery of Art

Jefferson Drive at 12th St SW ☎357-4880 or 357-2700; Smithsonian Metro. Daily 10am–5.30pm. Admission free.

Opened in 1923, the **Freer Gallery of Art** was the first Smithsonian museum devoted exclusively to art. The airy Italian Renaissance *palazzo* of granite and marble, designed by Beaux-Arts architect Charles Adams Platt, has long been considered one of the city's most aesthetically pleasing museums, with small, elegant galleries encircling a herringbone-brick courtyard furnished with splashing fountain. Design appeal aside, the gallery's abiding interest lies in its unusual juxtaposition of Asian and American art, including over 1200 prints, drawings and paintings by James McNeill Whistler – the largest collection of his works anywhere.

The collection, and the impetus for the gallery, was the work of **Charles Lang Freer**, an industrialist who made a fortune from building railroad cars in Detroit which he spent on what was then considered to be obscure Asian art. He bought his first piece, a Japanese fan, in 1887 and thirteen years later retired at the age of 44 to concentrate on his collection, adding Chinese jades and bronzes, Byzantine illuminated manuscripts, Buddhist wall sculptures and Persian metalwork during five trips to various Asian countries. Freer also began to put together a series of **paintings** by turn-of-the-century American artists whose work he considered complemented his Asian collection. Dwight William Tryon, Thomas Wilmer Dewing and Abbott Handerson Thayer benefited from Freer's patronage (indeed, the penurious Thayer was almost entirely dependent on him), though the most profitable relationship was with the London-based Whistler, practically all of whose works ended up in the hands of Freer. In 1912 Freer embarked upon a plan to endow and build a gallery to hold his collection. He was delighted with the plans drawn up by Platt but sadly never saw their fruition. Work began in 1916, but was interrupted by the outbreak of World War I; Freer died in 1919 and the gallery didn't open for another four years.

On the S level, a shared underground gallery leads through to the Arthur M. Sackler Gallery (p.68).

The **galleries** on the third level hold selections from the permanent collection, only a fraction of which is on display. It's grown since Freer's original bequest to around 28,000 works, but even when planning his gallery Freer wanted only to exhibit small samples of the works at any one time, though most of what's described in the following account is usually on display – pick up a current floor-plan at the **information desk** by the Mall entrance.

Whistler

Not unnaturally, it's **James Abbott McNeill Whistler** (1834–1903) who dominates proceedings. Born in Lowell, Massachusetts, he moved first to Paris as an art student, from which time dates a *Self-Portrait* (1857), with flat-brimmed hat, very much the man at ease in Left Bank life. Moving to London in the early 1860s, Whistler not only began to collect modish Japanese prints and *objets* but embraced their influences wholeheartedly in a series of vibrant works, starting with *The Golden Screen* (1865), depicting a seated woman in Japanese dress in front of a fine painted screen. Freer, attracted by the oriental flavor of Whistler's art, made a special journey to London to introduce himself, returning on several occasions over the years to buy more of the painter's work. There's an unfinished portrait of Freer (1902), started on his last visit just before Whistler's death. Other works include studies incorporating a red Oriental fan, a prop dear to Whistler's heart, and various examples of the tonal experiments that fascinated the artist, who constantly repeated and developed shades of color – purple and gold, blue and gold, rose and brown, red and pink – to harmonious effect. *Arrangement in White and Black* from 1873 contrasts the ghostly white dress and parasol of Whistler's mistress, Maud Franklin, with the dark shades of the background; *The Little Red Glove* harmonizes glove and bonnet with the subject's auburn hair. These and many other of Whistler's works in the Freer are signed with a butterfly monogram, a typically Japanese device (though one which the London *Times* of the day thought simply a "queer little label").

Besides these works, Whistler is also represented by the magnificent **Peacock Room** (permanently stationed in room 12), which started life as a mere commissioned painting, *The Princess From the Land of Porcelain*. This hung above the fireplace in the London dining room of Frederick Leyland, a Liverpudlian shipowner (and patron of Whistler) who had commissioned interior designer Thomas Jeckyll to add a framework of latticework shelves and gilded leather panels to the room's walls so that he might display his fine collection of Chinese porcelain. Whistler happened to be working on another project in the house at the time and, taking advantage of Leyland's absence on business, took it upon himself to restyle Jeckyll's work. Using a technique similar to Japanese lacquerware, he covered the leather-clad walls, ceiling, shelving and furnishings with rich blue- and gold-painted peacock feathers, gilt relief decor and green glaze, while above the sideboard he placed two golden painted peacocks trailing a stream of feathers; his famous butterfly monogram is visible in the corner. The idea, according to Whistler, was to present his art as a harmonious whole (the room's full title incorporates the phrase *Harmony in Blue and Gold*), much as the Japanese did; the room was at once a framed picture and an object of applied art, like an Oriental lacquer box. This artistic hijack outraged Leyland, who refused to pay Whistler for the work (his overriding gripe was the cavalier way that Whistler had entertained visitors in the room without his permission). Completed in 1877, the room met a mixed critical reception, though Whistler's friend Oscar Wilde, for one, thought it "the finest thing in color and art decoration the world has known". After Leyland's death, the room and its contents passed into the hands of a London art gallery, which later sold it to Freer. Restoration has returned the iridescent colors to their nineteenth-century best, the framed shelves filled with blue-and-white porcelain to show what Leyland's original dining room might have looked like.

Other American artists
The other American art is less gripping, though it is interesting to trace what attracted Freer to many of the works. Note the Oriental-style calligraphic brush strokes of the trees in the foreground of *Winter Dawn on Monadnock*, just one of the Impressionist land-scapes by **Abbot Handerson Thayer** (1849–1921), who was heavily influenced by Freer's Asian art collection, which he knew well. **Thomas Wilmer Dewing** comes closer to Whistler's mood with *The Four Sylvan Sounds* (1896), a folding painted screen clearly of Asian influence. Contemporaries considered Dewing to be elitist and Freer didn't have much competition for his works, though he doubt-less had to bid higher for paintings by the more popular John Singer Sargent, whose *Breakfast in the Loggia*, a scene in the arcaded courtyard of a Florentine villa, was bought to remind him of the gallery he planned to build in DC.

Oriental art
Things pick up again with the Freer's collection of **Japanese art**, in particular the painted folding screens that so delighted Whistler. Called *byobu* (protection from the wind), these tend to depict the sea-sons or themes from Japanese literature and range from two to ten panels long. Other choice items include the nineteenth-century porce-lain dish shaped like Mount Fuji and, one of the oldest pieces in the Japanese collection, a twelfth-century standing Buddha of wood and gold leaf. **Korean ceramics** – wine bottles, tea bowls, ewers – date mostly from the tenth to the fourteenth centuries and show a uniform jade-like glaze. They're remarkably well preserved, many having been retrieved from aristocratic tombs or having simply survived as vener-ated objects, handed down through the generations.

Other rooms are devoted to **Chinese art**, ranging from ancient jade burial goods to a series of ornate bronzes (1200–1000 BC), including ritual wine servers in the shape of tigers and elephants. There's also a stunning series of ink-on-paper handscrolls, though the calligraphy (literally "beautiful writing") isn't just confined to paper – jars and tea bowls, even ceramic pillows, are painstakingly adorned. Freer also made three trips to **Egypt**, whose ancient sculpture he came to think "the greatest art in the world". Many of the exhibits on display date from his last trip in 1909, when he bought a remarkable collection of richly colored glass vessels (used for scents and oils), bronze figurines and carved plaques, most around 4000 years old. Later Freer spread his net to incorporate pieces from **Buddhist, South Asian and Islamic art**. A remarkably well-preserved Pakistani stone frieze from the second century AD details the life of Buddha, while the South Asian art collection sports some of the most delicate pieces yet: temple sculpture, colorful devotional texts, and gold jewelry set with rubies and diamonds. Elsewhere, Turkish ceramics (many repeating garden motifs) are displayed alongside a fine inlaid Persian pen box (thirteenth century), emblazoned with animal heads and engraved with the name of the artist and the owner.

Hirshorn Museum and Sculpture Garden

Independence Ave at 7th St SW ☎357-2700; L'Enfant Plaza or Smithsonian Metro. Museum daily 10am–5.30pm; Sculpture Garden daily 7.30am–dusk. Admission free.

Gordon Bunshaft's windowless, cylindrical **Hirshorn Museum**, balanced on fifteen-foot stilts above a sculpture-littered concrete plaza, has been likened to everything from a monumental donut to a spaceship poised for takeoff. Inside – where, incidentally, you barely notice that the building is round – is contained the Smithsonian's extensive collection of late nineteenth- and twentieth-century art, based on the mighty bequest of Joseph H. Hirshorn, Latvian immigrant, stockbroker and uranium magnate. Hirshorn's vast fortune enabled him to collect art on a positively excessive scale: the original bequest in 1966 was of 4000 paintings and 2600 sculptures; by the time of his death in 1981, the overall number had risen to over 12,000 pieces, which Hirshorn was happy to see go to the country ". . . as a small repayment for what this nation has done for me and others like me who arrived here as immigrants".

It's both impossible for the museum to display more than a fraction of its collection at any one time and for the visitor to get much impression of what is on show in just one visit – there are also changing **exhibitions** of contemporary art, thematic shows, and a **Sculpture Garden**, which together with the *Full Circle* outdoor **café** (summer lunch only) provides respite when it all gets too much. There are free **guided tours** of the permanent collection (Mon–Fri

10.30am & noon, Sat & Sun noon & 2pm), and highly rated art films
shown a couple of evenings a week (☎357-1300 for details).

The museum

A much-needed top-to-bottom renovation was undertaken to celebrate the Hirshorn's first quarter-century. At the time of writing it
was unclear how exhibits from the permanent collection were likely
to be displayed, so you'll need to consult the **information desk** by
the entrance: there's exhibition space on the two upper floors as well
as on the lower level. What follows is a brief round-up of the
Hirshorn's highlights.

As far as it's possible to generalize about the collection – quite
simply, Hirshorn bought what he liked – if it has a recognized
strength it's in nineteenth-century French sculpture, considered the
best selection of its kind outside France. With a bit of backtracking,
it's possible to trace the transition from nineteenth-century natural-
ism to twentieth-century abstraction. Jean-Baptiste Carpeaux, principal French sculptor of the mid-nineteenth century, is represented,
along with Auguste Rodin, whom he directly influenced; for sheer
panache, however, seek out Honoré Daumier's raffish, crumpled,
bewhiskered gent, *Ratapoi*. By the turn of the century, developments in sculpture and art were going hand-in-hand – often literally
so, as painters became enamored of the possibilities of working in
another medium. Of various bronzes by Henri Matisse, most notable
is *The Serf*, a stumpy portrait of downtrodden spirit, while alongside
Edgar Degas' usual muscular ballerinas are energetic studies of
women washing, stretching and emerging from a bath. Masks and
busts by Picasso trace his (and sculpture's) growing alliance with
Cubism: contrast the almost jaunty bronze *Head of a Jester* (1905)
with the severe *Head of a Woman*, produced just four years later. A
similar exercise is possible with a series of five exemplary bronze
heads by Matisse of his wife Jeanette (1910–13), which show clearly
the journey from realism to Cubism.

Picasso and Matisse aside, you can spot Hirshorn's other
favorites a mile off. There are lashings of 1950s Henry Moore, from
the rather gentle *Seated Figure Against a Curved Wall* to the more
imposing *King and Queen*, a regal pair of seated five-foot-high
bronze figures whose curved laps and straight backs look as inviting
as chairs. Look, too, for the nastiest piece by far, *General Nuke*
(1984), Robert Arneson's snarling general's head with an erect missile for a nose, the neck sitting on a totem of entwined corpses.

Similarly, the **modern art collection** is a roll-call of the twentieth
century's great and good, with several strengths (de Kooning,
Bacon) and some weaknesses (few women, no Kandinsky paintings
and, despite his sculpture on display, no Matisse). American art
makes a particularly good showing: there are portraits by John
Singer Sargent, Mary Cassatt and Thomas Eakins (including a strong

*Most of the
artists repre-
sented in the
Hirshorn get
another crack
of the whip in
the National
Gallery's East
Building; see
p.95.*

study of Eakins' wife), and representative works by Winslow Homer, Albert Bierstadt, William Merritt Chase, Marsden Hartley and Edward Hopper. In addition, Hirshorn's collection of work by abstract-expressionist Willem de Kooning is one of the most impressive anywhere, although changing displays, loans and special exhibitions play havoc with formal viewing plans. Two or three are usually on display, though, like the elaborate swatch of lines and color that reveals itself to be *Two Women in the Country*. It's a fair bet, too, that you'll see at least some of the earlier European Surrealists; among them Max Ernst, Joan Miró, Yves Tanguy and Rene Magritte. In addition, there's a changing selection of paintings by Georgia O'Keeffe, Robert Motherwell, Robert Rauschenberg, Ellsworth Kelly, Louise Bourgeois, Clifford Styll, Piet Mondrian, Jasper Johns, Roy Lichtenstein, Gene Davis and Kenneth Noland – in short, just about anyone in the twentieth-century art world to whom Hirshorn could hand over money.

The Sculpture Garden

Much of the Hirshorn's monumental sculpture is contained in the **Sculpture Garden**, a sunken concrete arbor across Jefferson Drive on the Mall side of the museum. In May and October, there are special **free tours** (Mon–Sat at 12.15pm). Masterpieces come thick and fast: casts of Rodin's *Monument to the Burghers of Calais* and of Matisse's four human *Backs* in relief (1919–30) attract regular admirers. Many of those artists represented inside the museum appear in the garden, too – Henry Moore, naturally, but also Aristide Maillol (in particular, a graceful *Nymph* of 1930) and Henri Laurens, Joan Miró and David Smith. Of the lesser-known works, several stand out: Gaston Lachaise's proud, bronze *Standing Woman (Heroic Woman)* from 1932 is particularly fine and, nearby, there's great humor in Jean Ipousteguy's *Man Pushing the Door*. The pond, featuring a small Carl Milles' fountain, is fronted by Alexander Calder's static *Stabile-Mobile*; for a more impressive Calder, make for the Independence Avenue entrance to the museum, where his *Two Disks* (1965) sit on five spidery legs, tall enough to walk under.

National Air and Space Museum

Independence Ave and 7th SW ☎357-2700; L'Enfant Plaza Metro. Daily: June–Aug 10am–6.30pm; Sept–May 10am–5.30pm. Admission free.

If there's one museum people have heard about in DC, and just one they want to visit, it's the **National Air and Space Museum**. Since it opened in 1976, it's captured the imagination of almost ten million people every year, making it easily the city's most popular attraction. The frisson of excitement begins in the entrance gallery, which flirtatiously throws together some of the most celebrated flying machines in history, prompting even the most steadfast Luddite to consider a brief technological romance. Over twenty monstrous gal-

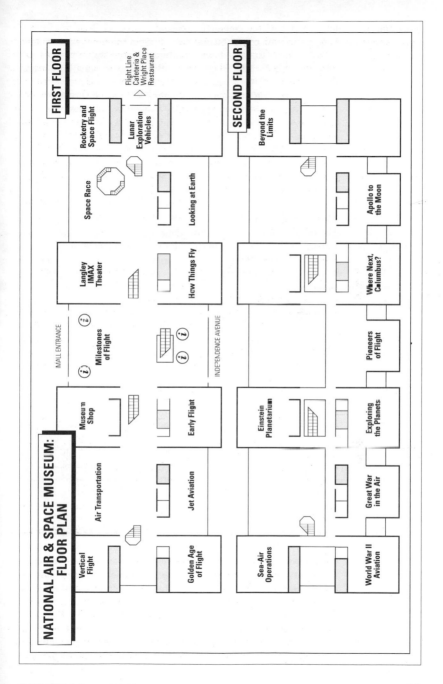

NATIONAL AIR & SPACE MUSEUM: FLOOR PLAN

FIRST FLOOR

Vertical Flight

Air Transportation

Museum Shop

Milestones of Flight

Langley IMAX Theater

Space Race

Rocketry and Space Flight

Lunar Exploration Vehicles

MALL ENTRANCE

Golden Age of Flight

Jet Aviation

Early Flight

How Things Fly

Looking at Earth

INDEPENDENCE AVENUE

Flight Line
Cafeteria &
Wright Place
Restaurant

SECOND FLOOR

Sea-Air Operations

Einstein Planetarium

Exploring the Planets

Great War in the Air

Pioneers of Flight

Where Next, Columbus?

Beyond the Limits

Apollo to the Moon

World War II Aviation

leries on two floors containing objects the size of, well, spaceships means that even on the busiest days, it's not too much of a struggle to get close up to the exhibits. You may have to wait a while to get into the Langley IMAX theater, but otherwise the worst lines are in the cafeteria.

However, there are disappointments. With some very honorable exceptions, many of the explanatory background displays are lack-luster and too reliant on a photo-video-text storyboard approach, which palls somewhat after an hour or two. Many of the most frequented exhibits are also physically worn, giving parts of the museum a tired air. With children in tow, if you get no further than the huge lobbies, take in the "Apollo to the Moon" exhibit and catch a movie, you'll have seen the best of the museum in an afternoon.

Visiting the museum

The **information desk** is at the Independence Avenue entrance; **free tours** leave from here (daily 10.15am & 1pm). If you want to visit the Einstein Planetarium ($4) or see an IMAX movie in the Langley Theater ($5.50), buy tickets when you arrive (☎357-1686 for times). Come early to **eat** in the self-service *Flight Line Cafeteria* or table-service *Wright Place Restaurant* since by noon both places are madhouses – incidentally, both also have great views of the Capitol dome. Finally, don't even think of entering the **museum shop** without wads of cash or the stamina to withstand repetitious demands from companions and kids for model spaceships, Klingon t-shirts and florid stunt-kites.

The first floor

Hanging from the rafters in the "**Milestones of Flight**" gallery, which confronts you upon entry, is the machine that started it all – the *Wright Flyer*, the handmade plane in which the Wright Brothers made the first powered flight in December 1903, at Kitty Hawk, North Carolina. They were an unlikely pair of pioneers, church-going, bicycle shop-owning bachelors who just happened to make themselves aerodynamic experts. The first flight – 20ft above the ground – lasted twelve seconds and covered 120ft, and within two years they were flying over twenty miles at a time, but there was curiously little contemporary interest in their progress. In part this was snobbery: in the rush for the skies, the Smithsonian Institution itself was supporting the efforts of a noted engineer (and, completely coincidentally of course, its third Secretary), Samuel Pierpoint Langley, who conspicuously failed to fly any of his experimental planes. It was forty years before the churlish Institution formally recognized the brothers' singular achievement, while the original *Wright Flyer* was only accepted into the Smithsonian fold in 1985.

Powered flight quickly caught the public imagination and prompted individual daring: on May 20, 1927, the 25-year-old

Charles Lindbergh made the first solo transatlantic crossing in the moth-like *Spirit of St Louis*, taking off from Long Island and landing near Paris almost 34 hours later. When he wanted to see where he was headed Lindbergh either had to use a periscope or bank the plane, since his gas reserve tank was mounted where the windscreen should have been. Just 59 years after the very first controlled, powered flight John Glenn became the first American to orbit the earth with the launch of *Friendship 7* in 1962. Glenn went around three times in five hours and saw four sunsets, in a craft barely big enough to swing an astronaut – his spacesuit is preserved upstairs in "**Apollo to the Moon**", as are the toothpaste tubes used to squeeze food into his mouth. Three years later, an American, Edward H. White, was walking in space for the first time, from the two-seater *Gemini 4*; while in July 1969, space travel came of age when the minuscule *Apollo 11* command module journeyed to the moon.

For more space bravado, head to the "**Space Race**" hall which traces the development of space flight with machines as diverse as a V2 rocket, Hitler's secret weapon and the world's first ballistic missile system, and the pioneering Skylab Orbital Workshop. Just 120ft long, this was base during 1973–74 for a three-person crew which stayed for up to three months at a time – the confined space can be seen better from a platform on the second floor. For relaxation, the astronauts played with velcro-covered darts and dartboard. With the thawing of relations between the Soviet Union and the US in the early 1970s came the Apollo-Soyuz Test Project, in which manned craft from the two countries docked in space for the first time (July 18, 1975). The docked craft are here, alongside various missiles, including an IBCM Minuteman whose sign, hardly comfortingly, states: "The Minuteman III displayed here has no nuclear warheads".

"**Lunar Exploration Vehicles**" displays the machines which in eight extraordinary years met President Kennedy's avowed aim of 1961 to land a man on the moon and return him safely. Unmanned probes – *Ranger*, *Lunar Orbitor* and *Surveyor* – finally gave way to the ludicrously flimsy lunar module *Eagle*, in which Neil Armstrong and Edwin "Buzz" Aldrin made their historic descent to the moon ("Houston . . . the *Eagle* has landed"). The *Eagle* itself isn't on display although the model that is, *LM-2*, was a back-up, built for the moon-landing program but never used: if told it was made out of tin foil, cans and coathangers, you could believe it. "**Rocketry and Space Flight**" traces the history of rocketry from the black-powder rockets used in thirteenth-century China to Robert Goddard's experiments with liquid-fuel in 1926, which pointed the way to eventual space flight. Light relief is offered by coverage of sci-fi stalwarts Jules Verne and Buck Rogers, and examples of spacesuit development (including details of exactly where the bodily waste goes).

To see the museum chronologically, you'd need to start with the galleries on the other side of "Milestones of Flight". None is essential

Museums and galleries

The museum's first director was Michael Collins, the often-overlooked "third man" in Apollo 11: he got to orbit the moon while Armstrong and Aldrin made history by walking on it.

– if time is limited, the most engaging is perhaps **"Early Flight"**, where you can see Otto Lilenthal's glider (1894), which first inspired the Wrights, whose success in turn provided the impetus for the resourceful Herman Ecker. Having taught himself to fly in 1911, a year later he built his *Flying Boat* using bits and pieces bought from hardware stores. The early technology explored by people like Ecker and the Wrights is covered in **"How Things Fly"**, one of the museum's few interactive rooms. It's also worth a quick glance at **"Looking at Earth"**, where aerial photographs include pictures of San Francisco after the 1906 earthquake (snapped from a kite camera), 1860 Boston from a balloon and German castles recorded by camera-carrying pigeons.

The second floor

Upstairs, you can look down to the exhibits in "Milestones of Flight" below, before stepping back to view the complementary **"Pioneers of Flight"** gallery. The balloon basket of Captain Hawthorne Grey makes a suitable place to reflect on the early pioneers: in it, in May 1927, in a wonderfully heroic but pointless gesture, he reached a height of 42,470 feet – only to run out of oxygen and expire. More successfully, the *Fokker T-2* was the first airplane to make a non-stop American transcontinental flight in 1923, a journey that took 26 hours 50 minutes. Just twelve years earlier – and after just twenty hours of flying lessons – one Cal Rogers had attempted to pick up the $50,000 prize offered by William Randolph Hearst to the first pilot to fly coast-to-coast in less than thirty days. He eventually managed the journey in a patched-up bi-plane, but it took him two months, seventy landings and several crashes. Perhaps the museum's most poignant airplane is the bright red *Lockheed Vega* flown solo across the Atlantic in May 1932 by Amelia Earhart; she disappeared five years later over the Pacific attempting a round-the-world flight.

On either side of "Pioneers of Flight", fairly uninspired rooms deal with **"Exploring the Planets"** and, in **"Where Next, Columbus?"**, the possibilities of future space travel. Most visitors make a beeline for **"Apollo to the Moon"**, perhaps the most fascinating room in the museum (and usually the most crowded). The main gallery centers on the *Apollo 11* (1969) and *17* (1972) missions, the first and last flights to the moon: there are Neil Armstrong and Buzz Aldrin's spacesuits; a Lunar Roving Vehicle (basically a golf cart with a garden seat); *Apollo 17*'s flight control deck, tools, navigation aids, space-food, clothes and charts; and an astronaut's survival kit (complete with shark repellent). If you want to touch a bit of moonrock, however, you'll have to go back down to "Milestones of Flight", where a four-billion-year-old sample brought back by *Apollo 17* astronauts is displayed – just a small chunk of the 250 pounds of material they collected. In a side room, each American space mission is detailed, from May 1961 onwards, when in *Freedom 7* Alan B.

The other great US space disaster, the explosion of the space shuttle Challenger, *is commemorated by a memorial plaque in Arlington cemetery; see p.251.*

Shepard Jr became the first American in space on a fifteen-minute flight to an altitude of 166 miles. A separate memorial commemorates the three men who died on the *Apollo* launchpad in 1967 – Virgil Grissom, Edward H. White II and Roger Chaffee.

This is all stirring stuff and although there's heroism on display in other second-floor galleries – like "**Great War in the Air**", bursting with dog-fighting biplanes, and "**World War II Aviation**" – it's hard to see the "Apollo" gallery as anything but the high point of the museum. Only "**Beyond the Limits**" raises much interest. Detailing how computers have affected flight, this at least has the advantage of being as up-to-date as the museum gets, featuring touch-screen workstations and a cockpit simulator.

National Gallery of Art

Constitution Ave, between 3rd and 7th St NW ☎737-4215; Archives-Navy Memorial Metro. Mon–Sat 10am–5pm, Sun 11am–6pm. Admission free.

The genesis of the **National Gallery of Art** lay in the vision of just one man, **Andrew Mellon**. An industrialist and financier, Mellon began to buy European old masters in his late 20s, and his connection with central government in the 1930s – as Secretary to the Treasury and ambassador to Britain – persuaded him that there was scope to create a national art gallery in Washington. His own collection certainly begged to be seen by a wider public: among the 121 paintings in Mellon's eventual bequest to the gallery were a score of masterpieces bought in 1931 from the government of the USSR, which plundered the works in the Hermitage to prop up its faltering economy.

The original National Gallery of Art, designed by John Russell Pope, was opened by President Franklin D. Roosevelt in March 1941. It wasn't (and still isn't) a government (or even Smithsonian) institution, despite its name, but building and collection were at once perceived to be of national importance and scope. Now known as the **West Building**, Pope's symmetrical, Neoclassical gallery is positively overwhelming at first sight, especially when approached up the sweeping steps from the Mall. On the **main floor**, two wings without external windows stretch for 400ft on either side of a central **rotunda**, whose massive dome is supported by 24 black Ionic columns. The central vaulted corridor of each wing does duty as a sculpture hall, both wings ending at an internal, skylit, fountain-and-plant-filled **garden court**. The entire floor contains almost one hundred display rooms, full of masterpieces ranging from thirteenth-century Italian to nineteenth-century European and American art; down on the **ground floor** are changing exhibitions from the gallery's virtuoso collection of prints, drawings, sculpture and decorative art.

Remarkably, at its inauguration in 1941 the West Building was virtually empty, since Mellon's bequest – substantial though it was – filled only five of the rooms. But such was the influx of gifts and pur-

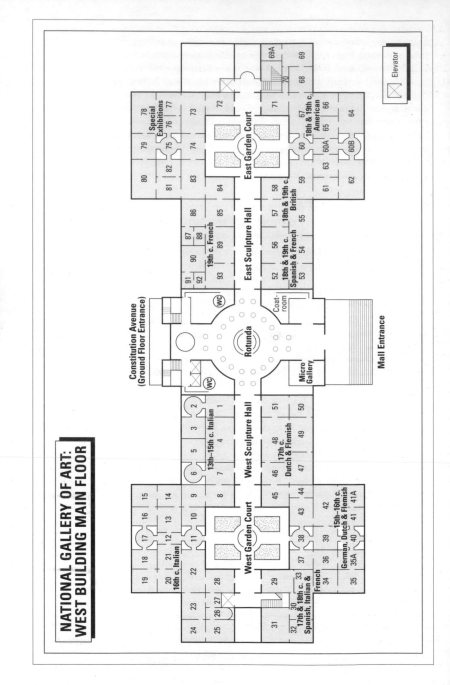

NATIONAL GALLERY OF ART:
WEST BUILDING MAIN FLOOR

Elevator

West Garden Court

13th–15th c. Italian

16th c. Italian

17th & 18th c.
Spanish, Italian &
French

German, Dutch & Flemish
15th–16th c.

West Sculpture Hall

17th c.
Dutch & Flemish

Constitution Avenue
(Ground Floor Entrance)

Rotunda

Micro
Gallery

Coat-
room

Mall Entrance

East Sculpture Hall

19th c. French

18th & 19th c.
Spanish & French

18th & 19th c.
British

East Garden Court

Special
Exhibitions

18th & 19th c.
American

chases that by the 1970s it was clear that the original building couldn't hope to hold them all. Consequently, I.M. Pei's thoroughly modernistic, triangular **East Building**, as it became known, was completed in 1978, utilizing a block of land between 3rd and 4th streets that Mellon had earmarked from the very beginning as the site of any future expansion. Pei's initial challenge was to deal with the awkwardly shaped block of land (truncated by Pennsylvania Ave), which he managed by making only the marble walls permanent; the rest of the internal structure can be shaped at will according to the dictates of the various temporary exhibitions. The East Building has a separate entrance on 4th Street, although an underground **Concourse**, with a moving walkway, connects the two buildings: in here there's more display space, a very good bookstore, an espresso bar and a large cafeteria – topped by pyramidal skylights and bordered by a glassed-in waterfall.

Visiting the National Gallery of Art

You can't hope to see the whole of the National Gallery in one visit, although it is surprisingly quick to move from West to East buildings using the Concourse, so visiting part of both collections in one go isn't out of the question. The most popular galleries (like the nineteenth-century French or American rooms) tend to be busiest in mid-afternoon and on weekends. To make best use of limited time, latch onto one of the informative daily **free tours and programs**; pick up a schedule from one of the gallery's **Art Information Desks** – located in the West Building on the main floor (Mall entrance) and on the ground floor (Constitution Ave at 6th St); in the East Building, at ground level central court.

It's vital to note that even in the permanent galleries of the West Building, parts of the collection are **rotated or sent out on tour**, while some rooms may be **closed for renovation**. To track down the specific location of a particular work – including any of those mentioned in the account below – visit the **Micro Gallery** in the West Building (main floor, Mall entrance), in which an interactive computer system allows you to locate and view around 1700 works in the gallery. The system can also access biographies of over 650 artists, and provide the historical and cultural background to an art work or artistic period – it can even print you a map of a self-selected tour.

Special **exhibitions and installations** are detailed in a monthly calendar, which also lists the **free classical music concerts** (Sept–June, usually Sun 7pm) held in the serene West Building West Garden Court. Ask at the information desks.

Thirteenth- to fifteenth-century Italian (rooms 1–15)

The gallery's oldest works are the stylized thirteenth-century Byzantine icons (holy images) in which an enthroned Mary, Queen of Heaven, holds the Christ-child who – as medieval art dictated – is a

*The collection
starts in room
1 of the West
Wing of the
West Building
and proceeds
chronologically.*

small adult figure. Not until the early fourteenth century did natural-ism and emotional range begin to manifest themselves in religious art. The Sienese artist **Duccio di Buoninsegna** was one of the first to move beyond strict Byzantine forms – there is genuine feeling in the faces of the subjects in his *Nativity*, a panel taken from the base of his masterpiece, the great *Maestà* altarpiece of Siena Cathedral. But while Duccio continued to work within flat Byzantine forms, his con-temporary in Florence, **Giotto**, was producing works whose new spirit of humanism would lead eventually to the Renaissance. His *Madonna and Child* (completed by 1330) marks an extraordinary departure in its attempt to create believable human figures.

The emphasis then switches to fifteenth-century Florence, the city in which the ideas of the Renaissance were first and most lastingly expressed. In Europe's pre-eminent banking and trading center, rich families – like the Medicis – had sufficient money to sponsor a new band of innovative artists. The prominent *tondo* (circular painting) depicting the *Adoration of the Magi* (c.1445) was probably commis-sioned by the Medicis, and though started by the monk **Fra Angelico** was substantially completed by **Fra Filippo Lippi**, who invested the biblical scene with his full range of emotive powers. The painting is full of symbolic content, from the oversized peacock on the stable roof (symbol of eternal life) to the dog in the foreground, representing Christian faith. **Domenico Veneziano**'s naked *St John in the Desert* (c.1445) would have been considered blasphemous before the Renaissance, when nudity was almost exclusively associated with the concept of sin. However, for dynamic realism there's nothing to com-pare with the decorative shield painted by **Andrea del Castagno** show-ing *The Youthful David* (c.1450) – muscles tensed, hair flowing – preparing to fling his sling. Goliath's decapitated head at his feet com-pleted the story for Florentine viewers, who would have understood the picture as a warning to the city's squabbling neighboring states.

In the "Florentine Portraiture" section all eyes are drawn to **Leonardo da Vinci**'s *Ginevra da' Benci* (c.1474), the only work by the artist in the United States. Painted when he was only 22, its sub-ject is a sixteen-year-old Florentine beauty with alabaster skin sitting before a spiky juniper bush – not only symbolizing chastity (this was commissioned as an engagement portrait) but also a visual pun on her name, Ginevra, and the Italian word for juniper, *ginepro*. Masterpieces by **Sandro Botticelli** include his devout rendering of the *Adoration of the Magi* from the early 1480s – one of the paint-ings Mellon appropriated from the Hermitage. The scene here is set in the ruins of a Classical temple from which the frame of a new structure, representing Christianity, is rising.

Among the Florentine sculpture is a bust of Lorenzo de Medici by Andrea del Verrocchio, commissioned from the Medicis' favorite sculptor to commemorate a failed assassination attempt. The **della Robbia** family and related artists (1475–1525) are represented by

their glorious glazed terracotta works that were popularly used as
devotional images. Luca della Robbia first developed the glazing
technique but it reached its height with his successors, particularly
his nephew Andrea, who by the 1480s was producing works of
exceptional sympathy, like his *Madonna and Child* and *Adoration
of the Child*. Other Renaissance developments come to light with
Andrea Mantegna's *Judith and Holofernes* – a calm Judith clutching the severed head of the Assyrian leader – less notable for its quality than for the obvious influence Mantegna had on his brother-in-
law, Giovanni Bellini.

Sixteenth-century Italian (rooms 16–28)

By the turn of the sixteenth century new artistic ideas were being
explored in other Italian cities, though not until the work of the
accomplished Bellini family did Venetian art thoroughly shake off its
erstwhile Gothic influences and produce its own Renaissance styles.
Nowhere is this seen better than in *The Feast of the Gods*, a powerful painting of mixed provenance. Commissioned by an Italian duke,
it was started by the great **Giovanni Bellini** between 1511 and 1514
(virtually his last work) and depicts deities feasting to bawdy excess
in a bucolic setting – among others, little Bacchus in his blue tunic
pouring wine and a predatory Priapus lifting a nymph's skirt. Bellini
died in 1516 and in 1529 Titian, his former pupil, was engaged to
restyle the painting, removing a grove of trees and adding the brooding mountain in the background. Bellini's contemporary in Venice,
Giorgione, made a similar use of color and shadow to accentuate his
subjects – his *Adoration of the Shepherds* contrasts the blackness
of the cave with the light-bathed garb of the doting family. This is one
of the few of Giorgione's works that survive: he died of the plague at
the age of 33, though like Bellini he had already managed to teach
and inspire **Titian**, who would later eclipse them both to become the
finest Venetian painter of all. His revealing portraits and visually
seductive mythological scenes made him one of the most famous
artists in Europe and eventually court painter to Charles V of Spain –
look for his superb *St John the Evangelist on Patmos*.

Back in Florence, painting of the Early and High Renaissance
periods culminates in several works by **Raphael**. Prime piece here is
the renowned *Alba Madonna* (1510), another of Mellon's purchases from the Hermitage. Unusually, the Virgin and Child are seated on
the ground, leaning against a tree-stump, emphasizing humility: the
perspective is breathtakingly accurate, while the figures of Jesus and
John the Baptist suggest that Raphael had studied the cherubic
sculpture of Michaelangelo. There's also a brief diversion into sixteenth-century Florentine **mannerism**, the style of painting which
largely succeeded the High Reniassance – the works (mostly for
ostentatious display at court) highly charged with emotion, and often
harsh and unharmonious.

**The seventeenth and eighteenth centuries: Spanish,
French and Italian (rooms 29–34 and 36–37)**

Crossing the lobby off the West Garden Court brings one to **Spanish**
works of the late sixteenth and seventeenth centuries. In the grip of
the Counter-Reformation, Spanish art – its themes and parameters
laid down by a zealous Catholic Church – remained deeply spiritual
in character, with individual works designed to inspire devotion and
piety. Paramount among these were the paintings of **El Greco**, "the
Greek", the Cretan painter who moved to Spain in the mid-1570s
(and is also said to have trained under Titian in Venice, which
explains his often startling use of color). *Christ Clearing the
Temple* (c.1570) portrays Jesus with leather whip in hand laying
into assorted traders and moneylenders. More typical, though, is the
dour *Laocoön* (1610–14), in which the eponymous Trojan priest and
his two sons are attacked by serpents sent by the Greek gods. A
storm rages above the city of Troy in the background (suspiciously
reminiscent of El Greco's home, Toledo). From the same period, *St
Jerome* – in retreat in the desert and about to beat his chest with a
rock – expresses perfectly the emphasis the Spanish Church placed
on the concept of penance.

*El Greco's
proper name
was Domenikos
Theotokopoulos;
the National
Gallery of Art
has the most
important col-
lection of his
work outside
Spain.*

Francisco de Zubarán, well known for his religious portraits,
was responsible for *St Lucy*, a typical spiritual study, though one
with an accompanying shock as your eyes are drawn to the saint's –
which have been plucked out and laid on a dish which she holds in
her hand. You'll also find work by Zubarán's contemporary, **Diego
Velázquez**, the finest Spanish painter of the seventeenth century. So
precocious was his talent, he was court painter to Phillip IV by the
time he was 24 and spent the rest of his life executing powerful court
and royal portraits for his patron. He did, however, return now and
then to domestic scenes; *The Needlewoman* from 1640 is a fine
(unfinished) example.

There are a limited number of **French** works from the same
period on show. *The Repentant Magdalene* by **Georges de la Tour**
(1640) is one of the most significant, its careful balance of form and
light typical of the early Baroque stirrings in France and Italy at this
time. The painting has an almost photographic quality, the pensive
subject's face lit by a candle hidden behind a skull. Work by popular seventeenth-century landscapist **Claude Lorrain** includes a typically ethereal *Landscape with Merchants* (c.1630). French he
may have been, but Claude's ideas of natural beauty (as represented in this picture) were firmly Italian – he spent much of his life in
and around Rome.

The emphasis is strictly **Italian** for the final few rooms of this
section, most notably in *River Landscape* (c.1590) by the
Bolognese artist **Annibale Carracci**, an example of early Baroque art
in which nature is the subject of the painting, rather than the backdrop. From here, the jump into the eighteenth century is fairly

abrupt, ending with a stream of interiors and landscapes. Italian painters were still much in demand throughout Europe and artists like Bernado Bellotto could make a handsome living producing commissioned works like *The Fortress of Königstein*, executed for Augustus of Poland. Meanwhile, back in Venice, highly accomplished artists were producing *vedutas*, or view paintings, for sale to the traveling gentry who wanted a memento of their Grand Tour. Giovanni Antonio Canaletto was the first acknowledged master of this genre, and the gallery contains paintings by him of the entrance to the Grand Canal and of St Mark's Square.

Early German, and Dutch and Flemish: fifteenth- and sixteenth-century works (rooms 35, 38–41)

Principal among early German masters of the Northern Renaissance is **Albrecht Dürer**. His visits to Italy had a direct influence on his art, something which can be seen in his splendid *Madonna and Child* (1496–99), which grafts realistic Renaissance figures – including a veritable squirming child – onto a landscape backdrop typical of northern European religious paintings of the time. Dürer's contemporary, **Matthias Grünewald**, had less time for the Italian niceties of proportion and perspective, but there's no doubting the power behind his agonized *Crucifixion*, completed a decade or so later – the only painting by Grünewald in the US (indeed, there are only twenty left in the world). The same scene is presented from an entirely different perspective by **Lucas Cranach the Elder**, whose small panel, *The Crucifixion with the Converted Centurion* (1536), emphasizes the ideas of faith and salvation which made him such a Reformation favorite. You'll also find portraits by **Hans Holbein the Younger**, who as an artist in Germany couldn't adapt to the religious turmoil of the Reformation and moved to England, where he became court painter to Henry VIII. In this role he executed the pudgy *Edward VI as a Child*, a portrait of Henry's heir and son of his third wife Jane Seymour: finished in 1538, it's thought it was given to Henry as a present on New Year's Day 1539, complete with added Latin inscription judiciously encouraging Edward to emulate the myriad virtues of his father.

The gallery's early Flemish and Dutch works show the new techniques made possible by the revolutionary change from painting with quick-drying egg-based tempera to using slow-drying oil, which allowed artists to build up deep color tones. Acclaimed fifteenth-century artist **Jan van Eyck** was one of the first to adopt the new technique – his *Annunciation* (1434) shows a remarkable grasp of color and texture. Even more striking is the tiny panel by **Rogier van der Weyden** of *St George and the Dragon*, also executed in the mid-1430s, which followed the realism pioneered by van Eyck and applied it to a medieval subject with incredible attention to detail: the artist probably used a magnifying glass to paint individual tree

branches and pin-prick windows. Also notable is **Hieronymous
Bosch's** *Death and the Miser* (1485–90), a gloriously ghoulish tour
de force. There are similar unsettling images at work in Quentin
Massys' *Ill-Matched Lovers* (1520), in which a grotesque beau fon-
dles a woman who is handing his stolen money pouch to an accom-
plice – like the Bosch panel, a moralistic tale familar to contemporary viewers.

Seventeenth-century Dutch and Flemish (rooms 42–50)

The mood changes with a swath of **Anthony van Dyck** portraits of
assorted Italian, English and Flemish nobility, covering the period
from 1618 to 1635. Van Dyck was an immensely popular portraitist,
perhaps due in part to his flattery of his subjects – elongating their
frames, painting them from below to enhance their stature, idealiz-
ing their features. He was duly knighted for his efforts in England by
Charles I, but his inherent artistic skill shines through even the most
overblown of his portraits; the earliest one here, *Portrait of a
Flemish Lady* from 1618, was painted when he was just nineteen.
Van Dyck's teacher, **Peter Paul Rubens**, is responsible for the one
real masterpiece in this section, *Daniel in the Lions' Den*
(1613–15), in which virtually life-sized lions bay and snap around an
off-center Daniel.

Raffish gentlemen in white collars and tall hats were bread-and-
butter work for a talented portrait-painter like **Frans Hals**. Not that,
ultimately, it did him much good – in his dotage, Hals was virtually
on the breadline, supported only by handouts from an almshouse
whose governors liked the portrait he'd once painted of them. For
portraiture there are few equals to **Rembrandt van Rijn**, amongst
whose works the gallery numbers a prized painting of his wife,
Saskia. Begun in 1634, but not completed for almost five years, it
shows a remarkable contrast between the unearthly shine of her
face, headdress, neck and necklace, and her deep black dress. After
Saskia died in 1642, Rembrandt fell into debt and was eventually
declared bankrupt; a second wife and his only son also died, though
a mournful Rembrandt lived on until he was 63. *The Mill* is a typical
later work, from 1650, a brooding study of a cliff-top mill, backlit
under black thunderclouds. It's a famous image, with its dark and
light connotations of good and evil, and one which influenced nineteenth-century British artists like J.M.W. Turner.

Although other seventeenth-century Dutch artists show flashes
of brilliance, few can compete with the scope of Rembrandt. Most of
his contemporaries settled for making a living from **genre painting**,
depicting people in everyday social and work situations. These
quickly became popular in seventeenth-century Holland, partly
because the paintings allowed the newly independent Dutch to celebrate a nascent national identity. Each artist had his particular spe-
cialization: as Hals (a Flemish immigrant to Holland) produced por-

traits, so **Peter de Hooch** depicted quiet domestic households – like *A Dutch Courtyard* or *The Bedroom*. With **Jan Steen**, the genre was typically festive, doubtless inspired by his experience as an innkeeper: witness his bacchanalian *The Dancing Couple*. Of all the genre artists, only **Johannes Vermeer** is still widely known. In his entire career he created just 45 paintings, only 35 of which survive. Of these, the gallery owns and displays in turn *The Girl With the Red Hat*, *Woman Holding A Balance* and *A Lady Writing*, contemplative scenes all set – like most of his works – in his parents' house, which he later inherited. A fourth, *Young Girl With a Flute*, may not be by Vermeer; the jury is still out.

Eighteenth- and nineteenth-century Spanish and French (rooms 52–56)

Back at the Rotunda there's a last showing of **Spanish art**, principally portraits by the flamboyant **Francisco de Goya**, Spain's greatest eighteenth-century artist, who after 1789 was court painter to Charles IV. The gallery owns several works, primarily the famous *Señora Sebasa García* in which he abandons background entirely to focus on the elegant *señora*.

Eighteenth-century **French** painting and sculpture is announced by the pair of marble busts of Voltaire by **Jean-Antoine Houdon**, sculptor of George Washington (see p.57). The main attraction, however, is the portrait of *Napoleon in His Study* (1812) by Neoclassicist **Jacques-Louis David**. Arch imperial propagandist David meant the sword, crisp uniform, military papers and imperial emblems to bolster Napoleon's heroic image, while his slightly disheveled appearance, the dying candles and the time on the clock in the background point to the fact that he's been up all night working for the good of the country. His portrait of *Madame David* (1813), on the other hand, won't have completely thrilled her with its honesty. Come the Battle of Waterloo in 1815, and the defeat of Napoleon, his career was over and he was forced to flee to Switzerland.

By way of contrast consider the still lifes and everyday scenes of **Jean Simeon Chardin**, who worked directly from the subjects, hardly ever making the prior detailed studies that contemporaries considered essential. *Soap Bubbles* (1733) is typically effusive. Works by **Antoine Watteau** include the delightfully absurd *Italian Comedians* (1720), a group portrait of clowns and players, whose characters and costumes he knew well, having once worked as a scene-painter. Watteau's highly decorative rococo style is seen to best effect, however, in the oval panel depicting *Ceres*, the Roman goddess of the harvest, surrounded by the signs of the summer zodiac, Gemini, Cancer and Leo.

There's also a major showing of **Jean-Honoré Fragonard**, who knocked out his so-called "fantasy portraits" in as little as an hour. In

Chronologically, the East Wing of the main floor starts at room 52; if you start across the corridor in 93 you're at the back end of nineteenth-century French works.

Museums and galleries	*A Young Girl Reading*, a reflective study halfway between a sketch and a portrait, the neck ruff and bodice are etched in the paint using the wooden end of the brush while the lines of the book are mere blurred traces of paint. *The Swing* (1765) is a more artful work, whose images of flounced dresses and petticoats had erotic connotations for contemporaneous viewers.

Eighteenth- and nineteenth-century British (rooms 57–59, 61, 63)

The gallery's few **British** works include individual pieces by William Hogarth, George Stubbs and George Romney, but the most interesting pieces are by contemporary eighteenth-century court rivals **Joshua Reynolds** and **Thomas Gainsborough**. Also usually on display are works by two American artists who enjoyed great popularity during their time in England: Benjamin West, the first American artist to study in Europe, and Gilbert Stuart, pictorial chronicler of the first American presidents. Stuart's *The Skater* (1782), produced during his time in London with West, depicts a nonchalant, black-clad ice-skating gent whose sheer cheek was beyond compare in Britain at the time.

Other works are firmly within the British tradition, particularly the harmonious landscapes by **John Constable** and the sea and river scenes of **J.M.W. Turner**, which run the gamut from a gentle, hazy *Approach to Venice* – which John Ruskin described as "the most perfectly beautiful piece of color of all that I have seen produced by human hands" – to *Keelmen Heaving in Coals by Moonlight* (1835), a light-drenched harbor scene set in the industrial north of England.

For the most comprehensive display of American art in the city, see the National Museum of American Art (p.197); there are significant collections, too, in the National Portrait Gallery (p.192) and the Corcoran Gallery of Art (p.159).

Eighteenth- and nineteenth-century American (rooms 60, 62, 64–71)

The enormously eclectic collection of eighteenth- and nineteenth-century **American art** is one of the most popular sections of the entire gallery. Pick of the collection for many is the line of portraits by **Gilbert Stuart** of the leading American men of his age. Born in Rhode Island, where he first studied painting, poverty forced him to London where he was taken on by fellow American Benjamin West. Stuart quickly became a success and set up his own studio, but later got into debt and returned after seventeen years abroad to a new United States, where he resolved to make his fortune by executing a portrait of the first president. In fact, he ended up painting the likeness of George Washington more than a hundred times during his career; the two examples here are the early *Vaughan Portrait* of 1795 and the more familiar *Athenaeum Portrait* (1810–15) – the latter eventually being used as the model for the portrait on the dollar bill. Following his success with Washington, Stuart became in effect the American court artist, painting the next four presidents –

Adams, Jefferson, Madison and Monroe – and over a thousand other
portraits (the National Gallery alone has 41), including private com-
missions such as the study of *Mrs Richard Yates*, whose crossed
eyes are partly concealed by the expedient of having her looking
sideways out of the picture.

In contrast to the youthful Stuart, **John Singleton Copley** was
already in his mid-30s when he decided to study painting in Europe.
The outbreak of the American Revolution kept him in England longer
than he had planned and his family joined him instead in London –
the *Copley Family* celebrates their reunion (the artist is in the rear
left of the painting). You'll also find work by **Benjamin West** who,
though born in Pennsylvania, studied first in Rome in the 1760s
before establishing himself as a history painter in England where he
succeeded Joshua Reynolds as President of the Royal Academy in
1792, an office he held for almost thirty years. Given this, it's debat-
able whether to consider him an American artist at all: certainly in his
splendid historical scenes, which he helped popularize as an art
form, West took subtle side with the British – in *The Battle of La
Hogue* (1778), which pits seventeenth-century English and French
naval forces against each other, the heroic English admiral directs
operations from close quarters while the French dandy is more concerned about losing his wig than with the hand-to-hand combat rag
ing around him.

There's more portraiture by two of West's former pupils, John
Trumbull (who was later responsible for the murals in the Capitol)
and Thomas Sully. Both were highly regarded, although the one
painting which most are keen to see, *The Washington Family* by
Edward Savage, is by a much inferior artist – his formal group portrait shows George, Martha and grandchildren sat around a table at
Mount Vernon in rather glum contemplation of a map of the new city
of Washington DC.

By the nineteenth century, American artists were tackling the
theme of territorial expansion head-on. *The Notch of the White
Mountains* by **Thomas Cole** (1839) – leading light in the Hudson
River School, in which human figures play second fiddle to their natural surroundings – is typical in its vibrant use of color. The subject
– settlers and stagecoach passengers threatened by dark clouds and
an imminent avalanche – was based on an actual event. You'll see a
similar awe of nature in Jasper Francis Cropsey's *Autumn – On the
Hudson River* (1860), in which auburn, yellow and faded green con-
spire to suggest an autumnal brown. At around the same time, the
German-born **Albert Bierstadt** brought his monumental eye to a
grand study of a shimmering, turquoise *Lake Lucerne*, framed by
mountains – the immediate progenitor of his startlingly successful
American landscapes (the best are in the National Museum of
American Art; p.197). Others, meanwhile, were recording the scale
of human progress in the wilderness, like **George Inness**, whose *The

Lackawanna Valley (1855), in which a steam train puffs through a Pennsylvanian landscape of felled trees, was commissioned by a railroad company. Inness hadn't wanted the job, but needed the money; at the company's insistence he included the "roundhouse" building in which the trains were turned around, a technological innovation of which they were especially proud.

After the landscapes, "**American Still Life and Genre Paintings**" is a minor triumph. There's a real spark in Caleb Bingham's *The Jolly Flatboatmen* – the dancing, fiddle-playing subjects amusing themselves on a dull journey down the Mississippi River – an immensely popular picture in its day, reminiscent of a scene from Mark Twain. Take a look, too at the initially unassuming portrait of *Rubens Peale with a Geranium*, an early work by Rubens' brother **Rembrandt Peale**. The Peales were an extraordinary family of seventeen children, with most of the eleven who survived into adulthood named after notable figures by their artist father Charles Willson Peale, whose work is also represented in the gallery. No fewer than eight of them, male and female, became artists (including Titian, who traveled to and painted western America), though Rembrandt was by far the most talented. The sickly Rubens was a keen botanist and the geranium he grips here is said to be the first grown in America (Jefferson had previously brought one back from France, but it died). As if the immediate family weren't precocious enough, a rather more conventionally named uncle, James Peale, weighs in with a *Fruit Still Life* in which the succulent grapes positively demand you pluck and eat them; in a flamboyant touch, this Peale includes his initials as a curling twig at the end of the grapevine.

The late nineteenth century is ushered in with a roomful of paintings by Philadelphia-based **Thomas Eakins**, whose light touch is atypical of the post-Civil War period, which tended to bring out a darker element in the works of contemporaries. **Winslow Homer** is a case in point: trained as a graphic artist, he worked during the Civil War for *Harper's Weekly*, recording battlefield scenes which had a profound influence on his later work. In the typically stormy *Lost on the Grand Banks*, all hope seems to have been abandoned by the occupants of the wave-tossed skiff. **James Abbott McNeill Whistler** is dominant, too; his stand-out work here is *The White Girl* from 1862, subtitled *Symphony in White No. 1*. The full-length study of his mistress is of secondary importance to his contrasting use of various shades of white, from dress to drapes to flowers, all subtly different in tone. There's a similar idea behind his self-portrait of 1900, *Brown and Gold: Self Portrait*. A more offbeat collection of works are those from the so-called Cartoon Collection by frontier artist **George Catlin** (for more on whom, see p.197), who certainly grabbed contemporary audiences' attention with his subject matter – notably himself sitting down to enjoy a feast of roast dog with his Sioux hosts.

Having a Break in the National Gallery of Art

For food and drink, you need to head down a level from the main floor or across to the East Building, noting as you go Salvador Dalí's *Last Supper*, which guards the escalators down to the Concourse.

Cascade Espresso and Gelato Bar, Concourse (Mon–Sat 10am–4.30pm, Sun 11am–5.30pm). Coffee, sandwiches, desserts, salads, ice cream and sorbets.

Concourse Buffet, Concourse (Mon–Fri 10am–3pm, Sat 10am–3pm, Sun 11am–3pm). Self-service breakfast (10–11am), salads, burgers, sandwiches and hot meals.

Garden Café, West Building, ground floor (Mon–Sat 11.30am–3pm, Sun noon–6.30pm). Lunch daily; later opening on Sunday for those attending the classical concerts in the Garden Court. Reservations on ☎216-2494.

Terrace Café, East Building, upper level (Mon–Sat 11.30am–3pm, Sun noon–4pm). Nicest lunch spot, with Mall views. Reservations on ☎216-2494.

The century turns with the last two rooms in the section, taking American art up to World War I. Childe Hassam's *Allies Day, May 1917* is a packed New York streetscape of flags and crowds, while the gallery also displays works by leading Impressionist William Merritt Chase. **George Bellows'** assured *Portrait of Florence Davey* in no way prepares you for his other paintings, notably the brutal prizefight pictures *Club Night* (1907) and *Both Members of This Club* (1909), in which you can almost feel the heat as the crowd bays for blood. There's a similar energy in the brilliantly realized *Blue Morning* (1909), set on a New York construction site.

Rooms 72–79 are usually devoted to special exhibitions.

Nineteenth-century French (rooms 80–93)

The most popular rooms in the West Building are those containing the exceptional collection of nineteenth-century French paintings, with every Impressionist, post-Impressionist, Realist and Romantic artist of note represented. For once the rooms don't follow an exact chronological order, so you may need to backtrack now and then to find some favorites.

There are always crowds for **Claude Monet** and his dappled European views, among them two facades of Rouen Cathedral. From 1892 onwards, he painted over thirty of these, almost all from the same close-up viewpoint but at different times of the day and in varied conditions, forming an integral part of his experimentation with light and color. They were reworked in his studio and a score of them finally exhibited in Paris in 1895. Significant, too, is *The Japanese Footbridge* (1899), whose waterlily theme he was to return to with spectacular success again and again until his death in 1926.

Impressionism continues with Monet's *Woman with a Parasol* (1875) – whose emphasis lies more on the vibrant summer light than its subjects, namely the artist's wife and child – and two of the dozens of studies he made of the town of Argenteuil, where he had a floating studio on the river in the 1870s. Honors, too, go to **Edouard Manet**'s *Gare Saint-Lazare* (1873), showing two contrasting figures before the station railings. Works by **Vincent van Gogh** include his *The Olive Orchard* and the rich honey and yellow tones of the *Farmhouse in Provence*, both portraying an intensity – like all his Provençal paintings – that echoed his ever-present mental turmoil. With **Auguste Renoir** you can contrast the subdued *Girl with a Watering Can* and *Girl with a Hoop* with the rather more dissolute *Odalisque*, stretched out in abandon on floor cushions. Here too are female portraits by the American-in-Paris **Mary Cassatt**, whose work you can usually count on finding with the French Impressionists – a term she decried as not reflecting her own careful technique and observation. It's easy to agree when studying the flat blocks of color and naturalistic models in *Mother and Child* (1905) and especially the earlier *Woman with a Red Zinnia* (1891) and *The Boating Party* (1894).

Symbolism and post-Impressionism are explored in later rooms. The powerful *Self-Portrait* (1889) by **Paul Gauguin**, complete with halo, apple tree and serpent, resembles an early Salvador Dalí. Gauguin's declared aim to depict himself outside of Western society, as an "outlaw", was taken to its logical extreme with his move to Tahiti in 1891, where he completed dozens of paintings detailing its people, culture and religion. The gallery's collection of works by **Paul Cézanne** contains still lifes, portraits and landscapes from most periods of his long life. Cézanne is often seen as the father of modern art, though he struggled to make an impression during his own lifetime, only ever selling around 50 of his 800 paintings – hostile criticism forced him to stop exhibiting in 1877, and his first one-man show wasn't held for another eighteen years. The invective he inspired is now difficult to conceive: Evelyn Waugh thought him a "village idiot who had been given a box of paints to keep him quiet". Cézanne was 27 when he completed *The Artist's Father* (1866) – Cézanne *père* had no time for his son's desire to become an artist and opposed his move to Paris in the 1860s; Paul retaliated by perching his father uncomfortably in a high-backed chair in front of a representation of one of his own paintings.

The later rooms finish with a flourish, highlighting varied works by **Henri de Toulouse-Lautrec**, portraying the dancers, madames and café patrons he observed in his peregrinations around the fleshpots of Montmartre. The most famous piece here by **Edgar Degas** is the dreamlike *Four Dancers* (1899), one of his last large paintings. It's a swirl of motion which could be four young ballerinas in different poses, or one single dancer moving through a routine – rather like a flick-book of sketches laid flat on the canvas.

Twentieth-century art

Although the National Gallery's **East Building** was opened in 1978 to make room for the ever-expanding collection of **twentieth-century European and American art**, there still isn't anything like enough exhibition space to display the entire collection. This is partly due to I.M. Pei's audacious design, which places a generous premium on public areas – since the exhibition spaces, squeezed in like an afterthought, are often taken up with special shows, it means that the gallery's own twentieth-century holdings may not be on display at all when you visit. If any of the artists or works below form part of your reason for visiting, be sure to call first.

Two or three items are always present, but that's only because they're too big to keep shifting around. Outside at the 4th Street entrance, **Henry Moore**'s bronze *Knife Edge Mirror Two Piece* is a male and female representation whose sensuous line and form contrast with the sharp angles of the building – Moore collaborated with Pei before deciding on its exact structure. Inside, dominating the atrium, a huge steel-and-aluminum mobile by **Alexander Calder** hangs from the ceiling, its red and black (and one blue) paddle-like wings moving slowly with the air currents. Also in the atrium, **Joan Miró**'s stunning tapestry *Woman* is usually on display.

When exhibitions from the twentieth-century collection are in place, they start chronologically on the upper level, which displays **pre-1945 art**, most of it European. The famous names are all here, none more so than **Pablo Picasso**, who is represented by several diverse works, including the blue-period *The Tragedy* (1903) and *Family of Saltimbanques* (1905), itinerant circus performers captured in reflective mood in a stripped landscape. By 1910, when he completed *Nude Woman*, Picasso had turned fully to Cubism – this piece particularly challenged contemporary audiences with a dissection of anatomy reminiscent of X-ray photography.

There's a similar range in the gallery's collection of paintings by **Henri Matisse**, with restrained early works giving way to the exuberant *Pianist and Checker Players* (1924), pictured in Matisse's own apartment in Nice. Technically the most interesting pieces, however, are those kept behind light-sensitive doors down on the Concourse level (Mon–Sat 10am–2pm, Sun 11am–3pm), the so-called Matisse "Cut-Outs". These late works, completed during the 1940s and early 1950s when illness prevented him gripping a paintbrush, involved Matisse cutting painted primary-colored sheets into assorted shapes which were then attached to a white background to form vibrant patterns.

Post-1945 art (mostly American, though with several honorable exceptions) is usually shown downstairs in the Concourse level galleries. **Andy Warhol**'s works are as familiar as they come, with classic serial examples of *32 Soup Cans*, *Let Us Now Praise Famous Men* and *Green Marilyn*. There's also usually work by **Roy**

For more Alexander Calder on the Mall, check out Stabile, *a black, angular piece at the northeast (14th and Constitution) corner of the National Museum of American History, his* Two Disks *stands outside the Hirshorn Museum on Independence Ave.*

Museums and galleries

Lichtenstein, **Clifford Still** and **Willem de Kooning**. Separate rooms are often set aside for the related works of those artists using huge color swatches: the gallery owns large, primeval canvases by **Mark Rothko**, as well as the thirteen hessian-colored *Stations of the Cross* by **Barnett Newman**, a series that took eight years to complete. There are various slabs of color, too, by **Robert Rauschenberg** (his *Blue Eagle* is more diverting, a motor oil can, old T-shirt and blue lamp affixed to a black-and-white smear) and a wealth of **Jasper Johns**, whose *Field Painting* (1963–64) sports cans, cut-out alphabet letters, knife and paintbrush. Other highlights include **Chuck Close**'s *Fanny/Fingerpainting* (1985), a mighty portrait of an elderly black woman realized from a brilliantly marshaled canvas of finger splodges. A more recent acquisition is the grim *Angel of History*, a warplane of lead and glass by the German expressionist **Anselm Kiefer** – 15ft long and embedded with dried poppy stalks. Much of Kiefer's work deals with the destruction of war; you can also look out for his landscape *Zim Zum*, which marries textured sheets of lead and a burned canvas marred by sand, ash and dust.

Sculpture, decorative arts, prints and drawings

Changing exhibitions of sculpture, decorative arts, prints and drawings take place on the **ground floor** of the West Building; the information desks can point out current highlights. The gallery owns over two thousand pieces of **sculpture**: many Italian and French pieces from the fourteenth to eighteenth centuries, as well as pieces from the excellent nineteenth-century French collection, with works by Rodin, Degas, Maillol, et al. Among the **decorative arts** are Flemish tapestries, eighteenth-century French furniture, Renaissance majolica, chalices and religious paraphernalia, Chinese porcelain, engraved medals, even stained-glass windows. Perhaps most impressive is the gallery's collection of **prints and drawings** – 65,000 works, from the eleventh to the twentieth centuries. Selections on show are necessarily limited and tend to be exhibited only for short periods, but if you're sufficiently clued up you can make an appointment to see particular works by calling ☎842-6380.

National Museum of African Art

950 Independence Ave SW ☎357-4600; Smithsonian Metro. Daily 10am–5.30pm. Admission free.

The **National Museum of African Art** – the nation's foremost collection of the traditional arts of sub-Saharan Africa – occupies the underground levels of one of the Mall's most appealing buildings. Its circular motifs and domes recall a traditional African dwelling, while providing an architectural counterpoint to the triangular lines of the neighboring Sacker Gallery. These are fine surroundings in which to view the collection, which runs to some six thousand diverse sculptures and artifacts from a wide variety of tribal

There's no café in the Smithsonian Castle, the Freer or Sackler galleries, or the African art museum; and the outdoor café at the Hirshorn is open summer only. Nearest refreshments are in the Air and Space Museum – or from the vendors on the street outside.

cultures, displayed in a series of permanent galleries and bolstered by special exhibitions.

In many ways, the museum is one of applied art, though the application of a particular piece is not always clear, not least to the curators. In part this is due to the techniques of early collectors, who tended not to concern themselves unduly with recording factual information about their loot. In most cases, even the artist's name isn't known, while dating a piece is fraught with difficulty, too. On the whole, most of the works are nineteenth or twentieth century – some are older, but because most African art is made from wood or clay, it tends not to survive for long.

For an overview of the collection, the free **guided tours** (daily except Fri) are an excellent introduction – pick up a schedule at the ground-floor **information desk**. It's also worth noting that the **gift shop** on the first level is one of DC's most intriguing, selling woven and dyed fabrics and clothes as well as the usual books and post-cards. The permanent **galleries** are downstairs on the first level.

The Kerma and Benin collections

The Nubian trading city of **Kerma**, 180 miles south of the present Egypt–Sudan border, flourished between 2500 and 1500 BC. Most of what is known about the city is derived from the excavations of royal tombs, discovered at huge cemeteries lost in the desert for centuries. On display are ceramic bowls (perfectly round, despite being hand-formed) and, more interestingly, carved legs and delicate ivory animal figures from the ceremonial beds used to carry the dead to the cemetery for burial. As in Egypt, Nubian royalty were buried with hundreds of what the museum likes to call "volunteers", who "allowed themselves to be buried alive" to serve their masters in the afterlife.

More coherent is the adjacent gallery's display of royal art from the **Kingdom of Benin**, home of Edo-speaking people in what is now Nigeria. It's a small collection of highly accomplished works relating to the rule of the *Oba*, or king, some dating back as far as the fifteenth century. Best pieces here are the copper alloy heads (made using the sophisticated lost-wax casting technique), some of which depict an erstwhile *Oba*, although one is of a defeated enemy – that he's not Edo is indicated by the four raised scars over each eye; the other heads have only three. There's a picture of the current *Oba* on the gallery wall, in resplendent orange, whose ceremonial headdress and neck-ruff echo those depicted on the copper heads – evidence that the same royal style has prevailed for over five hundred years.

The other galleries

The other galleries make valiant efforts to contextualize the objects on show. In **"Images of Power and Identity"**, the emphasis is on political, religious and ceremonial art – mostly from west and central Africa – which by its nature includes some of the most elaborate of the museum's holdings. The exhibition contains the museum's two oldest pieces – rounded, stylized, terracotta equestrian and archer figures from Mali (thirteenth–fifteenth century) – and also includes the only work in the museum where the artist is known. Olowe of Ise, an artist to royalty among the Yoruba people of Nigeria, was responsible for the carved wooden palace door, 6ft high and depicting in relief a king seated on a horse, his wives ranked above him, and soldiers and daughters below. Remarkably, the door was carved from a single piece of wood. Several works – fertility fetishes – represent a woman and child; note especially the worn wooden carving from Nigeria that would have sat at one end of a ceremonial drum. Unlike Western tradition, where Jesus is the dominant figure in any carving of Madonna and Child, here all the expressive power in the sculpture is with the woman – giver of life. In other cultures power is expressed in more abstract forms. From the Cameroon, a wooden sculpture of a regal male figure holds his chin in his hand (a sign of respect), his decorative bead **clothing** covered with symbolic representations of spiders (a wily opponent) and frogs (fecundity).

There's much to learn, too, about the varied African concepts of divinity or even beauty: a carved figure from the Ghanaian Asante people shows a seated male and female with disk-shaped heads, a form considered to be the aesthetic ideal. Not all concepts are completely alien to Western tradition, however. One of the most engaging works – a headrest from the Luba people of the Congo – is supported by two caryatid figures who (if you look around the back) have their arms entwined.

The "**Art of the Personal Object**" displays precisely that: chairs, stools and more headrests, mostly carved from wood using an adze; as well as assorted ivory snuff containers (two from Angola with stoppers shaped like human heads), beer straws (from Uganda), carved drinking horns, combs, pipes, spoons, baskets and cups.

National Museum of American History

14th St NW and Constitution Ave ☎357-2700; Smithsonian Metro. Daily: June–Aug 10am–6.30pm; Sept–May 10am–5.30pm. Admission free.

If there's one single museum in the United States that can begin to explain what it is to be American, it's the **National Museum of American History**. Behind a rather staid title hides a bizarre melange of artifacts that goes some way to recounting the lives and experiences of ordinary Americans by displaying the very stuff of life – from eighteenth-century farming equipment to computer chips; juke boxes to washing machines; harmonicas to train engines. Each floor is a serendipitous delight: George Washington's wooden teeth, Jackie K.'s designer dresses and the ruby slippers Judy Garland wore in the *Wizard of Oz* are set among didactic displays tracing the

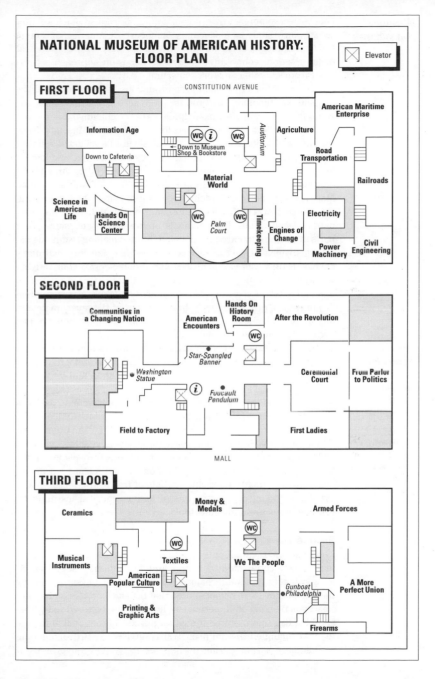

NATIONAL MUSEUM OF AMERICAN HISTORY: FLOOR PLAN

⊠ Elevator

FIRST FLOOR

CONSTITUTION AVENUE

Information Age

American Maritime Enterprise

Agriculture

Road Transportation

WC (i) WC

← Down to Museum Shop & Bookstore

Down to Cafeteria ↑

Auditorium

Railroads

Material World

Science in American Life

Hands On Science Center

WC
Palm Court

WC
Timekeeping

Electricity

Engines of Change

Power Machinery

Civil Engineering

SECOND FLOOR

Communities in a Changing Nation

American Encounters

Hands On History Room

After the Revolution

WC

Star-Spangled Banner

Washington Statue

(i) Foucault Pendulum

Ceremonial Court

From Parlor to Politics

Field to Factory

First Ladies

MALL

THIRD FLOOR

Ceramics

Money & Medals

Armed Forces

WC

WC

Musical Instruments

Textiles

We The People

American Popular Culture

Gunboat Philadelphia

A More Perfect Union

Printing & Graphic Arts

Firearms

country's development from colonial times. It's not so much a center for scholarly study as a sanctuary for vanishing Americana, though the museum looks forward, too, with its coverage of the white heat of information technology – where its hands-on approach sets its apart from any other "history" museum.

The museum's roots lie in the prodigious bequests made to the original Smithsonian Institution (see p.70), starting with the exhibits left over from Philadelphia's 1876 Centennial Exhibition. Each item collected was destined for the "National Museum" (now the Arts and Industries Building), but since this meant displaying stuffed animals alongside portraits, postage stamps and patent models, the Smithsonian was soon forced to specialize. An attempt was made to direct part of the collection by founding a National Museum of History and Technology in 1954, for which this traditional Beaux-Arts building – the last such on the Mall – was purpose-built a decade later. The emphasis proved important, since great parts of the museum are now devoted to the sweeping technological changes which helped mold modern America. But the final name change in 1980 was a belated acceptance of the constant underlying theme: that the museum of "American History" firmly relates its exhibits to the experiences of the American people. Not every item is domestic in origin – indeed, huge swathes of the museum deal in imported products and ideas – but each in its application has had both a personal and national effect.

Information desks at both Mall (second-floor) and Constitution Avenue (first-floor) entrances are staffed 10am–4pm.

You could easily spend a full day here; three to four hours would be a reasonable compromise, though to stick to this you'll have to be selective. There's an extremely good **museum shop and bookstore** on the lower level – the biggest of the Smithsonian stores (see p.321) – as well as the main self-service **cafeteria**. The ice-cream parlor is on the first floor, in the **Palm Court**, which is a table-service café – there's also a *Starbuck's* coffee bar just outside the Palm Court (next to a great 50s-style Horn and Hardart automatic vending machine) and a functioning **post office** counter inside a transplanted nineteenth-century general store (by the Constitution Avenue entrance). Ask at the information desks for details of free **tours, lectures and events**, including demonstrations of antique musical instruments, printing presses and machine tools.

Second floor

Entering from the Mall puts you on the second floor, where you are immediately confronted by a **Foucault Pendulum**, a seventy-foot-long swinging pendulum named for the French physicist who by these means in 1851 demonstrated that the earth rotates on its axis. Nearby is the Flag Hall, permanent home of the battered red-white-and-blue flag that inspired the writing of the US national anthem – the **Star-Spangled Banner** itself, which survived the British bombing of Baltimore harbor during the War of 1812. With dimensions of around 30 by 34 feet, and (backed by heavy linen) weighing 150 pounds, it sports fifteen stars and fifteen stripes (eight red and seven white), representing the fifteen states in the Union at the time of the hostilities. In the early life of the new republic, there was no fixed design for the national flag, as arguments raged over the relative prominence to be given to existing and future states. Congress eventually settled on the more familar thirteen stripes (for the number of original colonies), while adding a new star to the flag each time a state joined the Union. Following decades of exposure to light and pollution, the flag is currently under long-term restoration, though it's still on view in the conservation lab behind the George Washington statue; it should move back into the Flag Hall inside a climate-controlled case by 2002.

It's difficult to miss Horatio Greenhough's much-ridiculed **statue of George Washington**, commissioned in 1832 during the

---

The Star-Spangled Banner

O say, can ye see by the dawn's early light
what so proudly we hail'd by the twilight's last gleaming?
Whose bright stars and broad stripes through the clouds of the fight,
o'er the ramparts we watch'd were so gallantly streaming?

After the burning of the Capitol and White House in Washington DC in August 1814, the British turned their attention toward nearby Baltimore, then America's third largest city, which was defended by the garrison at **Fort McHenry**. To reinforce his defiance of the superior British force, the commander ordered the making of a large American flag, which was hoisted high above the fort in Baltimore harbor. The British finally attacked on the night of September 13, subjecting fort and harbor defenses to a ferocious bombardment, which was witnessed among others by **Francis Scott Key**, a 35-year-old Georgetown lawyer and part-time poet. Attempting to negotiate the release of an American prisoner, Dr William Beanes, Key was being held on board a British ship that night and come "dawn's early light" was amazed to see not only that the flag was still "so gallantly streaming" but that the cannons of the outnumbered Americans had forced the British to withdraw.

Key may have been a mediocre poet but he was no slouch. Taking the bombardment as his inspiration he rattled off a poem entitled "The Defense of Fort McHenry", which he set to the tune of a contemporary English drinking song. The first public performance of the song took place in Baltimore a month after the battle and it soon became an immensely popular rallying cry: Union troops adopted it during the Civil War and it became the armed forces' anthem in 1916, though not until a decree by Herbert Hoover in 1931 did it become the official **national anthem** of the United States. Despite Key's original title, the song seems to have become known as the "Star-Spangled Banner" almost immediately – indeed, the idea of the felicitous phrase had already occurred to Key in an earlier poem celebrating the exploits of Stephen Decatur against the Barbary pirates, which contained the words "the star-spangled flag".

---

centennial of Washington's birth. He was paid $5000 by Congress and in 1841 came up with an imperial, seated, toga-clad Washington with swept-back hair, bare torso and sandals – mothers reputedly covered their children's eyes at its public unveiling. Look past the ill-advised classic revivalism and the likeness actually isn't that bad; perhaps hardly surprising since Greenhough based it on the far more talented Jean-Antoine Houdon's earlier sculpture (see p.57).

Beyond here in the West Wing, the first main gallery details "**Communities in a Changing Nation**", with nineteenth-century America showcased through various social environments – slave cabin from South Carolina, indigent peddler's cart and wealthy Gothic-Revival bedroom interior. From here it's a quick move to the history of African-American migration from 1915 to 1940 in a display entitled "**Field to Factory**". The demand for unskilled labor stimulated by World War I saw an unprecedented move from the fields of the South to the factories of the North by hundreds of thousands of black Americans. The "Great Migration" proved a momentous change, establishing strong black communities in diverse northern cities – in DC, the hub of settlement was the Shaw neighborhood – and setting the framework for modern demographic patterns. Most of the documents, photographs and exhibits tell of the experience of individuals, from the recorded voices of migrants as they traveled north on the (segregated) trains to the re-creations of the new domestic situations they encountered on a farm in southern Maryland or in a Philadelphian tenement row. "**American Encounters**" focuses on New Mexico, looking at how sixteenth- and seventeenth-century Hispanic invasions and, later, tourism have affected the native communities – in particular, the pueblo Indians of Santa Clara and Chimayo. Traditional and contemporary applied art, in the shape of ornate rugs, chests, figurines and ceramics, sit alongside photographs, videos and recordings of narrative stories, music and dance.

The museum's chief strength lies in creating compelling images of ordinary life for Americans of different backgrounds through the ages. Nowhere is this more apparent than in "**After the Revolution**", whose walk-through displays detail the lives of three eighteenth-century families (of a Delaware farmer, a Virginia planter and Massachusetts merchant) as well as the wider concerns of three communities (African-Americans in Chesapeake, the Seneca people of New York State, and urban Philadelphia). Eager to efface difference and present a vision of consensus, the gallery tells of the same triumphs and difficulties in each community: the array of instruments and knives used for bleeding yellow fever victims in Philadelphia's 1793 epidemic is no more or less comforting than the brutal obstetrics equipment used on the Delaware farm.

The rest of the East Wing is devoted to presidential life in and beyond the White House. Its fulcrum is the walk-through **Ceremonial Court**, designed to resemble the Cross Hall of the White House as it appeared after its 1902 renovation; the Smithsonian managed to purloin some of the original architectural bits and pieces which are incorporated here into the design, as are displays of glass, porcelain, tinware and silver from the White House collections. More satisfying is the cabinet displaying personal items of the presidents: Washington's telescope*, Grant's leather cigar case, Nixon's gold pen, Wilson's golf clubs, Jefferson's eyeglasses and Theodore Roosevelt's toiletry set.

Museums and galleries

Off the Ceremonial Court, **"First Ladies"** begins with portraits of each one, from Martha (who liked to be known as Lady Washington) onwards. Though there's a game attempt to provide biographical padding, and exhibits exhort viewers to appreciate First Ladies as political partners (Eleanor), preservers of White House culture and history (Jackie), or advocates of social causes (Hillary), the real pleasure here is in the frocks. Helon Herron Taft was the first to present her inaugural ball gown to the Smithsonian for preservation, starting a tradition that allows the museum to display a backlit collection of considerable interest, if not always taste. Other outfits provide revealing historical snapshots: Jackie Kennedy's simple A-line brocaded dress and jacket raised hemlines in America almost overnight. There's access from the Ceremonial Court through to **"From Parlor to Politics"**, a worthy trawl through the history of women and political reform (1890–1925), with exhibits on women's clubs, the temperance movement and female suffrage.

First floor

Every technological change to affect America, from crop rotation to computers, is laid out with systematic and mind-bogglingly comprehensive clarity on the first floor. You know you're in for a treat when the central lobby, devoted to the **Material World**, throws up a veritable bazaar of handcrafted and machine-made artifacts, designed to show what things are made of and why. There's a great half an hour or so to be spent here picking out favorite items: a steel slot machine from 1940, a brass US Army bugle, ornate nineteenth-century marble balusters from a Boston bank, a cast-iron toy train, an aluminum softball bat, even astroturf. Adjacent displays trace the development of items like washing machines, from the earliest wooden tub to the first electrically operated model of the 1960s; bicycles get the same treatment, with the oldest example (from 1869) made of hickory and wrought iron.

The Constitution Avenue entrance leads directly into the first floor.

---

*George Washington's wooden false teeth, also on display here, are in fact a facsimile: the originals, which he used to soak in wine to improve their taste, were stolen in the 1970s. Washington had several handmade denture sets, crafted from materials as diverse as elephant and walrus tusks, lead, and human teeth.

"Science in American Life" fills in the background to many of the discoveries that made the artifacts possible in the first place. There's coverage of every scientific development you could think of, and several you've never even heard of; the interactive **Hands On Science Center**, contained within the gallery, explains many of them by letting you conduct basic experiments. The similarly interactive "Information Age" traces communications from Morse's first telegraph to modern information technology by way of a phalanx of radios, phonograms, telephones and computers of every age, shape and size. Some of the most remarkable relics are the early models from Alexander Graham Bell's first experiments with the telephone, a device he exhibited to universal amazement at the 1876 Centennial Exhibition in Philadelphia; only thirteen years later, the first public pay phone, a bulky box of tricks, was installed in Hartford, Connecticut. Among other multifarious diversions, you can hear excerpts from early radio programs, deal with a 911 emergency call, check out the state of contemporary communications in a re-created 1939 street scene, or sit in on a show in the Bijou Theater for archive newsreel and movie footage. The museum steps up a gear with its coverage of the development of computers: the thirty-ton ENIAC (Electronic Numerical Integrator and Computer) built for the US army during World War II could compute a thousand times faster than any existing machine but it takes up a thirty-by-fifty-foot room; by way of contrast, a dozen of its valves in a box are about the same size as the computer on which you can take part in an electronic opinion poll on recent government policies. There are up-to-the-minute computer-based presentations in the Multimedia Theater, and at the end of the section – if you can kick the kids off the consoles – you can explore the world of the "virtual Smithsonian".

For all the interactive goodies, it's the east side of the floor which, for many, is the most affecting, since here in glorious profusion are the artifacts and machines that have shaped America. Everyone will have their particular favorite, but the themes come thick and fast. "**American Maritime Enterprise**" is typical in its diversity, with the model boats and seafaring paraphernalia quite put in the shade by an entire ship's steam engine and a mock-up tattoo parlour; sea shanties warble away on tape in the background. The exhibits in "**Road Transportation**" are virtual icons of their various ages: a covered wagon from the mid-nineteenth century, a 1903 Oldsmobile (the first automobile to be built on an assembly line), a Ford Model T from 1913, Evel Knievel's Harley Davidson, and a solar-powered car which set a speed record of 75mph in 1988. In **Railroads**, an enormous Pacific-type locomotive from 1926 had to be shunted in through the museum window on a specially laid track. Galleries like "**Civil Engineering**" (bridges and tunnels through the ages), "**Power Machinery**" (big drills) or "**Timekeeping**" (railroad pocket watches to the atomic clock) will have their particular devotees. Of wider interest, though, is "**Electricity**", which celebrates not only the peculiar genius of Thomas Edison, who invented the light-bulb among other luminous discoveries, but concentrates, too, on Ben Franklin's early research on static electricity.

Third floor

Up on the top floor is everything else that had to go somewhere, and while the exhibits are divided into various themes, some items are simply unclassifiable and have ended up in a section entitled "**American Popular Culture**", on display in cases at the top of the escalators in the West Wing. Many make a beeline straight for these, gawking in reverence at – among other things – Dorothy's slippers from the *Wizard of Oz* (silver, incidentally, in the original Frank Baum stories, but changed to red to utilize the new capabilities of Technicolor), Muhammed Ali's boxing gloves, Michael Jordan's NBA jersey, a Babe Ruth autographed baseball, Dizzy Gillespie's trumpet and a Star Trek phaser. The third-floor exhibits proper start with "**Printing and Graphic Arts**", which shows temporary exhibitions from the museum's large collection of original prints alongside paper-making machines and printing presses. The west rooms then move around thematically, covering musical instruments, textiles, ceramics, and money and medals. Amid the eighteenth-century grand pianos, the racks of English and American porcelain or coins and notes from around the world, is the odd offbeat treat – President Clinton's first saxophone; a display devoted to the life and work of DC native and jazz legend Duke Ellington (see p.227); or the exhibit of *fai*, or circular stone money, of the West Pacific Yap Islands, which was up to 12ft in diameter and had to be carried around on poles. There were, needless to say, no very rich Yap islanders.

The East Wing is more consistently interesting, starting with "**We the People**", which has sections on extending the franchise, and on the Constitution itself, though most people are content to pick over the roomful of mementoes from presidential campaigns as far back as that for John Quincy Adams. Nineteenth-century straw boaters, pictures and commemorative plates give way to half-remembered button slogans – "LBJ: Light Bulb Johnson – turn him out in November" or "The Grin Will Win – Carter for President".

Star piece of the various military-related collections is the oak gunboat **Philadelphia**, the oldest US man-of-war in existence. In 1776, in a campaign against the British on Lake Champlain, 63 men lived on this tiny ship for three months, suffering extraordinary privation – there was no upper or lower deck and only a canvas cover to protect them from the elements. Also on display near here is General Washington's linen tent, his campaign headquarters during the Revolutionary War, alongside his camp chest complete with tin plate and coffee pot. Adjacent "**Firearms**" is a romp through weapons from the colonial era to modern machine guns, after which you'd do

*The Vietnam
Veterans
Memorial is
covered on
p.62.*

best to cross to "**Armed Forces**", which combines model ship displays and artillery pieces with a sympathetic look at the experiences of the American GI (named for their "Government Issue" gear) in World War II, from shipping out to homecoming.

Two final sections change the mood quickly and are the most moving parts of the whole museum. "**Personal Legacy: The Healing of a Nation**" brings together some of the 25,000 items left by relatives and friends at the Vietnam Veterans Memorial in DC. These deeply personal mementoes tell of the strict human cost of a detached foreign policy: each child's letter, wedding band, dog tag or forage cap represents a host of other lives touched by the war.

After two decades, the Vietnam vets can stand up and recount their experiences without fear of rancor, but it took even longer to rehabilitate another group of Americans in the public's eye. Throughout the nineteenth century, racist laws were passed to restrict American citizenship for Asian immigrants and there was little public opposition during World War II when Roosevelt agreed to the "evacuation" of Japanese-American citizens into "assembly centers" – basically concentration camps where people were interned solely on the basis of their race. FDR's Secretary of War, Henry L. Stimson, declared that "their racial characteristics are such that we cannot understand or even trust the citizen Japanese" – though no one ever suggested the containment of Italian- or German-Americans in the same period. "**A More Perfect Union**" deals with this shameful episode with commendable candor, pointing out for example that 25,000 Japanese-Americans served in the US forces, most of whom had family and friends in detention camps back home. Indeed, the largely Japanese 100th Infantry Battalion/42nd Regimental Combat Team was the most decorated military unit of its size at the end of the war. The displays contrast the dismal life in barracks at home with the valor of the combat units, who at the end of the war at least had their medals to prove their worth – the civilian Japanese-Americans, who had committed no crime other than to be born with the wrong "characteristics", got $25 and a ticket home.

National Museum of Natural History

10th St NW and Constitution Ave ☎357-2700; Federal Triangle Metro. Daily, June–Aug 10am–6.30pm; Sept–May 10am–5.30pm. Admission free.

The imposing three-story entrance rotunda of the **National Museum of Natural History** feels like the busiest and most boisterous crossroads in all DC, with troops of screeching school kids chasing each other non-stop around a colossal African elephant. Hundreds of other stuffed animals, tracing evolution from fossilized four-billion-year-old plankton to dinosaurs' eggs and beyond, are displayed on all sides. It's one of the oldest of DC's museums, founded in 1911, with its early collection partly based on the specimens that the Smithsonian commissioned from the game-hunting Theodore Roosevelt on his African safaris of 1909–10 – he collected (ie shot) thousands, from lions and rhinos to gazelles and cheetahs, many of which are still on display.

You'll need to go early to avoid the worst of the crowds, especially in summer and during school holidays; pick up floor plans at the **information desk** at the elephant's feet, check on any **temporary exhibitions** and ask about the **free guided tours** which show you the highlights in around an hour. Schedules and information about the films at the museum's **IMAX theater** are also available at the desk.

The collection

Given that the museum owns forty million specimens, it can be forgiven for failing to exhibit some of them with sufficient gusto: there are only so many things you can do with a trayful of pinned butterflies and turning them into an attention-grabbing, interactive exhibit is not one of them. Much, then, is as you might imagine, with halls full of stuffed mammals and birds placed in lifeless dioramas.

To be fair, though, when the museum does connect – particularly in the "Ocean to Dinosaur" sections on the first floor – it's among the finest in its field. In **"Exploring Marine Ecosystems"**, videos, aquariums and the odd furry seal illustrate life on the temperate rocky shore of Maine and a tropical coral reef from the Caribbean. Free behind-the-scenes tours of the model ecosystems afford a closer look (Mon, Wed & Sat 2pm); tickets are available from the first-floor information desk. If you prefer your attractions macro rather than micro, a life-sized model blue whale is on display along with a rare specimen of the giant squid; scientists don't know quite where it lives, but reckon it grows up to 50ft long. Naturally enough, the **"Dinosaurs"** section is the most popular part of the museum, with hulking skeletons reassembled in imaginative poses and accompanied by informative text, written with a light touch, accessible to children. The massive Diplodocus, the most imposing specimen, was discovered in Utah in 1923, at what is now Dinosaur National Monument. Stay in this section long enough to tour the related displays on the **Ice Age**, **Ancient Seas**, **Fossil Mammals** and **Fossil Plants** – each covering molluscs, lizards, giant turtles and early fish in exhaustive, engaging detail with the aid of diagrams, text and fossils.

Other highlights are upstairs on the second floor, where **"Reptiles"** and **"Bones"** give way to the splendid **"Insect Zoo"**, sponsored in a delicious irony by O. Orkin, the pest control company. Here, many of the exhibits are actually alive, which may or may not be a recommendation: behind screens – with notices pleading, unsuccessfully, "Please do not tap the glass" – are imprisoned tarantulas, roaches, crickets, bird-eating spiders, worms, termites, even a thriving bee colony. A member of staff with the most unenviable job in the world sits in one corner with assorted creepy-crawlies wandering up and down his arms; kids generally can't wait to grab a bug, while cowering adults try hard not to flinch. There's more hands-on

Less scary insects are on show in the Butterfly Garden, on the 9th Street side of the museum building. There are wetland, wooded, meadow and urban habitats featuring – as the brochure has it – "plant-insect interaction"; it's on view at all times.

participation for children in the first-floor "**Discovery Room**" (daily 10.30am–3.30pm), though this time it's rarely anything more alarming than old bones, pelts and stones to play with. You need a free pass to get in (available at the door); arrive early at peak times, since numbers are limited.

Since the museum's earliest days, "natural history" was deemed to embrace a broad remit, with the result that the museum's latest pride and joy is its revamped "**Hall of Geology, Gems and Minerals**", also on the second floor. Center of attention here are the astounding exhibits from the National Gem Collection, most importantly the legendary 45-carat **Hope Diamond**, once owned by Marie Antoinette – crowds also gather by a pair of her diamond earrings and a genuine crystal ball, the world's largest flawless quartz sphere, cut and polished in China in 1923. Further on are explanations of matters as various as why diamonds sparkle to full investigations of related geological phenomena – from plate tectonics and meteors to earthquakes and volcanoes – culminating in the museum's extraordinary mineral collection. Scientists have identified around 4000 different minerals so far and it seems like every single one is represented here in glorious shape, texture and color. Hunt around and you'll even find an example of Smithsonite – a needle-like crystal mined for zinc – named after Smithsonian Institution benefactor James Smithson, who first recognized it as a distinct mineral.

The museum has further to go before it deals successfully with its dated **ethnographical** collections; an early subtitle trumpeted it also as the "Museum of Man". There are moves to hive the ethnographical items off into their own museum, but for now entire galleries on the first and second floors continue to raise hackles with their 1950s-style attitudes and assumptions. Displays on "Native Cultures of the Americas" include the Lucayans, said to have "vanished" shortly after encountering Columbus, and static dioramas of the "primitive" pueblos of the southwest stand alongside bison, bighorn sheep and other once-wild things. Occasionally, a token disclaimer notice, pointing out contemporaneous inaccuracies and prejudices, drags the exhibits into the late twentieth century. The way forward is perhaps shown by the more imaginative treatment of the Seminole native people of Florida, which portrays contemporary facets of tribal life, culture and activities alongside the museum's own historic objects.

The Smithsonian Institution Building

1000 Jefferson Drive SW ☎357-2700; Smithsonian Metro. Daily 9.30am–5.30pm. Admission free.

Easily the most striking edifice on the Mall, the **Smithsonian Institution Building** resembles nothing so much as an English country seat, with its ruddy brown sandstone, nave windows and slender steeples – little surprise, then, that it's widely known as the

Smithsonian Castle. It's the headquarters of the **Smithsonian**
Institution (see p.67), an independent trust holding 140 million artifacts in sixteen museums (and one zoo) which, curiously, was
endowed by an Englishman. **James Smithson**, gentleman scientist
and illegitimate son of the first Duke of Northumberland, had never
even visited the US and yet on his death in 1829 left half a million
dollars "to found at Washington, under the name of the Smithsonian
Institution, an establishment for the increase and diffusion of
Knowledge" – provided, that is, his surviving nephew should die
without an heir. Luckily for future generations he did (in 1835),
though it took Congress until 1846 to decide, firstly, whether to
accept the money and secondly, quite what establishment would fit
the bill; John Quincy Adams, for one, favored an astronomical laboratory. In the end, the vote was for a multipurpose building that
would encompass museum, art gallery and laboratory: the original
Smithsonian Institution Building was duly completed in 1855.

For all its wealth, the **Smithsonian** had something of a shaky
start, since it wasn't at all clear quite how it should diffuse the knowledge proposed by its benefactor. Even just a few years after its opening, the collections were too large and varied to be able to be displayed thematically in the Castle. Matters slowly improved under the
stewardship of the Smithsonian's first Secretary, **Joseph Henry**, who
tried to direct the institute primarily toward scientific research. Even
the National Zoological Park had its origins here; a photograph
inside shows buffalo grazing in the grounds in 1889.

As the Castle shed its collections and bequests to specific museums, it took up duty as the Smithsonian administrative headquarters
and now houses the main **visitor center**, whose fine marble-pillared
Great Hall offers a foretaste of the Smithsonian attractions. Here,
too, are scale models of all the major city plans, from L'Enfant
onwards; twenty-minute video shows highlighting the role of the
Institution; interactive touch-screen Smithsonian information displays and electronic wall maps. You can pick up the latest details on
events at all the galleries at the information desk.

Incidentally, Smithsonian founder James Smithson, who never
visited America in life, found a place here in death: his ornate,
Neoclassical **tomb** stands in an alcove just off the Mall entrance,
placed here in 1904, 75 years after his death in Italy. In a neat counterpoint to the patent uncertainties of his life – which, not aware of
his true parentage, he started as James Lewis Macie – the tomb
records his age incorrectly, since he was 64 and not 75 when he died.
Out of the Mall itself, in front of the entrance, the resplendent robed
statue is not of Smithson, as you might suppose, but of first
Smithsonian Secretary, Joseph Henry.

Chapter 3

Capitol Hill

Everyone knows that Washington has a Capitol; but the misfortune is that the Capitol wants a city. There it stands, reminding you of a general without an army, only surrounded and followed by a parcel of ragged little dirty boys; for such is the appearance of the dirty, straggling, ill-built houses which lie at the foot of it.

Captain Frederick Marryat, 1839

For Capitol Hill listings, see the following pages: accommodation p.275; cafés p.283; restaurants p.290; nightlife p.301.

Although there's more than one hill in Washington DC, when people talk about what's happening on "The Hill" they mean **CAPITOL HILL**, the shallow knoll at the eastern end of the Mall topped by the giant white dome of the US Capitol. Home of both the legislature – Congress – and the judiciary – the Supreme Court – city planner L'Enfant's "pedestal waiting for a monument" is still the place where the law of the land is made and refined.

Yet, as Marryat observed, the neighborhood faced a lengthy clamber to respectability. When L'Enfant and his surveyors first put pen to paper, the cross drawn on what was then Jenkins Hill was the focus of a grand, Baroque city plan. The US **Capitol** building was duly erected, and Congress moved in in 1800. But this marshy outpost was slow to develop: it froze in the bitter winters and boiled in the harsh summers, and from their boarding houses around the Capitol legislators had to trudge the muddy length of Pennsylvania Avenue for an audience with the President in the White House. When the War of 1812 broke out the British weren't exactly spoiled for targets in Washington, and the Capitol was the first to burn, prompting many at the time to suggest abandoning the city altogether and setting up somewhere more hospitable. Later, Marryat was only the first in a long line of critics to point out the incongruity of the splendid ideal of the Capitol building and its rather dismal surroundings – ironically, at the time of his visit the "dirty, straggling, ill-built houses" of Capitol Hill comprised probably the most developed part of Washington.

However, as the capital and the federal government grew in stature, so did the Hill. Over the course of the nineteenth century appeared the rows of elegant townhouses that today form the key-

stone of Capitol Hill's status as a protected historic district. One, the **Sewall-Belmont House**, is open to the public. Eventually the major federal institutions, housed since 1800 in the ever-expanding Capitol building, moved into homes of their own: first the **Library of Congress** in 1897, whose oldest building has been skillfully refurbished; then the **Supreme Court** in 1935, which – like all the Hill's federal institutions – remains open for public visits.

Today the federal buildings reach as far as the two C streets, on either side of the Capitol, and east to 2nd Street – for many, that is the extent of Capitol Hill. But beyond the buildings lie diverse residential neighborhoods, where politicians, aides, lawyers, lobbyists and even ordinary people live. The early stretches of **Pennsylvania Avenue**, around **Eastern Market**, provide a few distractions, not least the market itself. **Lincoln Park**, with its memorial to the Great Emancipator, marks the eastern limit of the neighborhood, while to the north, the area around **Union Station** has been spruced up in the last decade or so.

The US Capitol

East end of the Mall, Capitol Hill ☎225-6827 for recorded tour information, ☎224-3121 general information; Capitol South or Union Station Metro, or bus #30, #32, #34, #36 from Pennsylvania Ave. Memorial Day–Labor Day daily 9am–8pm; rest of the year daily 9am–4.30pm. Admission free.

It's not by chance that the dome of the **US Capitol** is visible from all over the city. Like the White House, it's both a workplace and a monument. This is where Congress meets, the nation's law-makers and tax-takers, made up of the **Senate** and the **House of Representatives**; and it's from here that each president sets off on his inauguration parade, returning to give the annual State of the Union address. However, unlike the White House (where you get to see little more than museum-piece rooms), the US Capitol, with its grand halls and statues, committee rooms and ornate chambers, is one of the few places in the district where you get a tangible sense of the immense power wielded by the nation's elected officials.

Even if most visitors nowadays are a touch too worldly to accept that the goings-on here truly represent democracy at work, the US Capitol has remained a powerful symbol for two centuries. As early as 1812, Thomas Jefferson was trumpeting it as "the first temple dedicated to the sovereignty of the people, embellishing with Athenian taste the course of a nation looking far beyond the range of Athenian destinies". The foot of the US Capitol has always been an obvious convergence point for **demonstrations**. In 1894, Jacob S. Coxey led an "army" of unemployed from Ohio and points west to demand a public works program; he was arrested for trespassing and the few hundred men with him slunk off home. Unemployed soldiers set up camp outside the building after World War I, as did – fifty years later – the weary citizens of the Poor People's March of May 1968, whose makeshift tents and shelters they called "Resurrection City" (see p.62). More recently still, in 1995, Nation of Islam leader Louis Farrakhan harangued white America from the terrace steps while addressing the Million Men March. On occasion, the building itself has come **under attack**. Shots were first fired in the Capitol as early as 1835, while in 1915, 1971 and 1983 bombs were exploded by various aggrieved protestors, though no one was injured. The worst attack was in the summer of 1998, when a lone gunman stormed the building, killing two Capitol police officers and injuring several members of the public.

Modern security measures haven't impinged upon the right of open access to the seat of government. Even today, you can simply stroll into the Capitol for a look around (see "Visiting the Capitol" p.115). When Congress is **in session** (every year, from January 3, as prescribed in the Constitution, until close of business, usually in the fall) the lantern above the dome is lit, and flags fly above Senate or House wings.

Some history

A chaste plan, sufficiently capacious and convenient for a period not too remote, but one to which we may reasonably look forward, would meet my idea in the Capitol.

George Washington, 1792

In the best democratic fashion, the **design** of the US Capitol was thrown open to public competition in 1792. It was won by a dabbling amateur, **Dr William Thornton**, whose plan, it was agreed, brought a certain pomp deemed appropriate for the meeting place of Congress. In particular, he dreamed up the domed rotunda, the feature that two centuries later grants the building its towering authority over the city skyline. The cornerstone was laid by George Washington on September 18, 1793, but by the time the government moved to the city from Philadelphia seven years later, work was nowhere near completion. Not only did President John Adams move into an unfinished White House (see p.151), but on November 22, 1800, Congress assembled for the first time in the half-built brick-and-sandstone Capitol, which still lacked its rotunda and most of its offices: only a small north wing was ready, housing the Senate Chamber, the House of Representatives, Supreme Court and Library of Congress. What ceilings there were leaked, and the furnaces installed to heat the building produced intolerable temperatures. Adams' successor, Jefferson (the first president to be inaugurated inside the Capitol), appointed the respected **Benjamin Latrobe** as Surveyor of Public Buildings in an attempt to speed up work, and by 1807 a south wing had been built for the House of Representatives. In addition, Latrobe added a second floor to the north wing, allowing separate chambers for the Supreme Court and the Senate.

In 1814 the Capitol suffered the same fate as the President's house, as British troops burned the seat of government virtually to the ground. Indeed, with President Madison having fled the city, it was touch and go whether Washington – never a hugely popular choice as capital – would again house executive and legislative arms of the government. But with Madison later installed in The Octagon (p.168), Congress met for four years in a quickly built "Brick Capitol" – on the site of today's Supreme Court.

Restoration work continued on what was left of the original Capitol. It wasn't much. Latrobe found the interior gutted and the surviving exterior walls blackened by smoke; the British soldiers, it seemed, had stacked up all the furniture they could find in one of the rooms and lit a bonfire. Commissioned to rebuild and expand the Capitol, Latrobe's rather grandiose ideas found few admirers and in 1817 he was replaced by Charles Bulfinch. The reconstructed wings were re-opened in 1819 and, finally, in 1826 the Capitol appeared in a form that Thornton might have recognized, complete with central **rotunda**, topped by a low wooden dome wrapped in copper.

The US Capitol

By the 1850s Congress had again run out of space and plans were laid to build magnificent, complementary wings on either side of the building and to replace the dome with something more substantial. The new south wing, ready in 1857, now contained the **House Chamber**; two years later, the **Senate Chamber** moved to the new north wing. The Civil War threatened to halt work on the dome, but Abraham Lincoln was determined that the Capitol should be completed, recognizing the building as an enduring symbol of the Union he was pledged to defend. A cast-iron **dome** was painstakingly assembled, though the work was hampered by the presence of Union troops stationed in the Capitol; a company made up of enlisted firefighters insisted on shinning up and down hundred-foot ropes draped from the Rotunda walls for amusement. But in December 1863 the splendid project came to fruition. Hoisted on top of the white-painted dome was a nineteen-foot-high **Statue of Freedom** by sculptor Thomas Crawford, resplendent in feathered helmet and clutching a sword and shield (which gives it its alternative name of "Armed Liberty").

Give or take a few minor additions, the US Capitol building today shows little external change from this last burst of construction. The surrounding **terraces** were added after the Civil War, and when extra office space was required this century, separate **House and Senate office buildings** were built in the streets on either side of the Capitol, with tunnels to connect the legislators with their places of work. The Capitol's East Front was extended in 1962 and faced in marble to prevent the original sandstone from deteriorating further; thus far, the West Front – now the oldest original part of the building – has avoided modern accretions, though it too was restored in the 1980s.

The Brick Capitol

When the British marched into Washington in August 1814, they promptly burned down the Capitol and – in the words of Alistair Cooke – "the rest of the new public buildings that in those days were all that distinguished Washington from a fishing town on a marsh". It was a supreme humiliation, made more calamitous for the young republic in that it revived the often bitter debate about the suitability of Washington as the nation's capital. President Madison gave the Northern dissenters no chance to agitate: as well as returning to the city at the earliest opportunity he also directed the building of a temporary **Brick Capitol** to forestall any talk of a move away from the city. Hastily designed by Benjamin Latrobe, it was erected on the site of today's Supreme Court – land then occupied by a tavern and vegetable allotment. Here, in 1817, Monroe became the first president to take the oath of office in an outdoor public ceremony in Washington. When the US Capitol was finally restored in 1819 and the government moved back in, the Brick Capitol became home to the Circuit Court of DC until the new City Hall was finished; from 1824 to 1861 it was a lodging house, from 1861 until 1867 a prison, until finally being replaced by three row houses – which were in turn demolished to make way for the Supreme Court in 1935.

Visiting the Capitol

The Capitol is the only building in Washington DC not to have an address, since it stands foursquare at the centre of the street plan: the city quadrants extend from the building, and the numbered and lettered streets count away from its central axis. For the same reason, the building doesn't have a front or a back, simply an "East Front" and a "West Front": the **public entrance** is at the East Front, where, from 1829 to 1977, all presidents were inaugurated.

There's **free, walk-in access** all year to the Rotunda, Statuary Hall, the old Senate and Supreme Court chambers, and the Crypt. From April to September you can expect to have to wait in line for maybe one or two hours: lines are much shorter (or non-existent) in winter, and the place is generally less busy on Sunday and between noon and 1.30pm most other days. Once inside the Rotunda, you can join a **free guided tour** (every 15min 9am–3.45pm), though there's nothing to stop you wandering off on your own. That said, it's hard to find your way around, even with the information desks, signposts and the omnipresent Capitol police officers to keep you on the right track. Note that there's a split between the House side (to the south) and Senate side (north) inside the Capitol; for details on visiting the House and Senate chambers, see p.118.

The Rotunda and National Statuary Hall

Standing in the **Rotunda**, you're not only at the center of the US Capitol but at point zero of the entire city. It's a magnificent space: 180ft high and 96ft across, with the dome canopy decorated by Constantino Brumidi's almighty fresco depicting the *Apotheosis of Washington*. The painting took the sixty-year-old Brumidi almost a year to complete – like the Renaissance masters, he was forced to work lying on his back in a wooden cradle – and shows George Washington surrounded by symbols representing American democracy, arts, science, industry, and the thirteen original states; though they look lifesized from the floor, each of the figures is 15ft high. Brumidi had a hand, too, in the **frieze** celebrating American history that runs around the Rotunda wall, which starts with Columbus's arrival in the New World and continues clockwise, through the ages, finishing with Civil War scenes.

From the floor, it's hard to see much detail of either frieze or fresco, and eyes are drawn instead to the eight large **oil paintings** that hang below the frieze. Four depict events associated with the "discovery" and settlement of the country – Columbus again, and the embarkation of the Pilgrims among them – though the most notable are the four of the Revolutionary War period by John Trumbull, who trained under the celebrated Benjamin West. George Washington is represented with a fair accuracy; and so he should be, since Trumbull once served as his aide-de-camp.

The US Capitol

From Memorial Day to Labor Day, there are brass band concerts (Mon–Fri 8pm) on the east steps. And on the two holidays themselves, as well as July 4, the National Symphony Orchestra performs on the West Terrace.

US citizens can contact their representative or senator to arrange a climb up to the dome – not available to walk-in visitors.

Consciously or not, William Thornton, the Capitol's first architect, took Rome's Pantheon as his model, and it's fitting that busts
and statues of prominent American leaders fill in the gaps in the rest
of the Rotunda. Washington, Jefferson, Lincoln and Jackson are all
here, along with a modern bust of Dr Martin Luther King Jr and a
gold-and-glass facsimile of the Magna Carta (the original was loaned
to the Capitol during the 1976 Bicentennial). In such august surroundings, 29 prominent members of Congress, military leaders and
eminent citizens (including nine presidents from Lincoln to Johnson)
have been **laid in state** before burial; the most recently honored
were the two Capitol police officers slain in the July 1998 gun attack.

From the Rotunda, you move south into one of the earliest extensions of the building, the section that once housed the chamber of
the House of Representatives. The acoustics are such that, from his
desk, John Quincy Adams was supposed to have been able to eaves-
drop on opposition members on the other side of the room – something that is invariably demonstrated on the tour. When the House
moved into its new wing in 1857, the chamber saw a variety of temporary uses – Anthony Trollope bought gingerbread from a market
stall in here – until Congress decided to invite each state to contribute two statues of its most famous citizens for display in a
National Statuary Hall. Around forty are still on show in the hall,
with the others scattered around the corridors in the rest of the building; few are of any great distinction. That of suffragist Susan B.
Anthony (one of just six statues of women in the entire building) was
recently dusted off after years hidden in the Crypt to be placed in the
Rotunda – the only woman so honored.

The Old Senate Chamber, Supreme Court and the Crypt

North of the Rotunda, there's access to the **Old Senate Chamber**,
built in 1810 and reconstructed from 1815 to 1819 after the British
had done their worst. The Senate met in this splendid semicircular
gallery, with its embossed rose ceiling, until 1859 when it moved
into its current quarters. The chamber then housed the Supreme
Court (see p.120) until it, too, was given a new building in 1935,
after which the Old Senate Chamber lay largely unused until
restored to its mid-nineteenth-century glory in time for the
Bicentennial. Its furnishings are redolent of that period, during
which the Senate's membership increased from 46 to 64 (two senators for each state) in step with the number of states admitted to the
Union. In its heyday, the chamber made a formidable impression
upon visitors, like Anthony's pioneering mother Fanny Trollope,
whose travelog, *Domestic Manners of the Americans*, published in
1832, amused Europe but outraged America with its forthright
observations. Sorely unimpressed with the goings-on in the House
chamber, whose representatives were "sitting in the most unseemly
attitudes, a large majority with their hats on", she was considerably

more taken with the Senate, or at least the senators, who "generally speaking, look like gentlemen . . . and the activity of youth being happily past, they do not toss their heels above their heads". The members' desks today are reproductions, but the gilt eagle topping the vice president's chair is original, as is the portrait of George Washington by Rembrandt Peale.

Contemporary engravings helped restorers reproduce other features of the original Senate chamber, like the rich red carpet emblazoned with gold stars. As Charles Dickens noted when he visited, the original carpet received severe punishment from "tobacco-tinctured saliva" despite the provision of a cuspidor by every desk – the universal disregard of which led to "extraordinary improvements on the pattern which are squirted and dabbled upon it in every direction". If visitors dropped anything on the floor, they were enjoined "not to pick it up with an ungloved hand on any account". Yet, doubtless squelching underfoot as they stood to speak, members of this Senate chamber participated in some of the most celebrated debates of the era: in 1830 the great orator Daniel Webster of Massachusetts fiercely defended "Liberty and the Union" in a famous speech lasting several hours; over two days in 1850 Henry Clay pleaded his succession of compromises to preserve the Union (brandishing a fragment of Washington's coffin for emphasis); while in 1856, Senator Charles Sumner of Massachusetts – having, unwisely perhaps, talked too forthrightly against the Kansas-Nebraska Bill (extending slavery, which Sumner branded a "harlot", into the Great Plains) – was beaten senseless at his desk by an incensed congressman from South Carolina.

Before 1810, the Senate met on the floor below the Old Senate Chamber, in a room which architect Latrobe later revamped to house the Supreme Court. This sorely needed a permanent home: while the work was being carried out, sessions were often held in an inn opposite the Capitol, and once the British had delayed matters by burning the rest of the building, the nation's highest tribunal was forced to meet in rented townhouses on the Hill. However, by 1819 the Court was in residence in this chamber, where it remained until 1860, before moving again – confusingly, upstairs, to the chamber just vacated by the Senate. The **Old Supreme Court Chamber** served as a law library until 1950, after which it too was restored to its mid-nineteenth-century appearance, its dark, comfortable recesses resembling a gentleman's club – which, in many ways, it was. Again, some of the furnishings are original, including the desks, tables and chairs, and the busts of the first five chief justices.

Having viewed the historic chambers, spare a moment for the **Crypt**, on the same level as the Old Supreme Court Chamber, underneath the Rotunda. Lined with Doric columns, it was designed to house a tomb containing George Washington's body, a plan that was never realized; he's buried with his wife, Martha, at Mount Vernon.

For more on Rembrandt Peale and his remarkable family, see p.92.

The US Capitol

Both houses have their own unique lunch spots: Senate refectory (Mon–Fri 8am–4pm), House restaurant (Mon–Fri 8–11am & 1.30–2.30pm), and Dirksen Building buffet (1st and C NE; Mon–Fri 11.30am–2.30pm).

For more on the American system of government, see Contexts, p.337.

The office buildings all have street access; nearest Metros are Union Station for the Senate offices and Capitol South for the House offices.

The Crypt instead serves as an exhibition center, displaying details of the plans submitted for the 1792 architectural competition and snippets about the Capitol's construction.

The House and Senate chambers and office buildings

To gain entrance to the **visitors' galleries** of either the House or the Senate, **American citizens** must apply to their representative's or senator's office well in advance for a pass valid for the entire (two-year) session of Congress. **Foreign citizens** need to present their passport either at the House or Senate appointments desk, both on the first floor; they'll be given a day pass for either body. To find out where a particular office or desk is, ask any Capitol police officer, or call Capitol **information** (☎224-3121), the House sergeant-at-arms (☎225-2456) or Senate sergeant-at-arms (☎224-2341).

The **House and Senate chambers** may well be empty, or deep in torpor, when you show up, which is fine if all you want is a flavor of either place. Both chambers are suitably grand, and if you've already glimpsed the Old Senate Chamber you'll know what to expect. The **House chamber** is the most imposing, with its decorative frieze and oil paintings; from here the President addresses joint sessions of Congress, including making the annual State of the Union speech. If you're lucky, you may coincide with members introducing legislation or even voting on various bills or issues (or at least hear the bells and see the flashing lights summoning the members to vote). The **Senate chamber** is a little more widely recognized these days since being the setting for the final chapter of the impeachment trial of President Clinton.

Generally, most of the day-to-day fun and fireworks take place in committee rooms either in the Capitol or in the **House and Senate office buildings** on each side. The first of these six office buildings – named for past politicians – were built in 1908–09, the last in 1982, and they now house regular committee hearings, which have been open to the public since the 1970s. The buildings also contain the public and private offices of most representatives and senators. These follow the pattern of the Capitol in that the Senate office buildings (Russell, Dirksen and Hart) are to the north, the House office buildings (Cannon, Longworth and Rayburn) to the south: to reach them from the Capitol, head for the basement and ride the **Capitol subway** to the Senate offices or follow the pedestrian tunnels to the House offices. **Committee hearings** (usually held in the morning) are listed in the *Washington Post*'s "Today in Congress" section: unless you turn up early, you may not get in, especially to anything currently featured on the TV news. Of course, within reason you can simply wander around the buildings themselves, though there's little point unless you're a student of the minutiae of American politics, or have a wish to see the office of a particular senator or representative.

Only in the Senate **Hart Building**, on Constitution Ave NE at 2nd, is there anything to look at: dominating the atrium, Alexander Calder's monumental *Mountains and Clouds* was his last work – and the only one to combine a separate mobile and stabile. There are security checkpoints at the street-level entrances to the Hart Building, but visitors are free to pass through to see the sculpture.

West of the Capitol

Although, technically, the Capitol has no front (or at least no back), the **West Front** facade – facing the Mall – gets most photo calls, and from the terrace steps the views down the Mall to the Washington Monument are rightly lauded. Presidential **inauguration ceremonies** have taken place in the plaza here since 1981; before that, they were consigned to the more confined space at the East Front.

Two low-key memorials – to Peace and to assassinated twentieth President James Garfield (shot only four months after his inauguration) – flank the **Capitol Reflecting Pool**, added in 1970, a stretch of water which mirrors in style that in front of the Lincoln Memorial, more than a mile away. But the most significant structure here is the 250-foot-long **Grant Memorial**, a group statue honoring **Ulysses S. Grant**, general-in-chief of the Union forces under President Lincoln (and the first since George Washington to hold the rank). Dedicated in 1922, it's an overbearing martial monument depicting a somber Grant on horseback, facing the Mall, guarded by lions and overseeing an artillery unit moving through thick mud into battle (south side) and a charging cavalry unit (north side). Sculptor Henry Merwin Shrady took twenty years over the work, using uniformed soldiers in training as his models. The memorial is suitably single-tracked about Grant's achievements, focusing on his career as a soldier (as which he was formidable) rather than as twice-elected President (in which capacity he was undistinguished, verging on the corrupt; in the late nineteenth century, "Grantism" became a term synonymous with graft). In waging total war on the Confederate forces from 1864 to 1865 Grant secured final victory for Lincoln and the preservation of the Union, albeit at the cost of thousands of lives. Contemporaries talked of his personal shortcomings – he was once described as "an ordinary scrubby-looking man with a slightly seedy look" – and of his drinking habits: only Mrs Grant could keep him in check and when the general went on a drinking bout too far his aides would summon her to the front to sober him up. But Lincoln knocked back all complaints, recognizing his incalculable military worth: "You just tell me the brand of whiskey Grant drinks", thundered the President, "I would like to send a barrel of it to my other generals."

South of the Reflecting Pool, there's quiet relief in the **United States Botanic Gardens**, 100 Maryland Avenue SW at Independence Ave (daily 9am–5pm; free; ☎225-8333). The conservatory has been

under renovation for some time, but once it re-opens the popular
guided tours (call for times) around the colorful ranks of tropical,
subtropical and desert plants should be reinstated. Meanwhile,
there's a small demonstration garden on display across the avenue
next to the **Bartholdi Fountain** (at 1st St SW), a thirty-foot-high
marine-style work by French sculptor Frédéric Auguste Bartholdi,
who submitted it to the Centennial Exhibition in Philadelphia in
1876 – there's no hint here that Bartholdi would go on to create, just
a decade later, one of America's most enduring icons, the Statue of
Liberty. Congress bought the fountain in 1877 for display on the Mall
(it moved to this site in 1932), where its original gas lamps – illuminated at night – became a popular evening diversion. Walking north
instead, toward Union Station, skirting through the small park bordered by Constitution and Louisiana avenues, you'll pass the **Robert
A. Taft Memorial**, a statue and sixty-foot-high, rectangular concrete
belltower erected in 1958 to commemorate the veteran Republican
senator son of President William Howard Taft.

East of the Capitol

All the other notable buildings and institutions of Capitol Hill – like
the Supreme Court and the Library of Congress – lie on the east side
of the Capitol, within half a dozen blocks of each other. Unlike the
Capitol, you have to choose your day to tour these places: the
Supreme Court is closed on weekends, while other buildings are
closed on all or part of Sunday.

The Supreme Court

1st St and Maryland Ave NE ☎479-3211; Union Station or Capitol South
Metro. Mon–Fri 9am–4.30pm. Admission free.

*For an
account of the
various homes
occupied by
the Supreme
Court in
Washington,
see p.117.*

First stop after the Capitol for most visitors is the pseudo-Greek marble temple that houses the **Supreme Court of the United States**, the
nation's final arbiter of what is and isn't legal. Since it was established at the Philadelphia Constitutional Convention of 1787, the
Court has functioned as both the guardian and interpreter of the
Constitution, flexing its muscular, judicial arm of government in
favor of "Equal Justice For All" – the legend inscribed upon the archi-
trave above the double row of eight columns facing 1st Street.

Oddly, for such a crucial pin in the American political system, the
Supreme Court was forced to share quarters in the US Capitol until
1935, when on the prompting of William Howard Taft (then Chief
Justice and formerly President – the only man to hold both offices) it
was finally granted its own building. The architect, **Cass Gilbert**,
seventy years old at the time, was perhaps an odd choice, known primarily for his tongue-in-cheek Gothic Woolworth Building in New
York. But in Washington he behaved himself, creating in the

Supreme Court – completed after his death – a work of dazzling Corinthian harmony. So well did it fit with the spirit of the age that Cass was unnerved by the compliments bestowed upon him – "It is receiving so much favorable praise [he wrote in 1933] that I am wondering what is wrong with it."

The answer is: absolutely nothing. Outside, the building positively glistens as natural light bounces back off the bright white marble, while the wide steps down to 1st Street are flanked by **sculptures** (by James Earle Fraser) of the Contemplation of Justice and the Guardian of Law. Solemn, if not pompous, their effect is lightened somewhat when you cast your eyes up to the sculpted **pediment** over the main entrance; here, among allegorical Greek figures are relaxed representations of chief justices Taft (far left, portrayed as a Yale student) and Marshall (far right, reclining), while clad in togas are Gilbert (third from left) and sculptor Robert Aitken (second from right).

Inside, the main corridor – known as the **Great Hall** – features a superb carved and painted ceiling of floral plaques, while its echoing white walls are lined with marble columns, interspersed with busts of all the former chief justices. At the end of the corridor is the surprisingly compact **Court Chamber**, flanked by more marble columns and decorated with damask drapes and a molded plaster ceiling picked out in gold leaf. A frieze runs around all four sides, its relief panels depicting various legal themes, more allegorical figures and lawgivers ancient and modern. When in session, the Chief Justice sits in the center of the **bench** (below the clock), with the most senior justice on his right and the next in precedence on his left; the rest sit in similar alternating fashion so that the most junior justice sits on the far right (left as you face the bench); almost interestingly, the chairs for each justice are made in the Court's own carpentry shop.

Visiting the Supreme Court

The court is in session from October to June. Between the beginning of October and the end of April, oral arguments are heard every Monday, Tuesday and Wednesday from 10am to noon and 1pm to 3pm for two weeks each month. The cases to be heard are listed in the day's *Washington Post* (or call the Supreme Court for information) and the sessions, which last one hour per case, are open to the public on a first-come, first-served basis. They are rarely particularly illuminating for lay persons, but if you really want to witness an entire session you'll need to arrive by 8.30am to be sure of getting one of the 150 seats. Most casual visitors simply join the separate line, happy to settle for a brief, three-minute stroll through the standing gallery. In May and June on Mondays, fifteen- to thirty-minute public sessions deal with the rather less interesting reading of orders and opinions. When court is not in session, guides give informative **lectures** in the Court Chamber (Mon–Fri 9.30am–3.30pm; hourly on the half-hour).

The Functioning of the Supreme Court

*The duties of the Supreme Court are the simplest and best defined of
any part of government. The Supreme Court justices have to do nothing but sit and let others make ugly fools of themselves in front of the
Supreme Court bench.*

P.J. O'Rourke, *Parliament of Whores*

The Constitution established the **Supreme Court** in an attempt to oversee the balance between the federal government and the states, and
between the legislature and the executive; the Court itself (and the associated system of district courts) convened for the first time in February
1790. At the end of the following year, the ratification of the Bill of Rights
in effect gave the Supreme Court a further role – it was to defend the liberties enshrined in the Bill, directing the country as to what was and was-
n't constitutional. However, it wasn't until 1803 and the case of *Marbury
v Madison* that the Court's power of judicial review – the ability to declare
a law or action of Congress or the President unconstitutional – was established. Since then, the Supreme Court has repeatedly directed the country's political debate by declaring on the constitutionality of subjects as
diverse as slavery (as in the 1857 *Dred Scott* case), civil rights (1954
Brown v Board of Education, which outlawed school segregation), abor-
tion (*Roe v Wade* in 1973) or political freedom (Pentagon Papers and
Watergate tapes cases in the early 1970s).

Because of the vagueness of parts of the Constitution, and the fact that
the country relies on an eighteenth-century document as the basis of its
twentieth-century political structure, the Supreme Court has its work cut
out providing interpretive rulings. In practice, as O'Rourke points out, this
leads to a great deal of arguing in front of the Supreme Court justices. That
said, even though it's the country's final court of appeal, the Supreme
Court takes only about five percent of the seven thousand cases a year it's
asked to hear by lower courts (choosing which to take by the so-called
"Rule of Four" – the agreement of four justices to hear a case). These it
grants **certiorari** – the prospect of making a case "more certain" – and
then proceeds to hear written and oral arguments. After the deliberations,
one justice is made responsible for writing the **opinion**, which then forms
the latest interpretation of that particular constitutional issue. The justices
don't all have to agree: they can **concur** in the majority decision even if
they don't accept all the arguments; or they can produce a **dissenting
opinion**, which might be cited in future challenges to particular laws.

Contributing to these opinions are nine judges, or **justices**, who are
appointed by the President, though their positions have to be ratified by

On the **ground floor**, which has its own Great Hall overseen by a
mighty statue of Chief Justice John Marshall lounging in his chair,
there's a permanent **exhibition** about the Court: a free, short movie
fills you in on the political and legal background while architectural
notes, sketches and photos trace the history of the building itself.
You'll also find toilets, a gift shop, snack bar (10.30am–3.30pm) and
cafeteria (7.30–10.30am & 11.30am–2pm) on this level.

the Senate. One is named **Chief Justice**, though the position is not necessarily reserved for the most senior figure on the bench (or even for a justice already on the Supreme Court – a Chief Justice can be appointed from outside). Once appointed, they're in for life ("during good behavior" as the Constitution has it) and can only be removed by impeachment. And, at $160,000 a year ($170,000 for the chief), the justices are pulling in a federal salary second only to the President.

Given the system, it's obvious that the make-up of the Supreme Court is of the utmost relevance to the opinions it might produce. Not surprisingly, presidents down the years have thought it useful to have **politically sympathetic** justices on the bench and have made appointments accordingly. But the process is tinged with an element of luck, depending on the longevity of the existing incumbents: both Dwight D. Eisenhower and Richard Nixon, for example, got to appoint four justices, Jimmy Carter none. Controversial Supreme Court nominees can be rejected by the Senate – two of Nixon's were, as was Reagan's pet conservative judge, Robert Bork; Bush's second appointee, Clarence Thomas, only scraped through after the highly publicized hearings following allegations of sexual harassment against Anita Hill. And even when presidents do get the justices they want, they don't always want what they get: Earl Warren, appointed by the staunchly conservative Eisenhower, turned out to head the most liberal Court this century, his interpretation of the constitutional definition of "civil rights" aiding presidents Kennedy and Johnson in their radical domestic program. The current Court is considered a conservative-leaning force – seven out of the nine were Republican appointees – although it has proved unpredictable at times; in 1996, for example, it delivered a symbolic opinion in favor of respect for gay rights.

Whichever way the Court leans, and despite its firm roots in the Constitution, it depends ultimately on the mood of the people for its authority. If it produces opinions that are overwhelmingly opposed by inferior courts, or by the President or Congress, there's not much it can do to enforce them: indeed, Congress actually has the constitutional right (Article 3, Section 2) to restrict the Court's jurisdiction – a notion proposed by FDR when he tired of the Court's constant interference with his New Deal legislation. Strangely perhaps, and virtually unique among federal institutions, the Court has retained the respect of most of the population, not necessarily for the decisions of its justices (which are often viewed as confused or conflicting) but for its perceived impartiality in defending the Constitution against encroachment by that most hated of species: the politicians.

Sewall-Belmont House

144 Constitution Ave NE ☎546-3989; Union Station Metro. Tues–Fri 11am–3pm, Sat noon–4pm. Admission free.

North of the Court, across Constitution Avenue at 2nd Street, the red-brick townhouse known as the **Sewall-Belmont House** is among the oldest private residences in the city. Overwhelmed by the surrounding Senate Office monoliths, parts of the dainty building date back an astonishing – for Washington – 300 years. However, like most of historical Capitol Hill its aspect is firmly early nineteenth century, dating from the restructuring carried out in 1800 by its owner Robert Sewall. The house's next owner was Albert Gallatin, secretary of the Treasury under Jefferson. Gallatin took part in the negotiations for the Louisiana Purchase (1803), which was signed in one of the front rooms – and which, acquiring all land west of the Mississippi to the Rockies, at a stroke roughly doubled the size of the country for a mere $12 million. In 1814, while the Capitol was burning, a group of soldiers under Commander Joshua Barney retreated to the house and fired upon the British. It was virtually the sole act of resistance in Washington itself, but only stirred the British to have a go at setting the house ablaze too. Unlike the Capitol, it wasn't too badly damaged; enough survived, in fact, for Gallatin to negotiate the Treaty of Ghent – which ended the war – here.

Although negotiated in the Sewall-Belmont House, the Treaty of Ghent was signed in The Octagon; see p.168.

In 1929, the house was sold to the **National Woman's Party** and was home for many years to Alice Paul, the party's founder and author of the 1923 Equal Rights Amendment. The house is still the party headquarters, and maintains a museum and gallery dedicated to the country's women's and suffrage movements. A short film fills in some of the background and then you'll be escorted around on a short tour which makes much of the period furnishings; the carriage house, one of the oldest parts of the building, contains the country's earliest feminist library. There are portraits, busts and photographs of all the best-known activists, starting in the lobby with suffragist sculptor Adelaide Johnson's formidable busts of Susan B. Anthony, Elizabeth Cady Stanton, Lucretia Mott and Alice Paul. Other mementoes of the famous include the desks of both Alice Paul and Susan B. Anthony, while over the staircase hangs the banner used to picket the White House during World War I as the clamor for universal suffrage reached its loudest pitch. The women jailed for protesting were later presented with "jail-house pins" by Alice Paul – the one mounted on the wall here once belonged to Betsey Graves Reyneau.

Folger Shakespeare Library

201 E Capitol St SE ☎544-7077; Capitol South Metro or bus #40, 44 or 96. Mon–Sat 10am–4pm. Admission free.

On the south side of the Supreme Court, the renowned **Folger Shakespeare Library** provides an unexpected burst of Art Deco architecture, with a sparkling white marble facade, split by geometric window grilles and panel reliefs depicting scenes from the Bard's plays. Inside, however, the expansive 1930s mood is immediately transformed by a dark oak-paneled Elizabethan Great Hall, featuring carved lintels, stained glass, Tudor roses and a fine, sculpted ceiling. Founded in 1932, the Folger now holds over 300,000 books, manuscripts, paintings and engravings, accessible to scholars, and has also evolved over the decades into a celebration of Shakespeareana.

The Great Hall displays changing exhibitions about the playwright and Elizabethan themes; the reproduction Elizabethan Theater hosts lectures and readings, as well as medieval and Renaissance music concerts by the Folger Consort (see p.312); there's even an Elizabethan garden outside on the east lawn, growing herbs and flowers common in gardens of the sixteenth century.

For more background, aim to coincide with one of the free **guided tours** (Mon–Fri 11am, Sat 11am & 1pm; 1hr 30min); every third Saturday, from April through October, a guide also expounds upon the intricacies of the garden. You should be able to take a quick look inside the theater on most days; the library itself – another masterfully reproduced sixteenth-century room – is open to the public during the Folger's annual celebration of Shakespeare's birthday (usually the Saturday nearest April 23). Finally, as you'd expect, the **gift shop** sells everything from the Stratford lad's books to jokey T-shirts based on Shakespearean quotations, Elizabethan garden seeds, prints and postcards.

The Library of Congress

Jefferson Building, 10 1st St SE; Madison Building, 101 Independence Ave SE ☎707-8000; Capitol South Metro. Mon–Sat 10am–5.30pm. Admission free.

With Congress established in Washington in 1800 in its new, if incomplete, Capitol building, it was considered imperative to fund a library for the use of the members. Five thousand dollars was made available to buy books for a **Library of Congress**, which was housed in a small room in the original north wing. Calamitously, the carefully chosen reference works were all lost when the British burned the Capitol in 1814, an act which prompted Thomas Jefferson to offer his considerable personal library as a replacement. This was no empty gesture – at his retirement home at Monticello Jefferson was surrounded by over six thousand volumes, which he had accumulated during fifty years of service at home and abroad, picking up, he said, "everything which related to America". But neither was it an act of selfless charity: Jefferson's extravagant lifestyle always left him short of money so he was doubtless delighted when, in 1815, Congress voted to buy this stupendous private collection for almost $24,000, a massive sum at the time.

Jefferson's sale laid the foundation for a rounded collection, but another fire in 1851, this time accidental, caused severe damage. From that point, the library was forced to rely on donations and select purchases until it received two major boosts. In 1866, it acquired the thousands of books hitherto held by the Smithsonian Institution, and in 1870 was declared the national copyright library – adding to its shelves a copy of every book published and registered in the United States. Almost overnight, the Library of Congress was transformed into the world's largest library, and with time and technological progress books became the least part of its unimaginably large collection. Today, 110 million items (from books, maps and manuscripts to movies, musical instruments and photographs) are kept on 600 miles of shelving; it's said that on average ten items a minute are added to the library's holdings.

Hardly surprisingly, the library soon outgrew its original home and in 1897 the exuberantly eclectic **Thomas Jefferson Building** opened across from the Capitol, complete with domed octagonal Reading Room and flourishing hundreds of mosaics, murals and sculptures. This was projected to have enough space to house the library until 1975; by the 1930s it, too, was full, and in the surrounding blocks the **John Adams Building** was erected in 1939, followed by the **James Madison Memorial Building** in 1980. These three buildings today comprise the Library of Congress, which is open to the public either as readers, researchers or visitors.

Visiting the library

Visitors are directed toward the magnificent **Jefferson Building**, whose visitor center (ground-level entrance on 1st St SE) can point you to the library highlights and give you a calendar of events detailing forthcoming concerts and lectures. You're free to wander around inside, but you'd do well to catch one of the free library **tours** (currently Mon–Sat 11.30am, 1pm, 2.30pm & 4pm, but subject to change) or catch the continuously running twelve-minute **film** on the history of the library. Taking the buildings of the Italian Renaissance as their model, the Jefferson Building architects John L. Smithmeyer and Paul J. Pelz produced a peach, centered on a domed reading room and flaunting a **Great Hall** that, after a decade of restoration, is again looking its best: marble walls and floors that were once blackened by the smoke from coal fires and the cinders from Union Station are now pristine, with the medallions, inscriptions, murals and inlaid mosaics as clear as the day they were fashioned. A treasured copy of the **Gutenberg Bible** is on display, while upstairs the visitor's gallery overlooks the octagonal marble-and-stained-glass **Main Reading Room**, a beautiful galleried space whose columns support a dome 125ft high. The mural in the dome canopy, the *Progress of Civilization*, represents the twelve nations supposed to have contributed most to world knowledge.

The library's huge collection is showcased on the second floor in the **American Treasures** gallery, where themed cabinets – "Civil Society", "Mapping", "Invention and Film", "Technology", and so on – display some of the nation's most significant documents. The exhibits are periodically rotated, but you'll encounter such diverse pieces as Walt Whitman's Civil War notebooks, the original "I Have a Dream" typescript, a copy of Francis Scott Key's "Star-Spangled Banner" and a multitude of music scores, historic photographs, early recordings, magazines and baseball cards. Changing exhibitions (shown in an environmentally controlled cabinet) of especially significant documents, such as those associated with Washington, Lincoln and Jefferson, receive central billing. Other exhibit areas are downstairs on the ground floor, where a **Gershwin Room** preserves George's Steinway and Ira's typing table and typewriter, and the **Swann Gallery** puts on temporary shows extracted from the library's unrivaled collection of American caricature and cartoon art.

There's no real need to walk over to the massive marble **Madison Building** (Independence Ave between 1st and 2nd), though there is an information desk in the lobby, an exhibition about the **Copyright Office** on the fourth floor, a **snack bar** on the ground floor and, on the sixth floor, a **cafeteria** (Mon–Fri 9–10.30am & 12.30–3pm) with river views.

Using the library

Anyone over high-school age carrying photo-ID can use the library, and around a million readers and visitors do each year; to find out what's where, head for the information desks or touch-screen computers in the Jefferson or Madison buildings. The Main Reading Room in the Jefferson Building is just one of 22 reading rooms; the rules are the same in each. It's a research library, which means you can't take books out; in some reading rooms you have to order what you want from the stacks. You can also access papers, maps, and musical scores, and the advent of the **National Digital Library** means that many now come in machine-readable format – the desks in the Main Reading Room are wired for laptops and there are CD-ROM indexes. Major exhibitions, as well as prints, photographs, films and speeches, are also available online. To check out the Library of Congress online, access *www.loc.gov*.

For research advice, call ☎ 707-6500; for reading room hours and locations, call ☎ 707-6400.

Union Station and around

The Hill's northern limits incorporate **Union Station**, which stands at the center of a redevelopment plan designed to revitalize a formerly neglected part of the city. In addition to the station, a sight in its own right, you should try to make time for the Smithsonian's **National Postal Museum**.

Union Station

The city's main railroad station, **Union Station**, at 50 Massachusetts Ave NE, was built here in 1908 after the McMillan Commission decreed an end to the chaos caused by the separate lines and stations that crisscrossed the city. Its architect, Daniel H. Burnham, a member of the commission, produced a classic Beaux-Arts building of monumental proportions to house the train sheds and waiting rooms, alive with skylights, marble detail and statuary, culminating in a 96-foot-high coffered ceiling covered in gold leaf. The model

For Union
Station
listings, see the
following
pages: accom-
modation
p.280; cafés
p.285; restau-
rants p.298;
nightlife p.305.

Union Station
services:
arrivals p.38;
car rental
agencies p.6;
departures
p.327.

was no less than the Baths of Diocletian, the relaxation spot of the militarily bold and resolute third-century Roman emperor; the immense main waiting room is certainly imperial in scale if not in bathing appointments. For five decades, the station sat at the head of an expanding railroad network that linked the country to its capital: hundreds of thousands of people arrived in the city by train, catching their first glimpse of the Capitol dome through its great arched doors – just as the wide-eyed James Stewart does at the beginning of Frank Capra's *Mr Smith Goes to Washington.* Incoming presidents arrived at Union Station by train for their inaugurations (Truman was the last), and were met in the specially installed Presidential Waiting Room; some, like FDR and Eisenhower, left in a casket after lying in state at the Capitol.

Come the 1960s, though, and the gradual depletion of train services, Union Station was left unkempt and underfunded. An ill-conceived scheme turned it into a visitor's center during the Bicentennial in 1976, and it wasn't fully **restored** until 1988. The exterior is of a piece with much of monumental Washington, the facade studded with allegorical statuary and etched with prolix texts extolling the virtues of trade, travel and technology. Enter through the main, triple-arched portico and you're immediately confronted by the soaring vastness of its dimensions – the only other single-roofed space in America to touch it is New York's Grand Central Station, which is over 20,000 square feet smaller.

Although you can still catch **trains** at Union Station – there's a Metro station on the east side of the building as well as Amtrak and MARC departures – the renovation project wouldn't have succeeded without its commercial adjuncts: the lower-gallery food court and movie theater, and upper-floor stores, restaurants, money-exchange offices, car rental agencies, ticket counters and parking garage. Take a look at the statue near Gate D honoring **A. Phillip Randolph**, founder of the Brotherhood of Sleeping Car Porters union and one of the prime movers in the 1963 March on Washington for Jobs and Freedom.

It's also worth taking a turn outside in **Union Station Plaza**, the landscaped approach to the station that stretches all the way down to the Capitol grounds. In the middle, slap bang in front of the station (and destroying the sight lines to the Capitol), the **Columbus Memorial Fountain**, dedicated in 1912, features a statue of the old mercenary standing on the prow of a ship, between two lions and male and female figures representing old world and new. A replica of Philadelphia's Liberty Bell stands nearby.

City Post Office: the National Postal Museum

Having unwrapped the design for Union Station, Burnham turned his attention to a new **City Post Office** opposite the station (at Massachusetts Ave and N Capitol St); built between 1911 and 1914, it was used until 1986, when it was renovated at a cost of $200 million, in part to house a fascinating new National Postal Museum. Before you descend to the lower-level galleries, spare time for a quick look at the building itself, whose white Italian marble reaches are some of the most impressive in the city. In the style of the day, it is adorned with improving texts for the edification of the public: look up and read how the postal service is "Messenger of Sympathy and Love . . . Consoler of the Lonely . . . . Enlarger of the Common Life" and "Carrier of News and Knowledge" among other treacly attributes. Inside, the main lobby has been restored to its 1914 appearance, full of burnished marble, though the bulk of the building on this level has been taken over by a brew-pub.

Union Station and around

For city post office locations, see p.22.

The museum

The **National Postal Museum** (daily 10am–5.30pm; free; ☎357-2700) is one of the Smithsonian's quiet triumphs. The collection, from the National Museum of American History, includes sixteen million artifacts, though since many of these are stamps, only a few of which are displayed, it's not that daunting a show. Indeed, the museum's strength is its selectivity, judiciously placing the history of the mail service within the context of the history of America itself.

Escalators down to the galleries dump you in "**Moving the Mail**", basically an excuse to stack up some rattling pieces of machinery, from a Concord mail coach to a bi-plane. Beyond here you follow the first postal route, the seventeenth-century King's Best Highway between New York and Boston, while tracing the development of the postal system – interactive video panels allow you to create your own route between two towns in the 1850s, your choices determining whether the mail gets through or not. It was soon clear that established overland mail routes helped attract commerce and settlers, with President Buchanan envisaging a "chain of living Americans" along the roads from east to west. Yet some of the most famous of the pioneering stories turn out to be more hype than substance. The relay-rider system of the famed Pony Express lasted for only two years (1860–61), and although it cut mail delivery times in half – from San Francisco to New York in thirteen days – the founding partners lost $30 on every letter carried; in the end, without government backing, the private enterprise collapsed.

It was seventh president Andrew Jackson who first realized the political importance of being able to rely on the mail, which could disseminate information – and propaganda – quickly and efficiently to even the most isolated communities; for a century after him, whenever the party in power lost a presidential election, the employment patronage system led to a huge turnover in postal workers. Photos and text trace the early racial make-up of the service, from the opportunities offered to blacks during Reconstruction to the segregation measures introduced in 1913, which in DC led to the establishment of a post office on T Street in Shaw, staffed only by black workers.

Elsewhere, there are examples of weird and wonderful rural mailboxes, including one made from car mufflers in the shape of a tin man; while in a section devoted to "**Postal Oddities**" you'll find a paddle punch used to fumigate letters during Philadelphia's yellow fever outbreak of 1890, as well as the uniform of the supremely annoying Cliff Clavin, bar-fly and postie in *Cheers*. Only in "**Stamps and Stories**" does the philatelic collection finally get a look-in – up until this point, there's barely a stamp to be seen. Along with some splendid rarities, you learn among other things about the research that went into producing a gum that could be licked by those following a vegetarian or kosher diet.

Before leaving (allow ninety minutes or so), print out your free personalized postcard at the machines in the lobby and buy a stamp from the stamp store in order to mail it home.

East to Lincoln Park

East Capitol Street, one of the city's four axes, runs off between the Supreme Court and the Library of Congress' Jefferson Building. One of the first streets on the Hill to be settled, its wide tree-lined reach presents a fine aspect for the first ten blocks or so, studded with frame and brick townhouses, some dating from before the Civil War, others sporting the trademark turrets and "rusticated" (roughened) stonework so beloved of DC's turn-of-the-century builders.

Close to the Supreme Court, the typical row house at 316 A St NE was home to black orator and writer **Frederick Douglass** when he first moved to the capital in 1870 to take up the editorship of the *New National Era*, a newspaper championing the rights of African-Americans. His family owned no. 318, too, and Douglass lived here with his first wife Anna until 1877, when they moved to the rather grander Cedar Hill in Anacostia, which is where you'll have to go to discover more about his life (see p.144).

Bus #96 runs down 1st St NE, from Union Station via the Supreme Court, along East Capitol St to Lincoln Park.

From here, it's just a few blocks north to **Stanton Park**, centered on its equestrian statue of Revolutionary General Nathanial Greene, though there's more interest in **Lincoln Park** further east along East Capitol Street, between 11th and 13th. In 1876, on the eleventh anniversary of Lincoln's assassination and in the presence of President Grant, Frederick Douglass read out the Emancipation Proclamation to the assembled thousands as the "Freedom Memorial" was unveiled in the center of the specially designed park. It was paid for by funds collected from freed men and women; the first contributor, Charlotte Scott of Virginia, gave $5, "being her first earnings in freedom". To contemporary eyes it seems a paternalistic work, the bronze statue portraying Lincoln – proclamation in one hand – standing over a kneeling slave, exhorting him to rise. But it was considered rather daring in its day: working from a photograph, sculptor Thomas Ball re-created in the slave the features of one Archer Alexander, the last man to be seized under the Fugitive Slave Act, which empowered slaveowners to recapture escaped slaves – under Lincoln's gaze Alexander is breaking his own shackles.

East to Lincoln Park

It was a century, however, before any monument was erected in DC specfically to honor the achievements of a black American, or, indeed, a woman. Facing Lincoln, across the park, a second memorial – dedicated in 1974 – remembers **Mary McLeod Bethune**, educationalist, black women's leader and special advisor to Franklin Delano Roosevelt. Just as significant as the Lincoln statue, it is possibly even more striking: Robert Berks (responsible for the head of JFK in the Kennedy Center) provides an inimitable study of a stout Bethune, leaning on her cane, reaching out to two children, passing on, as the inscription says, her legacy to youth.

For more on Mary McLeod Bethune, see p.229.

East of the park the neighborhood degenerates. Come here in daylight and peer up East Capitol Street to the **RFK Stadium** in the distance (home of DC United, see p.327), but don't head there on foot.

Along and around Pennsylvania Avenue

Along the first few blocks of **Pennsylvania Avenue**, between 2nd Street and Eastern Market (at 7th), lie a score of bars and restaurants, including some notable Hill institutions: they're reviewed on p.301 (bars) and p.290 (restaurants). **Eastern Market** itself (7th and C, south of N Carolina Ave SE; Tues–Sat 7am–6pm, Sun 9am–4pm) makes a grand target, a red-brick edifice constructed in 1873 by Adolph Cluss, with rather less flamboyance than his Arts and Industries Building on the Mall. What it lacks in visual stimulus outside, though, it makes up for inside, where the traders continue to do roaring business: on the weekend, the stalls spill onto the sidewalk, when you can buy produce and flowers (Sat), or antiques and junk (Sun). On either side, along 7th Street, delis, coffee shops with outdoor seating, antique stores and clothes shops make it one of the more appealing hangouts on the Hill.

Transport: Eastern Market Metro, or bus #30, #32, #34, #35, #36 down Pennsylvania Ave.

There are more restored townhouses in the vicinity of Pennsylvania Avenue, and green splashes at places like Folger Square, Seward Square and Marion Park, but on the whole, the district south of E Street is not one to wander around on your own. Two churches stand out, though, and in daylight at least there should be no problem in visiting them. The utilitarian red-brick **Ebenezer United Methodist Church** at 420 D St SE (Mon–Fri 8.30am–3pm, Sun service 11am; ☎544-1415) is the oldest black congregation in the neighborhood. Founded in 1805, the church was the site of DC's first public school for black people, a short-lived affair (1864–65) though a pioneering one, since the teachers were paid out of federal funds; the current building dates from 1897 and if you call in advance someone will be on hand to show you around. On the 4th Street side stands a wooden model of "Little Ebenezer", the original frame church which stood on this site. Further south, but unlikely to be open, **Christ Church** at 620 G St SE is an early work (1806) by Capitol architect Benjamin Latrobe.

Chapter 4

Southwest, Waterfront and Southeast

T
he **Southwest** quadrant, cut into by the encroaching curve of
the river and East Potomac Park, is the most compact in the
city: it's easy to loop through on your way from the Capitol to
the Jefferson Memorial. This is the least distinguished of the city's
areas – locals know it as the home of various federal agencies, while
most visitors are hardly aware of its existence. Indeed, the district's
two principal sights, the **Holocaust Memorial Museum** and the
Bureau of Engraving and Printing, sit just off the Mall itself, neces-
sitating only the briefest diversion.

Museums aside, the bright spots are all down at the district's
southwestern edge, by the restored **Waterfront**, which runs along
Water Street on the north side of the Washington Channel. Modern
waterside apartment buildings have replaced nineteenth-century
slum housing, and the area today is defined by its smart marina,
promenades and seafood restaurants – useful lunch stops before
walking back to the Mall or on to the monuments and memorials. The
original fish market still survives at the Fish Wharf on Washington
Channel, though in a much more regulated and less offensively
smelly fashion than its eighteenth-century predecessor.

It's more of an effort (involving Metro, bus or taxi rides) to
explore the limited attractions contained in the blighted neighborhoods of Washington's **Southeast**. Visitors are advised to head directly to the three individual sights – the Navy Museum, the former home
of black orator and writer Frederick Douglass, and the neighborhood
Anacostia Museum – and then come straight back again. To attempt
any further exploration would be fruitless and possibly dangerous.

Southwest

In the early nineteenth century, **SOUTHWEST** was a fashionable
residential area, thriving on its proximity to the Capitol. But the

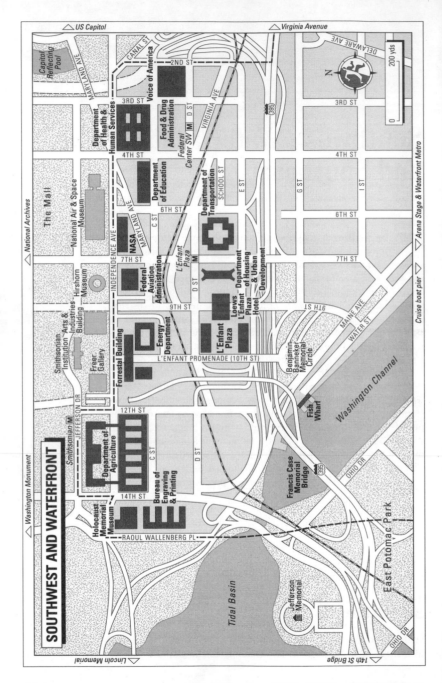

SOUTHWEST AND WATERFRONT

arrival of the railroad in the 1870s, whose tracks cut right through the district – and still do – diminished its social cachet and the wealthy moved north of the Mall. Those left were mostly poor blacks, an additional influx of whom soon turned Southwest into the largest black neighborhood in the city, its inhabitants working at the briefly flourishing goods yards, storage depots and wharves. As the work dried up, the swamp-ridden housing became ever more dilapidated, and by the 1920s the district had degenerated into a notorious slum. However, the federal government, looking for centralized office space, saw underutilized potential in the Southwest. The low-rent housing was demolished and families displaced to make room for federal agencies, including the Department of Agriculture and the Bureau of Engraving and Printing, both of which remain in situ; more buildings were added in the 1930s (to complement the work being undertaken across the Mall in Federal Triangle) and the 1960s. While these developments undoubtedly rescued Southwest from neglect, they also firmly stamped "federal" across its streets – there's little life here after 6pm on weekday evenings, even less on weekends, and few places to grab a coffee or sandwich that aren't brimming with office workers. There's a lack of architectural cohesion within the northern part of the quadrant too, certainly when compared to the public-works grandeur of Federal Triangle, just four blocks north.

Almost all the agencies are contained within a rectangle of land bounded by Independence Avenue, 3rd Street, E Street and 14th Street, and are served by two Metro stations, Federal Center SW and, further west, L'Enfant Plaza.

Federal buildings

Heading west from the Capitol, you're not missing anything by sticking to Independence Avenue as far as 4th Street. The block between 3rd and 4th is taken up by the Department of Health and Human Services, whose imposing bulk makes it one of the few in Southwest to stand comparison with the Classical entities of Federal Triangle; it dates from the same (late 1930s) period. It's the only federal building hereabouts open for public visits; part of the building houses the offices of the Voice of America (free 40-min tours Mon–Fri 10.30am, 1.30pm & 2.30pm; ☎619-3919); the entrance is around the back, on C Street between 3rd and 4th.

Along with the BBC and Radio Moscow, the VOA is one of the world's three biggest international broadcasters, established in 1942 as part of the war effort and given its own charter in 1960 (as part of the US Information Agency) to transmit programs overseas giving a flavor of US life and values. In theory, the VOA Charter is as admirable as they come: "VOA will serve as a consistently reliable and authoritative source of news . . . [which] will be accurate, objective, and comprehensive." But, whichever way you cut it, its intention to "present the policies of the United States clearly and effectively" makes it a valuable propaganda tool for the government – which is why the VOA's broadcasts have often been on the receiving end of jamming by various disaffected foreign powers. This, of course, is not something you hear too much about on the tour, in which you're walked through the corridors and studios from where broadcasts are made in 48 different languages to 90 million listeners in 120 countries. It's only really of interest if you've never been in a radio studio before, in which case you'll be happy to get up close to broadcasters and journalists at work (or at least reading the *Washington Post* and eating donuts). The two most interesting discoveries are that you can call collect to the *Talk to America* chatshow from anywhere in the world, a fact that unsurprisingly isn't widely advertised; and that, as evidenced by the photograph gallery of the personalities who've appeared on VOA over the years, Telly Savalas once had a fine head of hair.

The other federal buildings – large, and largely unappealing structures – occupy a no-man's-land between 4th and 14th streets. Presumably, it wasn't for want of trying that the area appears so dreary: the **Department of Transportation** building (between D and E at 7th) was designed by Edward Durrell Stone, who managed to make the Kennedy Center (see p.173) stand out in similarly unpromising surroundings; while even I.M. Pei has had a hand in the regeneration of the various plazas and streetscapes. The closest thing here to modern swagger, though, is the curving double-Y-shaped concrete structure from the late 1960s which holds the **Department of Housing and Urban Development** (D St between 7th and 9th), whose architect, Marcel Breuer, gave more than a nod to his Bauhaus origins. The only semblance of style, however, comes with the oldest (and westernmost) agency, the **Department of Agriculture** (Independence Ave between 12th and 14th): sited here since 1905, the original building on the north side of Independence Avenue is connected by slender arches to the much larger, 1930s Classical structure across the avenue.

L'Enfant Plaza to Benjamin Banneker Memorial Circle

The main focus of development in Southwest in the 1960s and 1970s was **L'Enfant Plaza**, at D Street between 9th and 10th, where there's now also a useful Metro station. The buildings surrounding the plaza are no more gripping than their neighbors, but from the Metro station there's direct access into a huge underground shopping mall and up into the luxurious **Loews L'Enfant Plaza** Hotel, which occupies the entire east block of the plaza. Quite apart from being the one decent place in the district where you can get a cup of coffee (in the *Café Pierre*), the outdoor terrace which wraps around the hotel has great views. Nonetheless, it's easy to feel a twinge of sympathy for Pierre L'Enfant – alone of the city's spiritual founders, he gets not a monument but a windswept 1960s concrete square and Metro station as his memorial.

From the plaza, 10th Street is immediately accessible, forming a landscaped mall (known as L'Enfant Promenade) which heads south to the **Benjamin Banneker Memorial Circle**, where there's a viewpoint over the Washington Channel and Waterfront. The African-American Banneker, born in Maryland in 1731 to a former slave and a servant girl, was a remarkable figure. Almost entirely self-taught, he distinguished himself as a mathematician, astronomer (he accurately predicted a solar eclipse) and inventor (of, among other things, a striking clock with every part made of wood) before, extraordinarily for the time and at the age of sixty, being invited to assist in the surveying of the land for the new capital. He followed this coup by publishing several editions of a successful almanac and spent his last years (he died in 1806) in correspondence with Thomas Jefferson, whom he hoped would abandon his "narrow prejudices" against the native intelligence of African-Americans.

United States Holocaust Memorial Museum

100 Raoul Wallenberg Place SW; entrance on 14th St ☏488-0400; Smithsonian Metro. Daily 10am–5.30pm; closed on Yom Kippur. Admission free.

Nothing in DC is more disturbingly unforgettable than the large and symbolically sited **United States Holocaust Memorial Museum**. Just a step from the Mall, and within the triangle formed by the Washington, Lincoln and Jefferson memorials, the museum commemorates in a uniquely provocative fashion the persecution and murder of six million Jews by the Nazis. Upon entry, each visitor is given the ID card, containing biographical notes, of a real Holocaust victim, whose fortunes are followed as the museum unfolds. This personalizes the fate of the affected individuals, while never losing sight of the wider historical machinations which allowed Hitler to assume power in the first place. The detail throughout is perfectly pitched – highly informative and pulling no punches, without being overly emotive. No knowledge of the events of the Holocaust is assumed, and this too is deliberate: indeed, however much you already know, nothing prepares you for this relentless, remorseless documentation of systematic brutality. The solemn mood throughout is reflected by the museum's design, overseen in part by noted Holocaust survivors. Half-lit chambers, a floor of ghetto cobblestones, an obscenely cramped barracks building, and an external roofline which resembles the guard towers of a concentration camp – all add to the overwhelming feeling of oppression. The themed displays are a mix of personal possessions and photographs alongside historical montages and video presentations, before which visitors stand visibly moved. And on this level, certainly, the museum passes the acid test: personal remembrance of an international horror.

The museum

Crowding can be a problem. To control the flow of people, **tickets** for fixed entry times are available free from 10am (limited to four per person) at the 14th Street entrance. You can also book in advance through Protix (☎1-800/400-9373; fee charged). If you arrive without a ticket any later than mid-morning, you're unlikely to get into the permanent exhibition that day, but a certain number of temporary displays are usually open to all. Note that the main exhibitions are not considered suitable for **children** under the age of eleven, though the less forbidding gallery, "Daniel's Story: Remember the Children", is designed for those over the age of eight.

The **permanent exhibitions** are on the second, third and fourth floors; you start at the top and work your way down. The 14th Street entrance is at first-floor level, where you'll find the information desk, *There's a café in the Administrative Center, around at the Raoul Wallenberg Place (15th St) entrance, open 9am–4.30pm.* children's exhibit and museum **shop**; stairs lead down to the auditoriums and **special exhibition** area at concourse level.

The first rooms on the fourth floor chronicle the **Nazi rise to power** from 1933 to 1939 through story boards, newspapers and film clips. The point that prejudice soon sweeps all before it is forcefully made: what started with the boycott of Jewish businesses and book-burning was swiftly followed by the organized looting of Jewish shops and the parading of German women who had "defiled" their race by associating with Jews. From there, anyone who didn't fit the Nazi ideal, like homosexuals (who were forced to wear a pink triangle), gypsies and even Freemasons were persecuted and imprisoned. Beyond a glass wall etched with the names of the hundreds of Eastern European Jewish communities wiped off the map forever, a towering stack of photographs records the breadth of life in just one of them. Domestic life in the *shtetl*, or community, of Eishishok (in what's now Lithuania) is vividly shown in street scenes, ceremonies, parties, family groups and portraits taken between 1890 and 1941.

The third floor covers the era of Hitler's **Final Solution**, beginning with the first gassing of Jews to take place at a death camp in Poland in December 1941. The Jews were transported to the camps from the ghettos in which they'd been incarcerated, most infamously at Warsaw. Even in the ghettos, there was resistance – although it's clear from the displays just how ultimately futile that proved to be. The slaughter at Babi Yar in Kiev (1941) claimed 33,000 Jewish lives in retaliation after Soviet saboteurs had blown up buildings in the city; in the Warsaw uprising of 1943, the resistance held out, remarkably, for a month but had no real weapons, no supplies and no hope. In the end, all the surviving ghetto Jews were taken to the camps in packed rail freight cars; the one that you can walk through in this section stands on railroad tracks taken from the camp at Treblinka.

The most harrowing part of the exhibition deals with life and death in the **concentration camps** themselves. There's an overwhelming poignancy in the pile of blankets, umbrellas, scissors, cutlery and other personal effects taken from the hundreds of thousands who arrived at the various camps expecting to be forced to work – most were gassed within hours. A re-created barracks building from Auschwitz provides the backdrop for the oral memories of some survivors, as well as concealing truly shocking film of gruesome medical experiments carried out on selected prisoners.

Many histories claim that it was only after the war had ended that the full scale of these atrocities became apparent, but as the museum clearly – and uncomfortably – shows, the Americans knew of the existence of Auschwitz as early as May 1944 and yet refused to bomb it; Assistant Secretary of War John J. Mclloy argued that its destruction "might provoke even more vindictive action by the Germans". It's a moot point now, though it's instructive that contemporary American Jewish organizations repeatedly demanded that the camps be bombed, while survivors later testified that they would have welcomed such terminal liberation – "Every bomb that exploded . . . gave us new confidence in life", records one witness. The third floor also ends with photographic coverage of the Eishishok *shtetl*, this time relating it to the Final Solution. The pictures show a town and community that had existed for over nine hundred years completely destroyed, and its inhabitants (including two of the photographers) shot, in just two days.

As the Nazi front collapsed across Europe during 1945, many different groups became involved in efforts to save the Jews. The **Last Chapter** on the second floor recounts the heroism of particular individuals and the response of governments, among whom the Danes have most reason to feel secure that they did all they could to save their Jewish citizens. Much of the floor is taken up with details of the **liberation of the camps** by the Allied forces: film reels show German guards being forced to bury mountains of bodies in mass graves, while locals were made to tour the camps to witness the extent of the horror. If people later looked to the **war trials** in Nuremberg to draw a line under this evil, little comfort was offered there either. Despite the imprisonment and execution of various high-profile Nazis, and a continuing trickle of prosecutions over the years, most people responsible for the planning, maintenance and administration of the camps were never tried; thousands of others were treated leniently or acquitted altogether.

The sheer amount on display requires most visitors to spend at least three hours in the museum. There are rest areas throughout, and a contemplative **Hall of Remembrance** on the second floor. The **Wexner Learning Center**, on the same floor, has computer stations that allow you to access text, photographs, film and other sources.

The Bureau of Engraving and Printing

14th and C streets SW ☎622-2000; Smithsonian Metro. Mon–Fri 9am–2pm; closed Christmas to New Year. Admission free.

Half a million visitors a year wait patiently in line at the **Bureau of Engraving and Printing** before being led through narrow corridors for a tantalizing glimpse of the nation's money-making process. It must be the avaricious thrill of being close to so much money that drags in the crowds, because it certainly isn't the twenty-minute tour of what is, effectively, a large printing plant. The difference is that the presses here crank out millions of dollars in currency every day, $120 billion a year (95 percent of which is replacement currency for money already in circulation).

The Bureau is the federal agency for designing and printing all US currency, government securities and postage stamps (of which it produces 30 billion a year). It was established in 1862, when Abraham Lincoln empowered six employees to start up business in the attic of the Treasury Building, sealing up blocks of $1 and $2 bills that had been printed by private banks. By 1877, all US currency was produced by the Bureau, which finally moved into this building in 1914. Nowadays, almost three thousand employees either work here or at a second plant in Fort Worth, Texas.

So much for the history, much of which is served up on video as you wait in line in the main corridor. What everyone wants to see is the cash, which is quickly revealed during the march through claustrophobic viewing galleries looking down upon the printing presses. It's a surprisingly low-tech operation: hand-engraved dyes are used to create intaglio steel plates, from which the bills are printed in sheets of 32, checked for defects and loaded into large barrows. On a separate press, they're then over-printed with serial numbers and seals, sliced up into single bills by ordinary paper cutters, and stacked into "bricks" of four thousand notes before being sent out to the twelve Federal Reserve Districts which issue the notes to local banks. Star facts, fired out amid lame jokes by the guides, include the Trivial Pursuit-winning knowledge that the notes aren't made from paper at all, but from a more durable fabric three-quarters cotton. Even so, the most-used note, the dollar bill, lasts only eighteen months on average. Those whose job it is to spot flaws in the currency get short shrift from federal-employee-baiting visitors, who see only a line of people with their heads in their hands gazing at bundles of notes. What you don't see in the two-minute gaze through the window is the rigor of the two-year apprenticeship that all undergo, or the eight-hour daily shift worked staring at one sheet a second, with just two twenty-minute breaks and a thirty-minute lunch. Yet they catch all but one in a thousand of misprinted bills. As a finale, guides deftly usher you into the **visitor center** (Mon–Fri 8.30am–3.30pm), which sells souvenirs like small bags of shredded currency – it's cheaper to provide yourself with two dollar bills and a pair of scissors from WalMart.

Despite the relative ordinariness of the process, the tour is immensely popular and between Easter and Memorial Day you must pick up **tickets** in advance; note that these have often all gone by 11.30am. At other times, you can simply turn up, though you'll still have to wait in line.

The Waterfront

Downtown Washington has always been rather removed from the rivers (Potomac and Anacostia) on which the city stands. They meet at a Y-junction some considerable way from the Mall and the other central axes, and for a century after the city was founded, the nearest accessible riverbanks (in today's West Potomac Park) were too marshy and malarial to develop anyway. The only practicable wharves and piers were those built along the Washington Channel, the thin finger of water that sheers off from the Potomac, but this too had a tendency to stagnate – at least until the Tidal Basin was created this century, the opening of whose gates now serves to flush the channel clean after every tide. The rather haphazardly developed commercial buildings and piers that lined the north bank of the Washington Channel were finally redeveloped during the 1960s as the **WATERFRONT**, a project designed to convince Washingtonians that they didn't have to go to Georgetown when they wanted a riverside stroll. Despite lacking Georgetown's natural advantages, the development has succeeded admirably, in part due to the proximity of so many office workers. Most people come here to eat seafood at one of the restaurants which line the waters of the Channel, along Maine Avenue or the parallel Water Street SW, west of 7th; all have terraces and patios with views across to East Potomac Park. The district even has its own Metro stop, at 4th and M.

The two main attractions are next to each other, near the bridge that crosses the Channel to East Potomac Park. The **Washington Marina** is the usual tangle of pricey nautical hardware, and provides a backdrop for various summer fairs and events. Adjacent lies the **Fish Wharf** (daily 7.30am–8pm), the oldest continuous fish market in America, conducted from permanently docked boats and trailers. This puts on a great spread, with huge trays of Chesapeake Bay fish, shrimp, clams, oysters and, especially, crabs, which you can buy live or steamed. There's nowhere to sit and eat, but there's nothing to stop you heading down the waterside promenade for a picnic.

A couple of cruise boats sail out of Pier 4 at 6th and Water streets – see "City tours", p.47, for details. For reviews of the Waterfront restaurants, see p.207.

Further down Maine Avenue, east of 7th Street, the **Waterfront** Metro station is closest if you're heading for the Arena Stage (see p.314). To the south, there's little specific to venture out for, but it's a nice walk along the Channel past the cruise boat docks and DC harbor patrol as far as the Titanic Memorial. Set back, opposite the Spirit Cruises dock, the **Thomas Law House** (built 1794–96) is one of DC's oldest surviving federal townhouses, and if you cut through past here to 4th Street, you can see another row of federal houses, called **Wheat Row** (1315–1321 4th St SW), maintained within the **Harbor Square** development at 4th Street between N and O.

Channel and river collide just to the south of here, with the strategic spit of land occupied by the military (and subsequently off-limits) since the city's earliest days. Now known as **Fort McNair**, the

The
Waterfront

base – originally fortified in 1791 – became home to the **Washington Arsenal** in 1804, though its buildings were blown up by the British in 1814 and later destroyed by an explosion which killed 21 people in 1864. At the US Penitentiary, built in the 1820s in the arsenal grounds, the conspirators in the Lincoln assassination (see p.204) were imprisoned, tried and executed.

Southeast

Run-down, impoverished **SOUTHEAST** Washington makes its presence felt just a few blocks south of the US Capitol; visitors shouldn't stroll around too far south of Eastern Market Metro or east of Waterfront Metro. Not that you'd have cause to: the only attraction hereabouts is the enclosed military campus of **Washington Navy Yard**, which can be reached directly by Metro or by bus (#90 or #92

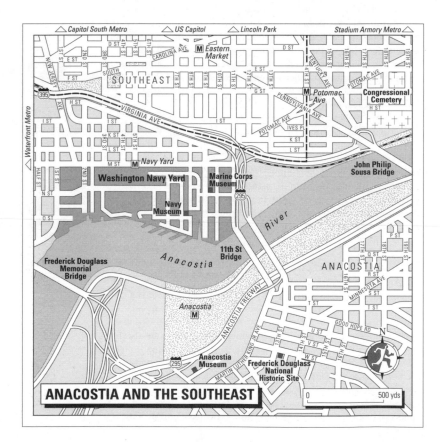

ANACOSTIA AND THE SOUTHEAST

down 8th St SE from Eastern Market Metro, #V6 along M St SE from
Waterfront Metro). There's parking inside the compound.

Navy Yard

NAVY YARD is the US Navy's oldest shore establishment, building
ships and producing weaponry for the fleet continuously from 1799
until 1961 – interrupted only in 1812 when the commander was
ordered to burn the base to prevent the British capturing it. Since the
1960s the base has acted as a naval supply and administrative center, and would be of no interest whatsoever were it not for its splendid Navy Museum. While you're within the confines of the Yard you'll
probably also look into the Marine Corps Historical Center and the
Navy Art Gallery, though both are very much an afterthought. You'll
need photo ID to show the guard at the main gate at 9th and M.

Navy Museum

Housed in the Navy Yard's former gun factory is the **Navy Museum**
(☎433-4882; Mon–Fri 9am–4pm, June–Aug until 5pm, Sat & Sun all
year 10am–5pm; admission free), whose focused and illuminating collection traces the history of the US Navy from its foundation in 1794 in
response to attacks on American ships by Barbary pirates – a painting
illustrates the exploits of early naval hero Stephen Decatur (see p.156),
who captured three boats during hand-to-hand fighting at Tripoli in
1804. Dress uniforms, ship figureheads and vicious cat-o'-nine-tail
whips, and a walk-through frigate gun-deck, illustrate the gradual development of the navy as a fighting force, while separate galleries deal with
every conflict the US Navy has taken part in – from the War of 1812 to
the Gulf War. The World War II displays are particularly affecting, featuring anti-aircraft guns in which you can sit, crackly archive film
footage and an account of the sinking by a Japanese destroyer of a
PT109 patrol boat on August 2, 1943: its commander, one John
Fitzgerald Kennedy, his back badly injured, swam ashore towing the
boat's badly burned engineer, an act for which he was later decorated.

The museum gets the balance just right, mixing informative text and
glass-case displays with huge pieces of hardware which you're encouraged to explore – not least the *USS Barry*, a destroyer docked outside the
museum, whose mess room, bridge and quarters are open to the public.

Anacostia

Washington's most notorious neighborhood, **ANACOSTIA**, is also
one of its oldest, the name deriving from that of the area's original
Native American inhabitants, the tobacco-growing Nacotchtanks.
They were supplanted by nineteenth-century merchants seeking
homes close to the Capitol, who in turn were displaced in the 1850s
by a white working and middle class encouraged to settle in what the
developers called Uniontown. Post Civil War Reconstruction saw the

neighborhood thrive, boosted by the building of the 11th Street Bridge which connected Anacostia with the rest of DC. But the white flight to the suburbs gathered pace in the 1950s, and by 1970 over 95 percent of Anacostia's residents were black – and largely abandoned by the city authorities. The 1968 riots did as much damage to infrastructure and confidence here as in Shaw, and it's been a long clamber back for the embattled community, which still suffers grievously from underfunding, poor housing, unemployment and crime – the last fueled by the city's spiraling drug problem.

None of which makes for a neighborhood you should visit lightly. There are, of course, handsome pockets of old houses, revitalized commercial areas and worthy community projects in

---

Frederick Douglass (1818–95)

He stood there like an African prince, majestic in his wrath, as with wit, satire and indignation he graphically described the bitterness of slavery.

Elizabeth Cady Stanton, 1895

Frederick Douglass was born into slavery as Frederick Bailey on a Maryland estate in 1818; the exact date is unknown, as is the identity of his father (Bailey was his mother's name), though it was rumored to be a white man, perhaps his owner. At the age of eight, he was sent to work as a house servant in Baltimore, where, although it was illegal to educate slaves, the owner's wife taught him to read, and he secretly taught himself to write. By 1834 he had been hired out to a nearby plantation where he was cruelly treated; his first attempt to escape, in 1836, failed. Later, apprenticed as a ship caulker in Baltimore docks, Frederick attended an educational association run by free blacks, where he met his first wife, Anna Murray. With money borrowed from her and equipped with a friend's passbook, he fled to New York in 1838 disguised as a free seaman. Anna followed him and they were married later that year, moving to Massachusetts where Bailey – now working as a laborer – became Douglass (after a character from Sir Walter Scott's *Lady of the Lake*) so as to confound the slave-catchers.

Douglass became active in the **abolition movement**, lecturing about his life for the Massachusetts Anti-Slavery Society during the 1840s and risking capture when, aged just 27, he published his early autobiography, *Narrative of the Life of Frederick Douglass, an American Slave*, in 1845. It was a resounding success, forcing the increasingly famous Douglass to leave for England (which had a strong abolitionist movement) for fear he'd be recaptured. After two years on the lecture circuit, friends raised the money to buy his freedom and Douglass returned home. His views were slowly changing and in a break with pacifist white abolitionists (particularly William Lloyd Garrison), he founded his own newspaper, the *North Star*, in Rochester, New York, in 1847 (later renamed *Frederick Douglass' Paper*) – in this, Douglass began increasingly to explore the idea of political rather than moral reform as a means of ending slavery. His reputation grew as a compelling orator and writer; another autobiography,

Anacostia – people, after all, *do* manage to live perfectly ordinary lives here – but there's no reason to come as a tourist. Much of it is dangerous to outsiders who don't know where they're going; the two attractions reviewed below are best reached by cab from Anacostia Metro station.

Frederick Douglass National Historic Site

Frederick Douglass – former slave, abolitionist leader and blistering orator – was sixty when in 1877 he moved to the white, brick house in Anacostia he knew and loved as **Cedar Hill**. Its mixed Gothic Revival-Italianate appearance, 21 rooms and 15 acres were typical of the quality homes built in Uniontown twenty years earlier, though at

Southeast

Abraham Lincoln's assassin, John Wilkes Booth, escaped on horseback through Anacostia after shooting the President in 1865; see p.204.

My Bondage and My Freedom, appeared in 1855. Meanwhile, he extended his interests to women's suffrage (a bold move at the time), debating issues with such luminaries as Susan B. Anthony, Lucretia Mott and Elizabeth Cady Stanton.

When Lincoln issued the Emancipation Proclamation during the Civil War, the country's most respected black leader turned his attention to urging "Men of Color" to join up, which backfired somewhat when it became clear that his fiery recruitment speeches promised black soldiers an equality in service and conditions that the Union Army didn't offer. With slavery abolished in 1865, and Reconstruction set in place, Douglass turned to pressing for black suffrage. He campaigned for Ulysses S. Grant and the Republicans in 1868 and played a major role in pushing through the Fifteenth Amendment (granting all "citizens" the right to vote) – though this caused a temporary rift with his suffragist colleagues since "citizens" still didn't include women. Frederick and Anna moved to DC in 1870, buying a house on Capitol Hill, where Douglass continued to earn his living lecturing and writing and, for a while, editing the progressive *New National Era* newspaper. Appointed to the largely ceremonial position of marshal of Washington DC in 1877, his last move was to Cedar Hill in Anacostia the same year.

He was made recorder of deeds for the city in 1880 and in 1881 published his third autobiographical work, the *Life and Times of Frederick Douglass*. Anna died a year later, but Douglass was quickly remarried – to Helen Pitts, a quick-witted white secretary almost twenty years his junior, whom he had met in the records office. More controversy followed as Douglass was accused of cosying up to successive political administrations that had been deemed to have betrayed the aspirations of black Americans ever since Emancipation. Quitting his post as recorder, Douglass regained his reputation with a series of searing attacks on injustice and, in 1889, at a time when others might have considered retirement, he accepted the post of consul-general in Haiti, where he served for two years. Back at Cedar Hill, but by now in ill health, he continued to write and speak publicly until his death from a heart attack on February 20, 1895, at the age of 77. His funeral, effectively a state occasion, was held at the Metropolitan AME Church in downtown DC; his writings continued to inspire a new generation of black leaders who took his fight into the twentieth century.

that time they were restricted to whites. Douglass, newly appointed US marshal in DC, was the first to break the racial ban, paying $6700 for the property and living out the last eighteen years of his life here.

Tours of what is now known, rather cumbersomely, as the **Frederick Douglass National Historic Site** (1411 W St SE ☎426-5961; daily: May–Sept 9am–5pm; Oct–April 9am–4pm; tours every 30min; admission $3) begin in the visitor center below the house, where a short docudrama and a few static exhibits fill you in on Douglass's life. You're then led up the steep green hill for a rather dry tour around the house. It was a substantial property for the time, in which Douglass received all the leading abolitionist and suffragist lights of the day, talking in the parlors or eating in the dining room. Many brought him mementos which are on display – President Lincoln's cane, given to him by Mary Lincoln, and a desk and chair from Harriet Beecher Stowe. Family portraits loom large: of his first wife Anna, who died in 1882; his second wife Helen, much younger and – more shockingly for hidebound DC – white; and his five children, two of whom served with distinction in the black Massachusetts 54th regiment during the Civil War.

Most of the fixtures and fittings are original and give a fair idea of middle-class life in late nineteenth-century Washington. Douglass kept chickens and goats outside in the gardens and the only water source was a rainwater pump, but inside the kitchen the domestic staff had access to all the latest technology, like the cranky Universal wrangler ("giving universal satisfaction"). Frederick himself worked either in his study, surrounded by hundreds of books, or in the outdoor "Growlery" – a rudimentary stone cabin he used for solitary contemplation.

Returning to the Metro **by bus**, the #B2 (which drops you right outside the door on the way *from* Anacostia Metro) heads back *to* the Metro from Good Hope Road SE, three blocks down 14th Street from the house; cross Good Hope Road and wait for the bus (every 15min) on the other side, outside the grocery-deli. It's much less hassle to arrange for a taxi to pick you up from the house.

Anacostia Museum

The Smithsonian's least-known outpost, the **Anacostia Museum** (1901 Fort Place SE ☎357-2700; daily 10am–5pm; admission free) devotes itself to recording African-American history and culture, with particular reference to the life of blacks in the upper South (DC, Maryland, Virginia and the Carolinas). There's no permanent collection and instead the museum holds renowned temporary exhibitions on themed topics: either call to see what's on or ask for details at the Smithsonian Castle on the Mall. The museum is well worth an hour or two of your time, but don't even think of walking here from the Metro; buses #W1 or #W2 from Howard Road (outside the Metro) stop at the museum, though it's less unnerving by far to come by taxi. As it's not far from the Frederick Douglass home, you could even get the same taxi to take you to both.

Chapter 5

The White House and Foggy Bottom

F ew residences in the world are as recognizable as the patrician outline of the **White House**. With an impeccable lineage – oldest public building in Washington DC, home of the President since 1800, and, with the Capitol, one of the two original cornerstones of L'Enfant's masterplan for the city – it stands as perhaps the most enduring symbol of democracy in the nation, a symbol bolstered by the extraordinary public access granted since the time of Thomas Jefferson.

Around the White House are genteel squares and streets fashionable since the early nineteenth century. To the west, in the high ground of **Foggy Bottom** – basically, the leafy area north of Constitution Avenue and west from the White House to the river – the chattering classes entertained the political elite in houses like **The Octagon**. Washington's first art gallery opened just a block from the White House in what is now the Smithsonian's **Renwick Gallery** of decorative arts and crafts; later, the art collection was moved into the larger **Corcoran Gallery of Art**, still one of the most respected art foundations in the country.

Today, Foggy Bottom is best known for the federal institutions which have their headquarters here. However, the students of **George Washington University**, set bang in the heart of Foggy Bottom, add a certain life to the otherwise nine-to-five flavor of the streets, and there are a handful of minor museums and galleries. The biggest draws, though, are the **Kennedy Center**, the city's major cultural complex, and – though there's little actually to see – the nearby **Watergate** building, scene of the infamous burglary that led eventually to the toppling of President Nixon.

The White House

1600 Pennsylvania Ave NW ☎ 456-7041; McPherson Square or Farragut West Metro. Continuous tours Tues–Sat 10am–noon; additional tours at other hours in summer; closed some holidays and official functions. Admission free.

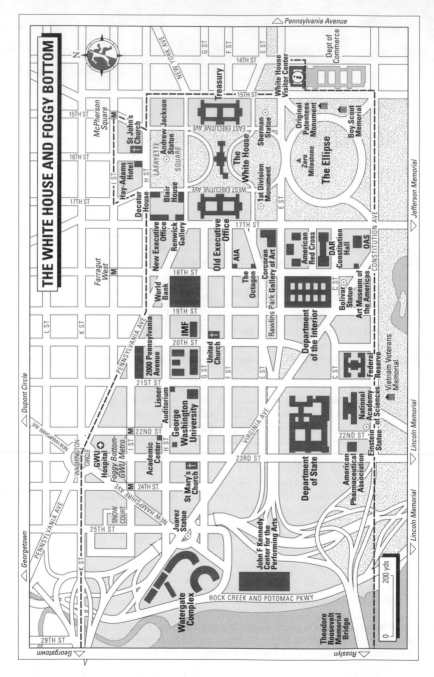

THE WHITE HOUSE AND FOGGY BOTTOM

For two centuries, the **White House**, 1600 Pennsylvania Avenue NW, has been the most famous house at the most famous address in America. For millions, the notion of touring the White House, residence and office of the **President of the United States**, has an almost totemic quality. Quite apart from relishing the freedom to stand in the same building, for a moment at least, as the chief executive of the nation, the person with their finger on the button, there's the undeniable thrill of nosing around the home of the closest the country has to royalty.

In the end, however, if it's domestic curiosity that brings you to the White House, you're likely to go away disappointed. Many are surprised by how small it is – "I think I may say that we have private houses in London considerably larger", sniffed Anthony Trollope in 1862 – while tours tend to consist of a lot of waiting around followed by a quick shuffle past railed-off rooms filled with portraits of ex-presidents.

Public access (see "Visiting the White House", p.150) isn't affected except during official functions, but **security** is every bit as tight as you'd imagine. In 1995 the stretch of Pennsylvania Avenue immediately outside the White House was permanently closed to vehicles, following two incidents in which shots were fired at the house and a light aircraft crashed into one of the outer walls. The Oklahoma City bombing shortly afterwards only served to heighten the fear of terrorist attack. Balancing security requirements with the historic right of access is not a new problem: in the nineteenth century, though there were armed sentries at every door and plainclothes policemen mingling with the visitors, virtually anyone could turn up at the President's house without an introduction. In his diary, naval novelist Captain Frederick Marryat deplored the way a visitor might "walk into the saloon in all his dirt, and force his way to the President, that he might shake him by the one hand while he flourished the whip in the other". As late as the 1920s, the general public was allowed to saunter across the White House lawns and picnic in the grounds. President Warren Harding even used to answer the door himself.

Some history

From the outset, the White House – or **President's Mansion**, as it was first known – was to be the focal point of executive government, connected to the proposed Capitol building by the broad diagonal sweep of Pennsylvania Avenue. L'Enfant was fired before he could make a start on the house, however, and its design was thrown open to an architectural competition in 1792. The winner, Irish immigrant and professional builder **James Hoban**, picked up a $500 prize for his Neoclassical design, which was influenced by the Georgian manor houses of Dublin. It coincided exactly with President Washington's requirement for a mansion that would command respect without being extravagant and monarchical – attributes the

The White House

For a roll-call of US presidents, see p.341. For an account of the role of the President within the American political system, see p.154.

Visiting the White House

*We entered a large hall, and, having twice or thrice rung a bell which
nobody answered, walked without further ceremony through the
rooms on the ground-floor, as diverse other gentlemen (mostly with
their hats on, and their hands in their pockets) were doing very
leisurely. Some of these had ladies with them, to whom they were
showing the premises; others were lounging on the chairs and sofas;
others, in a perfect state of exhaustion from listlessness, were yawn-
ing drearily. The greater portion of this assemblage were rather
asserting their supremacy than doing anything else, as they had no
particular business there, that anybody knew of. A few were closely
eyeing the movables, as if to make quite sure that the President . . .
had not made away with any of the furniture, or sold the fixtures for
his private benefit.*

Charles Dickens, American Notes (1842)

Long gone are the days when you could simply stroll into the White House.
During high season you must call first for tickets at the **White House Visitor
Center** (1450 Pennsylvania Ave NW ☎208-1631; daily 7.30am–4pm),
housed in the Department of Commerce, a couple of hundred yards southeast of the White House itself. In **high season** (April–Sept and the two weeks
before Christmas), the line snakes right around the outside of the building
by 7am; from the 15th Street edge the wait averages thirty to forty minutes.
You'll be given free tickets (maximum of six per person) for entrance at a
fixed time later that morning; the 4500 tickets available have usually all
gone by 8.30am. The first group of visitors is admitted at 10am: assemble in
good time at the bleacher seats on the Ellipse and wait for your number to
be called, at which point park rangers will lead your group to the gate on
East Executive Avenue. From October to March (apart from the two weeks
before Christmas), when there are fewer visitors, advance tickets are not
required – simply join the line at the gate – though you'll still need to get
there early. **American citizens** can arrange special tours by writing to their
congressperson at least six months in advance. If you get a ticket this way,
you'll be given a more in-depth VIP tour. Other parts of the White House are
accessible on occasion throughout the year. In April and October the **gardens** are opened for afternoon tours; at **Christmas** there are special evening
tours of the festively decorated interior; while on **Easter Monday**, the traditional Easter Egg Roll takes place on the South Lawn, a ceremony introduced during the nineteenth-century administration of Rutherford B. Hayes.
Finally, whenever your visit, it's best to call the visitor center or the White
House tour information line first – public access can be restricted at short
notice. The **flag** flies above the house when the President is in residence.

The visitor center is worth a visit in its own right – preferably after mid-
morning when the lines have disappeared – for its photos and film footage
of First Families and their distinguished guests, and the inaugural portraits, in which a succession of drawn and exhausted presidents hand over
power to their beaming successors.

White House recorded information lines:

Special events ☎456-2200
Tours ☎456-7041
The President's daily schedule ☎456-2343

leader of the new republic was keen to avoid. A stone house, moreover, would give the crucial impression of permanence and stability, though unfortunately for Hoban the city had few skilled masons and no quarries. Advertisements were even placed in European newspapers before Scottish masons from the Potomac region and local slaves were recruited for the work. Progress was slow: the masons downed tools in 1794 in the city's first pay strike, and the house of gray Virginia sandstone wasn't completed in time for George Washington, whose second term in office ended in 1797.

John Adams was the first presidential occupant, moving into the unfinished structure on November 1, 1800: the family was reduced to hanging its laundry in the grand East Room while final touches were put to the mansion. East and west terraces were built during the administration of Thomas Jefferson, who, incidentally, had entered the original design competition under an assumed name; he also installed the first water closets and (true to extravagant form) introduced a French chef to the house. Under James Madison, the interior was redecorated by Capitol architect Benjamin Latrobe, who copied parts of Jefferson's earlier competition design with the defense that Jefferson's ideas were lifted in turn from "old French books, out of which he fishes everything". Occupying British forces burned down the mansion in August 1814, forcing Madison and his wife to flee; when the troops entered, they found the dining table set for forty, the wine poured in the decanters and the food cooked in the kitchen – they tucked in and then torched the building. Hoban was put in charge of its reconstruction after the war and it was again ready for occupation in 1817, but with one significant change: to conceal fire damage to the exterior, the house was painted white. Fitting, as – for obscure reasons – the mansion was already commonly known as the "White House".

Throughout the nineteenth century, the White House was decorated, added to and improved with each new occupant, though occasionally there were unforeseen setbacks: to celebrate his inauguration in 1829, the populist Andrew Jackson invited back the rowdier campaigning elements of his fledgling Democratic Party who, in overexuberant mood, wrecked the place; Jackson was forced to spend the first night of his presidency in a hotel. He atoned by having the first indoor bathroom installed, in 1833; later improvements included gas lights in 1848, central heating and a steam laundry in 1853, the telephone in 1877 and electric lighting in 1891. During the Civil War, troops were briefly stationed in the East Room, cooking their dinner in the ornate fireplace, while the South Lawn was used as a field hospital; at the end of the war in 1865, following his assassination, Lincoln's coffin lay in state in the East Room (the first of seven presidents to be so honored). When a second president, James A. Garfield, lay dying from an assassin's bullet in 1881, enterprising naval engineers cooled his White House bedroom by concocting a prototype air-conditioner from a fan and a box of ice; full air-conditioning didn't follow until 1909.

Many of the house improvements were piecemeal and not until Theodore Roosevelt's administration (1901–09) was any serious attempt made to coordinate structural repairs and the expansion necessary for family and staff. Elevators were added for convenience (Teddy once had a pony called Algonquin brought up in one to delight his sick son*) and an executive West Wing built, which incorporated the President's personal **Oval Office**. The famous **Rose Garden** was planted outside the Oval Office in 1913 on the orders of Ellen Wilson, and became used for ceremonial purposes. An entire residential third floor was added in 1927, an East Wing followed in the 1940s, while World War II saw additions as diverse as an air raid shelter, swimming pool (which the lame FDR used for exercise) and movie theater. Roosevelt, though, refused to entertain the idea of painting the White House black in order to foil enemy bombers. All these works were completed while the presidential family of the day was in residence. This meant that additions and expansions tended to be finished too quickly, so that by 1948 the entire building was on the verge of collapse. Harry Truman – who had already added a poorly received balcony ("Truman's folly") to the familiar south side portico – had to move into nearby Blair House (see p.156) for four years while the structure was stabilized; new foundations were laid, all the rooms were dismantled and a modern steel frame inserted. The Trumans moved back in 1952, since when there have been no significant alterations – unless you count Nixon's bowling alley, Ford's outdoor pool and Clinton's jogging track. Jimmy Carter contented himself with converting part of the house to solar energy.

The interior

Pick up a leaflet at the visitor center and you're set to steer yourself around the **self-guided tour**, which concentrates on the core of rooms on the ground and state (principal) floors. The Oval Office, family apartments and private offices on the second and third floors are off-limits; posted guards make sure you don't stray from the des-

---

* Theodore Roosevelt's children were the last presidential kids permitted to impose themselves on the often stifling formality of the White House, sliding down the banisters, chasing their pet rat and flying squirrel, and interrupting state dinners. They were encouraged by the prank-loving Teddy himself – "the very embodiment of noise", according to Henry James – who was happy to join in most of the rowdy pastimes, whatever the occasion. As the British ambassador at the time wrote home, rather wearily, "We must never forget that the President is seven years old." But even Roosevelt couldn't keep up with his eldest, wildest daughter Alice, later to be a famous Washington socialite. Asked if anything could be done to curb her high spirits, he allegedly replied: "I can be President of the United States, or I can control Alice. I cannot possibly do both."

ignated route. Once inside, your group is allowed to wander one-way through or past half a dozen furnished rooms. It's not exactly conducive to taking your time, though guards will answer questions if they can, and in many rooms you can't get close enough to appreciate the paintings or the furniture; caught up in the flow, most people are outside again well within thirty minutes. As if this weren't enough, there's a paucity of quality fixtures and fittings on display, and not just because much of the best stuff is kept in private quarters. Until Jackie Kennedy and her Fine Arts Committee put a stop to the practice, each incoming Presidential family changed, sold or scrapped the furniture according to individual taste, while outgoing presidents took favorite pieces with them – you're just as likely to come across White House furniture and valuables in places like Dumbarton House or the Woodrow Wilson House.

Visitors enter the East Wing from the ground floor and traipse first past the Federal-style **Library**, paneled in timbers rescued from a mid-nineteenth-century refit and housing 2700 books by American authors. Opposite is the **Vermeil Room**, once a billiard room but now named for its extensive collection of silver gilt; the portraits are of recent First Ladies. Regular tours don't go any further on this floor, while VIP tours head next to the **China Room** – used to display china and glass since Wilson's presidency, and the spot where Annette Bening and Michael Douglas first kiss in the movie *The American President*. Beyond, in the oval **Diplomatic Reception Room**, where panoramic wallpaper depicts American landscapes, new ambassadors present themselves to the President. Eight days after his inauguration in 1933, this was the room from which Franklin D. Roosevelt broadcast the first of his so-called "Fireside Chats", popularizing the New Deal. The adjacent **Map Room** was FDR's private retreat during World War II, where he and Winston Churchill sank into the Chippendale chairs to chart the progress of the war. It's now used as a private reception room for the President: in 1998, Bill Clinton testified from here by video link during the Grand Jury hearings into the Lewinsky affair.

The regular tour moves upstairs to the State Floor, to the **East Room**, the largest in the White House, which has been open to the public since the days of Andrew Jackson. Used in the past for weddings, various lyings-in-state and other major ceremonies, it's on a suitably grand scale for once, with long, yellow drapes, a brown marble fireplace and turn-of-the-century glass chandeliers. Between the fireplaces hangs the one major artwork on general display: Gilbert Stuart's celebrated 1797 portrait of a steely George Washington, rescued from the flames by Dolley Madison when the British burned the White House.

The last rooms on the tour are more intimate in scale. The **Green Room**, its walls lined in silk, was Jefferson's dining room and JFK's favorite in the entire house. Portraits line the walls, Dolley Madison's French candlesticks are on the mantelpiece, and a fine matching

The White House

The Presidency

The executive Power shall be vested in a President of the United States of America.

Article 2, Section 1, Constitution of the United States

The President is simply chief enforcer of American financial interests.

Gore Vidal

When they created the role of **President of the United States**, the delegates at the Constitutional Convention in Philadelphia in 1787 had no intention of replacing a discredited but all-powerful British monarchy with an American version. The federal system of government they devised separated executive, legislative and judicial powers (see p.337 for more) and prescribed precisely the limits of their authority. The President was made chief executive, though one whose role was within, rather than above, the uniquely balanced federal system. Indeed, the relative importance the Founding Fathers placed upon the position is clear from its place in the Constitution – presidential powers were detailed in Article 2, after full discussion of the more fundamental role of Congress in Article 1. At first, the President wasn't even directly **elected**, but chosen instead by an electoral college appointed by the states, the idea being to free the presidency from factional influence. The 12th Amendment (1804) opened up the ballot for President (and Vice-President) to popular election.

The President's place within the Constitution may be strictly defined, but the Constitution has very little to say about the presidency itself. Specific, enumerated **powers** are few – to make treaties, appoint federal officers, act as commander-in-chief, etc – and this may have reflected the fact that the Constitution's authors couldn't agree themselves exactly what the President's role should be. The subsequent elevation of the role is due in part to the succession of extraordinarily able leaders who occupied and enhanced the post in the late eighteenth and nineteenth centuries, from George Washington to Abraham Lincoln. The presidency has subsequently been molded beyond recognition as incumbents have thrust themselves forward as head of state, leader of their particular party and even national symbol – in fact, the almost monarchical figure the Constitution's authors desperately tried to avoid creating.

No longer simply chief executive, the President is the embodiment of American power. Although the President's constitutional powers have barely expanded since the eighteenth century, the real influence available to him has. For example, under the President, the government's work is carried out by fourteen **executive departments**, whose appointed secretaries form the **Cabinet**. This is less a collective policy-making body than an advisory forum. Constitutionally, the President has sole executive responsibility, albeit he is assisted by special advisors, private White House staff and co-opted experts. Incoming presidents routinely change the staff at scores of federal agencies and advisory bodies, from the Post Office to the National Security Council, to ensure political consistency within the new administration (and also, more deep-seatedly, to reward loyal camp followers); these days, something approaching two thousand people work directly or indirectly for the Executive Office of the President, providing great scope for presidential patronage, while another 100,000 non-strategic federal posts are technically within the presidential gift.

green dinner service occupies the cabinet. The room is now often called upon to host receptions, as is the adjacent, oval **Blue Room**, whose ornate French furniture was bought by President Monroe after the 1814 fire. In 1886, Grover Cleveland was married in here, the only time a president has been married in the White House. The **Red Room** is the smallest of the lot, decorated in early nineteenth-century Empire style and sporting attractive inlaid oak doors. Finally, the painted-oak-paneled **State Dining Room** harks back to the East Room in scale and style, and hosts banquets for important guests. At one time, Theodore Roosevelt used to stick his big game trophies in here, though the most enduring item is the inscription engraved on the mantelpiece, part of a quotation from a letter by John Adams to his wife – "May none but honest and wise men ever rule under this roof". Some hope. You then loop back through the cross halls and exit on the north side of the White House, opposite Lafayette Square.

The Ellipse

The **Ellipse** – the large grassy expanse south of the White House – forms an integral part of the city plan's symmetry: due north is the rounded portico and porch of the White House, with the axis of 16th Street beyond; south, the Washington Monument and Jefferson Memorial.

You'll probably have considerable time to kill in summer waiting for your White House tour – bleacher seats and occasional concerts help maintain the spirits, though the same can't be said of the group of nearby sights. On the northern edge of the Ellipse, at E Street opposite the South Lawn, the **Zero Milestone** marks the point from which all distances on US highways are measured. Here, too, is the rather stumpy **National Christmas Tree**, its lamps lit by the President every year to mark the start of the holiday season. If you can stand the excitement, keep to the east (15th St) side of the Ellipse and walk south, passing the simple granite **Monument to the Original Patentees**, commemorating the eighteenth-century landowners who ceded land so that the city could be built; a few yards away a bronze boy scout marks the site of the **Boy Scout Memorial** – the flanking figures entirely unsuited to moral guardianship, at least until they put some clothes on. At the southeastern corner of the Ellipse, the stone **Bulfinch Gatehouse** at Constitution and 15th was one of a pair that once stood at the western entrance to the Capitol grounds. Its partner stands over the Ellipse at Constitution and 17th.

Lafayette Square and around

Originally part of the White House gardens, spick-and-span **Lafayette Square** was known until 1824 as President's Square and lined with the houses of cabinet members and other prominent citizens. Jefferson later turned it into a public park, at the same time as

*Nearest Metro
stations for
Lafayette
Square are
Farragut
North,
Farragut West
or McPherson
Square.*

the White House was opened to visitors, since when it's remained the most attractive approach to the President's house beyond. **Redevelopment** threatened the surrounding houses on several occasions, until the Kennedys took a keen interest in their preservation in the 1960s, saving them from further interference. However, cosmetic changes are imminent in "America's Town Square", as it's referred to rather self-importantly. The banning of traffic on Pennsylvania Avenue outside the White House has prompted proposals to extend the square's parameters, introducing shops, galleries and cafés as part of a fully pedestrianized zone between H Street and the White House. In the meantime, roller-bladers take advantage of the lack of traffic by organizing scratch games of street hockey in front of the President's house.

The square

Regularly patrolled by the police, **Lafayette Square** is one of the safest places to stretch out on the grass in downtown DC. It's also the closest that protesters are allowed to get to the White House; there's a knot of banner-clutching citizens in place most days with various points to make.

For many decades in the nineteenth century, the only statue on show was the central figure of **Andrew Jackson**, astride a rearing horse and doffing his hat – soldiers encamped here during the Civil War used to hang their washing from it – though this was framed this century by the addition of four corner-statues, all of foreign-born revolutionary generals. Most famous of all, in the southeast corner, is the Frenchman, the **Marquis de Lafayette**, who – inspired by the Declaration of Independence and his friendship with Benjamin Franklin, American minister in Paris – raised an army on behalf of the American colonists and was made a US general at the age of nineteen. Later imprisoned in France as a "traitor", he was never abandoned by America. He returned to the States an old man in 1824, a triumphal visit during which he was feted on the Mall and received various honors, including the naming of this square. His statue shows him flanked by French admirals and being handed a sword by a female nude, symbolizing America.

Built by the first surgeon-general in 1826, **Blair House**, in the southwestern corner of Lafayette Square, was where Robert E. Lee was offered – and refused – the command of the Union Army. It has served as the presidential guest house since the 1940s, hosting foreign dignitaries, while both the Truman and Clinton families used it while White House renovations were underway.

Oldest house on the square is **Decatur House** at 748 Jackson Place NW, at the corner with H Street (Tues–Fri 10am–3pm, Sat & Sun noon–4pm; $4; ☎842-0920). Dating from 1819, this red-brick house was built by Benjamin Latrobe (who had already worked on the White House) for Stephen Decatur, another precociously young

American hero who performed with distinction as a navy captain in the War of 1812. As things turned out, Decatur lived here for little more than a year, since he was killed in a duel with one Commodore Barron; the Federal-style first floor, studded with naval memorabilia, is decorated in the fashion of the day. Most of the other period rooms owe their inlaid floors, furnishings and decorative arts to the successive owners' penchant for heavy-handed Victorian style. Short guided tours run throughout the day; pick up tickets around the corner from the gift shop at 1600 H Street.

Walking east along the top of the square, you pass the Renaissance splendor of the **Hay-Adams Hotel** (at H and 16th), fashioned from the former townhouses of statesman John Hay (once President Lincoln's private secretary) and his friend, historian and author Henry Adams. Their adjacent homes were the site of glittering turn-of-the-century soirées, attended by Theodore Roosevelt and his circle, an association which appealed to hotshot society hotel developer Harry Wardman, who jumped at the chance to buy the properties in 1927. Since then, the hotel (which boasted the first air-conditioned dining room in the city) has been at the heart of Washington politicking – Henry Kissinger lunched here regularly, Oliver North did much of his clandestine Iran-Contra fundraising here, while the Clintons stayed over before Bill's first inauguration.

For details of the Hay-Adams, see p.276.

Immediately across 16th Street the tiny, yellow **St John's Church** (Mon–Sat 8am–4pm; free tours after 11am Sun service; ☎347-8766) dates from 1816. Latrobe again did the honors, providing the neighborhood with a handsome domed church in the form of a Greek cross, with appealing half-moon windows in the upper gallery of the intimately proportioned interior. Unsurprisingly, St John's is commonly known as the "Church of the Presidents"; all since Madison have visited – sitting in the special pew (no. 54) reserved for them (the kneeling cushions are embroidered with their names) – and when an incumbent dies in office the bells of St John's ring out across the city.

Old Executive Office and Treasury buildings

The highly ornate, granite **Old Executive Office Building** at 17th Street and Pennsylvania Avenue NW (free tours Sat 9–11.30am; book in advance on ☎395-5895) was built (1871–88) to house the State, War and Navy departments. Its architect, Alfred B. Mullet, claiming to be inspired by the Louvre in Paris, produced an ill-conceived French Empire-style building with hundreds of free-standing columns, extraordinarily tall and thin chimneys, a copper mansard roof, pediments, porticos, and various pedantic stone flourishes. It was never terribly popular – Truman thought it a monstrosity – but schemes to renovate or rebuild came to nothing, mainly because of the expense involved in tackling such a behemoth. These days its gracefully aging facade is loved a little more, and the roomy interior

provides office space for government and White House staff: notoriously, the building was the base of the White House "Plumbers",
Nixon's dirty-tricks campaign team, and hosted several of the infamous tape-recorded Watergate meetings; it was also where the zealously patriotic Colonel Oliver North shredded documents central to
the Iran-Contra affair. You need to call well in advance to tour the
public rooms, ornate with marble-and-gilt, stained glass, tiled floors
and wrought-iron balconies.

It's a similar story if you want to see inside the **Treasury
Building** on the other side of the White House, whose long facade
interrupts the line of Pennsylvania Avenue; ring at least a week in
advance (☎622-0896) to fix a free guided tour (Sat only). Built – or
at least started – in 1836 (by Robert Mills, of Washington Monument
fame), this is commonly judged to be the finest Greek Revival building in the city: its thirty-column colonnade facing 15th Street is particularly impressive. During the Civil War, the basement was
strengthened and food and arms stored in the building, since Lincoln
and his aides were determined to hole up here if the city was ever
attacked. The **statue** at the southern entrance, facing Hamilton
Place, is of **Alexander Hamilton**, first secretary of the Treasury (and
the man on the front of the $10 bill; the Treasury Building itself is on
the back). One of the most highly respected members of
Washington's first administration, Hamilton later died in a duel with
Aaron Burr, Jefferson's Vice-President and scheming Northern
Confederalist, to whom Hamilton was implacably opposed.

The Renwick Gallery

Pennsylvania Ave at 17th St NW ☎357-2700; Farragut West Metro. Daily
10am–5.30pm. Admission free.

The Second Empire flourishes of the Old Executive Office Building
were directly influenced by the earlier, smaller and much more harmonious **Renwick Gallery** of American arts and crafts, which lies
directly opposite across Pennsylvania Avenue. Built by James
Renwick (architect of the Smithsonian Castle) in 1859, the red-brick
building was originally destined to house the private art collection of
financier William Wilson Corcoran. Work was interrupted by the
Civil War, during which the building was requisitioned for use by the
Union Army's quartermaster-general; Corcoran, a man with
Southern sympathies, had left for Europe in 1862, where he stayed
for the entire war. On his return, Corcoran finally got his gallery back
(and, having sued, $125,000 from the government as back rent) and
opened it to the public, but within twenty years his burgeoning collection had outgrown the site – which led to the building of the new
Corcoran Gallery, just a couple of blocks south (see opposite). After
several decades as the US Court of Claims, the now-decrepit building
was saved and restored in the 1960s by the Smithsonian, which uses
it to display selections from the National Museum of American Art.

The building itself is a treat: an inscription above the entrance announces it to be "Dedicated to Art", and the ornate design reaches its apogee in the deep-red **Grand Salon** on the upper floor, a soaring parlor preserved in the style of the 1860s and 1870s – featuring windows draped in striped damask, period portraits (including one of Corcoran), velvet-covered benches, marble-topped cabinets and splendid wood-and-glass display cases taken from the Smithsonian Castle. This was the main picture gallery in Corcoran's time; its lofty dimensions meant that there was no difficulty in converting it into a courtroom and judge's chambers during the Court of Claims' tenure. Opposite, the smaller **Octagon Room** was specifically designed to hold Hiram Powers' notorious nude statue *The Greek Slave* (now in the Corcoran Gallery itself).

Between the two rooms on the same floor are galleries devoted to American crafts, mostly modern jewelry and furniture but also sculpture, ceramics, abstracts and applied art in all its manifestations. The first floor hosts **temporary exhibitions** of contemporary crafts (daily tours by appointment).

South along 17th Street

Having seen the major sights around the White House, you can stroll south down **17th Street** toward Constitution Avenue, calling in at a clutch of buildings along the way. Main port of call is the **Corcoran Gallery of Art**, the city's earliest art gallery, and still among its finest, though there are smaller, more offbeat collections nearby. Keep an eye out, too, for a couple of other notable buildings: the five-story, iron-framed **Winder Building** (604 17th St NW), housing federal government offices, was in 1848 the tallest building in Washington and the first to incorporate central heating; while the white marble headquarters of the **American Red Cross** (between D and E streets) sports Tiffany stained glass in its second-floor assembly rooms.

The Corcoran Gallery of Art

500 17th St NW ☎639-1700; Farragut West Metro. Mon, Wed & Fri–Sun 10am–5pm, Thurs 10am–9pm; tours daily except Tues 10.30am, noon & 12.30pm, Thurs also at 7.30pm. Suggested donation $3.

When the **Corcoran Gallery of Art** shifted premises at the turn of this century, moving from what is now the Renwick Gallery, it took its collection and ideals with it. Ernest Flagg's Beaux-Arts design is a beautiful construction of curving white marble with a green copper roof, the light and airy interior enhanced by a superb double-atrium. When an extension was required in the late 1920s, the trustees, seeking continuity, looked to Charles A. Platt, who had done such a good job with the Freer Gallery of Art.

Along with New York's Met and Boston's Museum of Fine Arts, the Corcoran is one of the three oldest art collections in the US.

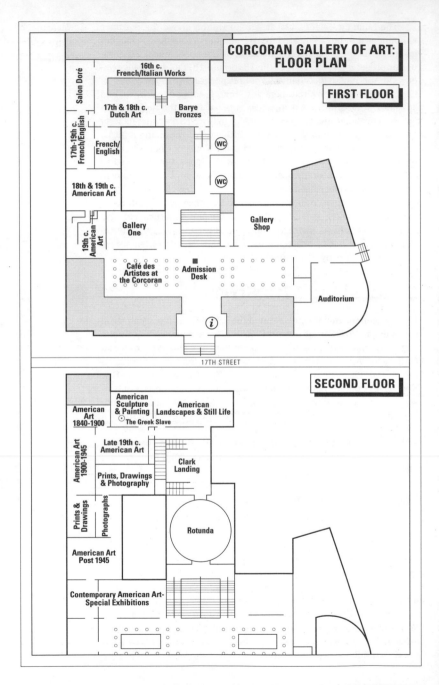

CORCORAN GALLERY OF ART: FLOOR PLAN

FIRST FLOOR

Salon Doré

16th c. French/Italian Works

17th & 18th c. Dutch Art

Barye Bronzes

17th-19th c. French/English

French/English

WC

WC

18th & 19th c. American Art

19th c. American Art

Gallery One

Gallery Shop

Café des Artistes at the Corcoran

Admission Desk

Auditorium

17TH STREET

SECOND FLOOR

American Art 1840-1900

American Sculpture & Painting
The Greek Slave

American Landscapes & Still Life

American Art 1900-1945

Late 19th c. American Art

Clark Landing

Prints, Drawings & Photography

Prints & Drawings

Photographs

Rotunda

American Art Post 1945

Contemporary American Art- Special Exhibitions

The Corcoran Gallery's American holdings are mighty: over three thousand paintings, from colonial to contemporary, alongside American Neoclassical sculpture and forays into modern photography, prints and drawings. Over the years, the permanent collection has expanded considerably to include European works (particularly seventeenth-century Dutch and nineteenth-century French), Greek antiquities and even medieval tapestries. Benefactors continue to bestow impressive gifts: in recent years Dr Armand Hammer has donated a large collection of Daumier lithographs, and there's been an important bequest by Olga Hirshorn (wife of Joseph of the eponymous gallery) of seven hundred works by two hundred nineteenth- and twentieth-century artists and sculptors, from Picasso to Calder.

Works from the permanent collection are rotated throughout the year and other pieces are sent out on tour; not everything mentioned below will be on display at any one time. Details of changing exhibitions are available at the **information desk**, inside the main entrance, which is also where you sign up for the **guided tours** of the permanent collection. The **gallery shop** has one of the city's better collections of posters, cards and books. The **café** (daily except Tues 11am–4.30pm, Thurs until 8.30pm) is decent too, especially during the gospel brunch (Sun 11am–2pm; $19), when the songs ring out through the gallery.

European art

The gallery's collection of **European art** is a very mixed bag, mainly comprising the 1925 bequest of Senator William A. Clark, an industrialist with more money than discretion. That's not to say there aren't some splendid pieces on display; rather that there's little overall cohesion, certainly in a gallery otherwise devoted to American art. Corcoran himself, though, had already blurred the edges of his collection by commissioning 120 animal bronzes by French sculptor **Antoine-Louis Barye** (1796–1875), a selection of which are usually on display. These are graphic representations, often of snarling, fighting animals: a horse attacked by a lion, a python crushing a gazelle.

Some of the most familiar names hang in the so-called **Clark Landing**, a two-tier, wood-paneled gallery accessed from the Rotunda on the second floor. Here, stacked on top of each other in nineteenth-century fashion, are paintings by Degas, Renoir, Monet and Pissarro. Perhaps the most prominent of the earlier **French and English** paintings of the seventeenth to nineteenth centuries are the sympathetic Thomas Gainsborough portraits of Lord and Lady Dunstanville. The only other European exhibits of real interest are the selection of sixteenth-century **French and Italian** works, including some outstanding Italian majolica plates depicting mythological scenes and two large, allegorical wool-and-silk French tapestries (1506), representing contemporaneous political and historical events.

However, the main European interest is not painting, but the corner room on the first floor known as the **Salon Doré** (Gilded Room), which originally formed part of an eighteenth-century Parisian home, the Hôtel de Clermont. Clark bought the entire room, intending to install it in his New York mansion: it came to the Corcoran after his death, where it now stands as a supreme example of French design. Framed mirrors (flanked by medallion-holding cherubs) make it seem larger than it actually is; the floor-to-ceiling hand-carved wood-paneling, gold-leaf decor and ceiling murals are perfectly judged.

American art

The bulk of the **American art** is usually displayed on the second floor. Approach through the Rotunda and Clark Landing and you'll be presented with a preliminary burst of minor paintings by early American artists like Gilbert Stuart, Thomas Cole, George Innes and Benjamin West. One piece with real spark is Rembrandt Peale's imperious, equestrian *Washington Before Yorktown* (1824), showing the general in the hours before the decisive battle for independence.

The gallery possesses a fine collection of **landscapes**, starting with the expansive *Niagara* (1857) by Frederic Edwin Church and Albert Bierstadt's splendid *The Last of the Buffalo* (1889), both masterpieces of immense scale. While Church concerned himself with the power of nature, Bierstadt here celebrated human endeavor in the natural world, portraying the Native American braves, pursuing buffalo so numerous they darken the plain in their thousands. In marked contrast, Thomas Cole's *The Return* (1837), a mythical medieval scene of an injured knight returning to a priory glowing in the evening light, has little to do with America, though it does display the Hudson River School theme of ethereal natural beauty. An interesting historical note is provided by artist-cum-inventor Samuel F.B. Morse's *The Old House of Representatives* (1822), which the artist finished in a studio at the US Capitol so that he could observe his subjects at work. For all his efforts, he failed to convey any sense of the urgency of debate and Morse lost money when he exhibited the painting – which led him to conclude he'd be better off sticking with inventing.

One room is devoted to nineteenth-century portraiture, with formal studies by renowned artists like John Trumbull (who painted the Capitol murals) and Charles Bird King. Most prominent, though, are the presidential portraits by **George Peter Alexander Healy**, commissioned by Congress in 1857 for display in the White House: van Buren, Tyler, Polk, Taylor, Arthur and a highly sympathetic Lincoln. This seems an odd room in which to display the gallery's most notorious piece of sculpture, **Hiram Powers'** *The Greek Slave* (1846), originally on show in the Renwick Gallery. Her manacled hands and simple nudity so outraged the sensibilities of contemporary critics

There are more Healy presidential portraits in the National Portrait Gallery.

that women visitors were prevented from viewing the statue while there were men in the room.

Moving into **late nineteenth-century** art, the gallery presents changing selections of work by John Singer Sargent, Thomas Eakins and Mary Cassatt among others. Society portraitist Sargent also produced one of the gallery's most loved pieces – the startling landscape of crags and boulders of *Simplon Pass* (1911). Few works, however, are as robust as Winslow Homer's depiction of sea folk: the brawny arms of the woman swathed in fishing nets in *A Light on the Sea* (1897) suggest the realities of her life better than any storm-tossed fishing scene. Working women are rare subjects indeed in works of this period, while American blacks were hardly ever considered an enlightening contemporary subject – exceptions include Richard Norris Brooke's beautifully lit family on the receiving end of *A Pastoral Visit* (1881). At the other end of the social scale, genre scenes of genteel domesticity are a popular Corcoran trait, seen in works by Edmund Charles Tarbell, Frank Weston Benson, William Paxton and others.

Pre-World War II paintings include works by Childe Hassam, George Bellows, Rockwell Kent, Thomas Hart Benton and, of course, Edward Hopper, whose yachting picture *Ground Swell* (1939) adds a real splash of color while providing a mere hint of menace. Meanwhile, realists Raphael Soyer (*Waiting Room*, 1940) and Ross Moffett (*Provincetown Wharf*, 1935) show an interest instead in the more mundane minutiae of daily working life. The remainder of the second-floor rooms are devoted to changing selections of prints, drawings and photographs from the permanent collection, as well as special exhibitions. Depending on space, **postwar and contemporary** American art gets a look-in too, and you can expect examples from all the big names, including Lichtenstein, Warhol and de Kooning.

Memorial Continental Hall: Daughters of the American Revolution

1776 D St NW ☎879-3239; Farragut West Metro. Mon–Fri 10am–4pm, Sun 1–5pm; tours Mon–Fri 10am–2.30pm, Sun 1–5pm; closed two weeks in April. Admission free.

The **National Society of the Daughters of the American Revolution** (DAR) has had its headquarters in Washington for over a century. Founded in 1890, membership of this thoroughly patriotic (if unswervingly conservative) organization is open to women who can prove descent from an ancestor (male or female) who served the American cause during the Revolution. Fueled by the motto "God, Home and Country", it busies itself with earnestly non-political good-citizen and educational programs, including one designed to promote "correct flag usage" throughout America: the Stars and Stripes adorning the rostrums in the Senate and the House in the US Capitol are gifts from the DAR, just two of over 100,000 given away since 1909.

The organization's original meeting place was the 1905 Beaux-Arts **Memorial Continental Hall**, facing 17th Street, whose main chamber hosted the world's first disarmament conference in 1921. Delegates now meet for their annual congress (the week of April 19, anniversary of the Battle of Lexington) in the massive adjoining **Constitution Hall** on 18th Street, designed with typical exuberance by John Russell Pope in 1929, but which you're unlikely to see unless your visit coincides with a concert (see p.307). It's one of the finest auditoriums in the city (indeed, until the Kennedy Center was built, the hall was the home of the National Symphony Orchestra), so it came as no surprise that when the peerless black contralto **Marian Anderson** (1902–93) was invited to sing in Washington in 1939, she was originally booked to appear here. What was shocking was that a racially hidebound DAR refused to allow her to perform at the hall: Eleanor Roosevelt resigned from the organization in outrage and Anderson gave her concert instead on Easter Sunday at the Lincoln Memorial to a rapt crowd of 75,000.

Visitors to the Memorial Continental Hall (entrance on D St) are shown first into the **gallery**, a hodge-podge of embroidered samplers and quilts, silverware, toys, kitchenware, glass, crockery and earthenware – in fact just about anything the daughters have managed to lay their hands on over the years. Although exhibits change, there's usually a particularly fine selection of ceramics, popular in the Revolutionary and Federal periods (from which most of the collection dates). On request, one of the docents will lead you through the rest of the building, starting off in the 125,000-volume genealogical **library** – once the main meeting hall, but now open to DAR members and the public ($5 a day) keen to bone up on such topics as *The History of Milwaukee* (in eight alarmingly large volumes) or *The Genealogy of the Witherspoon Family*.

What they're most proud of, however, are the **State Rooms**, a collection of no fewer than 33 period salons, mainly decorated with pre-1850 furnishings, each representing a different state. Few are of any historical or architectural merit, though occasionally there's a glimmer of relief: the New England room, containing a supposedly original lacquered wooden tea chest retrieved from Boston harbor after the Tea Party in 1773; the Californian adobe house interior; or the New Jersey room whose entire furnishings, paneling and furniture were fashioned from the wreck of a British frigate sunk off the coast during the Revolutionary War – the overly elaborate chandelier was made from the melted-down anchor.

Organization of American States Building

17th St at Constitution Ave NW ☎458-3000. Farragut West Metro. Mon–Fri 9am–5.30pm. Admission free.

Founded in 1890 "to strengthen the peace and security of the continent", the **Organization of American States** (OAS) is the world's oldest regional organization, with 35 member states from Antigua to Venezuela. Its headquarters occupy one of the more charming buildings in the city, a squat, white Spanish Colonial mansion built in 1910 and facing onto the Ellipse. From the main entrance on 17th Street – fronted by a gaunt statue of Queen Isabella of Spain, who sent Columbus on his New World voyage – you pass through fanciful iron gates to a cloistered lobby. The decor here turns almost to whimsy, with a fountain and tropical trees reaching to the wooden eaves and stone frieze above. Beyond the lobby, it's usually possible to catch temporary exhibitions of Latin American art; check in at the reception desk. Then climb upstairs, walk through the gallery of national flags and busts of OAS founder members, and take a peek in the grand Hall of the Americas.

A path leads from the Constitution Avenue side of the building through the so-called **Aztec Garden** to the smaller building behind. The **Art Museum of the Americas** – officially at 201 18th St NW (Tues–Sun 10am–5pm; free; ☎458-6016) – shows changing exhibits of Central and South American art, but again it's the interior that catches the eye. In the main brick-floored gallery, the walls are lined with lively Latin American ceramics reaching to a wood-beamed roof.

Foggy Bottom

Together with Georgetown, **FOGGY BOTTOM** – south of Pennsylvania Avenue to Constitution Avenue, between 17th and 25th streets – forms one of the oldest parts of DC. Settled as early as the mid-eighteenth century, the thriving town on the shores of the Potomac (which reached further north in those days) was known variously as Hamburg or Funkstown, after its German landlord Jacob Funk. Fashionable houses were built on the higher ground above today's E Street, though down by the river, in what is now West Potomac Park, it was a different story: filthy industries emptied effluents into the Potomac and the city canal, while workers' housing was erected on the low-lying malarial marshlands, blighted by plagues of rats, rampant poison ivy and winter mud and fog. It's not hard to see how the popular name originated.

The poor, predominantly black, neighborhood changed radically once the marshlands were drained in the late 1800s. Families and industries were displaced by the new West Potomac Park; the neighborhood's southern limit was now defined by the grand Constitution Avenue, which replaced the filled-in city canal. The smarter streets to the north formed the backdrop for a series of **federal and institutional organizations** which moved in during the years on either side of World War II, as the federal workforce rapidly expanded. Early city plans had made little provision for an influx of government support staff – in 1802, there were only 291 federal employees; by the 1970s the total number of civilians employed by the US government had risen to over two million, and entire districts like Foggy Bottom were appropriated to house DC's burgeoning share.

For Foggy Bottom listings, see the following pages: accommodation p.279; cafés p.285; restaurants p.295; nightlife p.304.

The cultural activities at the **Kennedy Center** and the various offices and institutions rather set the white-collar tone, but you can visit enough of the buildings to make a walk through the neighborhood worthwhile. The nearest Metro is **Foggy Bottom-GWU**, which is handy for George Washington University, Washington Circle and the Kennedy Center but is half a dozen blocks and fifteen minutes from Constitution Avenue. Consider, instead, approaching from the east, after touring the White House.

Constitution Avenue

From the OAS Building (see p.164) at the corner of 17th Street, **Constitution Avenue** – known as B Street until the 1930s – presents an attractive line of buildings framed by the greenery of Constitution Gardens across the way. First of any distinction is the enormous, eagle-fronted **Federal Reserve Building** of 1937, between 20th and 21st streets (Mon–Fri 11am–2pm; ☎452-3326), built by Paul Cret, who was also responsible for the OAS and the Folger Shakespeare Library on Capitol Hill. It's the headquarters of the Federal Reserve System – the organization which controls the money supply, issues government securities and is responsible for the country's gold reserves. If you want to know any more than that, weekly tours of the building are available, though you can walk in during the week to check out the special art exhibitions.

The Tourmobile bus runs along Constitution Avenue and up 23rd Street to the Kennedy Center.

The **National Academy of Sciences** (Mon–Fri 8am–5pm; free; ☎334-2000) is next, created by Congress in 1863 to provide the nation with independent, objective scientific advice. Again, there's exhibition space inside and the academy also hosts chamber recitals (see p.313). The style here is Neoclassical, the facade adorned with Greek inscriptions, but its cold lines are tempered by a grove of elm and holly trees at the southwest (22nd St) corner, in which sits a large bronze **statue of Albert Einstein**, by Robert Berks. Erected to commemorate the centenary of his birth, a rumpled Einstein lounges on a granite bench with the universe (in the shape of a galaxy map) at his feet; in his hand is a piece of paper inscribed with the famous formula ($E=mc^2$) from his Theory of Relativity. Finally, the corner plot of the avenue, at 23rd Street, is occupied by the building of the **American Pharmaceutical Association**, a severe Beaux-Arts construction by John Russell Pope, completed in 1933.

Department of State

Between 21st and 23rd streets NW, at C St ☎647-3241; Farragut West Metro. Tours by appointment only Mon–Fri 9.30am, 10.30am & 2.45pm. Reserve several weeks in advance. Admission free.

The **Department of State** received its own premises in 1960, following its move out of the Old Executive Office Building, and handsome they are too – the long, white, unblemished building occupying two entire blocks in the southwest corner of Foggy Bottom. The nation's oldest and most senior cabinet agency, established as early as 1789, the State Department is effectively the federal foreign office. It's also notoriously circumspect, and it's a wonder that visitors are allowed in at all. As it is, it's all but impossible for foreign tourists, as the hour-long tours must be booked several weeks in advance (up to two months in summer) – effort that is rewarded by a glimpse of one of the capital's more overblown interiors. During the 1960s, many of the rooms were redecorated and refurnished to provide a series of chambers suitable for the reception of diplomats and visiting heads of state. In came a wealth of eighteenth- and nineteenth-century paintings and furniture – including the desk on which the Treaty of Paris was signed, which ended the War of Independence.

Department of the Interior

Foggy Bottom-GWU Metro. C St NW, between 18th and 19th streets ☎208-4743. Mon–Fri 8.30am–4.30pm; call in advance for tours of the building and murals. Admission free.

For a walk-in tour of a government department, head further east down C Street to the **Department of the Interior**, the nation's principal conservation agency. One of the earliest federal departments to take up residence in Foggy Bottom, the Interior Department moved into Waddy Butler Wood's granite, square-columned building in 1937. Inside, grand WPA-era murals enliven the walls, including one commemorating Marian Anderson's 1939 concert at the Lincoln Memorial (see p.164).

Present ID at the reception desk and you'll be directed to the **Department of the Interior Museum**, a little-visited nook which throws some light on the various agencies that come under the department's auspices – notably fish, wildlife and geological services, the Bureau of Land Management and, most contentiously, the Bureau of Indian Affairs. The wood-paneled museum, opened in 1938, is very much of its time: then over 100,000 people a year toured its dioramas and exhibits; now you'll be on your own as you puzzle over fossil and mineral samples and examine stuffed bison heads, old saddles and paintings by nineteenth-century surveyors of the West. Like the National Museum of Natural History, the museum has trouble with its ethnographic content, particularly its coverage of the work of the Bureau of Indian Affairs which, it claims, holds Native American property – "lands, forests, minerals, funds – in trust for the Indian owners". Like the natural history museum, however, the entire collection is being reviewed, so in the near future you can expect revitalized, revisionist, and less rose-tinted displays. For now, probably the most arresting collection is that of contemporary Native American paintings and crafts, much of it by women artists. There's more of this, for sale this time, across the hall in the gift shop.

Inside the Department, the National Park Service information office (Mon–Fri 9am–5pm) has free leaflets about every NPS park, museum and monument in the country – in DC, all the major memorials along the Mall.

The Octagon

1799 New York Ave NW ☎638-3105; Farragut West Metro. Tues–Sun 10am–4pm. Admission $3.

When Virginian plantation owner John Tayloe had his Washington townhouse built in 1800, he picked a prime corner plot just two blocks away from the new President's Mansion. In those days the **Octagon**, as it became known, was set amid fields and flanked by a line of fir trees. Today, dwarfed by the office buildings behind, it still serves as a fine example of the type of private mansion that once characterized the neighborhood. Tayloe, a friend of George Washington, was so rich and well-connected that he could afford to spend the colossal sum of $35,000 on his house, engaging the services of William Thornton, winner of the competition to design the US Capitol.

The **War of 1812** guaranteed the house its place in history. Spared the bonfire that destroyed the White House – possibly because the French ambassador was in residence at the time – the Octagon was offered to the Madisons, who had been forced to flee the city. For six months in 1814–15, President Madison conducted the business of government from its rooms; on February 17, 1815, the Treaty of Ghent, making peace with Britain, was signed in the study (on a table still kept in the house). For much of the latter part of the nineteenth century, the Octagon was left to deteriorate, but at the turn of this century it was bought by the American Institute of Architects (AIA), which used it as its headquarters until 1973. The AIA – now ensconced in modern premises to the rear – still maintains the Octagon, which is open as both a historic house and **museum of architecture**, with changing exhibitions devoted to architecture, decorative arts and city history.

The **building** itself is not, in fact, an octagon – forced into an acute street corner, it has only six sides; the name was mis-assigned by the Tayloes when it was built. A rather simple brick exterior hides an example of period American Federal architecture unsurpassed in the city. The circular entry hall sports its original marble floor, while beyond, a swirling, oval staircase climbs up three stories; the house had two master bedrooms and five more for the Tayloe's fifteen children, most of which are now used as gallery space. In the dining and drawing rooms, period furnishings reveal how the house would have looked – light, with high ceilings, delicate plaster cornicing and Chippendale accompaniments. The two portraits in the dining room are of the architect and the owner; the beautifully carved stone mantel in the drawing room is an original, signed and dated 1799.

GWU to Washington Circle

The L'Enfant city plan allowed for the building of a university in the Foggy Bottom district, and it was certainly a development that

Washington himself was keen on; he even left money in his will to endow an educational establishment. A Baptist college founded by an Act of Congress in 1821 was the precursor of today's **George Washington University** (GWU), which moved into the neighborhood in 1912, since when it's played a crucial role in the city's development, buying up townhouses and erecting new buildings on such a scale as to make it the second biggest landholder in DC after the federal government. Famous alumni include Jacqueline Kennedy Onassis (who gets a building named after her), J. Edgar Hoover, General Colin Powell and crime author (and Harry's daughter) Margaret Truman. The main campus spreads over several city blocks between F, 20th and 24th streets and Pennsylvania Avenue; there's an information desk in the **Academic Center**, 801 22nd St NW (Jan–April & Aug–Oct Mon–Fri 9am–5pm, Sat 10am–3pm; ☎994-6602), on the H Street side. You can pick up a map of the campus here and ask about the occasional student-led historic **walking tours** of the neighborhood.

Foggy Bottom

GWU's main entertainment hall is the Lisner Auditorium; see p.307 and p.313 for details.

Although the student presence certainly enlivens the district, few of the university buildings are worth more than a passing glance; some people have kind words for the **Law Library** (716 20th St NW), which at least makes an attempt to fit in with its surroundings. This backs onto perhaps the nicest part of the campus, **University Yard** (between G and H, and 20th and 21st), a green, rose-planted park surrounded by Colonial Revival buildings; the statue of George Washington here is yet another copy of the famous Houdon image.

Nearby, on the southeast corner of 20th and G, the red-brick Gothic, Lutheran **United Church**, built in 1889 for the descendants of the neighborhood's Germanic immigrants, provides a solitary reminder of Foggy Bottom's antecedents. If you're heading back toward the White House, you may as well stick with G Street, which passes the concrete chicken-coop buildings of the twin peaks of international capitalism – the **International Monetary Fund** and, in the next block, the **World Bank**. For a glimpse of how modern development has encroached completely upon the remaining nineteenth-century pockets of Foggy Bottom, head instead up 20th Street to Pennsylvania Avenue. Between 20th and 21st, the **2000 Pennsylvania Avenue** complex of offices, shops and cafés preserves the original pastel-colored facades of a row of townhouses.

West of the university, en route to Foggy Bottom-GWU Metro station, you can swing by **St Mary's Church**, at 730 23rd Street, between G and H (daily 9.30am–3pm), the first black episcopal church in DC. Established in 1886, the church was paid for by a wealthy band of local citizens who stumped up $15,000 to hire the services of none other than James Renwick (of the Smithsonian Castle and Renwick Gallery), whose hand is clear in the church's careful Gothic proportions. Two blocks west, **25th Street** (north of H) gives a hint of Foggy

Bottom's historic charms with a carefully preserved run of attractive nineteenth-century brick houses picked out in pastels. The most interesting are those in **Snow Court** (off 25th, between I and K), the district's only surviving interior alley, where the houses are a bare twelve-feet wide – in the 1880s each one probably housed ten people; nowadays they change hands for a fortune.

One block north of the Metro, the northern limit of Foggy Bottom is marked by **Washington Circle**, L'Enfant's radial point for the major thoroughfares of Pennsylvania and New Hampshire avenues and K Street. In its center sits Clark Mills' equestrian statue of George Washington, erected at the outbreak of the Civil War and looking toward the White House and Capitol; not a thing of great splendor it's true, but quite how it aroused the particular ire of Anthony Trollope is a mystery. He thought it "by far the worst" equestrian statue he had ever seen, claiming "the horse is most absurd, but the man sitting on the horse is manifestly drunk".

Watergate

The Watergate Complex is named for the flight of steps behind the Lincoln Memorial, to the south, which lead down to the Potomac.

If there's a building that defines modern, political Washington, it's not the White House or the Capitol but the **Watergate Complex**, 25th Street NW, by Virginia Avenue, which gave its name to the most noxious political scandal ever to rock the country. This unassuming curving, Italian-designed mid-1960s residential and commercial complex has always been a much sought-after address, both for various foreign embassies and for city top-brass: the Doles and Caspar Weinberger have maintained apartments here for years, while a young White House intern called Monica Lewinsky also lived here before scandal forced her from DC. In 1972, its sixth floor housed the headquarters of the Democratic National Committee, the burglary of which led, two years later, to the resignation of a president.

The Watergate story

I lied to protect the Presidency – until it became clear that the President was frantically trying to preserve himself, not his high office.

Howard Hunt, Watergate burglar

The burglars who broke into the headquarters of the Democratic National Committee at the Watergate were in effect breaking into the home of every citizen of the United States. And . . . what they were seeking to steal was . . . their most precious heritage, the right to vote in a free election.

Sam Ervin, chairman of Senate Investigating Committee

The 1972 presidential election campaign was well underway when five men were arrested at the Watergate Complex on June 17.

Richard Nixon, running for re-election against the Democratic challenger Governor George McGovern, was determined to win a second term, elevating the election race into a moral, almost personal, struggle against encroaching liberal forces, who, crucially, were pushing the anti-Vietnam War message to the top of the political agenda.

After being spotted by a security guard on his rounds, the five men were apprehended in the offices of the Democratic National Committee in the act of tapping the phone of Lawrence O'Brien, the national party chairman. Once arraigned in court, it became clear that these were no ordinary burglars: one, **James McCord**, worked directly for the Committee to Re-Elect the President (known, delightfully, as **CREEP**), all had CIA connections, and some were later linked to documents which suggested that their escapade had been sanctioned by White House staffer **Howard Hunt** and election campaign attorney **Gordon Liddy**. To anyone who cared to look, the connections went further still: at the White House, Hunt worked for Charles Colson, Nixon's special counsel; while McCord's direct superior was the head of CREEP, John Mitchell, who also happened to be Attorney General of the United States.

Amazingly, at least in retrospect, hardly anyone looked further. The burglars, together with Hunt and Liddy, were indicted in September 1972 but continued to refuse to provide any collaborative detail. The Democrats, none more so than McGovern, complained loudly about dirty tricks, but the White House officially denied any knowledge. In the election in November, Nixon won a **landslide**, carrying 49 out of the 50 states (only Massachusetts and, ironically, the District of Columbia, went for McGovern).

From such commanding heights, it was remarkable how quickly things unraveled. Initially the only people asking questions were *Washington Post* reporters **Bob Woodward** and **Carl Bernstein**. As the months went by, and aided by a source known to Woodward only as "Deep Throat", the pair uncovered irregularities in the Republican campaign, many of which had tantalizingly close, but unprovable, links with the Watergate burglary. To the FBI's annoyance, the stories often relied on verbatim accounts of the FBI's own investigations – someone, somewhere, was leaking information. However, it still proved difficult to generate much interest outside Washington in the matter, and the story would probably have been forgotten but for the impetus provided by the trial of the defendants. All pleaded guilty to burglary, but before sentencing in January 1973 the judge made it clear that he didn't believe that the men acted alone; long sentences were threatened. Rather than face jail, some defendants began to talk, including James McCord, who not only implicated senior officials like John Mitchell for the first time but also claimed that secret CREEP funds had been used to finance an anti-Democrat smear campaign, which employed so-called "plumbers" – like the burglars – to work against domestic "enemies". This was precisely what Woodward and Bernstein had been trying to prove for months. As pressure on the administration for answers grew, the Senate established a **special investigating committee** under Sam Ervin and appointed a special prosecutor, Archibald Cox. The trail led ever closer to the White House. In a desperate damage limitation exercise, Nixon's own counsel, John Dean, was sacked and the resignations accepted of White House Chief of Staff Robert Haldeman and domestic affairs advisor John Erlichman; all, it seemed, were involved in planning the burglary.

In June 1973, the **Watergate hearings**, now broadcast on national television, began to undermine Nixon's steadfast denial of any involvement. The Watergate burglars had been promised clemency and cash by the White House if they remained silent, it transpired; the CIA had leaned on the FBI to prevent any further investigations; illegal wiretaps, dirty tricks campaigns and unlawful campaign contributions appeared to be commonplace. The President continued to stand aloof from the charges, but was finally dragged down by the revelation that he himself had routinely bugged offices in the White House and elsewhere, taping conversations which pertained to Watergate. It quickly became a matter of what the President knew, and when he knew it. The tapes were subpoenaed as evidence by Cox and the Senate committee, but Nixon refused to release them, citing his presidential duty to protect executive privilege. Soon after, he engineered the sacking of Cox, a move which led to the convening of the House Judiciary Committee, the body charged with preparing bills of impeachment – in this case, against the President for refusing to comply with a subpoena. To deflect mounting suspicion Nixon finally handed over edited transcripts of the tapes in April 1974; despite the erasure of eighteen minutes of conversation, rather than clearing Nixon of any involvement, the "smoking gun" transcripts simply dragged him further in. The President, it seemed, at least knew about the cover-up, and there was clear evidence of wrongdoing by key government and White House personnel. A grand jury indicted Mitchell, Haldeman, Erlichman, Dean and others for specific offenses, while the House Judiciary Committee drew up a bill of **impeachment** against Nixon for committing "high crimes and misdemeanors".

On August 5, 1974, the Supreme Court ordered Nixon to hand over the tapes themselves. These proved conclusively that he and his advisors had known about the Watergate burglary within days and had devised a strategy of bribes and the destruction of evidence to cover up White House and CREEP involvement. The President, despite his protestations, had lied to the people, and it was inevitable that he should face impeachment. Urged on by senior Republican senators, on August 8, 1974, Richard Milhous Nixon became the first President to **resign**. Combative to the end, he made no acknowledgment of guilt, suggesting instead that he had simply made errors of judgment.

Nixon was replaced by his deputy, **Gerald Ford**, but though the President changed, little else did. Secretary of State Henry Kissinger – architect of the bombing of Laos and Cambodia and the My Lai massacre, campaigns hidden from the American public – kept his job, while Alexander Haig, a key figure in withholding and doctoring the Watergate tapes, was promoted to become head of NATO. To top it all, Ford formally pardoned Nixon with unseemly haste, allowing him to live out his retirement without controversy in California. In a bizarre twist, Richard Nixon slowly rehabilitated himself in the eyes of the political establishment and even in the eyes of the press; when he died in 1995 there was a full turn-out at his funeral by leaders of all political hues.

The Kennedy Center

2700 F St NW, at Rock Creek Parkway ☎467-4600; Foggy Bottom-GWU Metro. Daily 10am–midnight; box office Mon–Sat 10am–9pm, Sun noon–9pm; tours daily 10am–1pm. Admission free.

Although government departments have been based in the capital for two centuries, it wasn't until 1971 that Washington got its national cultural center, a $78-million white marble monster designed by Edward Durrell Stone. Though the building has its detractors – travel writer Jan Morris dismissed it as "a cross between a Nazi exhibition and a more than usually ambitious hairdresser" – the **John F. Kennedy Center for the Performing Arts**, to give it its full title, continues to be the city's foremost cultural outlet. The National Symphony Orchestra, Washington Opera and the American Film Institute have their homes here, and there are four main auditoriums, various exhibition halls, and a clutch of restaurants and bars.

For details of performances at the Kennedy Center, see Chapter 16.

There's an **information desk** on your way in and you're free to wander around; provided there's no performance or rehearsal taking place, you should also be able to take a look inside the theaters and concert halls (most are open to visitors 10am–1pm). Free 45-minute **guided tours** depart daily from Level A (beneath the Opera House).

The **Grand Foyer** itself is some sight: 630ft long and 60ft high, it's lit by gargantuan crystal chandeliers and features a seven-foot-high bronze bust of JFK in the moon-rock-pimple style favored by sculptor Robert Berks. You can also drop by the **Hall of States** (flags of the states hung in the order they entered the Union) and **Hall of Nations** (flags of nations recognized by the US); while each of the theaters and concert halls has its own catalog of artworks, from the Matisse tapestries outside the Opera House or the Barbara Hepworth sculpture in the Concert Hall to the Felix de Welden bronze bust of Eisenhower above the lobby of the Eisenhower Theater.

The **Roof Terrace Level** holds the **Performing Arts Library** of scripts, performance information and recordings (Tues–Fri 11am–8.30pm, Sat 10am–6pm) and the center's eating places: the *Encore Café* and the much pricier *Roof Terrace Restaurant*. While you're up here, step out onto the terrace itself for scintillating views across the Potomac to Theodore Roosevelt Island, and north to Georgetown and the National Cathedral.

Chapter 6

Old Downtown and Federal Triangle

T he land between the Capitol and the White House, north of the Mall, was the only part of nineteenth-century Washington that resembled anything like a city. A convenient **downtown** developed in the diamond formed by Pennsylvania, New York, Massachusetts and Indiana avenues, where just a few blocks' walk from the seats of legislative or executive power, fashionable stores and restaurants existed alongside printing presses and shoeshine stalls, oyster sellers and market traders. Entertainment was provided by a series of popular theaters – not least Ford's Theater, where President Lincoln was shot dead as he relaxed just days after the end of the Civil War (see p.204).

By the 1960s, downtown was a shambling, low-rent neighborhood, later to be badly affected by the riots of 1968 following the assassination of Dr Martin Luther King Jr. As established businesses fled to the developing area north of the White House, the old neighborhood eventually became known, rather infelicitously, as **Old Downtown** (to distinguish it from the mushrooming buildings of New Downtown – see p.209).

In the nineteenth century, **Pennsylvania Avenue** marked the southern limits of civilized Washington society; the shops on its north side were as far as those of genteel sensibilities would venture. The area was given a new lease of life in the 1930s with the construction of the majestic buildings of **Federal Triangle**, though it wasn't until the 1980s that the avenue itself was finally rescued from years of neglect. An enormous amount of money has been pumped into renovation, especially in the easternmost area (south of G St, between 3rd and 12th), now being trumpeted by the authorities as the **Penn Quarter** – grafting a Left-Bank-like swatch of delis, restaurants, galleries and landscaping onto the existing historic buildings and cleaned-up streets. Just to the north of here, the opening of the **MCI Center** (at 7th and F) has sparked another revitalization – at present, this part of downtown DC is changing faster than any other.

For Old Downtown listings, see the following pages: accommodation p.278; cafés p.284; restaurants p.293; nightlife p.302.

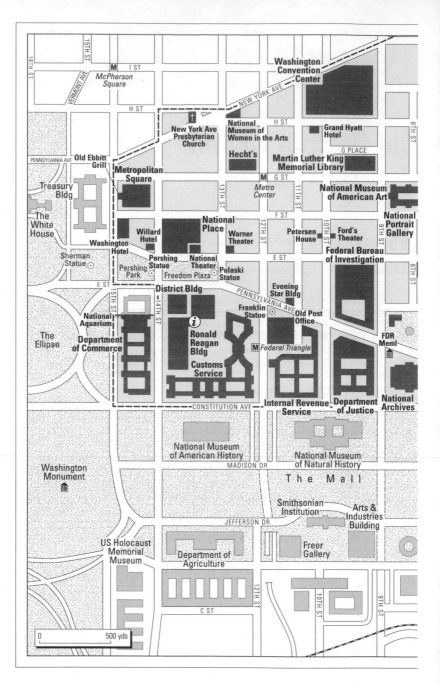

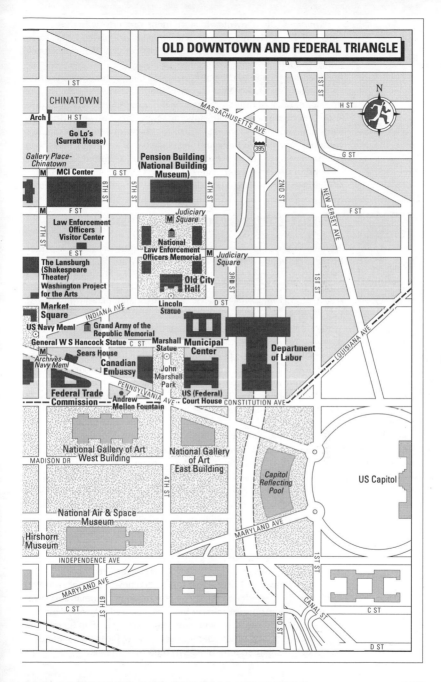

OLD DOWNTOWN AND FEDERAL TRIANGLE

Tours of Old Downtown start quite properly with the grand length of Pennsylvania Avenue and its landmark sights – the **Navy Memorial, FBI Building, Old Post Office** and **Willard Hotel**. Adjacent Federal Triangle has less to show, since so many of the buildings are closed to the public, save for the outstanding collection of manuscripts in the **National Archives**. Elsewhere, many of the grander municipal buildings have been converted into fine museums – the exceptional Pension Building, now the **National Building Museum**, and the Old Patent Office, split between the Smithsonian's **National Portrait Gallery** and the **National Museum of American Art**. Other sights include **Ford's Theater** and a unique **Museum of Women in the Arts**, from where it's only a short stroll to diminutive **Chinatown**, where you can lunch cheaply on noodles and *dim sum*.

Along Pennsylvania Avenue

A glance at the map shows **Pennsylvania Avenue** to be the backbone of the city, connecting the Capitol to the White House and, at its extremities, Georgetown to the Anacostia River. In its early days it was the only avenue in the city paved with federal funds, yet although it was the obvious focus for the new city's commercial life, it was hampered by the piecemeal development taking place all around. While fashionable shops traded along the north side of Pennsylvania Avenue, the swamp-ridden reaches to the south (today's Federal Triangle), close to the filth-ridden canal that isolated the city from the Mall, housed a notorious stew of slum housing, bordellos and cheap liquor joints. Often, the slurry washed onto the avenue itself; Anthony Trollope noted that in the 1860s there were "parts of Pennsylvania Avenue that would have been considered heavy ground by most hunting-men".

This account of the buildings along Pennsylvania Avenue starts from its south-eastern end at 6th Street NW; nearest Metro is Archives-Navy Memorial.

Turn-of-the-century additions to the avenue – notably the Post Office and the renowned Willard Hotel – formed part of an early attempt to transform the district's fortunes, but for much of this century Pennsylvania Avenue was in severe decline. In the 1970s the **Pennsylvania Avenue Development Corporation** (PADC) came into being, with whose assistance the area has become much livelier, dotted with small plazas, memorials framed by newly planted trees and with Victorian flourishes decorating lampposts and street furniture.

For the first time in years the avenue provides a suitable backdrop for that most Washingtonian of ceremonial processions – the triumphal **Inaugural Parade** that takes each new president from the Capitol to their residence for the next four years. Thomas Jefferson led the first impromptu parade in 1805; James Madison made the ceremony official; and every president since has trundled up in some form of conveyance or another – except Jimmy Carter who, famously, walked the sixteen long blocks to the White House.

From the Mellon Fountain to the Navy Memorial

The bronze, triple-decker **fountain** in the corner plot between 6th Street and Constitution Avenue commemorates former secretary of the treasury and art connoisseur Andrew Mellon, fittingly sited across from the West Building of the National Gallery of Art, which he funded and filled with paintings. It's overlooked by the ultra-modern stone-and-glass **Canadian Embassy**, on the north side of the avenue, a typical piece of contemporary braggadocio which cuts a neat bite out of its lower story and then props up the overhang on a circle of columns to form a covered piazza.

A little further up on the same side, the turreted, pink-stone **Sears House**, 633 Pennsylvania Avenue, once contained the studio of nineteenth-century photographer Matthew Brady, whose graphic photographs of the slaughter at Antietam in 1862 first brought home the full horror of the Civil War to the American public. The small plaza here at 7th Street, Indiana Plaza, is taken up by the memorial to the victorious **Grand Army of the Republic**, a triangular obelisk adorned with figures representing Fraternity, Loyalty and Charity. Across 7th Street, the gruff equestrian statue is of **General Winfield Scott Hancock**, commander-in-chief of the Union forces – aged 74 at the outbreak of war and ridden with gout, he barely left the War Department offices close to the White House.

Across Pennsylvania Avenue from here, in the green plot in front of the National Archives at 9th Street, a small marble memorial commemorates another war leader, **Franklin Delano Roosevelt**. It was his wish that any memorial to him erected after his death be "plain, without any ornamentation" and that's what he got: placed here in 1965 on the twentieth anniversary of his death, it's inscribed simply "In Memory of Franklin Delano Roosevelt 1882–1945".

Despite his wishes, FDR's supporters couldn't help themselves – the Mall's new FDR Memorial (p.64) is a grander affair altogether.

Market Square

In 1801 the city's biggest outdoor market opened for business at the foot of 7th Street. Known as **Center Market**, it backed onto the canal along the Mall where goods barges could be unloaded; out front, top-heavy carts and drays spilled across Pennsylvania Avenue and up 7th Street on the way out of the city. It was a notoriously noxious spot – presidential secretary John Hay in Gore Vidal's novel, *Lincoln*, "was haunted by the ghosts of the millions of cats who had given their lives that the nearby canal might exude its distinctive odor" – and there was little clamor when it was demolished in 1870. The National Archives (see p.185) were erected on the site in 1935. The concave, colonnaded buildings of the development opposite, known as **Market Square**, frame the view up 8th Street to the Old Patent Office Building. The ground floors are given over to café-restaurants and outdoor seating, while upper-floor apartments provide sweeping views over the revitalized Penn Quarter.

*There's a
regular series
of concerts by
the Navy Band
at the memori-
al (June–Aug
Tues 8pm).*

The US Navy Memorial

Market Square's circular plaza is entirely covered by an etched representation of the world, circled by low, tiered, granite walls lapped
by running water. These together make up the **US Navy Memorial**,
complemented by the statue of a lone sailor, kit bag by his side, and
inscribed naval quotations from the historic (Themistocles, architect
of the Greek naval victory during the Persian Wars) to the tenuous
(naval aviator Neil Armstrong's "That's one small step for man . . .").
Directly behind the memorial, in the easternmost Market Square
building at 701 Pennsylvania Ave NW, the **Naval Heritage Center**
(Mon–Sat 9.30am–5pm ☎737-2300) can tell you more about the
service with its changing exhibits and daily showing of the tub-
thumping *At Sea* movie (11am & 1pm; $4). Portraits honor the var-
ious presidents who have served in the US Navy: JFK famously com-
manded a motor torpedo boat and was awarded the Navy and Marine
Corps medal for heroism (see p.143), but Johnson, Nixon, Ford and
Carter all served with distinction, too, while George Bush, the Navy's
youngest bomber pilot, received the Distinguished Flying Cross and
three Air Medals for his endeavors.

The Federal Bureau of Investigation

9th St and Pennsylvania Ave NW ☎324-3447; Federal Triangle Metro.
Mon–Fri 8.45am–4.15pm. Admission free.

Disappointingly, the lightweight, partisan and ultimately tedious
hour-long tour of the **Federal Bureau of Investigation** does not
deserve its status as one of Washington's most popular attractions.
The building itself sets the tone: a 1970s concrete excrescence pon-
derously named after the organization's most notorious red-baiting,
cross-dressing chief, J. Edgar Hoover, it's hardly the most inspiring
structure in the city, and not one that provides any distraction for visitors who can expect to wait an hour (more in summer) before being
ushered into what is effectively a PR job for America's most mythol-
ogized law-enforcement agency.

Established in 1908 (motto: Fidelity, Bravery, Integrity) under
the auspices of the Department of Justice, the FBI owed its early
investigative techniques to those pioneered by the Pinkerton
Detective Agency in the 1870s, and made its reputation in the 1920s
and 1930s by battling gangsters and attempting to enforce
Prohibition. Today, ten thousand Special Agents are employed to
fight organized and white-collar crime, pursue drug-traffickers and
lurk in the shadowy world of counter-intelligence.

After an introductory video, the walk-through tour continues
with stilted presentations about FBI training and duties, led by
guides who have swallowed the textbook whole. After a brief exposition about drugs (bad) and FBI agents (good) – note that the phials
are filled with make-believe marijuana and crack, so as not to offend
– it's off to the next exhibit. The whole set-up is rife with contradic-

tions: while being led to condemn crimes of violence and their perpetrators, visitors are titillated with casefuls of confiscated, historic weaponry – "Pretty Boy" Floyd's Colt .45, John Dillinger's Winchester rifle – in a retrospective glorification of an age of cartoon villains. It is, if anything, even more problematic when looking to the future: systematic DNA sampling and the concept of a national fingerprint bank are championed as developments in the fight against crime, with not a mention of the encroachment upon civil liberties that each might bring.

Along
Pennsylvania
Avenue

The tour finishes down in the shooting range where an FBI agent fires semi-automatic handguns and assault rifles at a paper human target to approving gasps and whistles from the audience. The question-and-answer session afterwards tends to run, worryingly, along the lines of "how can I get one of those?", though to be fair the agent, when prompted, will claim that most FBI agents don't discharge their weapons during the entire course of their career. Neither, it turns out, do they have much contact with aliens, despite the high-profile exploits of the *X-Files*' Special Agents Mulder and Scully, who are often filmed running in and out of the building pursuing matters of life and death.

The FBI Building figures in dozens of movies, but doesn't survive Tim Robbins' car bomb in Arlington Road, which destroys it completely.

The Old Post Office

Built in 1899, the fanciful Romanesque **Old Post Office**, 1100 Pennsylvania Ave NW, at the junction with 12th Street, has survived various attempts to demolish it to become one of the most recognizable of downtown's monuments. For years, it served as federal offices, but since the mid-1980s it's been turned over to business. It's one of the city's great indoor spaces, with a glorious galleried interior, known as the **Pavilion** (mid-April to mid-Sept Mon–Sat 10am–9pm, Sun noon–8pm; mid-Sept to mid-April Mon–Sat 10am–7pm, Sun noon–6pm; information ☎289-4224), whose glass roof throws light down onto the restored iron support beams, brass rails, balconies and burnished wood paneling. There's a large food court in the first-floor courtyard (where clerks once sorted mail), and gift shops and stalls on the second. Check out the period **post office counter** (Mon–Fri 9am–5pm), still in use at the Pennsylvania Avenue entrance.

Signs point the way to the **clocktower** (mid-April to mid-Sept daily 8am–11pm, closed Thurs 6.30–9.30pm; mid-Sept to mid-April daily 10am–5.45pm; free; ☎606-8691), where park rangers oversee short tours up to the observation deck, 270ft above Pennsylvania Avenue. The glass-elevator ride allows you to see the interior in all its glory, and the viewing platform itself boasts a stunning city panorama. On the way down, walk the three flights to the glass elevator to see the Congress Bells, a Bicentennial gift from London, replicas of those in Westminster Abbey and installed here in 1983.

Back outside on the avenue, **Benjamin Franklin** – "Philosopher, Printer, Philanthropist, Patriot", as his statue has it – gives a cheery little wave. You can park yourself on a bench and look across to the Neoclassical facade of the **Evening Star Building** (1898), whose attractive balconies, pediments and carvings provide virtually the only exterior relief on any building on the north side of the avenue as far down as Sears House.

Freedom Plaza to the Willard Hotel

Where Pennsylvania Avenue kinks into E Street (at 13th), you've reached the large open space of **Freedom Plaza**, site of various festivals and open-air concerts. Lined in marble, it's inlaid with a large-scale representation of L'Enfant's city plan, picked out in bronze and colored stone, and etched with various laudatory inscriptions. The view down the avenue to the Capitol dome is splendid from here, but it's a scalding place to hang around in summer, the only shade provided by the statue of General Casimir Pulaski, Polish hero of the Revolutionary War, at the eastern end.

Freedom Plaza also offers a first-hand view of the development going on along Pennsylvania Avenue. On the south side the sculpted capitals and pediments of the Beaux-Arts District Building (see p.184) offer a sharp rebuke to the faceless behemoth which lines the plaza's entire north side. The *Marriott* hotel and restored facade of the **National Theater** (see p.314) – on this site since 1835, though the current building dates from 1922 – both form part of the **National Place** complex, whose unexciting exterior hides a three-level shopping mall. There's access to The Shops at National Place – (Mon–Sat 10am–7pm, Thurs until 8pm, Sun noon–5pm) through the hotel, as well as on 14th and F streets. At the northeastern corner of the plaza the historic **Warner Theater Building** (at 13th and E) forms part of the 1299 Pennsylvania Avenue development, whose carved stone latticework facade shines pink in the sun.

This section of the avenue ends at **Pershing Park**, named for the commander of the American forces during World War I whose statue stands alongside a sunken terrace that becomes a skating rink in winter. Just to the west, Hamilton Place marks the spot at which an earlier general, William Tecumseh Sherman (also honored by a statue), presided over the **Grand Review of the Union Armies** in May 1865; six weeks after Lee's surrender, the victorious troops marched proudly up Pennsylvania Avenue in the most stirring military parade ever seen in the capital. It was a show of Union strength tinged with sadness, since many at the time didn't think it appropriate to celebrate so soon after the assassination of Lincoln.

The Willard Hotel

Peering over the north side of Pershing Park at 14th stands one of the grand old ladies among Washington hotels, the **Willard**, a Washington landmark for 150 years. Though a hotel has existed on the site since the capital's earliest days, it was after 1850, when

Henry Willard gave his name to the place, that it became a haunt of Along Pennsylvania Avenue statesmen, politicians and top brass – not least Abraham Lincoln, who was smuggled in before his first inauguration (during which snipers were placed on the roof). Its opulent public rooms attracted placemen and profit-seekers anxious to press their suit on political leaders; it's claimed, with a bare smidgen of proof, that this is whence the word "lobbyist" derives. Somewhat less apocryphal is the story that Julia Ward Howe wrote *The Battle Hymn of the Republic* while closeted in her *Willard* room during the Civil War – supposedly inspired by Union soldiers marching under her window belting out their favorite song, *John Brown's Body*.

In 1901, Henry Hardenbergh – architect of some of New York's finest period hotels – was engaged to update the *Willard* and produced the splendid Beaux-Arts building which stands today; it went out of business after the riots of 1968, but a thorough restoration in 1986 has recaptured its early style. Drop by the galleried lobby and tread the plush carpets of the grand main corridor for a coffee in the Art Nouveau *Café Espresso*; other refreshment spots are the *Nest* bar and *Willard Room* restaurant.

While you're here, you may as well slip into the **Washington Hotel**, a little further along at 15th Street, less for its architectural attractions (though it's a decent enough building of 1917, with a fine lobby and handsome brown-and-white facade) than for its **rooftop bar** (May–Sept only; see p.303), from where there are splendid views across to the White House grounds.

For reservation details for both hotels, see p.278.

Federal Triangle

The wedge of land east of the White House between Pennsylvania and Constitution avenues, **FEDERAL TRIANGLE** makes one of the most coherent architectural statements in the city. Grand Neoclassical government buildings follow the lines of the avenues, presenting imposing facades to the Mall on one side and Pennsylvania Avenue on the other; all were erected in the 1930s in an attempt to graft an instant "imperial" look upon the capital city of the Free World. The district's nineteenth-century origins, however, were distinctly humble, as a canal-side slum known, graphically, as Murder Bay: hoodlums frequented its brothels and taverns, while on hot days the stench from Center Market drifted through the ill-fitting windows of the district's cheap boarding-houses. Few improvements were effected until the mid-1920s, when an increasing shortage of office space forced the federal government's hand. The triangle of land was bought and redeveloped in its entirety between 6th and 15th streets, following a Neoclassical plan with buildings opening onto quiet interior courtyards. Although never fully realized – the Old Post Office and the District Building intruded into the Triangle but were saved from successive attempts to knock them down – it's a remarkably uniform area, even today. Different architects worked on the buildings, but they all have the same characteristics: granite facades, stone reliefs, columns and worthy inscriptions.

Department of Commerce to the Federal Trade Commission

One of the first buildings completed, in 1931, was the thousand-foot-long **Department of Commerce**, which forms the western base of the Triangle, at 14th between E and Constitution. Its main interest today is as site of the White House Visitor Center (on the north side of the building; see p.150) and home of the **National Aquarium** (daily 9am–5pm; $2; ☎ 482-2825), tucked into the basement; the entrance is on the 14th Street side. Founded in 1873, it's the oldest aquarium in America, and even though it's had a home here since 1932 the gray federal corridors seem a strange environment for the fish; more surreal still are the dulcet tones of Dudley Moore drifting past the tanks from the aquarium theater, where he narrates an introductory video. There are 1700 creatures from 260 species kept down here, forced to listen to Dud day in day out; the sharks (Mon, Wed & Sat) and piranhas (Tues, Thurs & Sun) get fed at 2pm.

Also at 14th Street, with a facade fronting Pennsylvania Avenue, the Beaux-Arts **District Building** predates the other Triangle edifices; walk down 14th for a view of its mighty caryatids and bold corner shield emblems. Erected as city council offices in 1908, it escaped demolition during the decade of Federal Triangle construction and clung on until 1992, when the mayor's office was shifted to Judiciary Square. Since then, the District Building has been restored as part of the massive adjacent development, which stretches right down 14th Street. This, the **Ronald Reagan Building** (1300 Pennsylvania Ave/14th St NW) – despite being the US's second largest federal building after the Pentagon – hides its bulk well behind a facade that's broadly sympathetic to its neighbors. Walk in to look at the immense barrel-vaulted atrium: inside, along with the International Trade Center and other offices, is a basement food court, visitor's center, restaurant and exhibition space.

East along Constitution Avenue, between 14th and 12th streets, the large complex housing the **Customs Service Building** is as fussy as a building could be, its long colonnade and entablature of lazing nudes a stark contrast to the stripped facade of the National Museum of American History over the road. Across 12th Street is the **Internal Revenue Service Building**, the earliest (1930) federal building to grace the area; while across 10th Street stands the **Department of Justice Building**, in whose (enclosed) courtyard stands a bust of former Attorney General Robert Kennedy fashioned by Robert Berks – who was also responsible for the mighty bust of older Kennedy brother, John Fitzgerald, in the Kennedy Center (see p.173). The

National Archives (see below) are next, across 9th Street, and the is completed by the suitably triangular **Federal Trade Commission Building**, between 7th and 6th streets, where friezes over the Constitution Avenue doors depict agriculture and trade – and the control of trade, as shown by the twin exterior statues of a muscular man wrestling a wild horse (at the rounded 6th St side).

The National Archives

7th St and Pennsylvania Ave NW ☎501-5000; for guided tours call ☎501-5205; Archives-Navy Memorial Metro. Daily 10am–5.30pm, April–Labor Day until 9pm. Admission free.

As if bored with the restrictions of his brief, John Russell Pope's **National Archives** building completely subverts the tenets of the Federal Triangle plan. This is Neoclassical with knobs on, with 72 highly ornate Corinthian columns, each 50ft high, plain walls supporting a dome 75ft above floor level, and a sculpted pediment (facing Constitution Ave) topped by eagles. But then, unlike the other buildings, it was destined to hold a collection of national significance, namely the country's federal records dating back to the 1700s. When opened in 1935, the roll-call of the National Archives' holdings already made impressive reading; today they're of an almost unfathomable quantity. What everyone comes to see is the Holy Trinity of American historical record – the Declaration of Independence, the Constitution and the Bill of Rights – but the National Archives also encompass hundreds of millions of pages of paper documents, from war treaties to slave ship manifests, seven million pictures, 120,000 reels of cine film, almost 200,000 sound recordings, eleven million maps and charts, and a quarter of a million other artifacts.

The documents on permanent display are shown in the magnificent marble Rotunda, each in cases protected by bullet-proof glass, green light filters and a helium atmosphere; at night, they drop 20ft down into vaults for further protection. Visitors first file past the **Declaration of Independence**, rather faded now, but with its opening words and signatures still clear. The copy of the **US Constitution** is the one signed at the Constitutional Convention in Philadelphia in September 1787 by twelve of the original thirteen states (Rhode Island signed three years later). The later amendments to the Constitution became the articles of the **Bill of Rights**, of which this is the federal government's official copy.

Murals on the side walls bang home the significance of the documents, with pictures of Thomas Jefferson handing the Declaration to John Hancock, and James Madison presenting the Constitution to George Washington (who chaired the Constitutional Convention). The other document on display is one of the few extant copies of the English **Magna Carta**, this one a specimen revised in 1297 after its initial agreement by King John in 1215. Written in Latin, it seems out

The Declaration of Independence

We hold these truths to be self-evident: that all men are created equal, that they are endowed by their Creator with certain unalienable rights, that among these are life, liberty, and the pursuit of happiness . . .

Declaration of Independence, Second Continental Congress, 1776

We are the only nation in the world based on happiness. Search as you will the sacred creeds of other nations and peoples, read the Magna Carta, the Communist Manifesto, the Ten Commandments, the Analects of Confucius, Plato's Republic, the New Testament or the UN Charter, and find me any happiness at all. America is the Happy Kingdom.

P.J. O'Rourke, *Parliament of Whores*

Revolutionary fervor was gaining pace in the American colonies in the early months of 1776, whipped up in part by the publication of Tom Paine's widely read, coruscating pamphlet, *Common Sense*, which castigated monarchical government in general and George III of England in particular. In May, the sitting **Second Continental Congress** in Philadelphia advised the colonies to establish their own governments, whose delegates in turn increasingly harried Congress to declare independence. The die was cast on June 7 when **Richard Henry Lee** of Virginia moved in Congress that "these United Colonies are, and of right ought to be, Free and Independent States". Four days later, while debate raged among the delegates, Congress authorized a committee to draft a formal declaration of independence.

Five men assembled to begin the task: **Thomas Jefferson, Benjamin Franklin, John Adams, Roger Sherman** and **Robert Livingston**.

For more on the Constitution, see "The American System of Government", p.337.

of place here, but the privileges and freedoms it guaranteed (trial by jury, equality before the law, etc) were a precursor of those enshrined in the Bill of Rights. Incidentally, it's owned (and permanently loaned to the National Archives) by businessman and failed presidential candidate Ross Perot, who liked democracy so much he tried to buy it.

Given that the Archives hold items as diverse as Napoleon Bonaparte's signature on the Louisiana Purchase, the World War II Japanese surrender document, the Strategic Arms Limitation Treaty of 1972 and President Nixon's resignation letter, it's always worth checking the **temporary exhibitions**. To hear selections from the Watergate tapes (see p.170), which led to Nixon's downfall, a shuttle bus will take you to the Maryland depository where they're held (call the Archives for details).

You can see much more of the holdings by signing up for one of the excellent twice-daily **guided tours**, though you'll need to call well in advance. The **Central Research and Microfilm Rooms** (Mon & Wed 8.45am–5pm, Tues, Thurs & Fri 8.45am–9pm, Sat 8.45am–4.45pm) are also open to visitors, and are used for genealogical and research purposes – Alex Haley, author of *Roots*, spent a great many hours tracing his ancestry here.

Jefferson, an accomplished writer, was charged by the others to produce a draft, which was ready to be presented to Congress by June 28. Despite the evidence of most history books, though, Jefferson didn't simply rattle off the ringing declaration that empowered a nation. For a start, he lifted phrases and ideas from other writers – the "pursuit of happiness" was a common contemporary rhetorical flourish, while the concept of "unalienable rights" had appeared in George Mason's recent Declaration of Rights for Virginia. Moreover, his own words were tweaked by the rest of the committee and other changes were ordered after debate in Congress, notably the dropping of a passage condemning the slave trade in an attempt to keep some of the southern colonies on board. However, by the end of June, Congress had a document which spelled out exactly why Americans wanted independence, who they blamed for the state of affairs (George III, in 27 separate charges) and what they proposed to do about it. Read today, it's still a model of perfect clarity of political thought.

At this point, myths start to obfuscate the real chain of events. After a month of argument – not every delegate agreed with the proposed declaration – Congress finally **approved Lee's motion** on July 2, 1776. Technically, this was the day that America declared independence from Great Britain, though two days later, on **July 4, 1776**, Congress, representing the "thirteen United States of America", also approved Jefferson's explanatory declaration – and within a couple of years, and ever since, celebrations were held on the anniversary of the later date. The only man to sign the Declaration itself on July 4 was John Hancock (president of the Continental Congress) – hence the use of the colloquialism "John Hancock" for someone's signature; other signatures weren't added until August 2 and beyond, since many of the delegates had gone home as soon as the declaration was drawn up.

Judiciary Square

East of 5th Street, between E and F streets, **Judiciary Square** has been the focus for the city's judiciary and local government since 1800 when storehouses here served as rank jails for runaway slaves. Today, the mayor's new offices are at One Judiciary Square, while the unobtrusive **Old City Hall** on D Street, dating from the early nineteenth century, now houses courts and other offices – in 1881 it saw the trial for murder of Charles Guiteau, who shot President James Garfield in the back just four months after his inauguration. There's a rare outdoor **statue of Abraham Lincoln** in front of the building on D Street. Within a few blocks of here stand the US Tax Court, the District of Columbia Court House, the Municipal Center and the US (Federal) Court House, all without exception uniformly bland – nineteenth-century workers in the nearby Pension Building (see p.190) had a vastly superior working environment. All the courthouse galleries are open to members of the public interested in watching proceedings: the US (**Federal**) **Court House** (main entrance on Constitution Ave) sees the most high-profile action, from the trial of

Judiciary Square is served by Judiciary Square Metro station.

various Watergate and Iran-Contra defendants to that of former
mayor Marion Barry. This was also where the 1998 grand jury hearings on the Clinton-Lewinsky affair were played out, with all the main
players appearing to give evidence in person save for the President,
who testified via closed-circuit TV from the White House.

Governing DC

Washington DC has always had an anomalous place in the Union. It's a **federal district** rather than a state, with no official constitution of its own, and
its citizens are denied full representation under the American political system: they have no senator to pursue their interests and only a non-voting
representative in the House (a position the capital city shares, ingloriously,
with Samoa, Guam and the Virgin Islands). Perhaps most incongruously,
only since 1961, by virtue of the 23rd Amendment, have they been able to
vote in presidential elections; the first they participated in was that of 1964.

Local powers have been similarly disregarded. There's been a city mayor
and some sort of elected council since 1802 but in the early days, so many
inhabitants were temporary visitors – politicians, lobbyists, lawyers and
appointed civil servants – that there was no question of granting local tax-
raising powers. Congress simply appropriated money piecemeal for necessary improvements. Under President Grant in 1871 the District was given
territorial status: he appointed a governor and council, under whom
worked an elected house of delegates, and boards of public works and
health; all adult males (black and white) were eligible to vote. Many of the
most significant improvements to the city infrastructure date from this period of limited self-government, with the head of the Board of Public Works,
Alexander "Boss" Shepherd, instrumental in sinking sewers, paving and
lighting streets and planting thousands of trees. However, Shepherd's
improvements and a string of corruption scandals put the city $16 million in
debt. Direct control of DC's affairs passed back to Congress in 1874, which
later appointed three commissioners to replace the locally elected officials.

And that was the way matters stood for a century, until Congress passed
the **Home Rule Act** in 1973. Small improvements had already been effected – the first black commissioner (for a city now predominantly black) was
appointed in 1961; later, an elected school board was established. But
only in 1974, with the advent of the District's first elected **mayor** for more
than a century – the black Walter E. Washington, supported by a fully
elected thirteen-member council – did the city wrest back some measure
of autonomy. However, Congress still retained a legislative veto over any
proposed local laws, as well as keeping a close watch on spending limits.

Washington was succeeded as mayor in 1978 by **Marion S. Barry**, former civil rights activist and as picaresque a political leader as any city
could wish for. At first, he was markedly successful in attracting much-
needed investment; he also significantly increased the number of local
government workers, which gave him a firm support base among the
majority black population. But longstanding whispers about Barry's tur-
bulent private life – charges of drug addiction in particular – exploded in
early 1990, when he was surreptitiously filmed in an FBI sting operation,
buying and using crack cocaine. Barry spent six months in prison, being
replaced as mayor by the Democrat **Sharon Pratt Kelly**, a former corporate manager who, despite her undoubted expertise, signally failed to

National Law Enforcement Officers Memorial

Davis Buckley's impressive **National Law Enforcement Officers Memorial** occupies the whole of the center of Judiciary Square; one of the Metro entrances emerges right by it. Dedicated in 1991, the

---

improve the city's worsening finances. Nor did she endear herself to the city's employees, and in the mayoral election of 1994, Barry made an astounding **comeback**, admitting to voters the error of his ways. But a year later, Congress – influenced by the sweeping Republican gains in the previous year's general election – finally tired of the embarrassment of DC's massive budget deficit and **revoked the city's home rule charter**.

A Congressionally appointed **control board** was subsequently given jurisdiction over the city's finances, personnel and various work departments until 2003, and although its principal task is to balance the budget, the swingeing cuts and redundancies demanded gradually stripped away what little responsibility the mayor had left. Barry didn't stand in the 1998 mayoral elections and was succeeded, somewhat surprisingly, by the city's former chief financial officer, Democrat **Anthony A. Williams**, who won a resounding two-thirds share of the vote in his first political foray. Perhaps even more significantly, the election results produced for the first time a majority-white district council. This fact alone, together with the election of an avowed technocrat as mayor, signaled a shift away from the confrontation of the later Barry years and, within days of the election, Williams was negotiating with the financial control board to restore many of the mayoral powers. His was a strong hand, since – partly due to his efforts as financial chief – the city was running an annual surplus for the first time in many years. It seems now that full executive power may be returned to the city ahead of schedule, with Congress (which subsidizes the District) less fearful than before that the federal capital will simply collapse.

However, DC's problems go far deeper than simple financial mismanagement. The heart of the matter is the shrinking **tax** base: two-thirds of DC's workers live (and pay local taxes) in Virginia and Maryland; the continuing middle-class flight to the suburbs has left the city population at its lowest since the 1930s. Thirty percent of those left are on welfare (which jacks up the deficit), while the rest face increased local income taxes in a doomed attempt to raise funds for put-upon city services. The obvious solution to this vicious circle – a commuter tax – is a non-starter for political reasons. Instead, some propose to exempt DC residents from federal and capital gains taxes, and freeze property taxes, to promote business and population growth in the city, but the outcry against self-serving politicians would be enormous. Granting **statehood**, with all the political, tax and jurisdictional rights that would entail, is another option (last considered and turned down by Congress in 1993), though there's no real enthusiasm at local level, at least when it comes to voting – in the 1998 elections, the DC Statehood Party's mayoral candidate received just two percent of the vote. But the crux of the whole matter of granting statehood to DC is **race**. The predominantly black city pays federal taxes but has no representation in the predominantly white Congress; consequently, there's a distinct whiff of distrust – locals, with some justification, feel that the last thing the government wants is a black city in charge of its own affairs on the nation's doorstep.

---

walls lining the circular pathways around a reflecting pool are inscribed with the names of more than 14,000 police officers killed in the line of duty, starting with US Marshall Robert Forsyth, shot dead in 1794. With symbolic bronze lions overseeing their cubs at the end of the memorial walls, it's a poignant spot in the oft-claimed Murder Capital of the nation (though the state with the highest number of police, as opposed to civilian, deaths is actually California). New names are added each May to the memorial, which has space for 29,000 – at the present rate (a murdered police officer every other day on average), it will be full by the year 2100. There are directories at the site if you want to trace a particular name, or call in at the nearby **visitor center**, two blocks west at 605 E St NW (Mon–Fri 9am–5pm, Sat 10am–5pm, Sun noon–5pm; free; ☎ 737-3400).

The Pension Building and National Building Museum

In the late 1860s the sheer number of Civil War casualties put a huge strain on the government's pension system. New offices were required in which to process claims and payments to veterans and dependents; subsequently, in the 1880s, what became known as the **Pension Building** was erected between 4th and 5th streets, framing the entire north side of today's Judiciary Square. Emerging from the Metro up the escalators brings you face-to-face with its imposing red-brick facade.

Architect Montgomery C. Meigs' concern was to honor veterans of both sides with a building of distinction, and in this he succeeded admirably. The Renaissance-style palazzo is handsome in the extreme, its exterior enhanced by a three-foot-high terracotta **frieze** that runs around the entire building (between the first and second floors) and depicts the Union Army in all its manifestations: drilling soldiers and the walking wounded, horses pulling wagons, marines rowing in a storm-tossed sea, charging cavalry and thunderous artillery.

Inside, Meigs maximized the use of natural light and freely circulating air to produce a majestic **Great Hall**, inspired by the generous proportions of Rome's Palazzo Farnese, a stadium-sized interior centering on a working fountain. The eight supporting columns are 8ft across at the base and more than 75ft high; each is made up of 70,000 bricks, plastered and painted to resemble Siena marble. Above the ground-floor Doric arcade, the three open-plan galleried levels, 160ft high, were aired by vents and clerestory windows – opened each day by a young boy employed to walk around on the roof. In the upper-floor niches Meigs planned to put busts of prominent Americans, though this plan never came to fruition; today, the 244 busts are a repeated series of eight figures (architect, construction worker, landscape gardener, etc) representing the building arts. Hardly surprisingly, such a vast, sympathetic space has been in regular demand. Grover Cleveland held the first of many presidential inaugural balls here in 1885 (when there was still no roof on the building); a century later, it hosted President Reagan's second inaugural and then Clinton's first; while every year the *Christmas in Washington* special is filmed here.

The Pension Bureau moved out in 1926 and for a time the building served as a courthouse and various federal offices. It's now preserved as the **National Building Museum**, 401 F St NW (June–Aug Mon–Sat 10am–5pm, Sun noon–5pm; Sept–July closes 1hr earlier; free but $3 donation suggested; ☎272-2448), presenting changing exhibitions on all aspects of architecture and building history. The permanent exhibition on the second floor, "Washington: Symbol and City", usefully concentrates on the construction of the city itself. Free **tours** (Mon–Fri 12.30pm, Sat & Sun 12.30pm & 1.30pm) give you access to the otherwise restricted third floor (the best spot to view the towering column's curlicued capitals) and to the former Pension Commissioner's Suite on the second floor. There's also a monthly lunchtime concert program, and coffee and cookies served at **café** tables (Mon–Sat 10am–3pm, Sun noon–3pm) in the Great Hall – one of the most jaw-dropping spots in DC to take a break.

Old Patent Office Building

Three blocks west of the Pension Building, the older **Patent Office Building** houses two of the city's major art displays, the **National Portrait Gallery** and the **National Museum of American Art**, both of which come under the aegis of the Smithsonian.

The Greek Revival building, begun in 1836 by Robert Mills, is among the oldest in the city, though it wasn't completed for thirty years. It was designed to hold offices of the Interior Department and the **Commissioners of Patents**, displaying models of all patents taken out in nineteenth-century America. Thus it became one of the city's earliest museums, featuring models of inventions by Thomas Edison, Benjamin Franklin and Alexander Graham Bell as well as Whitney's cotton gin, Colt's pistol and Fulton's steam engine. Charles Dickens remarked that it was "an extraordinary example of American enterprise and ingenuity", although Anthony Trollope, hard to please as usual, was put out that he couldn't see what many of the inventions were supposed to be and thought the building "no better than a large toy shop". During the Civil War the echoing halls were pressed into emergency service as a **hospital** with over two thousand beds. One of the clerks in the Patent Office, a certain Clara Barton, abandoned her clerical duties to work in the hospital, going on to found the American Red Cross in 1881. The poet Walt Whitman worked here, too, as an untrained volunteer, dressing wounds and comforting injured soldiers, an experience which led directly to the long series of poems known as *Drum-Taps*, which was included in

Orient yourself in the building's Patent Pending *cafeteria (p.284), just off the court-yard, on the 7th St side.*

Old Patent Office Building

the fourth edition (1867) of *Leaves of Grass*. In March 1865, just before the end of the war, Whitman's "noblest of Washington buildings" hosted **Lincoln's second inaugural ball** with four thousand people in attendance for a night of dancing and feasting. "Tonight", wrote Whitman later, "beautiful women, perfumes, the violins' sweetness . . . then, the amputation, the blue face, the groan, the glassy eye of the dying."

Despite its heritage, the building was scheduled for demolition in the 1950s, before the Smithsonian stepped into the breach; the double museum opened in 1968. The galleries occupy separate wings: the Museum of American Art on the G Street side; the Portrait Gallery on F Street. There are separate main entrances, but since you can cross into either museum from the other once you're inside, it can occasionally get a little confusing.

National Portrait Gallery

8th and F streets NW ☎357-2700; Gallery Place-Chinatown Metro. Daily 10am–5.30pm. Admission free.

Portraits of prominent Americans formed the basis of many early art collections – Congress itself commissioned a series of presidential portraits for the White House in 1857 – but the country wasn't provided with a **National Portrait Gallery** until the 1960s, when the Old Patent Office Building was converted for artistic use. The permanent collection contains more than four thousand images of notables from every walk of life, and there are some excellent paintings on show – Gilbert Stuart's celebrated "Lansdowne" portrait of George Washington being the best known. But the strength of the collection is in the people it honors, from politicians, novelists and inventors to sports heroes, civil rights leaders and industrialists. The collection isn't restricted to paintings, either: there's a wealth of **sculptures** and **photographs**, including over five thousand plate-glass negatives of the Civil War era alone by Matthew Brady.

The **main entrance** is on F Street at 8th; the **information desk** is here, as is the gallery **shop**. Ask at the desk about **guided tours** of the permanent collection (usually on request Mon–Fri 10am–3pm, Sat & Sun 11am–2pm); you can also pick up a schedule of events.

First floor
The pick of the gallery's **recent acquisitions** are presented along the south corridor, which leads to one of the most popular sections in the gallery. **"Performing Arts"** presents a starburst of portraits: Paul Robeson as Othello by Betsy Graves Reyneau (see p.196); a regal portrait of singer Marian Anderson; photographs of Gloria Swanson and Boris Karloff; a bronze bust of Grace Kelly; and an almost three-dimensional metallic study of Ethel Merman as Annie Oakley by Rosemary Sloat. Perhaps most striking is Harry Jackson's terrific polychrome bronze sculpture of a *True Grit*-era John

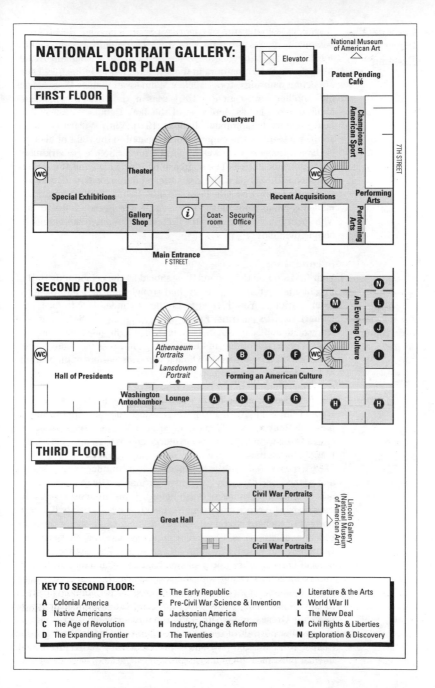

NATIONAL PORTRAIT GALLERY: FLOOR PLAN

⊠ Elevator

National Museum of American Art

FIRST FLOOR

Patent Pending Café

Courtyard

Champions of American Sport

7TH STREET

Theater

WC

Special Exhibitions

Recent Acquisitions

WC

Performing Arts

Gallery Shop

ⓘ Coat-room

Security Office

Performing Arts

Main Entrance
F STREET

SECOND FLOOR

Ⓝ

Ⓜ Ⓛ

An Evolving Culture

Ⓚ Ⓙ

WC

Athenaeum Portraits

Ⓑ Ⓓ Ⓕ

WC

Ⓘ

Landsdowne Portrait

Hall of Presidents

Forming an American Culture

Washington Antechamber

Lounge

Ⓐ Ⓒ Ⓕ Ⓖ

Ⓗ Ⓗ

THIRD FLOOR

Civil War Portraits

Lincoln Gallery (National Museum of American Art)

Great Hall

⊠

Civil War Portraits

KEY TO SECOND FLOOR:

A Colonial America
B Native Americans
C The Age of Revolution
D The Expanding Frontier

E The Early Republic
F Pre-Civil War Science & Invention
G Jacksonian America
H Industry, Change & Reform
I The Twenties

J Literature & the Arts
K World War II
L The New Deal
M Civil Rights & Liberties
N Exploration & Discovery

Wayne. In **"Champions of American Sport"**, beyond, the spot-the-personality games continue, with studies varying from a pugnacious Joe Louis (again by Betsy Graves Reyneau) to a poignant Arthur Ashe (Louis Briel), painted in the last few months of his life. There are action paintings, too – Mickey Mantle watching as Roger Maris hits another homer in the 1961 season and, best of all, James Montgomery Flagg's depiction of the Jack Dempsey–Jess Willard heavyweight championship fight of 1919. With Willard (in black shorts) in trouble, the eager reporter seated to the right of his knee is Damon Runyon, who was a sports reporter before embarking on his humorous stories. The staircase here provides one route up to the second floor, past the dramatic rendition of *Grant and His Generals* (1865) by Ole Peter Hansen Balling, a Norwegian who made his name painting the Union Army during the Civil War, and who spent five weeks during the Richmond campaign sketching officers in the field.

Second floor

Your first stop on the second floor should be the celebrated **"Hall of Presidents"**, which can be reached straight up the stairs from the main entrance. You'll emerge in the Rotunda, face-to-face with **Gilbert Stuart**'s portrait of George Washington (1796), an imperial study of an implacable man, head bathed in light, one hand clutching a swordstick, the other outstretched. It's known as the "Lansdowne" portrait after the person for whom it was commissioned: the Marquis of Lansdowne, who had earned American respect by defending the rebellious colonies in the British Houses of Parliament. Stuart based this full-length work on the portrait-head of Washington he had completed from life in April 1796, when he also took the opportunity to paint his only known likeness of Martha Washington – these so-called "Athenaeum" portraits of George and Martha are also usually hung in the Rotunda.

*For more on
Gilbert Stuart,
see p.90.*

On the west side of the Rotunda, the hall continues with portraits and sculptures of every American president (there's a separate antechamber for studies of Washington). Some are most notable for the artists who represent them: Norman Rockwell's overly flattering portrait of Richard Nixon is the most striking, while one of the more recent acquisitions is a bust of a relatively carefree, first-term Bill Clinton by Jan Wood, a sculptor otherwise best known for her depictions of horses. Other portraits illuminate the characters of the various presidents, starting with the work of George Peter Alexander Healy, who was first commissioned to produce presidential portraits in the 1850s. His pensive study of Abraham Lincoln manages to make the Great Emancipator rather more handsome than in virtually any other portrait of the time. Civil War painter Ole Peter Hansen Balling also managed portraits of presidents Chester A. Arthur and, in what must have been a rush-job, James Garfield, who, inaugurated in March 1881, was shot in July and died in September. Other artists faced different problems. Edmund Tarbell's Woodrow Wilson had to be painted entirely from photographs since Wilson was always too ill to pose, while one critic noted of Joseph Burgess's stern portrait of Calvin Coolidge that the subject looked as if, "without further provocation, he would bite the person . . . who, obviously, had been annoying him". English portraitist Douglas Chandor's rather raffish Franklin Delano Roosevelt has FDR in a chic fur-lined cape and sporting his trademark cigarette holder. This was to form part of a (never-completed) study of FDR with Churchill and Stalin at Yalta – which explains the alternative sketches of Roosevelt's hands, holding cigarettes, glasses and pens.

Old Patent Office Building

The rest of the second floor is taken up with the major collections – the **"Galleries of Notable Americans"**. First come portraits of Colonial America (including one of Pocahontas in English dress) and Native Americans, with several studies of braves and chiefs by George Catlin (there are more examples of his work in the American art museum; see p.197). There's a lithograph of Sitting Bull and, bringing the room up to date, a bust of Geronimo, sculpted by his distant relative, the Apache artist Allan Houser. In **"Industry, Change and Reform"**, industrialists, inventors and businessmen are pictured alongside churchmen and feminists, so together with Bell, Edison and Carnegie there's Belva Ann Lockwood, the first woman to stand for president (in 1884; she got 4149 votes), a bust of Susan B. Anthony by Adelaide Johnson (who sculpted many other suffrage leaders of the day) and a rather stuffy portrait of early feminist Elizabeth Cady Stanton.

Other early rooms highlight personalities from the Revolutionary War and, more interestingly, from **"Pre-Civil War Science and Invention"**: in the latter, Christian Schussele's *Men of Progress* depicts Samuel Morse, John Ericsson, Joseph Henry and Charles Goodyear among eighteen prominent scientists and inventors of 1862. The corridor display, **"Forming an American Culture"**, has portraits from the same period, including another Schussele work, *Washington Irving and His Literary Friends*, featuring Oliver Wendell Holmes, Longfellow, Emerson, Fenimore Cooper et al. In **"Literature and the Arts"** there's a distinct improvement in quality. Gems include a touching early photograph by Man Ray of Ernest Hemingway and his young son, and the extraordinary, bulky terracotta figure of Gertrude Stein, depicted by Jo Davidson as a tranquil, seated Buddha. Honors, too, for Edward Biberman's creepy study of Dashiell Hammett in a horrible wool coat, and to the staring Samuel Clemens (better known as Mark Twain) portrayed by John White Alexander in 1902; in 1889 the same artist painted Walt Whitman as a seated sage, with light streaming through his bushy beard. The most prized piece, however, is Edgar Degas' severe portrait (1880–84) of his friend, Impressionist Mary Cassatt, hunched over a chair with a sneer on her face – the subject hated it so much she had

There are more Adelaide Johnson busts on display in the Sewall-Belmont House, Capitol Hill; see p.123.

it sold on the express understanding that it wouldn't be allowed to go to an American collection where her family and friends might see it.

With **"The Twenties"** come photographs and prints of personalities that defined an era, from executed anarchists Sacco and Vanzetti to Babe Ruth – the "Sultan of Swat" – depicted as a baseball in *Vanity Fair* magazine. A further selection concentrates Roosevelt's **New Deal**. FDR is here, of course, in a portrait by Henry Hubbell, as is a rather kindly Eleanor, alongside most of their contemporaries. Betsy Graves Reyneau was commissioned in the 1940s by the Harmon Foundation to paint prominent African-Americans: here there's a sympathetic portrayal of Mary McLeod Bethune (see p.229), and of A. Phillip Randolph, President of the Brotherhood of Sleeping Car Porters and once regarded as the "most dangerous Negro in America" following his 1941 call for 50,000 blacks to march on Washington to protest against employment discrimination. Across the corridor, the **"World War II"** room mixes its portraits of generals with some interesting recruitment posters, like that of Private Joe Louis in uniform from 1942. Douglas Chandor's study of Winston Churchill – part of his proposed Yalta group with FDR and Stalin – may seem a puzzling inclusion in an American National Portrait Gallery, until you realize that Churchill was granted honorary US citizenship in 1963.

Final rooms take in **"Exploration and Discovery"**, in which Albert Einstein makes his mark as a kindly, twinkly uncle in a wonderful portrait by photographer Fred Stein, and **"Civil Rights and Liberties"**, which contains one of the strongest of all the gallery's sculptures. Marshall D. Rumbaugh chose to represent Rosa Parkes manacled between two law-enforcement officers after she had taken her seat on the bus in Montgomery, Alabama – their small heads and shaded eyes contrasting with the seamstress's defiant gaze as her handbag dangles beneath her handcuffs.

Third floor

Up on the third floor, the main staircase leads you straight into the beautifully restored Victorian **Great Hall**. This was originally used as a display area for the Patent Office, and the Declaration of Independence was on show here from 1841 to 1871; a selection of models of patented inventions still occupies two glass cases (the National Museum of American History has the other 10,000 models).

From the Great Hall, there's direct access through to the Lincoln Gallery of the National Museum of American Art.

The surrounding mezzanine brings together portraits of the **Civil War** era (Union and Confederate), centered on a full-length likeness by William Cogswell (1869), notable mainly for its poor proportions, of Lincoln in front of the Capitol. Far more striking is the copy of the notorious portrait of Lincoln taken in February 1865 by war photographer Alexander Gardner. A crack in the plate runs right across Lincoln's forehead – after the President's assassination, many observers saw this, in retrospect, as a terrible omen.

National Museum of American Art

8th and G streets NW ☎357-2700; Gallery Place-Chinatown Metro. Daily 10am–5.30pm. Admission free.

The **National Museum of American Art** holds one of the more enduring of the city's art collections. Even before the founding of the Smithsonian, the federal government had its own art collection which, together with pieces loaned by prominent Washington citizens, was displayed for a time in the 1840s in the Patent Office Building. These works were later transferred to the Smithsonian, which had yet to find premises for a planned "National Gallery" based on its expanding art collection. In the end the Smithsonian resorted to displaying its paintings in the Natural History Museum, receiving a second blow when Andrew Mellon's bequest to the nation resulted in the foundation of a quite separate National Gallery of Art. Not until the Patent Office Building became available did the Smithsonian finally find a home for its 38,000 paintings, prints, drawings and sculpture, photographs, folk art and crafts – the largest collection of American art, colonial to contemporary, in the world.

Not everything, of course, is on permanent display in this building, large though it is. Many of the museum's decorative arts and crafts, for instance, are shown in temporary exhibitions at the Renwick Gallery (see p.158). "American" here includes significant selections of African-American and Hispanic-American art, though there's no permanent exhibition of African-American works. You're also unlikely to see the museum's New Deal-era WPA murals or its unrivaled collection of portrait miniatures – the latter a happy consequence of the early Smithsonian's lack of space, which at one point forced the directors to acquire ever smaller paintings.

The **main entrance** is on G Street, marked by Luis Jiménez's bucking, multicolored fiberglass *Vaquero* sculpture. There's an **information desk**, which has floor plans and details of the free daily **guided tours** (Mon–Fri noon, Sat & Sun 2pm) and free **lectures**, and a gallery **shop** (daily 10am–5.15pm) just across the corridor.

First floor

The museum scores an early success with its presentation of the nineteenth-century **"Art of the American West"**. The collection includes almost four hundred paintings by George Catlin, who spent six years touring the Great Plains, painting portraits and scenes of Native American life which he later displayed as part of his "Indian Gallery". Catlin received no formal training, and certainly had his critics as an artist, but as an early anthropologist his work was invaluable. His paintings were the first contact many white settlers had with the aboriginal peoples of America, and viewers were fascinated by his lush landscapes showing buffalo herds crossing the Missouri, or those featuring tribes at work and play. The contrast between cultures is best seen in Catlin's 1832 painting of a warrior named Pigeon's Egg Head arriving in Washington DC in full traditional dress, only to return to his tepee encampment in frock coat and top hat, sporting an umbrella and smoking a cigarette. Perhaps Catlin is most interesting for recording civilizations and habitats that survived only briefly after the onslaught of the pioneers – soon after he visited and painted the Plains Mandan tribes, they were wiped out by a smallpox epidemic introduced by white settlers. Not all the scenes are of warriors or hunts: Catlin also produced many keenly observed domestic studies, like that of the woman with child in an elaborately decorated cradle, while Joseph Henry Sharp has a later picture (1920) of Blackfoots making medicine by burning feathers over an open fire. Catlin's contemporary John Mix Stanley concentrated on depicting Apache warriors, though he's also represented by the graphic *Buffalo Hunt* (1845). There's a remarkable bronze statue, too, of an *Indian Ghost Dancer* by Paul Wayland Bartlett (1888), the dancer clearly near total exhaustion after hours of trancelike dancing.

Changing displays of **folk art** on the first floor include some traditional pieces, notably Native American ceramics, but it's the contemporary works that stand out. Malcah Zeldis' *Miss Liberty Celebration* is typically exuberant – here, the Statue of Liberty, surrounded by a family group of Elvis, Einstein, Lincoln, Marilyn and Chaplin, was completed to celebrate the artist's recovery from cancer. Less easy to categorize are items like the painted swordfish bill (in a room of maritime folk objects) and the varied, modernistic animals, including a giraffe made entirely from bottle tops. Most extraordinary of all, though, is the room devoted to the so-called **Hampton Throne**, a mystic, cryptic cluster of foil- and gilt-covered lightbulbs, boxes, plaques, wings, altars and furniture capped by the text "Fear Not". The work of James Hampton, a solitary figure who referred to himself as "Saint James" and worked in a garage on N Street NW between 1950 and his death in 1964, it's full of obscure religious significance. It's also thought that it was unfinished at the time of his death, though quite how anyone could tell is a mystery.

The Hampton Throne's full title is The Throne of the Third Heaven of the Nations' Millennium General Assembly.

Second floor

Climb the staircase from the "American West" section and you're in for a highly enjoyable romp through paintings by the heavyweights of **nineteenth- and early twentieth-century** American art. The rooms aren't labeled too clearly, and paintings are occasionally moved, but working your way around to the main staircase should guarantee a view of most of the following.

An early picture by James McNeill Whistler of *Valparaiso Harbor* (1866) stands in the same room as a still life by his friend Abbott Handerson Thayer; for the best work of both men, though, you'll need to visit the Freer. There are significant chunks of work by Albert Pinkham Ryder, whose dark, often nightmarish paintings are full of symbolism, though there's more general appeal in those of Old Patent Office Building Winslow Homer, whether it's the rural studies of his *Bean Picker* or *A Country Lad*, or the leisurely antics of female models in his dappled *Sunlight and Shadow* and *Summer Afternoon*, all executed in the same prolific period during the 1870s. In the corner rooms, paintings are mixed with sculpture: accomplished society portraitist John Singer Sargent's direct study of the beautiful, taffeta-clad *Elizabeth Winthrop Chanler* (1893) and his later, jauntier *Betty Wertheimer* (1908) vie with ephemera such as Daniel Chester French's *The Spirit of Life* (1914), a winged sprite with laurel wreath fashioned by the man who produced the powerful statue in the Lincoln Memorial. You may also see a couple of other works by renowned artists: Mary Cassatt's *Spanish Dancer* (1873), showing little of her later Impressionist flair, and colonial master John Singleton Copley's infinitely more striking portrait of *Mrs George Watson* (1765).

The museum excels in American **landscapes**. *Among the Sierra Nevada Mountains* (1868) is a superb example of the dramatic power of **Albert Bierstadt**, whose three long trips to the American West between 1858 and 1873 provided him with enough material for the rest of his career – the detail is typical, with the ethereal light picking out distant waterfalls, ducks in flight and high snow-capped peaks. People rarely intruded into these romanticized landscapes: nowhere is this seen better than in the enormous, startlingly colored **Thomas Moran** landscapes at the top of the main staircase – two sweeping studies of Yellowstone Canyon, fully 12ft across, and *Chasm of the Colorado*, alive with multifarious reds. Elsewhere on the floor are similar, though smaller, expressions of grandeur in scenes from Lake Placid, the Colorado River and Niagara Falls, painted by Hudson River School artists (see p.91) such as Jasper Francis Cropsey and John Frederick Kensett, who cast their sensuous eye across what Americans soon came to regard as their own backyard. There is the occasional portrayal of the original inhabitants of these landscapes; look for **Charles Bird King**'s powerful picture of five Pawnee braves sporting red face-paint and ceremonial bead earrings. King studied in London under Benjamin West (see p.91) before moving to Washington DC, where he earned a comfortable living painting society portraits. The steady flow of Native Americans through the capital in the 1820s – there to sign away their land in a series of ultimately worthless treaties – prompted him to divert his attentions to recording their likenesses instead. Also rather extraordinary, though in quite a different fashion, is Charles Bird King's contemporaneous portrait of *Mrs John Quincy Adams*, obviously uncomfortable with the artist's suggestion that she sit at a harp in an ill-advised crown of feathers.

Beyond the Moran landscapes, the corridor contains examples from the noted collection of sculptures and models by **Hiram**

Powers. The surface of *America* (1848), a plaster model of crowned
Liberty, is punctured by the tips of a series of metal rods, inserted to
act as a guide for carving the eventual marble version. *Thomas
Jefferson* (1860) shows the same technique, unfortunately making it
look as if the frock-coated President has a severe case of acne.

Third floor

On the third floor, the museum moves into the **twentieth century**,
most spectacularly in the 260-foot-long **Lincoln Gallery**, which runs
down the east side of the building. It was here, amid the white marble pillars, that Abraham Lincoln and his entourage enjoyed his second inaugural ball. Now, in what can be seen as an adjunct to the
Hirshhorn and the National Gallery of Art's East Building, a kaleidoscopic selection from the Smithsonian's modern and contemporary
art collection is perfectly placed in this wonderful space.

Mostly, it's an exercise in name-spotting. Robert Motherwell,
Willem de Kooning, Robert Rauschenberg, Clyfford Styll, Ellsworth
Kelly and Jasper Johns all battle for attention. Often you're delayed by
less high-profile names and works, like that of Leon Golub, whose red,
raw *Napalm Head* is painted onto a torn canvas sack; or Marisol's
comical *Charles de Gaulle* (1967), which depicts the great French
President as a rectangular wooden box and head atop a small cart.
Louise Nevelson's *Sky Cathedral* from 1982 – fixed with retrieved
banister rails, cogs, handles, chair backs and metal frames – was originally commissioned for the lobby of the American Medical Association
in DC, her first public installation. The Hispanic-American sculptor
whose *Vaquero* stands outside the museum – Luis Jiménez – is represented here by the alarming, molded fiberglass *Man on Fire*, a red-
and-orange human figure slowly losing shape as the fire takes hold.

Finally, although not always on display, the museum owns a
decent selection of abstract works by the artists of the **Washington
Color School** – primarily Gene Davis, Morris Louis, Kenneth Noland,
Thomas Downing, Paul Reed and Howard Mehring. All tended to
stain their canvases with acrylic paint to give greater impact to color
and form, methods that first came to public attention in 1965 at a
ground-breaking Washington exhibition of modern art.

Around the MCI Center and Chinatown

The biggest engine of downtown change has been the construction
of the **MCI Center**, a 20,000-seater sports, concert and entertainment arena located opposite the Old Patent Office Building, on the
fringes of Washington's skimpy **Chinatown**. This has underpinned
the ongoing redevelopment around **7th and F streets**, part of a
concerted effort to breathe sustainable commercial life back into

DC's original downtown. By 2003 the main arteries of 7th, 9th and F streets – largely abandoned since the 1970s – will host a plethora of new office complexes, arts and leisure facilities, stores and apartments. The MCI Center has already succeeded in channeling sports fans and concertgoers into a series of new bars and restaurants that are currently among the city's most fashionable. The Gallery Place-Chinatown Metro gives direct access to the MCI Center, from where it's an easy eight-block walk back toward the White House, past historic Ford's Theater, where President Lincoln met his end.

The MCI Center and around

With the opening of the $200-million **MCI Center** (601 F St NW) at the end of 1997, professional sports came back to downtown DC – and with it, on game nights, the crowds and the buzz. Home of the NBA's Washington Wizards (formerly Bullets), the Women's NBA Washington Mystics and the Washington Capitals NHL team, suddenly there's a bit more to DC sports than not being able to get a ticket to a Redskins game. To serve the crowds, and to encourage extra visits, the center hosts several other attractions, including a sports bar-restaurant, the *Velocity Grill*, which overlooks the Wizards' practice court. There's also a huge, four-floor **Discovery Channel** showcase store (daily 10am–10pm; free), which while introducing you to the wonderful interactive, scientific world of Discovery Channel also just happens to sell every conceivable gift on the planet.

For sports fans, though, there's only one stop, and that's the **MCI National Sports Gallery** (3rd floor; daily 10am–6pm; $5; ☎661-5133), which displays a veritable pantheon of sports' greatest stars alongside historic mementos, photographs and sports gear. There's some attempt to present the history, so if you didn't know that baseball's first professional team was the 1869 Cincinatti Red Stockings or that football's "huddle" was invented by DC's own Gallaudet University team of deaf players (who didn't want opponents who could sign to steal their plays), this is where you'll find out. But most are just along for the vicarious thrill of touching Babe Ruth's bat, checking out the story of the great home run race of 1998, and seeing Joe Montana's last touchdown ball, Ali's boxing robe from the "Thriller in Manila", Sonny Liston's trunks, and more autographed baseballs and football jerseys than you can count. Foreign visitors are going to find it all a bit bewildering, and even English soccer fans will be puzzled to read the American take on their greatest moment in 1966 when "regulation time ended with a 2-2 tie . . . [but] eleven minutes into overtime a shot by Geoffrey [sic] Hurst bounced from the crossbar to the grass and away". *Sir* Geoffrey, please. Charge up your entrance card with extra dollar-credits and you can play on the dozen or so interactive games in the gallery – shooting hoops,

For sports ticket information, see p.327.

pitching a championship putt, throwing a winning ball or making a tricky downhill ski run.

Along 7th and F streets

Downtown transformation is taking place rapidly along **7th Street**, between F and D, whose spruced-up buildings form the focus of a nascent arts district studded with galleries. New cafés, bars and restaurants contribute to the area's growing appeal, perhaps best exemplified by the residents of 7th Street's finest building, **The Lansburgh**, at no. 420 (between D and E). Once a department store, the building's soaring Neoclassical facade now provides a grand frame for the **Shakespeare Theater** (see p.314) and the swish apartments above it – home to (or at least Washington mailing address of) various celebs including Betty Friedan. Improvements are being made along **F Street**, between 7th and 10th, though it still has a way to go before it resembles its thriving turn-of-the-century commercial self. The street lost its heart after the 1968 riots, when its core businesses moved west; these included Hecht's (see p.206), whose forlorn old store premises at 7th and F, with its beautifully carved facade, cries out for rescue. The street is still largely a run of parking lots, T-shirt stalls and boarded-up buildings, but some elegant facades survive, starting with the Greek-Revival **Tariff Commission Building** (7th between E and F), opposite the old Hecht's, used by the Post Office Department for many years. In 1814, following the burning of the Capitol by the British, Congress convened here briefly before moving into the temporary Brick Capitol (see p.114). Two blocks west, at 9th Street, the elegant former **Riggs National Bank Building** has been rescued by *Marriott* hotels, while there are more stirring facades – though no development yet – on F Street at no. 918 (the rustic National Union Building) and no. 930 (Atlantic Building).

Chinatown and around

For reviews of Chinatown's best restaurants, see p.291.

Washington's **Chinatown** isn't a patch on those in San Francisco, New York or even London, stretching no more than a few undistinguished city blocks along G and H streets NW, between 6th and 8th. The vibrant **triumphal arch** over H Street (at 7th), paid for by Beijing in the 1980s, is hopelessly at odds with the neighborhood since it heralds little more than a dozen restaurants and a few grocery stores. Come here to eat, by all means – restaurants are particularly thick on H Street – but don't expect much else, other than dodging the attentions of panhandling drunks at night. Washington DC's first Chinese immigrants, in the early nineteenth century, didn't live in today's Chinatown (which only became such at the turn of this century) but in the gloriously named slums of Swampoodle, north of the Capitol. At that time, H Street and its environs were home to small businesses and modest but respectable rooming houses. In one of these, during the 1860s, Mary Surratt presided over the comings and goings of her son John and his colleagues, including a certain John Wilkes Booth – all subsequently implicated in the assassination of Abraham Lincoln (see p.204). A plaque records the affair at the **site of the house** (then no. 541 H St), now *Go-Lo's* restaurant at 604 H St NW.

Around the MCI Center and Chinatown

At present, Chinatown is on the cusp as full-scale development encroaches on either side, slowly reviving the area – or rather tearing it down and starting again. The first moves were made in the 1980s, which saw the construction of the colossal **Washington Convention Center** (H St, between 9th and 11th) and the multistory **Grand Hyatt** (1000 H St NW) – the latter is worth popping into in order to experience its soaring atrium. The occasional remnant of former days survives: walk past the Convention Center up to **1100 New York Avenue**, where the sprightly Art Deco facade of the avenue's former bus terminal is now preserved within an office complex.

Southeast, heading back toward Gallery Place-Chinatown Metro, a stroll along the pedestrianized section of G Street at 9th brings you up hard against the **Martin Luther King Memorial Library**, at 901 G St NW (Mon–Thurs 9am–9pm, Fri & Sat 9am–5.30pm, Sun 1–5pm; ☎ 727-1186), whose sleek lines of brick, steel and glass announce it immediately as the work of Mies van der Rohe. Opened in 1972, it's the city's main public library, and you can walk in to see the large mural of the life of the assassinated civil rights leader, painted by Don Miller.

Ford's Theater and the Petersen House

The district north of Pennsylvania Avenue has been home to several theaters since the founding of the city, being little more than a stroll from the White House and mansions of Lafayette Square for Washington notables who fancied a night's entertainment. In 1861, the National (see p.182) was joined by **Ford's Theater**, at 511 10th St NW, opened in a converted church by theatrical entrepreneur John T. Ford. It proved just as popular as its near neighbor, until on April 14, 1865 – during a performance of *Our American Cousin* – it witnessed the dramatic **assassination of Abraham Lincoln** by John Wilkes Booth, actor and Southern sympathizer. During the play, which Lincoln was watching with his wife from the presidential box, Booth shot the President once in the head before escaping; pandemonium broke out and Ford lost his theater in one fell swoop. Initially draped in black as a mark of respect, it was closed while the conspirators were pursued, caught and tried; Ford later abandoned attempts to reopen the theater after he received death threats. The theater was converted into offices and only in the 1960s was it decided to restore it to its previous condition.

Nearest Metro stations are Gallery Place-Chinatown, Metro Center or Federal Triangle.

Today it's a rather heavy-handed period piece, furnished in the style of 1865, but although it still serves as a working theater it's more notable as a museum dedicated to the night that Lincoln died. Provided rehearsals or matinées aren't underway (usually Thurs, Sat

The Assassination of President Lincoln

Five days after General Ulysses Grant received Robert E. Lee's sword and surrender at Appomattox, effectively ending the Civil War, President Abraham Lincoln went to the theater. There was a celebratory mood in the city and on the evening of Good Friday, **April 14, 1865**, President and Mrs Lincoln opted to go and see top actress Laura Keene perform in the comedy *Our American Cousin* at Ford's Theater, a play about a yokel who travels to England to claim his inheritance. The President's advisors were never very keen on him appearing in public, but Lincoln, as on several previous occasions, overrode their objections. The Lincolns were accompanied by their acquaintances Major Henry Rathbone and his fiancée Clara Harris; the four took their seats upstairs in the presidential box, just after the play had started.

The conspirators had been planning for weeks. **John Wilkes Booth**, a 26-year-old actor with Southern sympathies and delusions of grandeur, had first conceived of a plan to kidnap Lincoln during the war and use him as a bargaining chip for the release of Confederate prisoners. Booth drew others into the conspiracy, notably John Surratt, whose mother owned a rooming house on H Street, where the conspiracy was hatched; John Surratt was already acting as a low-level courier for the secessionist cause. George Atzerodt from Maryland was recruited because he knew the surrounding countryside and its hiding places, as was David Herold, a pharmacist's clerk in DC; Lewis Powell (or Paine, as he was sometimes known) was hired as muscle. With Lee's surrender in April, Booth decided to assassinate the President instead; Herold, Atzerodt and Powell were to kill Secretary of State William Seward and Vice-President Andrew Johnson. Surratt had already left the group when the talk turned to murder, and the other attacks came to naught: Johnson was left alone by a fearful Atzerodt while Seward, although injured by Powell, later recovered.

At about 10.15pm, during the third act, when only one actor was on stage and the audience was laughing at a joke, the assassin struck. Lincoln's bodyguard had left the box unattended and Booth took the opportunity to step inside and shoot Lincoln in the back of the head. Major Rathbone grappled with Booth but was stabbed in the arm with a hunting knife and severely wounded. Booth then jumped the 12ft down onto the stage, catching one of his spurs and fracturing a bone in his left leg as he fell. But he was on his feet immediately – most of the audience still thought it was part of the play – and shouted "Sic semper tyrannis!" ("Thus ever to tyrants": the motto of the state of Virginia) before running off backstage, where in the alley he had a horse waiting for him.

& Sun), the theater hosts entertaining **talks** (hourly 9.15am–4.15pm; free), recounting the events of the fateful night. You can then file up to the circle for a view through glass of the damask-furnished presidential box in which Lincoln sat in his rocking chair; most of the items inside are reproductions. In the basement, the **Lincoln Museum** (daily 9am–5pm; free; ☎ 426-6924) puts more flesh on the story. The actual weapon – a .44 Derringer – is on display, alongside a bloodstained piece of Lincoln's overcoat, Booth's knife and keys, and his diary, saying "I hoped for no gain. I knew no private wrong. I struck for my country and that alone."

First into the box was Charles Augustus Leale, a young army doctor. Lincoln was unconscious and laboring badly and it was decided to carry him to the nearest house to care for him better. Once inside the Petersen House, Lincoln was placed in the small back bedroom, where Leale and the other doctors strived to save him. Soon the house was bulging at the seams, as Mrs Lincoln, her son Robert, Secretary of War Edwin Stanton, various politicians and army officers and, eventually, Lincoln's pastor, all arrived to do what they could. Lincoln never regained consciousness and died at 7.22am the next morning, April 15; Stanton spoke for all, declaiming "Now he belongs to the ages" (or, as some historians assert, to the "angels"). Lincoln's body was taken back to the White House, where it lay in state for three days before the funeral.

Booth, meanwhile, had fled on horseback through Maryland with David Herold, stopping at a certain Doctor Mudd's to have his injured leg treated. The pair hid out for several days, but after crossing into Virginia were eventually surrounded by Union troops at a farm. Herold surrendered, and on the same day, April 26, Booth was shot dead while holed up inside. All the other alleged conspirators were soon captured and sent for trial on May 10 in a military court at Fort McNair (see p.141). They were kept chained and hooded and, after six weeks of evidence, Herold, Powell, Atzerodt and Mary Surratt were sentenced to hang, the punishment being carried out on July 7, 1865. A last-minute reprieve for Mary Surratt – who, although she housed the conspirators, probably knew nothing of the conspiracy – was refused, and she became the first woman to be executed by the US government. Dr Mudd received a life sentence, while the stage hand who held Booth's horse at the theater got six years, though both were pardoned in 1869 by Andrew Johnson, Lincoln's successor. John Surratt, who had fled America, was recaptured in 1867 and also stood trial, but was freed when the jury couldn't agree on a verdict.

Much has been written about the effect on the country and its future of the assassination of Lincoln, who was at the start of his second term as President when he died. Many have held that the slavery question would have been settled with more skill and grace under his leadership. It's impossible to say, though it is interesting to note the personal effect that the close-quarters assassination may have had on the three other occupants of the presidential box that night: ten years later Mary Lincoln – never the most stable of people – was judged insane and committed; in 1883 Clara Harris (by now Clara Harris Rathbone) was herself shot, by her husband, Henry Rathbone, who died in an asylum in 1911.

The Petersen House

Having been shot, the President – now unconscious – was carried across the street and placed in the back bedroom of a house belonging to a local tailor, William Petersen. Lincoln never regained consciousness and died the next morning. Built of the same red brick as the theater, **Petersen House**, at 516 10th St (daily 9am–5pm; free), has also been sympathetically restored, and you can troop through its gloomy parlor rooms to the small bedroom to see a replica of the bed on which Lincoln died (laid diagonally, since he was too tall to lie straight). Period furniture aside, there's little to see – in a concession to taste, the original bloodstained pillow that used to be laid on the bed has been moved to the theater museum. However, it's interesting to note just how small the room is: Lincoln's immediate family and colleagues were present in the house during his last night, but not all could cram into the room at the same time – something ignored by contemporaneous artists who, in a series of mawkish deathbed scenes popular at the time, often portrayed up to thirty people crowded around the ailing President's bed.

Around Metro Center

The downtown hub of the Metro system is **Metro Center**, with separate exits along G and 12th streets. From either you emerge by the **Hecht Company Department Store**, in stunning modern premises on G Street (between 12th and 13th), but with decades of tradition behind it. Other aged department stores haven't done quite so well: a block east, at 11th and F, the venerable Woodward and Lothrop closed in 1995 – if the Washington Opera ever raises the money, the empty store is slated to be its future home – while Garfinkel's lost its fight for survival in 1990, though its location at 14th and F forms part of the **Metropolitan Square** and **Hamilton Square** development. This retains various historic Beaux-Arts facades along 15th Street (facing the Treasury Building), notably the turn-of-the-century B.F. Keith's Theater and the National Metropolitan Bank; there's also access to the historic **Old Ebbitt Grill** (see p.293).

Around the corner on the south side of F Street, there's an entrance to The Shops at National Place (see p.320); the facade incorporates the original, highly decorative half-rotunda entrance of the **National Press Club**.

National Museum of Women in the Arts

1250 New York Ave NW ☎783-5000; Metro Center Metro. Mon–Sat 10am–5pm, Sun noon–5pm. Suggested donation $3.

The museum's airy Mezzanine Café (Mon–Sat 11.30am–2.30 pm) is one of the most appealing lunch spots in the city.

The **National Museum of Women in the Arts** houses the world's most important collection of art of its kind – over 2500 works by 600 artists, from the sixteenth century to the present day. Incorporating silverware, ceramics, photographs and decorative items, as well as paintings, the museum opened in 1987 and proved an instant hit. This is partly to do with the building itself, converted from – of all things – a former masonic lodge built by Waddy Butler Wood.

The **permanent collection** is on the third floor. Rotating selections of **contemporary works** are displayed in the mezzanine level, and there are **temporary exhibitions** on the ground, second and fourth floors. The **information desk** and **shop** are on the ground floor as you enter.

The collection

The collection runs chronologically, starting with works from the Renaissance, like those of Sofonisba Anguissola (1532–1625), who was considered the most important woman artist of her day. From a noble family, she achieved fame as an accomplished portraitist before becoming court painter to Phillip II of Spain; her well-judged *Double Portrait of a Lady and Her Daughter* is on show, along with the energetic *Holy Family with St John* by her contemporary, Lavinia Fontana (who had a head start by being the daughter of a successful Bolognese artist). A century or so later, **Dutch and Flemish** women like Clara Peeters, Judith Leyster and Rachel Ruysch were producing still lives and genre scenes that were the equal of their more famous male colleagues – witness the vivacity of Peeters' *Still Life of Fish and Cat*. Women broke out of their restricted environment on occasion too, as demonstrated by the superbly crafted natural-science engravings of German-born Maria Sybilla Merian, the result of her intrepid explorations in Surinam in 1699. Meanwhile, in France, women like Elisabeth-Louise Vigé-Lebrun (1755–1842) held sway as court painters, depicting the royalty fluttering around Marie Antoinette. But as a woman artist she was marginalized, her paintings denied the respect accorded those of her male contemporaries – who kept her out of the Académie des Beaux-Arts until the 1780s.

In the **nineteenth century**, American women artists began to enter the fray. Lilly Martin Spencer was inordinately popular as a producer of genre scenes: *The Artist and Her Family at a Fourth of July Picnic* (1864) is typically vibrant. As Impressionism widened the parameters of art, painters like Berthe Morisot (1841–95) and particularly **Mary Cassatt** (1844–1926) produced daring (for the time) scenes of nursing mothers, young girls and mewling babies. Cassatt, like many of her contemporaries, was intrigued by the forms and colors of oriental art; *The Bath* (1898), an etching of mother and baby using crisp swatches of pale color, was influenced by an exhibition of Japanese woodblocks she had seen in Paris, where she lived from an early age. Cecilia Beaux (1863–1942), also inspired by her stay in Paris, was sought after for her rich, expressive portraits – so much so that she was honored with a commission to paint Theodore and Mrs Roosevelt in 1903.

Edgar Degas befriended Cassatt in Paris – his portrait of her hangs in the National Portrait Gallery (see p.195).

Twentieth-century artists and works include the Neoclassical sculpture of Camille Claudel (1864–1943), the occasional painting by Georgia O'Keeffe and, most boldly, a cycle of prints depicting the hardships of working-class life by the socialist and feminist **Käthe Kollwitz** (1867–1945), part of her powerful *A Weaver's Rebellion* (1893–98). Self-portraits add some interesting insights into character: Kollwitz appears drained by her work in an etching of 1921, while **Frida Kahlo** (1907–54), dressed in a peasant's outfit and clutching a note to Trotsky, dedicates herself to the Revolution. The

last gallery brings you into modern times, with contemporary pieces
by sculptor Dorothy Dehner, minimalist Dorothea Rockburne and
abstract expressionists Helen Frankenthaler and Elaine de Kooning
among others: should these appeal, you'll need to set off for the
Hirshorn, National Gallery East Wing and National Museum of
American Art, whose holdings are all more substantial.

The New York Avenue Presbyterian Church

Half a block west of the museum, at 1313 New York Avenue at H
Street, the red-brick **New York Avenue Presbyterian Church** (daily
9am–1pm; guided tours Sun after 9am & 11am services; ☎393-
3700) is a clever 1950s facsimile of the mid-nineteenth-century
church in which the Lincoln family worshipped. The pastor, Dr
Gurley, was at Lincoln's bedside at the Petersen House (see p.205)
when he died and conducted the funeral service four days later at the
White House. Ask in the office on the New York Avenue side and
someone should be on hand to show you the President's second-row
pew, while downstairs in the "Lincoln Parlor" you can see an early
draft of his Emancipation Proclamation and portraits of Lincoln and
Dr Gurley.

Chapter 7

New Downtown to Adams-Morgan

W hile the tourists zigzag back and forth through the cultural triangle formed by the Mall, White House and US
Capitol, the business brain and artistic heart of the city
tick away in the very different neighborhoods to the north. Not all
will be high on everyone's vacation agenda – many locals visit parts
infrequently if at all, and some districts probably shouldn't be inves-
tigated by anyone with a desire to live a long and fruitful life. But to
go home without sampling any of downtown Washington beyond the
Mall would be a mistake.

Closest to the center, **New Downtown** – for the want of a better label – has least to recommend it, though visitors, perversely,
often end up seeing more of these few blocks between K Street and
Scott Circle than any others, since they contain most of the city's
central mid-range hotels. Here, L'Enfant's grid contains some of
the city's least inspiring architecture, and although as many political and economic decisions are made in these white-collar offices
as in Congress, a stately hotel, a church or two and a couple of offbeat museums are about the limit of New Downtown's interest.
Things pick up at nearby **Dupont Circle**, DC's major arts corridor,
with a score or more of private galleries and the **Phillips
Collection**, the first modern art museum in America. There's
enough to keep you in the neighborhood for a day at least: avenues
of imposing turn-of-the-century mansions (several open to the
public), the buildings of **Embassy Row**, the townhouse museums
of neighboring **Kalorama**, and some of the city's best shopping
and nightlife. To the north, ethnically mixed **Adams-Morgan** has
more soul and less pretension, and is one of the few areas in the
city with a safe, democratic and inexpensive nightlife; dine out at
least once here, since the area's run of ethnic restaurants is
unbeaten in the city. Only in **Shaw**, to the east, do you have to pick
your spot carefully. Once *the* thriving black neighborhood, and
home of a vibrant 1920s and 1930s music scene, the area is still

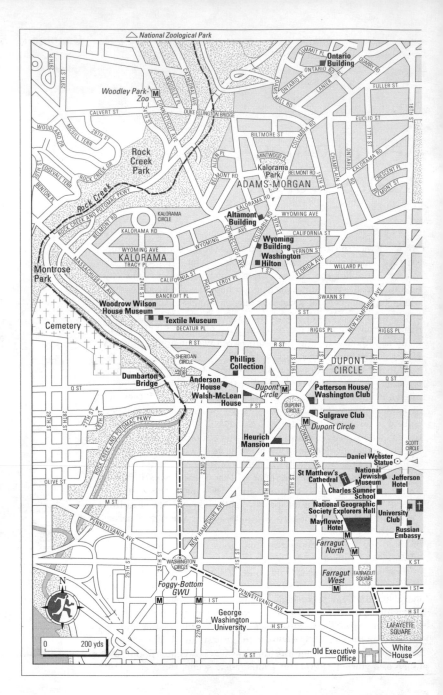

△ National Zoological Park

Ontario
Building

Woodley Park-
Zoo

Rock
Creek
Park

Kalorama
Park

ADAMS-MORGAN

Altamont
Building

Wyoming
Building

Washington
Hilton

KALORAMA

Montrose
Park

Woodrow Wilson
House Museum

Cemetery

Textile Museum

Phillips
Collection

DUPONT
CIRCLE

Dumbarton
Bridge

Anderson
House

Walsh-McLean
House

Dupont
Circle

Patterson House/
Washington Club

Sulgrave Club

Dupont Circle

Heurich
Mansion

Daniel Webster
Statue

St Matthew's
Cathedral

National
Jewish
Museum

Jefferson
Hotel

Charles Sumner
School

National Geographic
Society Explorers Hall

University
Club

Mayflower
Hotel

Russian
Embassy

Farragut
North

Farragut
West

Washington
Circle

Foggy-Bottom
GWU

George
Washington
University

Farragut
Square

LAFAYETTE
SQUARE

Old Executive
Office

White
House

N

0   200 yds

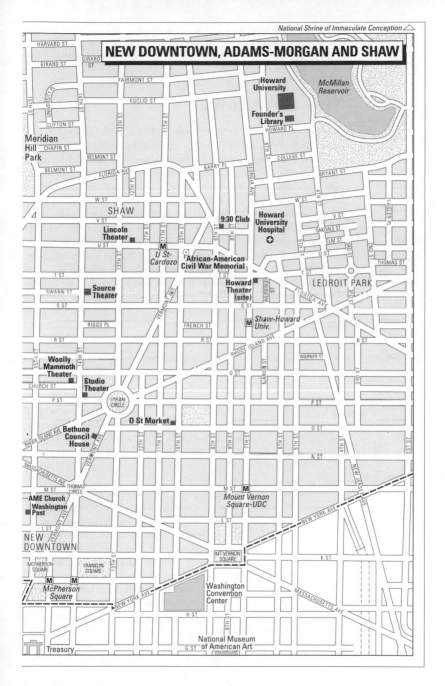

National Shrine of Immaculate Conception △

NEW DOWNTOWN, ADAMS-MORGAN AND SHAW

HARVARD ST

GIRARD ST

GIRARD ST

FAIRMONT ST

EUCLID ST

Howard University

Founder's Library

HOWARD PL

COLLEGE ST

McMillan Reservoir

CLIFTON ST

Meridian Hill Park

CHAPIN ST

BELMONT ST

BELMONT ST

FLORIDA AVE

BARRY PL

BRYANT ST

W ST

SHAW

V ST

Lincoln Theater

9:30 Club

Howard University Hospital

OAKDALE ST

ELM ST

THOMAS ST

U ST

U St-Cardozo

African-American Civil War Memorial

T ST

LEDROIT PARK

Source Theater

SWANN ST

S ST

Howard Theater (site)

FLORIDA AVE

RIGGS PL

FRENCH ST

Shaw-Howard Univ.

R ST

R ST

RHODE ISLAND AVE

WARNER ST

Woolly Mammoth Theater

Studio Theater

CHURCH ST

P ST

LOGAN CIRCLE

O St Market

O ST

P ST

O ST

Bethune Council House

MASSACHUSETTS AVE

N ST

AME Church

THOMAS CIRCLE

M ST

Mount Vernon Square-UDC

NEW YORK AVE

Washington Post

L ST

L ST

NEW DOWNTOWN

K ST

MCPHERSON SQUARE

FRANKLIN SQUARE

MT VERNON SQUARE

McPherson Square

NEW YORK AVE

Washington Convention Center

MASSACHUSETTS AVE

H ST

Treasury

National Museum of American Art

G ST

feeling the effects of its rapid postwar decline, though pockets are slowly being dragged back toward respectability: the odd museum, a fringe theater scene and booming bar-life on U **Street** offer rare diversions.

New Downtown

DC's business district, or **NEW DOWNTOWN**, is the off-center diamond north of Lafayette Square formed by Pennsylvania, New Hampshire, Massachusetts and New York avenues. Some of its thoroughfares, like 16th Street and Connecticut Avenue, were developed early by businessmen and hoteliers who saw the advantage in being just a few blocks from the White House, but these streets really took off after the panicked flight from the old downtown areas to the east after the 1968 riots. In part the district has paid the price for this shotgun arrangement: there's little sense of history and virtually no sense of a meaningful neighborhood. In this, of course, New Downtown resembles the anonymous downtown ghettos of other modern American cities – largely white, largely sterile and largely deserted after 6pm.

For New Downtown listings, see the following pages: accommodation p.276; cafés p.284; restaurants p.291; nightlife p.301

Along K Street

K Street – spine of New Downtown's corporate business and political lobbying district – is DC's Wall Street in spirit only. When the companies first moved in during the 1970s, local zoning ordinances prevented them from aping New York's soaring urban streetscape. Restricted to a maximum height of 130ft, the buildings are generally production-line boxes of little distinction in which lobbyists, lawyers, brokers and bankers beaver away from dawn till dusk. Between 13th and 20th streets there's barely a building to raise the pulse, though street traders do their best to inject a bit of life, hustling jewelry, T-shirts, silk ties, hot dogs and bath-salts from the wide sidewalks.

Use McPherson Square Metro for McPherson Square, Franklin Square, K St and 16th St; Farragut West and Farragut North Metros for Farragut Square, K St, 16th St and 17th St.

Most agreeable of the trio of squares on the south side of K Street is **Franklin Square** (between 13th and 14th), its large, tree-covered expanse broken up by paths, benches and a central fountain.

A block west, **McPherson Square** is named for the commander of the Tennessee Army during the Civil War. Here, at least, late nineteenth- and early twentieth-century architects injected a modicum of style and wit into their buildings' facades, as in the Neoclassical Investment Building (15th and K), the Southern Railway Building (1500 K St, opposite the square) and, best of all, the scrupulously carved capitals and lion's head plaques of the Southern Building (805 15th St).

Two blocks further west, **Farragut Square** (at 17th) is the least prepossessing of K Street's open spaces, a small green stain beneath the gaze of Admiral David Farragut, whose statue celebrates his reck-

less heroism ("Damn the torpedoes. Full speed ahead") during the
Civil War Battle of Mobile Bay.

Connecticut Avenue and 17th Street

North of K Street the business-oriented boulevards of **Connecticut
Avenue** and **17th Street** march four long blocks to Dupont Circle.
Connecticut Avenue is the grander, graced since 1925 by the double
bay-fronted **Mayflower Hotel** (no. 1127), whose first official function was President Coolidge's inaugural ball. Designed by the New
York architects responsible for Grand Central Station, it has the
same glorious height and space: inside, the remarkable 500-foot-
long Promenade – effectively a lobby connecting Connecticut
Avenue to 17th Street – could comfortably accommodate an army
division or two. It's rich in rugs, oils, sofas, gilt and mirrors, as is the
hotel's Grand Ballroom, in which a dozen incoming presidents have
swirled around the dancefloor over the years. FDR even lived in the
Mayflower for a while after his inauguration, J. Edgar Hoover
lunched here every day during his tenure at the FBI, while Monica
Lewinsky was interviewed in her suite by House prosecutors during
the Clinton impeachment proceedings.

Cut through to 17th Street, then head north for one block to M
Street, where the **National Geographic Society** maintains its
Explorers Hall at 1145 17th St NW (Mon–Sat 9am–5pm, Sun
10am–5pm; free; ☎857-7588). Founded in 1888, the Society started off by funding important expeditions to various uncharted terri-
tories, but its greatest asset was Gilbert Hovey Grosvenor, founding
editor of *National Geographic* magazine, who first conceived that
geography could be presented in an exciting fashion, primarily by
commissioning spectacular illustrations. The yellow-bordered magazine is now recognized the world over. The Explorers Hall presents
special exhibitions and child-friendly geography exhibits. The walk-
through **"Geographica"** features interactive panels and videos
explaining weather systems, evolution, planet-forming and fossil
finds – many of the subjects are illustrated with splendid photography from the magazine – whilst in **"Earth Station One"** a giant
video screen and revolving eleven-foot globe combine to present a
fifteen-minute interactive show on the workings of the earth, its
seas, atmosphere and natural features.

Across M Street, the **Charles Sumner School**, at 1201 17th St
(Mon–Fri 10am–5pm; free; ☎727-3419), was named for the nineteenth-century senator beaten up in the Old Senate Chamber by pro-
slavery Congressman Preston Brooks of South Carolina, who violently
objected to Sumner's more enlightened views (see p.117). To improve
the education offered to black children, a separate public high school –
the first in the country – was established in the city in 1870; for a period it was located here at 17th Street. A harmonious red-brick building
of 1872 with a handsome central clocktower, the school is largely used

*JFK was, of
course, buried
at Arlington;
see p.252.*

today for conferences, but sign in at the desk and check the list of current exhibits, which range from temporary shows by African-American artists to displays relating to the city's school system.

Half a block further north, turn left down Rhode Island Avenue for princely **St Matthew's Cathedral**, 1725 Rhode Island Ave NW (Mon–Fri & Sun 6.30am–6.30pm, Sat 7.30am–6.30pm; tours Sun 2.30–4.30pm; free; ☎347-3215), where JFK's funeral mass was held in 1963; there's a memorial in front of the altar.

B'nai B'rith Klutznick National Jewish Museum

1640 Rhode Island Ave NW ☎857-6583; Farragut North Metro. Daily except Sat 10am–5pm. Admission $2.

On the corner of Rhode Island Avenue and 17th Street, the exemplary **B'nai B'rith Klutznick National Jewish Museum** presents a captivating look at Jewish life through historical, ceremonial and folk art objects. The galleries cover every aspect of the Jewish experience, from birth to Bar Mitzvah, marriage and death – eighteenth-century circumcision instruments and tax permits, painted Italian marriage contracts and linen Torah (liturgical scroll) binders are all on display. The oldest items are two-thousand-year-old incantation bowls, whose Hebrew inscriptions were believed to cast a protective spell over whoever the words were dedicated to. Other pieces show extraordinary workmanship, like the silver spice containers adorned with turrets or the micrographic writing on miniature Bibles. Enthusiastic docents point out the significance of silver amulets, Torah crowns and various parchment scrolls; slender metal Torah pointers, for example, in the shape of a hand, are designed to avoid a human hand touching the sacred scroll itself. The museum also displays changing exhibits of Jewish art and has a hall of fame celebrating the Jewish-American contribution to sports. There's also an excellent museum shop.

Along and around 16th Street

If New Downtown has a street to match the grandiloquence of Pennsylvania Avenue it's **16th Street**, the wide boulevard that starts at Lafayette Square and runs north to the border with Maryland six miles away. Most of the area above K Street was scantily populated until well into the nineteenth century, but post-Civil War expansion changed 16th Street completely, replacing a ramshackle black neighborhood with large mansions, gentlemen's clubs and patrician hotels, reveling in their proximity to the White House.

The best of the buildings in the lower reaches are between K Street and Scott Circle, starting with the imposing **Russian Embassy** (1125 16th St NW); across the street from here, the original mansion facade of the **National Geographic Society** is far more appealing than its modern 17th Street addition. Further up come the equally grand **University Club** and, opposite, the stately **Jefferson Hotel** (1220 16th St NW), before you reach Scott Circle itself.

There was a time, at the end of the nineteenth century, when Scott Circle was a fashionable park at the center of a residential neighborhood. Now the traffic is thick and the park is non-existent – the only diversion being provided by the Union commander General Winfield Scott astride a prancing horse. The views, though, are majestic, particularly those south to the White House.

New Downtown

Off 16th: Metropolitan AME Church and the Washington Post

Half a block to the east at 1518 M St, the large Gothic red-brick **Metropolitan African Methodist Episcopal (AME) Church** – built and paid for in 1886 by former slaves – saw the funeral of statesman and orator Frederick Douglass in February 1895, brought to lie in state in the church in which he had often preached. On the day of the funeral, crowds swamped the street outside, black schools closed for the day and flags in the city flew at half mast. The church isn't open for visits, though you may be able to take a look around if the doors are open, or after a service.

For more on Frederick Douglass, see pp.144–145.

Walk around the block onto 15th Street for the offices of the **Washington Post**, at 1150 15th St NW (tours Mon 10am, 11am, 1pm, 2pm & 3pm; free; ☎334-7969; reservations recommended). Together with the *New York Times*, the *Post* likes to imagine that it informs the informed in America. Its reputation is based squarely on the investigative coup of its reporters Bob Woodward and Carl Bernstein, who brought to light the Watergate scandal that led ultimately to the resignation of President Nixon (see p.170). Tours show you how the paper is produced not, it has to be said, a deeply exciting experience, and unless you're hot on the Watergate trail, it's one you can probably live without.

Dupont Circle, Embassy Row and Kalorama

Until the Civil War, Pacific Circle – as **Dupont Circle** was first known – marked the western edge of the city, beyond which the nation's capital petered out into a series of farms, slaughterhouses and barns. With the postwar boom, however, came something of a transformation, as streets were paved and a bridge was built across Rock Creek to nearby Georgetown. The British Embassy was built here in the mid-1870s, followed by lawyers and businessmen who installed their families in substantial brick Victorian houses. By the turn of the century, Dupont Circle was where all self-respecting industrial barons and high-flying diplomats built their city mansions, often in the favored Beaux-Arts style of the time. Massachusetts Avenue, northwest of the Circle, became so popular with foreign legations that it acquired the tag **Embassy Row**, while the even more secluded residences north of S Street developed into the exclusive neighborhood of **Kalorama** – named (in Greek) after the "beautiful view" it afforded of the Rock Creek Valley.

Dupont Circle's golden age of soirées, socialites and selectivity ended at roughly the same time as World War II. Many of the wealthy residents had already been hard hit by the 1929 stock market crash and had sold up; other mansions were torn down or, the ultimate ignominy, turned into rooming houses for the postwar influx of federal workers. The Circle became solidly middle-class and, during the 1970s, even vaguely radical, as a younger crowd moved in, attracted by a dilapidated housing stock in which they could strip pine, throw down weave rugs and demonstrate against Vietnam.

Rampant gentrification has long seen off the Dupont Circle hippies and it's once more a very definitely upmarket address, but the neighborhood has managed to retain something of a cultural edge. There's a thriving **gallery district** (around Q and R streets, between 20th and 22nd), while Dupont Circle is also center of the city's **gay scene**, with bars and clubs along 17th Street (east of the circle) and P Street (west). Washington's influx of designer coffee shops began here, and there are more impressive restaurants and bookshops than in any other part of DC. One of the best days to visit is the first Saturday in June when the **Dupont–Kalorama Museum Walk** (☎667-0441) sponsors free concerts, historic house tours and various craft activities.

Dupont Circle

For Dupont Circle listings, see the following pages: accommodation p.278; cafés p.284; restaurants p.294; nightlife p.303.

Dupont Circle itself is one of the city's major intersections, with New Hampshire, Massachusetts and Connecticut avenues converging at a large traffic island centered on an allegorical **fountain** whose frolicking nude figures – representing sea, stars and wind – were designed to honor the Civil War naval exploits of Admiral Samuel Dupont. In modern times the Circle itself has always looked a little ragged at the edges – hip thriller writer George P. Pelecanos, writing about the 1970s, pictured it full of "girl-watching businessmen, stoners, cruising homosexuals, short-skirted secretaries, doe-faced chicken hawks eyeing little boys, the whole Dupont stew", a tableau that's not entirely outdated today – but on the whole it's an easygoing hangout with chess-players hogging the permanent tables in the center of the circle, and a multitude of cafés, bookstores and restaurants within a few minutes' walk. There are **Metro** entrances to the north and south.

It's hard to imagine Dupont Circle in its prime since most of the surrounding mansions were razed by developers in the 1950s and 1960s. Two survivors are the Beaux-Arts specimen at the corner with Massachusetts Avenue (now the **Sulgrave Club**), and the Neoclassical building at no. 15 – now the Washington Club but once the **Patterson House** where, famously, the Coolidges, camping out while White House renovations took place, entertained Charles Lindbergh, fresh from his solo transatlantic crossing.

The Heurich Mansion

Built in 1894 for German-born brewing magnate Christian Heurich, the Romanesque **Heurich Mansion**, 1307 New Hampshire Ave NW, a block south of the Circle, announces its owner's origins and wealth loud and clear with its turret, castellations and richly carved wood-and-plaster interior. The building is now occupied by the **Historical Society of Washington DC** (Wed–Sat 10am–4pm; $3; ☎785-2068), which allows visitors to take a self-guided tour through many of the restored rooms, dwelling on the mansion's lavish decor and the lifestyle of its occupants. On display are the formal parlor, drawing room and dining room, a music room with a mahogany musicians' balcony, and the basement *Bierstube* (beer room) where the family had breakfast, carved with clunky Teutonic drinking mottos ("He who has never been drunk is not a good man"). Temporary exhibitions also highlight aspects of city history and architecture, and there's a good bookstore, devoted to works about the city.

Embassy Row

Embassy Row – as it still likes to think of itself – starts in earnest a few paces northwest up Massachusetts Avenue, where the Indonesian Embassy at no. 2020 (opposite the *Embassy Row Hilton*) occupies the magnificent Art Nouveau **Walsh-McLean House**, built in 1903 for gold baron Thomas Walsh. It's a superb building, with colonnaded loggia and intricate, carved windows, and saw regular service as one of Washington society's most fashionable venues, with soirées presided over by Walsh's daughter Evalyn, the last private owner of the Hope Diamond (now in the National Museum of Natural History).

The Goodwill Embassy Tour (May; ☎636-4225) is a unique chance to see inside DC's embassies – see p.47.

A block further up – past the stately red-brick *Westin Fairfax* hotel (formerly the *Ritz-Carlton*) – the **Anderson House** at 2118 Massachusetts Ave NW is a similarly impressive pile, a veritable palace built between 1902 and 1905 as the winter residence of Larz Anderson, who served as ambassador to Belgium and Japan. As a Beaux-Arts residence it has no equal in the city, its gray-stone exterior sporting twin arched entrances with heavy wooden doors and colonnaded portico. Inside, original furnishings – cavernous fireplaces, inlaid marble floors, Flemish tapestries, diverse murals and a grand ballroom – provide a suitably lavish backdrop for ambassadorial receptions. Some of this you'll be able to see for yourself since the house was bequeathed in Anderson's will to the **Society of the Cincinnati** (Tues–Sat 1–4pm; free; ☎785-2040), which maintains a small museum of Revolutionary memorabilia. The society is the oldest patriotic organization in the country, established in 1783 – Anderson's great-grandfather was a founder-member – and all its members are direct descendants of Revolutionary War officers. George Washington was the first President-General of the Society; there's a white marble bust of him in the entrance hall, by Thomas

Crawford, who sculpted the Freedom figure on top of the Capitol. Probably the best time to come to the Anderson House is for one of the regular **free concerts** (see p.313).

This far up the avenue, virtually every building flies a national flag outside its front door and security is discreet but tight. With time on your hands, you may as well stroll the block or so further northwest to **Sheridan Circle**, whose equestrian statue of Union General Phillip H. Sheridan was erected in 1909. It's quite a dainty representation of the general astride a boisterous horse – restrained in the extreme compared to the sixty-foot-high heads of Washington, Jefferson, Lincoln and Roosevelt that its sculptor Gutzon Borglum went on to carve at Mount Rushmore. On the south side of the Circle, the **Turkish Embassy** (1606 23rd St) is awash with Near Eastern motifs – oddly, it wasn't commissioned by the Turks at all but by one Edward Everett, the man who patented the fluted bottle-top. Finally, from the Circle, duck briefly down 23rd Street to see **Dumbarton Bridge**, guarded on either side by enormous bronze bison. The bridge provides the quickest route into northern Georgetown, emerging on Q Street by Dumbarton House, about twenty minutes from Dupont Circle.

The Phillips Collection

1600 21st St NW ☎387-2151; Dupont Circle Metro. Tues–Sat 10am–5pm, Sun noon–7pm; tours Wed & Sat 2pm (reserve in advance). Admission $6.50; tours free.

The **Phillips Collection**'s much trumpeted claim to be "America's first museum of modern art" is based on its opening eight years before New York's Museum of Modern Art. It's one of the most congenial galleries in Washington: the oldest part of the brownstone Georgian-Revival building was the family home of founder Duncan Phillips, who lost his father and brother in little over a year and established a memorial gallery in the house in 1921 in their honor. Financed by the family's steel fortune, Phillips bought nearly 2500 works over the years: during the 1920s, he and his artist wife Marjorie became patrons of young painters like Georgia O'Keeffe and Marsden Hartley, while there are works by everyone from Renoir to Rothko (and several by distinctly non-modern artists like Giorgione and El Greco, in whose work Phillips saw the sources of modern art). Highlights are picked out below, but note that not everything can be displayed at any one time: changes of paintings and temporary exhibitions are common, which can frustrate particular viewing plans but can also throw up unexpected delights.

The **main entrance** is in the Goh Annex, on 21st Street. The permanent collection is exhibited on the first two floors of the annex and on the first and second floor of the original building; annex and original building are connected by an enclosed "skywalk". The annex's third floor is used for **special exhibitions**, while the ground level of the main building also holds the **museum shop**. There's a full program of cultural events: in particular, **classical music recitals** (Sept–May Sun 5pm; free with admission) and so-called **"Artful Evenings"** (June–Sept Thurs 5–8.30pm; $5), with live music, lectures and a bar.

The Goh Annex

The permanent collection on the **first floor** of the Goh Annex makes for a rather low-key introduction, usually featuring a handful of Abstract-Expressionist works from the 1950s, including a characteristically gloomy set of paintings by Rothko. Things cheer up no end once you climb the stairs to the **second floor**: a wistful Blue Period Picasso, Matisse's *Studio, Quai St-Michel*, a Cézanne still life and no fewer than four van Goghs, including the powerful *Road Menders* (1889). Pierre Bonnard gets a good showing – you have to stand well back to take in the expansive and assertive *The Terrace* (1918) and *The Palm* (1926). Top billing generally goes to *The Luncheon of the Boating Party* (1891) by Renoir, where straw-boatered dandies linger over a long and bibulous feast – Phillips bought the painting in 1923 for $125,000 as part of a two-year burst of acquisition that also yielded Cézanne's *Mont Saint-Victoire* and Honoré Daumier's *The Uprising*. There's an interesting spread of works by Degas, too, from early scenes like *Women Combing Their Hair* (1875) to a late ballet picture, *Dancers at the Bar* (1900), in which the background and hair of the subjects collide in an orange frenzy.

The English landscapes of John Constable include the fine *On the River Stour* (1835), where a fisherman battles against the elements, alongside other nineteenth-century works by artists including Gustave Courbet and Eugène Delacroix – the latter responsible for a wonderful picture of the violinist Paganini in full fiddle, with the light falling only on his white hands and expressive face. Phillips' catholic taste comes to the fore with the juxtaposition of two paintings of the *Repentant Peter*: one, fat and bluff, by Goya, the second – two centuries older – a more familiar, biblical study by El Greco. An odd pictorial choice on the face of it, this last was bought by Phillips for his modern art museum for the very good reason that he considered El Greco "the first impassioned expressionist".

Main building

Across the skywalk and down the stairs to the **first floor** of the main building brings you into the oak-paneled **"Music Room"**, where Cubist works by Georges Braque (a particular favorite of Phillips, who owned thirteen) vie for attention. *Round Table* (1929) is the most famous, piled high with guitar, dagger, apples, books, clay pipe and wallet – the sort of stuff lying around the average Cubist's kitchen. Beyond here the collection begins to concentrate more on late nineteenth-century American artists, with Winslow Homer's bleak *To The Rescue*, James McNeill Whistler's gentle *Miss Lilian Woakes* and moody Albert Pinkham Ryder landscapes to the fore.

The **second floor** features artists championed by Phillips in the 1920s and 1930s including Milton Avery (who influenced the young Rothko) and Jacob Lawrence – the latter represented by extracts from a powerful series known as *The Migration of the Negro*. Better-known names abound, too, notably Edward Hopper, whose works include the faintly menacing *Sunday* (1926) and the much later *Approaching a City*, viewed from the vantage point of sunken train tracks. A separate **Klee Room** displays a stunning collection of paintings by the Bauhaus teacher and artist, from the stick figures embellishing *Arrival of the Jugglers* (1926) to the abstract *The Way to the Citadel* (1937), where red arrows point the way through a kaleidoscopic maze of rectangles, triangles and trapezoidal shapes.

Woodrow Wilson (1856–1924)

He was the perfect prototype of the seventeenth-century Puritan reincarnated.

Alistair Cooke, *America*, 1973

Born **Thomas Woodrow Wilson** in Stanton, Virginia, to a plain-living Presbyterian family, the future president dropped the "Thomas" at a very early age, convinced that the new version would sound better when he was famous. He attended law school and, though he didn't take his final exams, practiced law in Georgia for a year, only to discover that it wasn't his *métier*. Wilson returned to graduate school to take his doctorate (making him the only American president to have earned his PhD) and taught law and political economics for twelve years, eventually rising to become a reforming president of Princeton. Known and respected as an academic writer on political science and stern critic of government corruption, there he might have stayed but for the Democratic Party's need for progressive candidates to run against the splintering Republicans. In 1910 Wilson won election as the **Governor of New Jersey** and two years later received the Democratic nomination for President. The split in the Republican Party – with Theodore Roosevelt running against the incumbent William Howard Taft – gave the Democrats both houses in Congress and let Wilson into power.

A stirring orator (and the last president to write his own speeches), in his two terms of office Wilson saw through a batch of **reforming legislation** that wouldn't be matched until the days of FDR: the Federal Reserve Bank was established to better regulate the banking system, anti-trust laws were strengthened, the 19th Amendment (for women's suffrage) passed, and labor laws enacted that at least gave a nod to workers' rights. But, with Congress dominated at least at first by Southern Democrats, Wilson also presided over rather darker deeds – not least the violent breaking of the Colorado coal strike, leaving 66 people dead, and the entrenchment of segregation in the federal system. Indeed, it's misleading to see Wilson as any kind of liberal; his reforms made capitalism safe in a period of con-

---

Kalorama

North of Sheridan Circle, in the exclusive district of **Kalorama**, quiet, crisp, lawned streets stretch out to meet Rock Creek Park. Here, the city's diplomatic community sits behind lace curtains and bullet-proof glass in row after row of multimillion-dollar townhouse embassies, private homes and hibiscus-clad gardens. If you wanted an immediate object lesson in the inequalities of life in downtown DC, just ten blocks to the east you can buy crack on the street in Shaw.

As in all rich American ghettos there is very little to see (the only similarity they have, in fact, with poor American ghettos). But for an agreeable stroll in quite the nicest neighborhood this side of Georgetown, head up 24th Street toward **Kalorama Circle**, from where there are splendid views across Rock Creek Park. Just to the east, the **French Embassy** at 2221 Kalorama Rd NW is the most ambitious building hereabouts, a Tudor-style country manor

Dupont Circle, Embassy Row and Kalorama

---

siderable turmoil and were very much part of the turn-of-the-century strengthening of federal power at the expense of individual freedom. It's no coincidence that the 18th Amendment sanctioning Prohibition was passed during his presidency.

If Wilson was blind to the narrow concerns of workers and minorities, he had a keen political eye for the wider picture, mixed with a high moral tone that brooked no argument. Inspired by his sound analysis of the mood of the American people, and perhaps also by a gut pacifism, he managed to keep America out of **World War I** until 1917 – the politician in him happy to win re-election on the pacifist ticket. Within four months, however, the country was at war, prompted ostensibly by unprovoked German attacks on American shipping, though later critics would claim that the government wanted Allied war orders to stimulate the economy. Abandoning his pacifist stance, Wilson instead declared a war "for democracy" and devoted his considerable energies to ending it quickly and imposing a new moral order on the world. This manifested itself in his championing of a **League of Nations**, which idea he took to the peace conference in Paris, seeing it as a "matter of life or death for civilization". Returning in June 1919 to sell the idea to the American people (and more importantly to the Senate, which has to ratify any treaty by a two-thirds majority), Wilson undertook a draining speaking tour. After a series of blinding headaches he had to cut it short, returning to DC where, on October 2, 1919, he suffered a huge stroke that half-paralyzed him.

His cherished treaty was finally rejected by the Senate in March 1920, but by then Wilson was almost completely incapacitated. Few people outside government were informed of this, and in what today looks suspiciously like a cover-up, his wife Edith – sixteen years his junior – took on many of the day-to-day decisions in the White House, prompting critics to complain of a **"petticoat presidency"**. As inflation rose and the economy slumped, Warren Harding was swept into power in the 1920 presidential elections. Wilson, old and infirm, and his wife left the White House for S Street, where crowds greeted him on the steps. There he died, three years later on February 3, 1924, and was buried in Washington National Cathedral.

built originally for a mining magnate and sold to the French in 1936 for the then ludicrously expensive sum of almost half a million dollars.

Woodrow Wilson House

2340 S St NW ☎387-4062; Dupont Circle Metro. Tues–Sun 10am–4pm. Admission $5.

Many presidents-to-be have lived in Washington DC before their stint in the White House; all but one of them left the moment they had passed on the presidential baton. Only Woodrow Wilson, the 28th President, stayed on in the city, moving into a fine Waddy Butler Wood-designed Georgian-Revival house on S Street that is now open to the public as the **Woodrow Wilson House**. It's a comfortable home – light and airy, with high ceilings, wooden floors, a wide staircase and solarium – which, despite his incapacitating stroke in 1919, Wilson aimed to use as a workplace where he could write political science books and practice law. That his second wife Edith, a rich jeweler's widow, wanted to stay in DC near her family and friends probably had something to do with the decision to remain; she lived in the house for over 35 years after his death.

Visitors are first ushered into the front parlor, where Wilson liked to receive guests, to watch a hagiographical film narrated by Walter Cronkite. There's plenty to see in the house itself, not least the elevator – powered from the nearby streetcar supply – installed to help the enfeebled ex-President move between floors, and the bedroom, furnished by Edith as it had been in the White House. The canvas-walled **library** of this most scholarly of presidents once contained eight thousand books (they were donated to the Library of Congress after his death); those that remain are the 69 volumes of Wilson's own writings (the only president to have written more was Theodore Roosevelt – who, incidentally, Wilson used to impersonate, unflatteringly, to amuse his children). The silent-movie projector and screen were given to him after his stroke by Douglas Fairbanks Sr. Frozen in the 1920s, the fully equipped **kitchen** is a beauty, with blacklead range and provisions stacked in the walk-in pantry.

Textile Museum

2320 S St NW ☎667-0441; Dupont Circle Metro. Mon–Sat 10am–5pm, Sun 1–5pm. Suggested donation $5.

Next door to the Woodrow Wilson House, in two equally grand converted residences, the **Textile Museum** presents temporary exhibitions drawn from its 15,000-strong collection of textiles and carpets. The museum had its roots in the collection of George Hewitt Myers, who bought his first Oriental rug as a student and opened the museum with three hundred other rugs and textiles in 1925. Based in his family home, designed by no less an architect than John Russell Pope, the museum soon expanded into the house next door and today both buildings, and the lovely gardens, are open to the public. Displays – in some of the most pleasingly presented galleries in town – might take in pre-Columbian Peruvian textiles, Near and Far Eastern exhibits (some dating back to 3000 BC) and rugs and carpets from Spain, South America and the American Southwest.

It's best to call for a schedule of exhibitions; better still, aim to coincide with a free **tour** (Sept–May Wed, Sat & Sun 2pm) or the weekly **rug/textile appreciation** mornings (Sat 10.30am; free).

Dupont Circle, Embassy Row and Kalorama
The museum shop (see p.321) is an excellent place to buy textiles and fabrics.

Adams-Morgan

Nowhere is gentrification faster undermining the original, ethnic character of a Washington neighborhood than in **ADAMS-MORGAN**, DC's trendiest district. With every passing month new designer restaurants, stylish bars and hip stores march further into the area, if not – for the time being – displacing, then at least beginning to outnumber the traditional hispanic businesses which have thrived here since the 1950s. Spanish signs and notices are still much in evidence, and the neighborhood certainly celebrates its heritage fulsomely at the annual Latin American Festival (July) and Adams-Morgan Day (Sept) shindigs, but these days its character is better defined by the burgeoning number of cafés where asking for a *latte frappé* won't be met by a blank stare. For a night out largely free from the braying collegiate antics of Georgetown, you'll find Adams-Morgan's 18th Street strip a refreshing change – laidback, open-to-the-sidewalk bars, restaurants, cafés and clubs with an ethnically mixed, cross-class clientele.

For Adams-Morgan listings, see the following pages: accommodation p.274; cafés p.283; restaurants p.287; nightlife p.299.

Ironically, this middle-class influx into the neighborhood is simply turning Adams-Morgan full-circle. In the last decades of the **nineteenth century** its hilly, rural reaches were colonized by wealthy Washingtonians looking for a select address near the power-housing of Dupont Circle. Impressive apartment buildings were erected in the streets off Columbia Road, boasting fine views and connected to downtown by streetcar. Until World War II some of the city's most prominent politicians and business people lived here, and many of their mansions survive intact. After the war, the city's accommodation shortage meant that many buildings were converted into rooming houses and small apartments; well-to-do families moved further out into the suburbs and were replaced by a growing blue-collar population, black and white, and, crucially, by an increasing number of Latin American and Caribbean **immigrants**, whose numbers grew rapidly in the 1960s. Concerned that the area was becoming too segregated, a local group fashioned a symbolic name from two local schools: one all-white (Adams), one all-black (Morgan).

Today, Adams-Morgan is regarded as the most racially mixed neighborhood in the city, and for the most part there's a good-natured atmosphere in the streets, where grocery stores and corner cafés rub shoulders with arty boutiques and sharp bars. Undoubtedly, the yuppies have "discovered" Adams-Morgan, or at least discovered that it's a relatively cheap, fairly groovy, reasonably central place to live; but they're not the only recent immigrants. As any quick glance at the shop-fronts will tell you, Adams-Morgan's **restaurant scene** is the most eclectic in the city – Ethiopian arrivals are responsible for some of the neighborhood's most highly rated places, but you can eat anything from Argentinian to Vietnamese.

Adams-Morgan orientation

Adams-Morgan frequently pops up in establishing shots in the movies – In the Line of Fire, Dave, A Few Good Men and Enemy of the State all feature scenes shot in the neighborhood.

Adams-Morgan is generally thought of as being bounded by Connecticut and Florida avenues and 16th and Harvard streets, although in practice most visitors see little more than the few blocks on either side of the central **Columbia Road/18th Street intersection**, where most of the bars and restaurants are situated. The eastern boundary of the neighborhood is marked by 16th Street and **Meridian Hill Park** – don't stray further east than 16th Street into Shaw. To the west, the boundary is formed by the National Zoological Park and Connecticut Avenue NW, which is where you'll find the nearest **Metro**: from Woodley Park-Zoo Metro on Connecticut Avenue, it's a fifteen-minute walk across the Duke Ellington Bridge to the Columbia Road/18th Street junction. From Dupont Circle Metro it's a steep twenty-minute hike up 19th Street to Columbia Road. By **bus**, take the #L2 from McPherson Square, which travels up 18th Street to Calvert Street.

A neighborhood tour

Adams-Morgans' hispanic legacy is at its strongest in the stretch of Columbia Road northeast of 18th Street, a good place to check out the street stalls, tape and jewelry sellers, and thrift stores; 18th Street south of the intersection with Columbia Road is lined with the best of the bars, clubs and restaurants. A Saturday market occupies the southwestern plaza where the two meet. For most visitors that's more than enough, though the streets east and west of the two main drags contain a fair amount of interest – Anthony Pitch's walking tours of the district (see p.46) can show you more.

The **Wyoming Building**, 2022 Columbia Rd NW, is a classic example of the marvelous apartment houses built early this century, its mosaic floor, molded ceilings and marble reception room forming one of DC's loveliest private interiors. The Eisenhowers lived here between 1927 and 1935. Up the street the Italian-Renaissance-style **Altamont Building**, 1901 Wyoming Ave NW, at 20th, is similarly well endowed, with a baronial reception room and a top floor that once incorporated its own roof-terrace restaurant. Often, the historical associations and **former occupants** are more diverting than a building itself: Admiral Robert Peary, first to reach the North Pole in 1909, lived at 1831 Wyoming Ave; Tallulah Bankhead spent her teenage years in the Norwood building, 1868 Columbia Rd (her father was speaker of the House of Representatives); while Lyndon Baines and Mrs Johnson spent the early years of their marriage at the Woburn building, 1910 Kalorama Rd. Ronald Reagan was shot in Adams-Morgan, surviving an assassination attempt in 1981 as he left the *Washington Hilton*, at the southern end of Columbia Road. Most glamorous of all the Adams-Morgan buildings is the cupola-topped **Ontario** building (2853 Ontario Rd, at 18th), built between 1903 and 1906, whose roll-call of famous residents has numbered five-star generals Douglas MacArthur and Chester Nimitz, journalist Janet Cooke, whose Pulitzer Prize-winning story about youth and drugs was later discredited, and Bob Woodward, who could afford to live here once Watergate had made his reputation. At the time of Watergate, his partner Carl Bernstein lived in Adams-Morgan too, in a much less grandiose apartment in the Biltmore apartment block, 1940 Biltmore St, off 19th St, just a couple of blocks south.

Shaw

East of Adams-Morgan, the historic district of **SHAW** has an upbeat past and the stirrings of a future, but is meantime still sorely affected by three intervening decades of neglect. The neighborhood – roughly north of M Street between North Capitol and 15th streets – is one of the oldest residential areas in DC, its first settlers immigrant whites who built shanty housing along **7th Street** after the Civil War. The district was one of the booming city's main commercial arteries and remained busy during the Depression when the low-rent housing in the alleys on either side began to attract countless black immigrants from the rural southern states in search of work. Pool halls, churches, cafés, theaters and social clubs sprang up; a shopping strip developed across on **14th Street**; while U Street evolved into the "Black Broadway". For years the neighborhood was known simply as "14th and U", taking the name Shaw at the turn of the century after Colonel Robert Gould Shaw, the (white) commander of the first black regiment (the Massachusetts 54th) in the Union Army. With the all-black **Howard University** at 6th Street and **Griffith Stadium** (now Howard University Hospital, 2401 Georgia Ave) attracting massive crowds to its black baseball games, there was a rare vibrancy to this corner of DC.

Segregation – entrenched in Washington since the late nineteenth century – only secured Shaw's prosperity, since the local blacks stayed within the neighborhood to shop and socialize. Conversely, **desegregation** (starting with the Supreme Court's overturning of the "separate but equal" schools policy in 1954) opened

For Shaw listings, see the following pages: restaurants p.297; nightlife p.304.

up the varied attractions of downtown Washington for Shaw's black inhabitants, and decline was swift. Black middle-class flight to the periphery had been taking place since the turn of the century, with larger Victorian properties bought from suburb-bound whites in fringe neighborhoods like LeDroit Park, Logan Circle and the so-called "Striver's Section" of U Street (between 15th and 18th). By the 1960s, the older black streets in Shaw were feeling the pinch, while the **riots** of 1968 finished them off. News of the assassination of Dr Martin Luther King Jr sparked three days of arson, rioting and looting which destroyed businesses and lives along 7th, 14th and H streets. A dozen people were killed, millions of dollars of property lost and the confidence of nearby businesses in Old Downtown jolted so severely that within a decade that area, too, was virtually abandoned.* The three decades since have done little for Shaw, much of which has become indistinguishable from the crack-infested neighborhoods to the northeast and southeast. Signs of **revival** are there for those who look close enough – revitalized U Street has a Metro station and once again features on the city's nightlife scene, while 14th Street has blossomed as an alternative theater district. There's no harm in a night out on U Street or a stroll around some of the peripheral historic sights and landmarks covered below, but heed the fact that you're away from the safer parts of Northwest. Drugs (and the crime that goes with them) are still very prevalent, many buildings are run-down and the atmosphere is often oppressive. Don't wander aimlessly and alone in the neighborhood, which can change from borderline to downright threatening in a block or two; head straight for your destination, take cabs when necessary and keep your wits about you.

U Street-Cardozo Metro is named after Francis Cardozo Sr, renowned Washington educationalist and first principal of the M Street High School – successor to the Charles Sumner School on 17th St, the nation's first public high school for black students.

U Street and around

The only part of Shaw most visitors see – and the safest to visit – is the thriving section of **U Street** in the blocks near **U Street-Cardozo Metro**, where more trendy bars and clubs move in with every passing year. Between the wars, U Street – known locally as "You" Street – ranked second only to New York's Harlem as the center of black entertainment in America. At the splendid **Lincoln Theater**, 1215 U St, built in 1921, vaudeville shows and movies were bolstered by appearances from the most celebrated jazz performers of the day: Count Basie, Billie Holiday, Cab Calloway, Ella Fitzgerald and DC's own Duke Ellington among them. The theater now serves as a per-

---

*The 1968 riots weren't the first to tear Shaw apart. Immediately after World War I, returning black servicemen were dismayed to find segregation forcefully applied in DC. In the summer of 1919, prompted by the violent antics of vigilante white ex-soldiers, five days of racial rioting left thirty people dead, after fierce fighting on U, 7th and T streets, as well as in areas of southwest Washington.

Duke Ellington (1899–1974)

Edward Kennedy Ellington was born in Washington DC (on 22nd St NW), and grew up in Shaw at 1212 T Street (not open to the public). A precocious child, nicknamed "Duke", at fifteen he was playing ragtime in scratch bands at local cafés; he wrote his first composition, *Soda Fountain Rag*, in 1914. Also an accomplished young artist, Ellington turned down a scholarship to New York's Pratt Institute to form instead "The Washingtonians", a trio with which he played extensively in DC before making the big move to New York in 1923. By 1927, his trio had expanded to become **The Duke Ellington Orchestra**; a year later, it was a permanent fixture at Harlem's Cotton Club, where Ellington made his reputation in five tumultuous years, writing early, atmospheric classics like *Mood Indigo* and *Creole Love Call*. Composer and band appeared in their first feature film, *Check and Double Check*, in 1930; by 1932, the Duke Ellington Orchestra had made over 200 recordings. Established as one of America's finest jazz composers and bandleaders, Ellington set off on his first European tour in 1933, where he went down a storm. The following decade saw the penning of his most celebrated works – from *Sophisticated Lady* and *Take the A Train* to *Don't Get Around Much Anymore*. The Ellington style was unmistakeable: melodious ballads and stomping swing pieces alike employed inventive rhythmic devices and novel key changes to devastating, creative effect. In 1943, he was the first popular musician to perform at Carnegie Hall (where he premiered the ambitious *Black, Brown and Beige*) and, despite a decline in big-band popularity after World War II, managed to keep both his band and personal following largely intact. He spent much of the 1950s and 1960s touring and diversifying his output – writing soundtracks for (and appearing in) movies, and composing extended pieces which mixed jazz with classical music. In 1969 he received the Presidential Medal of Freedom for his services to music and the arts. By the time of his death in 1974, Duke Ellington had arranged or composed over six thousand works. Duke married Edna Thompson in 1918 and they had one son, Mercer, though the couple later separated. Mercer went on to play trumpet in his father's band and, after Duke's death, led the Duke Ellington Orchestra.

In DC, the city remembers its favorite son with a week-long festival of his music each year around April 20: the **Duke Ellington Birthday Celebration**. The Calvert Street Bridge between Woodley Park and Adams-Morgan was renamed Duke Ellington Bridge in his honor, while the city established the **Duke Ellington School of the Arts** in Georgetown (35th and R streets NW; ☎337-4022) as a public high school, with a four-year course for artistically talented youths; free tours are available once a month (except June–Sept) – call for details.

forming arts center. Next door, *Ben's Chili Bowl* (see p.297) is a forty-year-old institution frequented by the likes of Bill Cosby and Denzel Washington.

Leave the Metro by the 10th Street exit and you'll emerge right by the **African-American Civil War Memorial**, honoring the more than 200,000 African-American soldiers (and their 7000 white officers) who fought for the Union. It's still unfinished, and work is likely to continue over the next couple of years; in time, plaques should record all their names. For anyone especially interested in the subject, there's a more dramatic artistic memorial in the National Gallery on the Mall, where Augustus Saint-Gaudens' masterpiece, his *Memorial to Robert Gould Shaw and the Massachusetts 54th Regiment*, is on display.

The elegant **Howard Theater**, 624 T St, a few blocks east of the U Street scene, was the neighborhood theater with the proudest pedigree. Opened in 1910, it was the first theater in DC built strictly for black patrons, though that didn't stop hip whites flocking here to see the shows – an unknown Ella Fitzgerald won an open-mike contest, 1940s big bands filled the place, and later artists like James Brown, Smokey Robinson, Gladys Knight and Martha and the Vandellas were lining up to appear; in 1962 the Supremes played their first headlining gig here. The theater survived the riots in one piece but closed soon after and still stands abandoned today. There's not much to see now, and for safety you're advised to come in a taxi, if at all.

See pp.304–5 for reviews of U Street's bars and clubs.

Howard University and LeDroit Park

Famous Howard alumni include Toni Morrison, Jessye Norman, Thurgood Marshall, David Dinkins, Andrew Young and Shaka Hislop.

Perhaps the most prestigious black university in the country, **Howard University** – named for General Otis Howard, commissioner of the Freedmen's Bureau – was established in 1867 by a church missionary society to provide a school for blacks freed after the Civil War. Its first faculties were in law, music, medicine and theology, though nowadays hundreds of subjects are taken by almost 13,000 students from over a hundred countries. Sadly, none of the original campus buildings remain; the earliest structure was replaced by the **Founder's Library** in the 1930s, which now maintains the Moorland-Spingarn Research Center (Mon–Thurs 9am–4.45pm, Fri 9am–4.30pm, Sat 9am–5pm) housing the country's largest selection of literature relating to black history and culture. This is open to the public, but as a casual visitor, you're more likely to come for a campus **tour** (call ☎806-6100 in advance); the **main entrance** is at 2400 6th St NW. Nearest **Metro** is Shaw-Howard University, half a dozen blocks south down Georgia Avenue – don't walk, take a taxi to the gates.

Short of money just a decade after its inauguration, the university sold a plot of land to the south (in the shallow angle formed by Florida and Rhode Island avenues) to developers who built an exclusive parkland-suburb of sixty detached houses. White university staff were the first to take up residence in **LeDroit Park**, as it was known, though the addition of brick row-houses in the 1880s and 1890s signaled the advance of well-to-do black families. By 1920 LeDroit Park was established as a fashionable black neighborhood and though much of it has decayed over the decades, the area has been declared a historic district, with the best surviving group of original houses along the 400 block of U Street. Prominent black citizens continue to be associated with the area – the family of DC's first black mayor, Walter Washington, has owned a house here for years, while Jesse Jackson also maintains a property in the district. Perhaps it was LeDroit Park that blues musician Leadbelly had in mind when he wrote his *Bourgeois Blues* in the 1930s; to an ex-jailbird, these rarefied streets must have seemed miles away from the basement jazz and blues clubs on U:

> Look a here people, listen to me,
> Don't try to find no home in Washington DC
> Lord, it's a bourgeois town, it's a bourgeois town.

Logan Circle and 14th Street

At the same time as LeDroit Park saw a black middle-class influx, so too did the roomy Victorian houses around **Logan Circle**, at the southern edge of Shaw. Nearby 14th Street was the black community's swankiest shopping thoroughfare; in the 1930s, the blocks between P and U streets were known as "Auto Row" after the rash of car showrooms which opened up, eager to sell vehicles to the upwardly mobile residents. Fashionable Iowa Circle, as it was then known, became Logan Circle in 1930, named after the Civil War general whose impressive equestrian statue still lords over it. The surrounding Victorian houses have miraculously survived the neighborhood's slow decline since the 1950s – turrets, terraces, balconies and pediments in various states of repair signal the fact that this, too, is a protected historic district.

14th Street, half a block west, was almost completely lost to the 1968 riots, but its rough edges have been tamed by the arrival of various fringe **theater companies** and **bars** that have set up here and in the surrounding streets. It's still a bit risky at night – don't wander around alone – but the fact that it's already known to some as "Dupont East" is probably symptomatic of the way the neighborhood's going.

The Bethune Council House

Just off Logan Circle, the **Bethune Council House**, 1318 Vermont Ave NW (Mon–Fri 10am–4pm; free; ☎673-2402), based in one of the district's restored Victorian townhouses, serves as a memorial to one of DC's most prominent African-American inhabitants. **Mary McLeod Bethune** was born on a cotton farm in South Carolina in 1875, one of seventeen children of poor parents, both ex-slaves. A bright, inquiring child, she was sent to a local school and later entertained thoughts of becoming a missionary in Africa (she was turned down on account of her race), before moving to Florida in 1904 to found the Daytona Educational and Industrial School for Negro Girls (later the Bethune-Cookman College). Starting in a rented room and using homemade materials, Bethune persevered with her

The memorial to Mary McLeod Bethune in Lincoln Park (see p.131) records more of the "Legacy".

intention to train teachers who would serve the African-American community. In 1935, recognition came with the award of a prize by the National Association for the Advancement of Colored People (NAACP), swiftly followed by a call from President Roosevelt to serve as special advisor on minority affairs. Later, as the director of the Division of Negro Affairs in the National Youth Administration, she became the first African-American woman to head a federal office, and was the only woman to work in the ad-hoc "Black Cabinet" which advised FDR on the implications for blacks of his New Deal policies. In 1945, under the aegis of the NAACP, Bethune was invited to San Francisco to attend the conference which established the concept of the United Nations.

The house on Vermont Avenue was bought by Bethune in 1942 to serve both as her home (she lived there for seven years) and as headquarters for the National Council for Negro Women, which she had founded in 1935, bringing together various organizations in order to fight discrimination more effectively. Her work here formed the basis of her "Legacy", finished just before her death in 1955, in which she encapsulated the meaning of her life's work in a stirring series of messages for those who would follow: "I leave you a thirst for education. I leave you a respect for the use of power. I leave you faith. I leave you racial dignity." Now administered by the National Park Service, the house still serves as a research center and archive, though you're welcome to tour the restored rooms, which contain a few mementos of Mary McLeod Bethune alongside period photographs and changing exhibitions.

The best way to the house is the fifteen-minute walk straight up Vermont Avenue from McPherson Square Metro, past Thomas Circle.

Chapter 8

Upper Northwest

N one of the fluctuating fortunes that have afflicted DC's other neighborhoods have ever ruffled the well-to-do feathers of the districts of the **Upper Northwest**. The upper- and middle-class flight up Connecticut, Wisconsin and Massachusetts avenues began with a series of nineteenth-century presidents who made the cool reaches of rural **Woodley Park** – across Duke Ellington Bridge from Adams-Morgan – their summer home. Grover Cleveland later bought his own stone cottage a little further north in an area which, as a consequence, became known as **Cleveland Park**. Few others could afford the time and expense involved in living a four-mile carriage-ride from the city center until the arrival in the 1890s of the streetcar; within three decades both Woodley Park and Cleveland Park had become bywords for fashionable, out-of-town living, replete with apartment buildings commissioned from the era's top architects. The tone is no less swanky today, with a series of ritzy suburbs stretching into Maryland. Politicians and media people choose to live in the safe streets of Cleveland Park; President Clinton sent Chelsea to school in neighboring Tenleytown; while the gleaming malls and power-shoppers of Friendship Heights, on the DC/Maryland boundary, are second only to those of New York's Fifth Avenue.

For Upper Northwest listings, see the following pages: accommodation p.281; restaurants p.298; nightlife p.306.

For all its pedigree, however, this part of town has relatively little to offer visitors. You can only view the most celebrated mansions from the outside while the surrounding streets, though pleasing, are hardly exciting. The three major targets are the excellent **National Zoological Park**, the furthest-flung of the Smithsonian attractions; **Washington National Cathedral**; and the expanses of **Rock Creek Park**, largest and most enjoyable of the city's green spaces.

The area is most easily reached using the **Metro** Red Line. Alternatively, bus #L2 runs up Connecticut Avenue from McPherson Square via Adams-Morgan (18th St) to Chevy Chase, while buses #30, #32, #34, #35 and #36 travel up Wisconsin Avenue from Georgetown to Friendship Heights.

Woodley Park and Cleveland Park

Architect Harry L. Wardman designed many of the apartment buildings and townhouses in **WOODLEY PARK**, his most adventurous construction being the massive **Wardman-Park Hotel** (Connecticut Ave NW and Woodley Rd) in 1918, whose tower dominated the local skyline (it's now part of the 1500-room *Sheraton Washington*). It proved a resounding success, attracting high-profile politicians and social gadflys who entertained guests in the grand public rooms and rented apartments for themselves. Within a decade a second landmark followed, the hybrid Art Deco-Renaissance-style **Shoreham** on Calvert Street (now the *Omni Shoreham*), designed by Joseph Abel for owner-builder Harry Bralove. Built in 1930 at a cost of $4 million, this has held an inaugural ball for every president from FDR to Clinton; here Truman played poker, JFK courted Jackie, Nixon announced his first cabinet and, in the hotel's celebrated *Blue Room*, Judy Garland, Marlene Dietrich, Bob Hope and Frank Sinatra entertained the great and the good.

For a view of where the generally more staid nineteenth-century presidents passed their summers, head up Connecticut Avenue to Cathedral Avenue and walk west past 29th Street to the white stucco Georgian **Woodley Mansion**. This was built in 1800 for Philip Barton Key, whose nephew Francis was later to pen the "Star-Spangled Banner". Its elevation meant it was a full ten degrees cooler in the summer than downtown, and presidents Van Buren, Tyler and Buchanan needed no second invitation to spend their summers here; it's now a private school.

Back on Connecticut Avenue and heading north past the zoo you're soon, and imperceptibly, in **CLEVELAND PARK**. For sheer exuberance, the **Kennedy-Warren** apartment building (3133 Connecticut Ave NW) on the east side takes the local honors – this soaring Art Deco evocation of 1930s wealth is home today to P.J. O'Rourke, among others. Slightly further north, just before Cleveland Park Metro station, the Art Deco movie house, the **Uptown** (3426 Connecticut Ave NW), now part of the Cineplex Odeon chain, has been showing movies since 1936.

Backtracking from Cleveland Park Metro down Connecticut Avenue you can make your way to the cathedral along **Newark Street** and **Highland Place**. These hold the area's highest concentration of upper-class residences, dating from its great turn-of-the-century expansion: Robert Head, Waddy Butler Wood and Paul Pelz all built houses here, and it was on Newark Street that Grover Cleveland's (long-demolished) summer house – the one that prompted the whole influx – once stood.

Washington National Cathedral

Massachusetts and Wisconsin aves NW ☎537-6200; Woodley Park-Zoo or Cleveland Park Metro; bus #30, #32, #34 or #36 from Pennsylvania Ave

For reviews of the Sheraton Washington *and the* Omni Shoreham, *see p.281; for restaurants in Woodley Park and Cleveland Park, see p.298.*

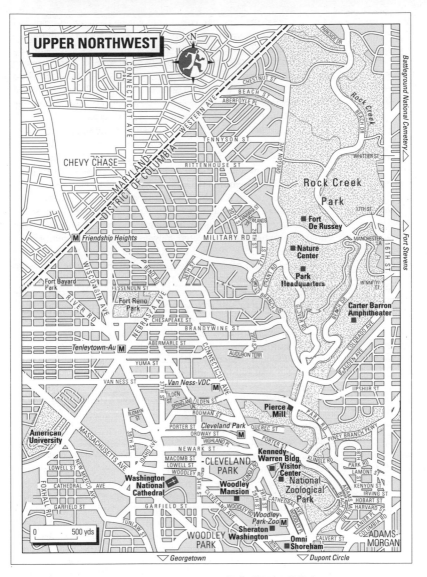

(downtown) or Wisconsin Ave (Georgetown), or #N2, #N4 or #N6 from Farragut Square. April–Sept Mon–Fri 10am–9pm, Sat 10am–4.30pm, Sun 12.30–4.30pm; Oct–March Mon–Sat 10am–4.30pm, Sun 12.30–4.30pm. Suggested donation $2.

The twin towers of **Washington National Cathedral** – the sixth largest cathedral in the world – are visible long before you reach the

*From Woodley
Park-Zoo
Metro (20min
walk), turn
left from
Connecticut
Ave into
Cathedral Ave
and right into
Woodley Rd to
reach the
lower-level
information
center; the
west door is
around the
corner on
Wisconsin Ave.
The
Tourmobile
(p.46) runs
here too.*

church itself. Turn the final corner and you're confronted by one of the city's most surprising edifices, a monumental building so medieval in spirit it should surely rise from a dusty European old town plaza rather than from a two-car-two-kid suburb. It comes as no surprise in this planned city, however, that the siting of the cathedral was intentional: here, on the heights of Mount St Alban, unaffected by the District's zoning restrictions, the architects could have free rein to produce their anachronistic Gothic masterpiece.

George Washington first proposed the establishment of a "national" church in the city, but it was a century before Congress finally granted a charter for what is officially known as the Cathedral Chuch of St Peter and St Paul. President Theodore Roosevelt graced the foundation ceremony in 1907 and architects George Bodley (a noted English church architect) and Henry Vaughan set to work, suceeded after their deaths by **Philip Hubert Frohman**, who spent the next fifty years completing the design. Frohman died in 1972; the cathedral was finally completed only in 1990, though parts have been in use since the 1920s. It's a Protestant church, the seat of the Episcopal Diocese of Washington, yet is conceived of as a national church, and also hosts services for other denominations.*

Built from Indiana limestone and modeled entirely in the medieval English Gothic style – its great spaces supported by flying buttresses, bosses and vaults – it's a supreme achievement. Unfortunately, there are more similarities with the hoary, crumbling relics of Europe than appearances alone suggest: although it looks brand new – and indeed, some parts are – the cathedral is already undergoing restoration. The decorative bosses have been attacked by lichen, while Washington's freezing winters have cracked the gutters and the roofing and damaged some of the exterior gargoyles.

The interior

*Cathedral
services:
Mon–Sat
7.30am, noon
& 4pm; Sun
8am, 9am
(10am
Sept–June),
11am, 4pm &
6.30pm.*

The center portal in the west facade isn't always open and you may have to **enter** from the northwest cloister; for a floor plan and information, descend to the crypt floor, where there's an **information desk** and gift shop. **Guided tours** are available on request at the west entrance (Mon–Sat 10am–3.15pm, Sun 12.45–2.45pm; suggested donation $2); ask one of the purple-hatted docents.

Place yourself first at the west end of the **nave** (completed as recently as 1976) to appreciate the immense scale of the building; it's more than a tenth of a mile to the high altar at the other end, and the

*Thoroughly Roman Catholic but similarly immense in scale is DC's other major church, the Basilica of the National Shrine of the Immaculate Conception (4th St and Michigan Ave NE), a striking hilltop Marian shrine in NE, three blocks west of Brookland-CUA Metro. It's an architectural hodge-podge compared to the National Cathedral, but the majolica-tiled dome and mosaics are spectacular.

Music in the Cathedral

Carillon recitals: Sat 12.30pm, ten-bell peal Sun 11am.

Cathedral choristers: Mon, Tues & Wed 4pm (school year only).

Concerts: summer choral and classical concerts, indoors and out.

Organ recitals/demonstrations: Wed 12.30pm, Sun 5pm.

only reason you can see the gold cross on the altar from this distance is because it's 6ft tall. Along the south side, the first bay commemorates **George Washington**, whose marble statue proclaims him to be "First Citizen, Patriot, President, Churchman and Freemason", while five bays down is the sarcophagus of **Woodrow Wilson** – the only president to be buried in the District (although Eisenhower's funeral was also held in the cathedral). Much of the work on the building took place during Wilson's presidency, a process which so fascinated him he used to visit the construction site in his chauffeur-driven limousine. In the adjacent bay, look up to the **Space Window**, whose stained glass incorporating a sliver of moon rock commemorates the flight of Apollo II, and resembles nothing so much as the cover of a Robert A. Heinlein paperback. On the north side, across from Washington, the **Abraham Lincoln Bay** is marked by a bronze statue of Abe with Lincoln-head pennies set into the floor. The next berth down is for cathedral architect **Philip Hubert Frohman**, a Catholic whose family received special dispensation to have him buried in this Protestant church. Last bay before the North Transept features a small likeness of **Dr Martin Luther King Jr** above the arch, inscribed "I Have A Dream": on Sunday March 31, 1968, the reverend preached his last sermon here before heading for Memphis where he was due to lead a march of striking black workers; four days later he was dead, assassinated by a bullet fired by James Earl Ray.

At the **High Altar** there's a splendid view back down along the carved vault to the west rose window. The beautifully intricate reredos features 110 figures surrounding Christ in Benediction. An elevator from the south porch at the west end of the nave (near the Washington statue) ascends to the **Pilgrim Observation Gallery**, which affords stupendous city views.

The 57-acre grounds or **Cathedral Close** – virtually a small fiefdom – hold cathedral offices, three schools, a college, sports fields and a swimming pool, not to mention a **Herb Cottage** selling dried herbs and teas, a **Greenhouse** and the attractive **Bishop's Garden**, a walled rose-and-herb garden laid out in medieval style.

National Zoological Park

3001 Connecticut Ave NW ☎ 673-4800; Woodley Park-Zoo Metro, or bus #L2 from McPherson Square or 18th St (Adams-Morgan). Grounds daily: May to

National
Zoological
Park

mid-Sept 6am–8pm; mid-Sept to April 6am–6pm. Buildings daily: May to mid-Sept 10am–6pm; mid-Sept to April 10am–4.30pm. Admission free.

The enormously entertaining **National Zoological Park** forms part of the Smithsonian ensemble – which apart from anything else means that admission is free. Sitting between Woodley Park and Adams-Morgan, it sprawls down the steep slopes of the gorge cut by Rock Creek, with trails through lush vegetation leading past comparatively humane simulations of the home environments of over three thousand creatures. Although founded in 1889 as a traditional zoo, it likes to think of itself these days as a "BioPark", combining the usual menagerie of giraffes, elephants, lions and tigers with botanic gardens, a prairie and a wetlands zone, "Amazonia" (a re-creation of a tropical river and rainforest habitat), as well as aquariums and natural history displays.

A café, restaurant, concession stands, paid parking, police post and restrooms are scattered throughout the park.

The **main entrance** on Connecticut Avenue is ten minutes' walk north from the Metro station; just inside the gates, the **visitor center** has a map and list of the day's events, including feeding times. From here, two trails loop downhill through the park to Rock Creek itself: the **Olmsted Walk**, passing most of the indoor exhibits, and the steeper **Valley Trail**, with the major aquatic exhibits, birds and "Amazonia". Head down one and back up the other, visiting the side exhibits on the way, and you'll walk over two miles – allow a minimum of three hours to do the park justice.

Park highlights

The scales outside the **Cheetah Conservation Station** provide the first interaction between visitor and captive. Weigh yourself, check the chart to see with which animal your weight corresponds – and then read just how quickly the apparently somnolent cheetahs and hyenas in the paddock beyond would take to kill and eat you. The first celebrity is a little further on, the **panda** Hsing Hsing, one of a pair presented by the People's Republic of China during Richard Nixon's 1972 visit. His mate, Ling Ling, died in 1992, and Hsing Hsing has had a rough ride since then, surviving surgery for testicular cancer in 1997 – you can usually only see him at feeding times.

Hsing Hsing is fed at 11am & 3pm.

The path winds down past elephants, giraffes, hippos and rhinos to perhaps the saddest relic in the zoo, Hsing Hsing included. Before the European settlement of America, millions of **bison** roamed the country; now, along with the couple here, just 140,000 or so survive in scattered parks, refuges and private ranches, their numbers boosted by the modern success in breeding bison for its low-calorie and minimum cholesterol meat. An **"American Prairie"** exhibit puts the beasts in context, providing some explanation of the natural and cultural histories of the nation's grasslands. The first of the zoo's garden areas, the **American Indian Heritage Garden**, celebrates the natural history knowledge of the Native Americans, whose lives were sustained by the bison herds before they and the animals became surplus to white American requirements. Here you learn about the healing properties of herbs and plants like the coneflower (used to treat insect bites, venereal disease and rabies) and the gloriously emetic Indian tobacco plant: should you ever be tempted to make cigarettes out of this, bear in mind that it's also known as vomitweed, pukeweed and gagroot.

Some of the zoo's most adventurous work is taking place with its primates. The orangutans are encouraged to leave the confines of the **Great Ape House** and commute to the **"Think Tank"** and back down the **"O Line"** – overhead cables strung from towers across public areas of the zoo, with only the depth of the fall (and some low-voltage electric wires on the towers) to deter them from leaping off. At the Think Tank, scientists and orangutans come together to hone their communications skills and discuss world events in the fascinating Orangutan Language Project: if in any doubt about the relative intelligence of ape and human, take a look at the glass case in the Great Ape House, which displays the ludicrous items visitors have thrown into the enclosures over the years – from cans of soda to plastic crocodiles.

Between Ape House and Think Tank is the **"Reptile Discovery Center"** (opens 10am), with a full complement of snakes, turtles, crocs, alligators, lizards and frogs, and some enterprising interactive displays, though quite how interactive you want to be with said beasts is open to question. Ponder here on the remarkable komodo dragon, the first to be born in captivity outside Indonesia: it currently eats two rats a week, but will eventually grow to be more than 9ft long and weigh over 200 pounds – at which point they'll have to start rat rationing. The adjacent **"Invertebrate Exhibit"** (Wed–Fri opens 10am, Sat & Sun opens 9am) covers the lives and loves of everything from ants to coral and octopus – admission to these two popular centers can be restricted at busy times; check first at the visitor center. Beyond here, the special moated island with the **lions and tigers** marks the end of the big animals, though you might want to duck in and out of the thoroughly unpleasant **bat cave** before heading back up the Valley Trail.

Best thing on the Valley Trail is undoubtedly **"Amazonia"** (opens 10am), the indoor tropical river and forest habitat. A cleverly constructed undulating aquarium gets you close to the fish – piranhas included – while bombarding you with informative notes; you then climb up a level into the humid, creeper-clad rainforest, above the water you've just walked along, familiarizing yourself with roots, leaf mold, forest parasites and birdcalls.

Outside again, seals and sea lions splash in an outdoor pool, and then it's a slow pull uphill, past beaver dams, an impressive **bird house**, an artificial wetland replete with cranes and herons, and assorted eagles, bongos and tapirs. If there's some jiggery-pokery in

the bushes as you go, it'll be the **golden lion tamarins,** or South
American marmosets, the successful breeding of which is one of the
zoo's quiet triumphs – they've been released into a cageless enclo-
sure to prepare them for eventual return to the wild in Brazil.

Rock Creek Park

Most visitors and many Washingtonians overlook the attractions of
the city's major park, **Rock Creek Park,** the bulk of which stretches
between the quiet suburbs of the Upper Northwest. Established by
mandate from Congress in 1890, its 1800 acres cut a generous six-
mile-long swath, tracing the line of the eponymous creek from its
early meanderings through Georgetown and Woodley Park to the
northernmost DC-Maryland border. Little more than a narrow gorge
in its southern reaches, the park spreads out above the National Zoo
to become a mile-wide tranche of woodland, west of 16th Street.

A road shadows the creek for much of its length, called the **Rock
Creek Parkway** until it reaches the zoo, north of which it's known as
Beach Drive. A car is the easiest way to get in and around the park;
by **public transit,** your only real choices are the Metro to Cleveland
Park, which provides access to the section of the park just north of
the zoo; or the Metro to Tenleytown-AU, from where buses #D31,
#D33, #D34, #W45 or #W46 run up Nebraska Avenue NW and
along Military Road through the middle of the park; for the east side
of the park, buses #S1, #S2, #S3, #S4 and #S5 all run straight up
16th Street from anywhere north of K Street NW.

The park is open during **daylight hours,** which in practice means
from around 7.30am: it's not a wise idea to come on foot, on your
own, at night, though traffic is permitted 24 hours a day.

Inside the park

There are fifteen miles of **trails and paths** in the park, along both
sides of the creek, including tracks and workout stations, bridleways
(in the wooded, northern section) and a **cycle route** that runs from
the Lincoln Memorial, north through the park and into Maryland; to
the south, Arlington Memorial Bridge links the route to the Mount
Vernon Trail in Virginia (see p.260). On weekends (from 7am Sat to
7pm Sun), Beach Drive between Military and Broad Branch roads is
closed to cars, when the **rollerblading** crowd comes out to primp
and preen. The park also features ballparks and thirty **picnic areas,**
some of which have barbecues – bring your own fuel, and take everything away with you afterwards.

*There are a
variety of
summer
concerts at the
Carter Barron
Amphitheater
(16th St and
Colorado Ave
NW); see
p.307.*

The sights start at the southern end of the park, a mile above the
zoo, where the serene, granite **Pierce Mill** (Wed–Sun 10am–4.30pm;
free; ☎426-6908) stands in a beautiful riverside hollow on Tilden
Street, near Beach Drive. One of eight nineteenth-century gristmills in

the valley, and the last to shut down (in 1897), it has been restored by the National Park Service and today produces cornmeal and wheat-flour for sale to visitors. You can observe the process, and even have a go yourself with small hand-grinders and sifters. Just across the way, the old carriage house serves as the **Rock Creek Gallery** (Mon–Thurs & Sun 11am–4pm; ☎244-2482), which displays local art.

The **Nature Center** on Glover Road, just south of Military Road (Wed–Sun 9am–5pm; free; ☎426-6829), acts as the park visitor center, with natural history exhibits and details of weekend guided walks and self-guided nature trails. Finally, just on the other side of Military Road, the remains of **Fort De Russey** stand as a reminder of the network of defenses that ringed the city during the Civil War. Guarding against Confederate attack from the north, this was just one of 68 forts erected around the city. The sites of others – notably forts Reno, Bayard, and Stevens (see below) – have been appropriated as small parks on either side of Rock Creek Park proper.

Fort Stevens and Battleground National Cemetery

Drive east on Military Road from the park to 13th Street NW where **Fort Stevens** marks the spot at which the city came closest to falling to Confederate troops during the Civil War. An army of 15,000 men crossed the Potomac in July 1864 and got within 150 yards of the fort before the hastily reinforced Union defense drove them back under a barrage of artillery fire. President Lincoln was in the fort during the attack and mounted the parapet for a better look at the Confederate line, drawing a stinging rebuke from a nearby soldier who is said to have shouted "Get down you damned fool" at his commander-in-chief. Lincoln, to his credit, heeded the advice, but not all his troops were so lucky. Seven blocks further north on Georgia Avenue is **Battleground National Cemetery** (sunrise–sunset), in whose restricted confines lie the remains of the Union soldiers killed in the battle to defend the fort. Buses #70 and #71 run here, up 7th Street (which becomes Georgia Ave NW) from the Mall, but given Georgia Avenue's rather fearsome reputation you're advised to come and go by taxi.

Chapter 9

Georgetown

For a map of Georgetown, see the color section at the back of the book.

Socially, politically and culturally, **GEORGETOWN** sits at the center of Washington high life. Geographically, of course, it's out on a limb, way to the west of downtown, off the Metro line and beyond the divide of Rock Creek. This relative isolation has engendered an elitism that isn't entirely imagined: to stroll around the area's steep, leafy streets, past rows of million-dollar chocolate-box houses, is to step inside what Jan Morris has called "the most obsessively political residential enclave in the world". The Kennedys moved here before Jack made it to the White House and were followed by a cocktail-party full of establishment figures who have counted Georgetown as their home (or, more usually, one of their homes): Bob Woodward, Katherine Graham (former *Washington Post* publisher), Ben Bradlee (executive editor of the *Post* during Watergate), Bill Clinton as a student, Secretary of State Madeleine Albright, art collector and philanthropist Paul (son of Andrew) Mellon, biographer Kitty Kelley, novelist Herman Wouk, even Elizabeth Taylor during her marriage to Senator John Warner – the list goes on and on.

For Georgetown listings, see the following pages: accommodation p.280; cafés p.285; restaurants p.295; nightlife p.304.

There is, of course, more to Georgetown than its upper-crust inhabitants. The area is at its vibrant best along the spine of **Wisconsin Avenue** and **M Street**, with their enjoyable saloons, coffee shops, fashionable restaurants and antique bookstores in which students of Georgetown University rub shoulders with staid old power-brokers. Its history is diverting too, and many of the district's buildings date back to the early eighteenth century, making it older than the capital itself. Genteel Federal-era and shuttered Victorian townhouses hung with flower baskets stud the streets, while **north of Q Street** lies a series of stately mansions and handsome parks, gardens and cemeteries. Down on the **C&O Canal**, below M Street, horse-drawn boats fill the waterway while the tree-shaded towpaths have been turned over to cyclists and walkers; to the east, the boardwalk, cafés and restaurants of the **Washington Harbor** development provide views down the Potomac to the Kennedy Center.

Georgetown's most annoying anomaly is that it's not on the **Metro** (Rock Creek and its valley are in the way). And don't even think of driving: there's nowhere to park. The nearest Metro station is **Foggy Bottom-GWU**, from where it's fifteen to twenty minutes' walk up Pennsylvania Avenue and along M Street to the junction with Wisconsin Avenue. Alternatively, approach from Dupont Circle, a similar-length walk west along P Street (or over the Dumbarton Bridge and along Q St; see p.218), which puts you first in the ritzier, upper part of Georgetown – in which case you might want to start with the mansions, parks and gardens of northern Georgetown (see p.247). **Buses** #30, #32, #34, #35 and #36 run up Pennsylvania Avenue from Washington Circle (and other points downtown), along M Street and Wisconsin Avenue; #D2 and #D4 run from Union Station via Dupont Circle to Q Street; and #G2 runs from Dupont Circle to P and Dumbarton streets. At night you'll find **taxis** relatively easy to come by on the main drags; it's a $6–7 ride to most downtown destinations.

Some history

In the early eighteenth century, when this area was part of Maryland, **Scottish merchants** began to form a permanent settlement around shoreside warehouses on the higher reaches of the Potomac River (or "Patowmack", as it was then known). Here they oversaw a thriving trade, exporting the plentiful tobacco from nearby farms and importing foreign materials and luxuries for colonial settlers. In 1751 the Maryland Assembly granted a **town charter** to the merchants, who named their flourishing port after their royal protector, George II. Within a decade, "George Towne" was a runaway success, attracting other merchants who built large mansions on estates to the north of the river, and by the 1780s, it was America's largest tobacco port.

Once George Washington had pinpointed the Potomac region as the site of the new federal capital, it seemed logical that such a thriving port be included in the plans. In 1791, together with Alexandria in Virginia, the town was incorporated within the federal district. And while for many years the new city of Washington remained little more than an idea, Georgetown itself continued to prosper – by 1830 it had a population of nine thousand, and boasted streets of Federal-style brick houses, fashionable stores, well-tended gardens and even a university (founded in 1789). By the time of the **Civil War**, Georgetown was still separate enough from Washington to be considered suspect in Union eyes. Many of the town's early landowners came from the South and during the war there was strong support (by the "Sessesh" – or secessionists – as they termed themselves) for the Confederate cause. But Georgetown's proximity to the capital (and the Union troops stationed in the town) kept the lid on any overt secessionist feeling.

The war and Georgetown's commercial prospects flickered and died at about the same time. The tobacco trade had already faltered due to soil exhaustion, while the steady growth of Baltimore and Washington itself badly affected the town's prosperity. The **Chesapeake and Ohio (C&O) Canal**, completed in 1850, represented an attempt to revive trade with the interior and for a time Georgetown became a regional center for wheat, coal and timber shipment. But the canal was soon obsolete: the coming of the railroads was swiftly followed by the development of larger steamboats which couldn't be accommodated by Georgetown's canal or harbor. After losing its charter in 1871, relegated to a mere neighborhood in the District of Columbia, Georgetown was delivered another insult in 1895 when most of its old **street names** – some in use for over 150 years – were abandoned by order of Congress in favor of the numbers and letters of the federal city plan; there was even a suggestion that Georgetown become known as "West Washington".

For much of the late nineteenth and early twentieth centuries, Georgetown was anything but a fashionable place to live. Water-powered foundries and mills provided employment for a growing, predominantly black population, based in the neighborhood of Herring Hill, south of P Street and close to Rock Creek. Gardens were lost to speculative row housing and many larger mansions were subdivided; a noisy streetcar system was installed; and M Street became a workaday run of cheap stores and saloons owned by immigrant families. However, a mass influx of white-collar workers to DC during the New Deal era and World War II reversed Georgetown's rather down-at-heel image. Black and immigrant families were slowly pushed out of the Victorian streets, apartments were knocked back into houses and Federal mansions renovated. Part of the charm for newcomers was that Georgetown's natural boundaries – southern river, eastern creek, western university grounds and northern estates – had prevented wholesale, indiscriminate development. Despite the disruption, a certain smalltown character had survived the years.

Now, of course, this character is zealously preserved by Georgetown residents who, since the 1950s and 1960s, have included ever-increasing numbers of DC's most fashionable and politically well-connected inhabitants. Certain historic houses have been lost to developers and some of the streets are overwhelmed by traffic, but since 1967 Georgetown has been registered as a **national historic landmark** – new buildings and renovations have to be sympathetic to their surroundings, house facades are color-coordinated, and the canal has been landscaped and preserved as a national historic park.

Along the C&O Canal

On a summer's day there's no finer part of Georgetown than the **Chesapeake and Ohio (C&O) Canal** – whose eastern extremity feeds into Rock Creek at 28th Street NW – overlooked on both sides by restored red-brick warehouses, spanned by small bridges, lined with trees and punctuated by occasional candy-colored towpath houses. The prettiest central stretch starts at 30th Street, where the adjacent **locks** once opened to allow through boatloads of coal, iron, timber and corn from the Maryland estates upriver.

The Potomac River had been used by traders since the earliest days of settlement in the region, but a series of rapids and waterfalls – like those at Great Falls, just fourteen miles from Georgetown – made large-scale commercial navigation all but impossible. A canal was proposed (George Washington was one of the shareholders) that would follow the line of the river and open up trade as far as the Ohio Valley, but when construction finally finished in 1850, the C&O reached only as far as Cumberland in Maryland, 184 miles and 74 locks away. Confederate raiding parties found the barges and locks easy targets during the Civil War and much of the traffic dried up for the duration – doubtless to the satisfaction of the Union troops stationed in Georgetown, who used to swim naked in the canal, offending local sensibilities. Even after the war the canal never attracted sufficient trade, mainly because of competition from the railroads; the last mule-drawn cargo boat was pulled through in the 1920s, after which severe flooding from the Potomac destroyed much of the canal infrastructure. The C&O's historical importance was recognized in 1971 when its entire length was declared a national historical park, and today scores of visitors hike, cycle and horseride along the restored towpaths; canoeing and boating are allowed in certain sections, too. Massive **flooding** in 1996 caused serious damage and while the towpath itself has now been largely restored, certain sections of the canal have not yet been re-flooded. This doesn't affect access for hikers and bikers (though it's a bit unsightly in parts), or the National Park Service passenger **canal boat** services (see p.244).

One of the most appealing stretches of the canal is the short section between Thomas Jefferson Street and 31st Street, where artisans' houses dating from the building boom of the mid-nineteenth century have been handsomely restored as shops, offices and, occasionally, private homes. Thomas Jefferson Street itself is lined with attractive brick houses, some in the **Federal style**, featuring rustic stone lintels, arched doorways with fanlights and narrow top-floor dormers. On the south side of the canal, **The Foundry**, 1050 30th Street, is just one of the many brick warehouses that line the canal, originally built as a machine-shop and later serving as a veterinary hospital to care for the mules that worked the boats. It's been sympathetically restored and expanded, and now houses the Odeon Foundry cinema (see p.311), as well as shops and a restaurant-bar (the *Music City Roadhouse*; see p.304). Other warehouses have received similar treatment – like the shops and offices at **Canal Square**, 1054 31st St – and frame either side of the waterway as far up as Francis Scott Key Bridge, five blocks west. Various steps and paths from the towpath connect with the

Canal Boats and Other C&O Activities

It is 184 miles from Georgetown to the canal terminus at Cumberland, MD, passing through highly varied scenery, past waterfalls, through forests, and skirting the ridges and valleys of the Appalachian Mountains.

Canal boats

To sign up for trips on the ninety-foot, mule-drawn **canal boats** – accompanied by park rangers in nineteenth-century costume who work the locks – stop in at the Georgetown **C&O Canal Visitor Center**, 1057 Thomas Jefferson St NW (April–Oct daily 10am–4pm; ☎653-5190). Tickets cost $7.50 and there are usually two to four daily departures (Wed–Sun) from mid-June to mid-September, with reduced services from April to mid-June and the last couple of weeks of September.

Along the canal

A number of outlets along the canal rent boats, canoes and bikes, including several in the first twenty-mile stretch from Georgetown (see p.46). For a day-trip by **bike**, Great Falls (see below) – an easy, flat fourteen miles away – is a reasonable destination. You'll need to observe a 15mph speed limit on the towpath, wear a helmet and give way to all pedestrians and horses – it takes most people a couple of hours from Georgetown and the only slightly tricky bit is just before lock 15 where you'll have to carry the bike for a couple of hundred yards. **Canoes** and **boats** are limited to specific areas (visitors centers and rental outlets can advise) and should not venture onto the Potomac River, which can be very dangerous; you also shouldn't **swim** in the canal or river due to unpredictable currents. You can **picnic** anywhere you like, but only light fires in authorized fireplaces; first-come, first-served basic campsites are dotted along the entire length of the canal; the one closest to the city is at Swain's Lock, twenty miles from Georgetown.

Great Falls

At **Great Falls**, fourteen miles from Georgetown, the Great Falls Tavern Visitor Center, 11710 MacArthur Blvd, Potomac, MD (April–Oct daily 8.30am–5pm; ☎301/299-3613), has a museum covering the history of the canal. This is the starting point for guided local tours, walks and canal boat trips (same prices and schedules as in Georgetown); nearby, a boardwalk offers terrific views of the falls themselves. There's a snack bar but no other eating or rental facilities. By car, take MacArthur Boulevard, signposted from Georgetown, or exit 41 off the Beltway; outside rush hour, it's a twenty-minute drive. There's also a visitor center on the Virginia side of the falls (☎703/285-2965) – though no access between the two sides of the canal and the Potomac River – featuring more tours and trails, though no boat trips. Get there by following Route 193 (exit 13 off the Beltway) to Route 738, from where it's signposted (parking $4).

backstreets off M Street, and there's also direct access to Georgetown Park shopping mall (see p.320).

At **Wisconsin Avenue**, south of the canal, you're at the oldest part of Georgetown. This was the first road built from the river into

Maryland during colonial times, and was a major route for farmers and traders who used the slope of the hill to roll their barrels down to riverside warehouses. Later, canal boatmen would be enticed into the Gothic Revival **Grace Church** on South Street, just off Wisconsin Avenue, by promises of salvation from the earth-bound drudgery of hauling heavy goods from barge to warehouse. Others sought solace in nearby Suter's Tavern, where, it's claimed, George Washington met Maryland landowners to discuss the purchase of property so that work could start on the federal city; the inn was knocked down long ago, but there's a plaque marking its approximate site at 31st and K streets.

K Street itself was once known as Water Street for the very good reason that it fronted the Potomac River, though land reclamation has now pushed the water a hundred yards or so further south. Its most noticeable feature is what's above it, namely the **Whitehurst Freeway**, the elevated road built in the 1950s to relieve traffic congestion on M Street. Cross the road under the freeway and you reach the riverside development of **Washington Harbor** (east of 31st), its interlocking towers and capsules set around a circular, terraced plaza with spurting fountains. The waterfront on either side is due to be landscaped as part of a new Georgetown Waterfront Park, and there are views upriver to the Francis Scott Key Bridge, and downriver to Theodore Roosevelt Island and Bridge as well as of the backs of the Watergate Complex and Kennedy Center. The restaurants and bars in the complex are all fairly expensive, but there's nothing more relaxing than a summer evening's drink on the terrace watching the boats sculling by.

Along and around M Street

The central artery of Georgetown for two centuries, **M Street** cuts through the lower town before crossing Rock Creek into the city of Washington. As elsewhere in Georgetown, the street retains many of its original Federal-style and later Victorian buildings, though the ground floors have all long since been converted to retail use. Where new buildings have filled in any gaps they've tended to follow the prevailing red-brick style, none more noticeably than the elegant and supremely luxurious **Four Seasons Hotel** between 28th and 29th streets. Built in 1979, it regularly garners awards as one of the most exclusive hotels in America.

Though the **Old Stone House**, 3051 M St (Wed–Sun 8am–4.30pm; free; ☎426-6851), facing Thomas Jefferson Street, has the very real accolade of being the only surviving pre-Revolutionary house in DC (it was built in 1764 by a Pennsylvania carpenter, Christopher Layman), the only thing that saved it from demolition in the 1950s was the fanciful suggestion that L'Enfant used it as a base while designing the federal city. Today it has been restored to the state it probably resembled in the late eighteenth century, and short guided tours lead you through kitchen and carpenter's workshop downstairs, paneled parlors and bedrooms upstairs.

Shops, restaurants and bars proliferate around the main M Street/Wisconsin Avenue junction, whose useful landmark is the gold dome of the Riggs National Bank. Just beyond, the late twentieth century imposes upon the late nineteenth in the shape of **Georgetown Park**, a high-profile shopping mall at 3222 M St (Mon–Sat 10am–9pm, Sun noon–6pm). As a deskbound designer's idea of what a Victorian architect might have come up with given the money, material and tools it's just about a success – wrought-iron fencing and balconies, glass lanterns and skylights, potted ferns and polished brass all add to the image, though no Victorian marketplace was ever this clean. There's a food court inside, too, and one exit from the mall leads directly to the canal towpath. A block west, at Potomac Street, the triple-arched, red-brick **Market House** has been the site of a public market since the 1860s, even if today the butchered carcasses and patent medicines have made way for a celebrated *Dean & Deluca* deli.

The café at Dean & Deluca is a favored lunch spot, with conservatory-style sidewalk seating, decent coffee and a good salad and pasta bar.

Potomac Street is as good a point as any to detour north to **N Street** – known as Gay Street until the late nineteenth century – which contains some of Georgetown's finest federal-era buildings. None are open to the public, but there are several particularly attractive facades between 29th and 34th streets. At 3014 N St, Robert Todd Lincoln (President Lincoln's son) lived out the last decade of his life – the house is now owned by *Washington Post* stalwart Ben Bradlee. Four blocks along, JFK and Jackie owned no. 3307 from 1957 to 1961 – Jackie also moved briefly into no. 3017 after the assassination. Other historic houses cluster on **Prospect Street**, one block south, where late-eighteenth-century merchants built mansions like those at nos. 3425 and 3508; as the street name suggests they once possessed splendid views down to the river from which they derived their wealth.

Back on M Street, aim for the junction with 34th Street, from where the **Francis Scott Key Bridge** shoots off across the river to Rosslyn. Francis Scott Key, author of the "Star-Spangled Banner", moved to Washington in 1805 and lived in a house here at M Street which was demolished to make way for the Whitehurst Freeway – an act of sacrilege only belatedly acknowledged by the establishment of the **Francis Scott Key Park**, just off the street. There's a bronze bust of the man, a sixty-foot flagpole flying the Stars and Stripes, a wisteria-covered arbor and a few benches from which to peer through the break in the buildings to the river. Walk down the steps here and you're standing on the point at which, in September 1781, General Washington and his ally, Jean-Baptiste de Rochambeau, Commander-in-Chief of the French Army in America, prepared to cross the Potomac en route to Mount Vernon and, ulti-

Georgetown in the Movies

Georgetown crops up in many movies which are only incidentally set in Washington DC. Although the house in **The Exorcist**, in which a vomiting, pustulating Linda Blair swiveled her head, was a stage set, the steep flight of steps down which Father Damien is thrown exists (at 36th between M and Prospect); author-screenwriter William Peter Blatty knew it well since he lived nearby. Other scenes were filmed on campus at Georgetown University. Student Georgetown also gets an outing in cult 1980s bratpack movie **St Elmo's Fire**, in which Demi Moore, Emilio Estevez, Rob Lowe, Andrew McCarthy, Judd Nelson, Ally Sheedy and Mare Winningham primp, preen and throw tantrums all over town as they come to terms with life and love after college; scenes in the bar, *St Elmo's*, were actually filmed in *Third Edition*. Lawyer-turned-fugitive Will Smith gets an extremely agreeable Upper Georgetown pad in **Enemy of the State** (though not much time to enjoy it as he's confusingly pursued from Adams-Morgan to Baltimore). The pseudo-Victorian elegance of the Georgetown Park Mall on M Street has turned up in key scenes in Jean-Claude van Damme's **Timecop** and Arnold Schwarzenegger's **True Lies**, though top Georgetown thriller honors go to Kevin Costner's underrated **No Way Out**. Although largely set in the Pentagon, the film has Costner jogging along the C&O Canal and later pursued along the Whitehurst Freeway before it loses the plot entirely and has him escaping into the "Georgetown Metro" station – there is, of course, no such thing.

mately, Yorktown – to a decisive victory the following month against the British which turned the course of the Revolutionary War.

Before you leave lower Georgetown you may as well swing by **Georgetown University**, splendidly sited on the heights above the river; the main gate is at 37th and O streets. Founded in 1789 as the Jesuit Georgetown College (the oldest Catholic university in the US), it, and its six thousand students, are what gives the neighborhood much of its buzz. No one will mind if you pop in for a look around, though apart from treading in the footsteps of exorcized priests and excitable college kids (see "Georgetown in the Movies" above), there's little incentive to do so. The architecture is a bit of a hybrid, ranging from the plain facade of the building known as Old North, which dates from 1795, to the Romanesque niceties of Healy Hall, finished ninety years later.

Northern Georgetown

Set above the rest of Georgetown on "The Heights" (above Q Street), the grand mansions and estates of **northern Georgetown** sat out the nineteenth- and twentieth-century upheavals taking place below. Owned by the richest merchants, the land here was never exploited for new building when Georgetown was in the throes of expansion.

Northern
Georgetown

*For details of
the annual
Georgetown
garden tour
(May; fee
charged), call
☎333-4953.*

Today several of the fine mansions are open to the public, their grounds and nearby cemeteries forming a pleasing backdrop.

From the middle of Georgetown, the easiest access is straight up Wisconsin Avenue (bus #30, #32, #34, #35 or #36 from M St). Alternatively, approaching from Washington, crossing Dumbarton Bridge from Massachusetts Avenue NW (Dupont Circle Metro) puts you directly on Q Street.

Mount Zion Cemetery

Five minutes from Dumbarton Bridge, hidden away down an offshoot of 27th Street (northern side of Q St), the headstones scattered through the tangled undergrowth form part of **Mount Zion Cemetery**, the oldest burial ground in the city. Formerly the Old Methodist Burying Ground, the land was bought in 1842 by a women's association known as the Female Union Band for the burial of members of the Mount Zion Methodist Church (whose fine red-brick church building still stands at 1334 29th St, at Dumbarton St). The cemetery has been neglected over the years, though a start has been made in tidying up the grounds and restoring some of the monumental gravestones. There's still a long way to go, though, before it matches the pristine grounds of the adjacent (white) Oak Hill Cemetery (see opposite), whose tiered gravestones you can glimpse through the trees beyond.

Dumbarton House

Past 27th Street, **Dumbarton House**, one of the oldest houses in Georgetown, built between 1799 and 1804, comes into view at 2715 Q St NW (tours Tues–Sat 10am–12.15pm; closed Aug; $3; ☎337-2288). Known for a century as "Bellevue", its elegant Georgian proportions housed Georgetown's first salon, as political leaders of the day came to call on Joseph Nourse, registrar of the US Treasury, who lived here until 1813. The following year, as the British overran Washington, Dolley Madison watched the White House burning from Bellevue's windows – the house was the first sanctuary for the fleeing presidential couple. It's a period that the guides from the National Society of Colonial Dames of America (whose headquarters Dumbarton House now is) make much of, and you'll be escorted slowly through period rooms, filled with Federal furniture, early prints of Washington and less-than-accomplished portraits. If you don't have an hour to spare, or an insatiable interest in decorative porcelain that once, possibly, adorned the White House, content yourself instead with a seat in the restful garden and contemplate perhaps the most remarkable fact about the place: that the building of the bridge over Rock Creek in 1915 necessitated the house's removal, brick-by-brick, from further down Q Street to its present position.

Oak Hill Cemetery

Endowed by banker and art collector William Wilson Corcoran, the exclusive **Oak Hill Cemetery** (Mon–Fri 10am–4pm; free; ☎337-2835) began receiving the wealthy dead of Georgetown in 1849. Dating from that time is the brick gatehouse at 30th and R streets, where you enter the lovingly kept grounds which spill down the hillside to Rock Creek. Within the grounds, the diminutive brick-and-sandstone Gothic chapel is the sprightly work of James Renwick (architect of the Smithsonian Castle, among other works), while to the west stands a marble plinth with a bust of John Howard Payne – author of the treacly "Home Sweet Home". Ask at the gatehouse for directions to the cemetery's other notable inmates, among them Corcoran himself, Edwin Stanton, Secretary of War under President Lincoln, and former Secretary of State Dean Acheson.

Dumbarton Oaks

If one estate typifies both the success of the early Georgetown merchants and the durability of their property it's **Dumbarton Oaks**. In 1703, Scottish pioneer Ninian Beall was granted almost 800 acres of land, stretching from the river to Rock Creek, and proceeded to make himself a fortune from the tobacco trade. Although much of the land was later sold by his descendants, more than enough of the coveted northern reaches remained for incomer William H. Dorsey to build a grand red-brick mansion in 1800, surrounded by gardens and woods. This was added to and renovated down the years, before being acquired by diplomat Robert Woods Bliss in 1920 to house his significant collection of Byzantine and pre-Columbian art. In 1940 the house was handed on to Harvard University (the current owners) and in 1944 its commodious Music Room saw a meeting of American, Russian, British and Chinese delegates whose deliberations led directly to the founding of the United Nations the following year.

The house (entrance at 1703 32nd St), restored to its Federal glory, contains a beautifully presented **museum** (Tues–Sun 2–5pm; suggested donation $1; ☎339-6400). Eight connected circular glass pavilions, added in 1963, display selected carvings, sculpture, jewelry and textiles of Olmec, Inca, Aztec and Mayan provenance – ceremonial axes, polychrome vases depicting palace scenes, jade pendants, goldwork recovered from graves and bluff stone masks of unknown significance. Bliss was equally fascinated by the Byzantine Empire; the silver Eucharist vessels, decorated ivory boxes and various painted icons stand out. Perhaps most extraordinary is the celebrated miniature fourteenth-century mosaic icon of the Forty Martyrs, so-called because it depicts – in cubes of enamel paste and semiprecious stone – forty Roman soldiers left to freeze to death because they refused to recant their Christian beliefs.

Outside, the ten acres of formal **gardens** (entrance at 3101 R St; daily 2–5pm; closed in bad weather; free), with their beech terrace, evergreens, rose garden, brick paths, pools and fountains, provide one of DC's quietest backwaters.

Tudor Place

The area's final mansion is stately **Tudor Place**, 1644 31st St NW, between Q and R streets, designed by William Thornton, who won the competition to design the US Capitol. Commissioned by Thomas Peter (descendant of one of the original Scottish tobacco merchants and son of Georgetown's first mayor) and his wife Martha Custis (granddaughter of Martha Washington), the house displays a pleasing incongruity, rare for the period – a fundamentally Federal-style structure which Thornton embellished with a Classical domed portico on the south side. The exterior has remained virtually untouched since and, as the house stayed in the same family for over 150 years, the interior is considered rather fine, too, being saved from the constant "improvements" wrought in other period Georgetown houses by successive owners. **Tours** (Tues–Fri 10am, 11.30am, 1pm & 2.30pm, Sat on the hour 10am–3pm; $6; ☎965-0400) point out highlights including furnishings lifted from the Washington's family seat at Mount Vernon. You're supposed to reserve in advance for the tours, but ringing the bell at the front gate gives you access to the **gardens** (Mon–Sat 10am–4pm; free) during the day – walk up the path and bear to the right where a white box holds detailed plans ($2 donation) of the paths, greens, box hedges, arbors and fountains.

Chapter 10

Arlington

A cross the Potomac River from DC lies the Virginian county of Arlington, which formed part of Washington itself until 1846 when Virginia demanded back the thirty square miles it had contributed to the capital city. The river here was always more than a geographical boundary: for many people in the nineteenth century, Arlington was where the South started, and it was to prove significant that Confederate commander Robert E. Lee had his home for many years on the Arlington heights, overlooking the Potomac and the capital city beyond. In the 1930s, as a final act of reconciliation, **Arlington Memorial Bridge** was dedicated – symbolically connecting the Lincoln Memorial with the dead of both sides buried in Arlington National Cemetery.

For a map of Arlington, see the color section at the back of the book.

It might be in Virginia, but modern Arlington is still effectively part of Washington DC, with easy access from the capital via four bridges and the Metro to the commuter and shopping belt that stretches from Rosslyn and Clarendon to Crystal City. Planes land at **National Airport**, the closest airport to downtown DC, while locals descend on the mega-**malls** at Pentagon City or Crystal City, refueling on Southeast Asian food in the burgeoning number of **restaurants** along Wilson Boulevard in Clarendon. For most visitors, though, the area is defined by three high-profile attractions: **Arlington National Cemetery**, burial place of John, Jackie and Robert Kennedy; the **Pentagon**, the country's military headquarters; and the **Newseum**, dedicated to the history of news and journalism.

For Arlington listings, see the following pages: restaurants p.289; nightlife p.300.

Note that the **area telephone code** for Arlington is ☎703.

Arlington National Cemetery

Across Arlington Memorial Bridge, Arlington, VA ☎703/979-0690; Arlington Cemetery Metro. Daily: April–Sept 8am–7pm; Oct–March 8am–5pm. Admission free.

The grand monuments of the capital across the river are placed into sharp perspective by the vast sea of identical white headstones which spreads across the hillsides of **Arlington National Cemetery**. The city's celebration of the life of a few prominent Americans – Lincoln, Washington and Jefferson – gives way at Arlington to the commemoration of the deaths of many thousands of others, including the assassinated Kennedy brothers, the presence of whose graves here elevates the cemetery to the status of a pilgrimage site. Primarily a military burial ground – the largest in the country – Arlington's 600 landscaped acres contain the graves of almost a quarter of a million war dead and their dependents, as well as those of a panoply of other national heroes with military connections from boxer (and ex-GI) Joe Louis to the crew of the doomed space shuttle *Challenger*. In some ways it's America's pantheon, a fact that partly excuses the constant stream of visitors on sightseeing tours which elsewhere might be considered unseemly in a cemetery. What saves it is not only its size – far too large to take in every plot on a single visit – but also the dignity inherent in the democratically similar lines of simple markers and unadorned headstones. Paris's Père Lachaise it's emphatically not; there's a restrained, understated ambience here which honors presidents, generals and enlisted personnel alike.

The **Metro** takes you right to the main gates on Memorial Drive. The **visitor center** by the entrance issues sketch maps indicating some of the more prominent graves, while various guidebooks on sale at the center offer more thorough coverage; alternatively, call the grave-site office (☎ 703/607-8052) for information about particular graves. The cemetery is absolutely enormous, so if you simply want to see the major sites without doing too much walking, buy a **Tourmobile** ticket ($4.75) from the booth inside the visitor center, for a narrated, shuttle-bus tour – you can get on and off as many times as you like.

Combined Tourmobile tickets are also available, including sights in DC and transportation to Arlington; see p.46.

The cemetery

In good weather the cemetery is busy by 9am. A good portion of the crowds heads straight for the Kennedy gravesites, though few realize they're bypassing Arlington's only other presidential occupant. Through Memorial Gate, just to the right, lies **William Howard Taft**, the poorly regarded 27th President (1909–13) who, in a heartfelt outburst toward the end of his administration, said "the nearer I get to the inauguration of my successor [Woodrow Wilson], the greater the relief I feel"; Taft – uniquely – enjoyed a second, much more personally rewarding, career as Chief Justice of the Supreme Court between 1921 and 1930.

The focus of attention, though, is the marble terrace further up the hillside where simple name plaques mark the graves of **John F. Kennedy**, 35th US President, his wife Jacqueline Kennedy Onassis (laid to rest here in 1994), and a son, Patrick, and an un-named daughter who both died shortly after birth. The eternal flame was lit at JFK's funeral by Jackie, who ordered the funeral decor to be copied from that of Lincoln's, held a century earlier in the White House. When it's crowded here, as it often is, the majesty of the view across to the Washington Monument and the poignancy of the inscribed extracts from JFK's inaugural address – "Ask not what your country can do for you . . ." – are sometimes obscured; come early or late in the day if possible. In the plot behind Jack a plain white cross picks out the gravesite of his brother Robert, assassinated in 1968 during the presidential primaries.

The **Tomb of the Unknowns**, a white marble block dedicated to the unknown dead of two world wars and the Korean and Vietnam conflicts, is guarded 24 hours a day by impeccably uniformed soldiers, who carry out a somber **Changing of the Guard** (April–Sept every half-hour, otherwise on the hour) on the sweeping steps; the circular, colonnaded Memorial Amphitheater behind is the site of special remembrance services. DNA testing in June 1998 provided positive identification of the remains of the previously unknown soldier in the Vietnam tomb, which – for now – stands empty.

The cemetery began as a burial ground for Union soldiers, though as a national cemetery it was subsequently deemed politic to honor the dead of both sides in the Civil War. The **Confederate Section**, with its own memorial, lies to the west of the Tomb of the Unknowns; other sections and memorials commemorate conflicts from the Revolutionary War to the Gulf War. The highest concentration of notable individual graves is found in the myriad plots surrounding the Tomb of the Unknowns; with a map, and an eye for knots of camera-toting tourists, you'll find the graves of **Audie Murphy**, most decorated soldier in World War II, and boxer **Joe Louis** (born and buried here as Joe Louis Barrow), world heavyweight champion from 1937 to 1949. Elsewhere, among others and in no particular order, are buried Robert Todd Lincoln, Abraham's son; John J. Pershing, commander of the American forces during World War I; Arctic explorer Robert Peary; civil rights leader Medgar Evers, shot in 1963; astronauts Virgil Grissom and Roger Chaffee of the ill-fated 1967 *Apollo* flight; actor Lee Marvin; thriller-writer Dashiell Hammett; and William Colby, former director of the CIA.

The most photographed of the many memorials is that to the **Space Shuttle Challenger**, immediately behind the amphitheatre; adjacent is the memorial to the **Iran Rescue Mission**, whose failure doomed Jimmy Carter at the polls. Both stand close to the **mast of the USS Maine**, whose mysterious destruction in Havana harbor in 1898 prompted the short-lived Spanish-American War – the war itself is commemorated by both a memorial and a monument to the **Rough Riders**, a devil-may-care cavalry outfit in which a young Theodore Roosevelt made his reputation. More controversial is the

Arlington National Cemetery

The drums and bugle played at JFK's state funeral are on show in the "First Ladies" room of the National Museum of American History

.

The main Arlington services and ceremonies take place at Easter, Memorial Day and Veterans Day.

memorial inscribed with the names of those killed over **Lockerbie**, Scotland, in the 1988 terrorist explosion; some felt its siting in a military cemetery inappropriate. The most recent memorial to be dedicated, situated at the main gateway, honors **Women in Military Service** – the country's first national monument to American servicewomen.

Arlington House

The entire cemetery stands on land that formerly belonged to George Washington Parke Custis, the grandson of Martha Washington by her first marriage. Custis built an imposing Georgian-Revival mansion known as **Arlington House** on the high ground above the Potomac, which passed to his daughter, Mary, on his death. Her marriage in 1830 to Lieutenant **Robert E. Lee** (1807–70) of the US Army was later of enormous consequence: in 1861, Lee was at home at Arlington House when he heard the news of the secession of Virginia from the Union. Coming from a proud Virginian family, whose number included two signatories of the Declaration of Independence, the West Point-trained Lee was torn between loyalty to his native state and to the preservation of the Union which he served. His decision was made more acute when he was also offered command of the Union Army by Lincoln, who greatly respected his ability. But familial loyalty held out and Lee resigned his US Army commission and left Arlington for Richmond, where he took command of Virginia's military forces. Mary fled Arlington a month later as Union soldiers consolidated their hold on DC and the estate was eventually confiscated by the federal government. The Lees never returned to Arlington (though the family was later compensated for the estate's seizure) and as early as 1864 a cemetery for the Union dead of the Civil War was established in the grounds of the house. A year later, Lee – now general-in-chief of the Confederate armies – surrendered to General Grant at Appomattox.

Since the 1950s Arlington House has stood as a memorial to the Lee family. The house is immediately above the Kennedy gravesites and you can look around during cemetery opening hours on a self-guided **tour** (information on ☎703/557-0613), though note that some rooms may be under restoration. Highlights include the principal bedroom, where Robert E. Lee wrote his resignation letter, and the family parlor below, in which he was married from home. A fair proportion of the furnishings are original.

Outside, the views across the river to the Mall are exemplary. Fittingly, the grave of city designer **Pierre Charles L'Enfant** was belatedly sited here in 1909 after the city forgave his feuding about low pay for his services. No less a man than the Marquis de Lafayette, a guest at Arlington House in 1824, thought the aspect "the finest view in the world", and who's to say that's still not the case.

The Marine Corps Memorial and Netherlands Carillon

Lying to the north, just outside the cemetery walls, the hugely impressive, 78-foot-high, bronze **Marine Corps Memorial** (open 24hr; free; ☎703/285-2601) shouldn't be missed. It's a twenty-minute walk north of the cemetery's main section, through the Ord-Weitzel Gate, though the easiest approach is actually from Rosslyn Metro, from where it's a ten-minute, signposted walk. The affecting memorial commemorates the marine dead of all wars – from the first casualties of the Revolutionary War to those who fell in Somalia in 1994 – but it's more popularly known as the Iwo Jima Statue, after the "uncommon valor" shown by US troops in the bloody World War II battle for the small Pacific island which cost 6800 lives. In a famous image – inspired by a contemporaneous photograph by Robert Rosenthal – half-a-dozen marines raise the Stars and Stripes on Mount Suribachi in February 1945; three of the survivors of the actual flag-raising posed for sculptor Felix W. de Weldon.

The US Marine Corps presents a parade and concert at the memorial every Tuesday (June–Aug) at 7pm, and the annual Marine Corps Marathon starts here each October.

Nearby, to the south, rises the **Netherlands Carillon**, a 130-foot-high steel monument dedicated to the Netherlands' liberation from the Nazis in 1945. Given by the Dutch in thanks for American aid, the tower is set in landscaped grounds featuring thousands of tulips which bloom each spring. The fifty bells of the carillon are rung on Saturdays and holidays from May to September (call ☎703/289-2530 for times), when visitors can climb the tower for superlative city views.

The Newseum and Freedom Park

1101 Wilson Blvd, Arlington, VA ☎703/284-3544; Rosslyn Metro. Wed–Sun 10am–5pm. Admission free.

Under the auspices of the Freedom Forum, in whose headquarters it stands, the **Newseum** provides an interactive look at the history, theory and practice of news. Drawing on the Freedom Forum's own experience – its chairman, Allen H. Neuharth, founded *USA Today* – the museum draws visitors in with an imaginative 126-foot-long video wall displaying live satellite newsfeeds and daily front pages from around the world, before honing in on the way news has evolved in a "News History Gallery" which, in many ways, takes up where similar exhibits in the National Museum of American History leave off. A storyboard time-line provides gripping historic front pages (JESSE JAMES ASSASSINATED! NIXON RESIGNS!), newscasts and background exhibits alongside artifacts including printing presses, Thomas Paine's writing kit, and a stuffed carrier pigeon. If you can get in ahead of the school-groups then touch-screen computers let you try your hand at being a reporter, editor or TV announcer; films and vintage newsreels are shown daily, and there is on-line access from the terminals in the *Newseum café*.

Museum and park are just a couple of minutes' signpost-ed walk from Rosslyn Metro, an easy stop on the way to or from the Iwo Jima Statue.

**The
Newseum
and
Freedom
Park**

Outside, a section of elevated freeway adjoining the museum has been landscaped and turned into **Freedom Park** (daily dawn to dusk; free), with views across the river to DC's monuments, memorials and Capitol dome. Various "icons" of freedom – parts of the Berlin Wall, a bronze casting of Dr Martin Luther King Jr's jail-cell door, a South African ballot box, a toppled statue of Lenin – march up to the central focus here, the **Journalists Memorial**, the world's first memorial to journalists killed while reporting. The 24-foot-high spiraling glass prism is etched with the names of almost a thousand journalists of various nations, beginning with James M. Lingan, trampled to death in Baltimore in 1812 during a mob attack on a printing press, and continuing with well-known names including World War II foxhole reporter Ernie Pyle, killed by a Japanese sniper in 1945, and renowned photographer Robert Capa, who stepped on a landmine in Vietnam in 1954.

The Pentagon

Along I-395, Arlington, VA ☎703/695-1776; Pentagon Metro. Tours on the half-hour Mon–Fri 9.30am–3.30pm. Admission free.

The headquarters of the US military establishment, the **Pentagon** is one of the largest chunks of architecture in the world, with a total floor area of 6.5 million square feet (three times that of the Empire State Building) and five 900-foot-long sides enclosing 17.5 miles of corridors. Unfortunately, facts like these, churned out ad nauseum by tour guides and Pentagon pamphlets, are as much of the story as you'll ever get from a visit to this lair of the Department of Defense. While invisible tacticians in isolated operation rooms target Tripoli and Baghdad, they'd rather you heard about the 284 restrooms and 1700 pints of milk used every day by the 25,000 employees.

There are five armed forces of the United States. The one everyone forgets is the Coast Guard.

The wonder is not that the Department of Defense allows visitors to the Pentagon, but why it bothers in the first place. Almost everyone bar statistics junkies goes away disappointed since, aside from a short introductory film and very brief stops at selected military portraits, model craft and memorial bays, the guided tour imparts next to no information worth having. What you do get for the ninety-minute investment of your time is the chance to walk very quickly through one of the famed seventeen miles of corridors behind a service personnel-guide who – in the one novel departure from the norm – walks backwards the entire time to ensure that disguised foreign agents don't slip off into one of the aforementioned restrooms.

The most interesting thing about the Pentagon is the structure itself, which was thrown together in just sixteen months during World War II to consolidate seventeen different buildings of what was, in those days, known less euphemistically as the War Department. Efficiency dictated the five-story pentagonal design: with so many employees, it was imperative to maintain quick contact between separate offices and departments – for someone versed in the arcane numbering system, it takes just seven minutes to walk between any two points in the building. Built on swamp- and wasteland, the building was constructed entirely of concrete (fashioned from Potomac sand and gravel) rather than the marble that brightens the rest of Washington; President Roosevelt thus neatly avoided boosting the Axis war effort since Italy was then the world's foremost supplier of marble. The design has barely been tampered with since, save for the oak cladding around some of the higher echelon offices. Naturally, modern technology has transformed communications within the Pentagon over the years and the 100,000 miles of telephone wires laid down since 1943 are gradually being replaced by fiber-optic cables – it's unclear whether this will hinder the 71 successful daily attempts to hack into the Pentagon's computer system (an alarming fact they have no intention of sharing as part of the general tour).

Crossing the Potomac by bridge, the yellow line Metro affords great views of the Pentagon's famous outline. The **Metro station** debouches right into the Pentagon lobby area where you sign up for the **tours**; you'll need photo ID. At peak times (generally, after 11.30am), there may be a thirty-minute wait for the next tour – before it leaves, the "security briefing" informs you that there are no cameras allowed and no restroom stops during the ninety-minute tour.

Chapter 11

Out of the City

Arlington aside, the other forays into northern Virginia made by virtually every visitor to Washington are to the historic port-town of **Old Town Alexandria**, six miles south of the capital, and to **Mount Vernon**, country seat of George Washington, another ten miles beyond. Virginia was the first and biggest British colony on the continent, generating the bulk of its wealth in a tobacco industry that relied on the forced labor of thousands of imported slaves. When the Civil War came, Virginia declared for the Confederacy, its forces led by Robert E. Lee, scion of one of the state's most venerable families. Alexandria – a solidly Southern town – was occupied by federal forces.

A generation earlier, before the great divide, Alexandria had been a typical town in the heartland of Virginia. The state had a habit of producing great leaders and here the Lee family socialized with the Washingtons in the local churches and parlors. Tours of northern Virginia provide fascinating glimpses of their private lives: especially at Mount Vernon, where the daily experiences of George Washington, farmer, are laid bare.

Access to both places is easy, either by public transportation, car or the Mount Vernon Trail. You could see the best of either in half a day, though at Alexandria, in particular, you'll probably want to spend more time.

Old Town Alexandria

ALEXANDRIA, six miles south of Washington DC, predates the capital considerably, and its preserved old town district gives a good idea of what eighteenth-century life was like for the rich tobacco farmers who lived here. First settled by Scotsman John Alexander in 1699, Alexandria was granted town status fifty years later – according to tradition, a seventeen-year-old George Washington assisted in the preliminary survey (a claim bolstered by the existence of a contemporaneous parchment map with his name on it in the Library of

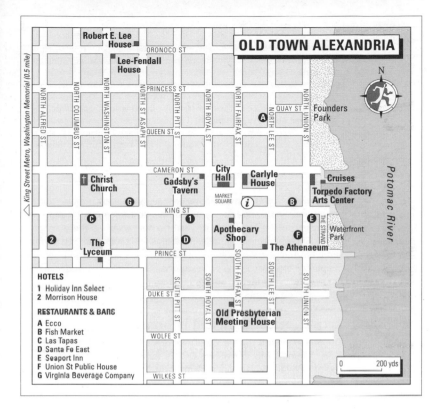

OLD TOWN ALEXANDRIA

Robert E. Lee House
Lee-Fendall House
ORONOCO ST

PRINCESS ST

QUEEN ST

N

North Alfred St
North Columbus St
North Washington St
North St Asaph St
North Pitt St
North Royal St
North Fairfax St
North Lee St
North Union St

King Street Metro, Washington Memorial (0.5 mile)

QUAY ST
Founders Park

CAMERON ST

Christ Church
Gadsby's Tavern
City Hall
Carlyle House
Cruises
Torpedo Factory Arts Center

MARKET SQUARE

KING ST

The Lyceum
Apothecary Shop
The Athenaeum
THE STRAND
Waterfront Park

PRINCE ST

SOUTH FAIRFAX ST

HOTELS
1 Holiday Inn Select
2 Morrison House

RESTAURANTS & BARS
A Ecco
B Fish Market
C Las Tapas
D Santa Fe East
E Seaport Inn
F Union St Public House
G Virginia Beverage Company

DUKE ST

SOUTH PITT ST
SOUTH ROYAL ST
SOUTH FAIRFAX ST
SOUTH LEE ST
SOUTH UNION ST

Old Presbyterian Meeting House

WOLFE ST

WILKES ST

0   200 yds

Potomac River

Congress). By the time of the Revolution, Alexandria was a booming port and trading center, exporting wheat and flour to the West Indies, with a thriving social and political scene. With the establishment of the new capital in 1791, the town was incorporated into the District of Columbia very much against the wishes of its Southern, estate- and slave-owning inhabitants, and few were sorry when in 1846 Virginia demanded its land back from the federal government. Alexandria's Confederate sympathies led to it being occupied by Union troops during the Civil War, from when dated its decline: the new railroad tracks used to move troops and supplies throughout northern Virginia were later employed to carry freight, destroying Alexandria's shipping business at one fell swoop.

What's now known as **Old Town Alexandria** – the compact downtown grid by the Potomac – was left to rot for a generation. Many of the warehouses and wharves were abandoned, while other buildings became munitions factories during both world wars. Today, after twenty years of spirited renovation, the preserved colo-

**Old Town
Alexandria**

*For
Alexandria
listings, see the
following
pages: accom-
modation
p.275; restau-
rants p.289;
nightlife p.300.*

> **Mount Vernon Trail**
>
> The 18.5-mile **Mount Vernon Trail** – a biking-and-hiking route – runs
> parallel to the George Washington Memorial Parkway, from Arlington
> Memorial Bridge, south via Alexandria (7 miles) to Mount Vernon in
> Virginia. In DC, you can pick up the trail near the Lincoln Memorial, from
> where an offshoot also runs north to Rock Creek Park. The trail sticks
> close to the Potomac for its entire length (diverting around the west side
> of National Airport) and runs past a number of sites of historic or natural
> interest. There are picnic areas en route. For more **information**, and a
> free trail guide, contact the National Park Service in Washington
> (☎202/619-7222).

nial-era streets and converted warehouses are hugely popular tourist
attractions, and although the gift shops, costumed guides and endless insistence on "authenticity" can become wearing, there are still
plenty of fascinating buildings, museums and tours. Nor is it all preserved in theme-park isolation, since it forms part of the booming
commuter town of greater Alexandria. Consequently, you can get
here easily on the Metro, and there's more than a fair share of decent
cafés and restaurants.

Arrival, orientation and information

The **Metro** station for the Old Town is King Street (Yellow and Blue
Lines; 25min from downtown DC), a mile or so from most of the
sights. Outside the station, pick up local DASH bus #2 or #5, which
runs down King Street, and get off at Fairfax Street – alternatively,
it's about 20 minutes' walk. **Drivers** should follow the George
Washington Memorial Parkway south from Arlington and take the
East King Street exit. Metered **parking** in the Old Town is limited to
two hours, though a free 24-hour parking pass is available by taking
ID and car registration to the visitor center (see below) – insert
enough money to cover the time between parking the car and returning with the pass. Cyclists or walkers can get here using the **Mount
Vernon Trail** (see above); in town, **Big Wheel Bikes** (2 Prince St
☎703/793-2300) can rent you a bike to ride to Mount Vernon, ten
miles away, and back.

The Old Town is laid out on a grid plan and most of the sights lie
within the same ten blocks. A good first stop is the **Ramsay House
Visitor's Center**, 221 King St, at Fairfax Street (daily 9am–5pm;
☎703/838-4200), where you can pick up dozens of leaflets and
brochures and book various **tours** – guided walks ($5), ghost tours
($5) or river cruises (from $7) all operate from the end of March to
the end of November. There's a **combination-museum** ticket available for some of the most visited attractions ($9; valid indefinitely),
or you can pay as you go. Note that many sights are **closed on
Monday**, and that opening hours are limited on Sunday.

Alexandria's Festivals

Alexandria has a full **festival** calendar, many of them based either around its original settlers' Scottish connections or on the Washington and Lee families. Call the visitor center (☎ 703/838-4200) for exact dates.

January (3rd Sun): music, house tours and other entertainment to celebrate the birthday of Robert E. Lee.

February (3rd weekend): George Washington's birthday, with a ball at *Gadsby's Tavern*, a parade, and mock battle at nearby Fort Ward.

March St Patrick's Day parade.

April Special homes and gardens tours in old town.

June Waterfront festival, with music, fireworks, tours, cruises and entertainment.

July (last weekend): Virginia Scottish Games, featuring highland dancing and Celtic games, sports and pastimes.

December (1st Sat) Scottish Christmas Walk with more dancing and parades; (2nd Sat) candlelit tours of museums and historic houses, accompanied by traditional music.

Around the town

It's a relief, after the expansive boulevards and monuments of DC, to walk around a town built on a more human scale. Although the main drags – particularly King Street – are top-heavy with traffic, it's not hard to find eighteenth-century peace and quiet. Cobbled, tree-lined streets with herringbone brick sidewalks are lined with pastel-washed houses featuring boot-scrapers and horse-mounting blocks outside the front door, and cast-iron drainpipes stamped "Alexandria, DC". The angled second-floor mirrors allowed the occupants to see who was calling.

A convenient starting point is the visitor center on King Street, which occupies **Ramsay House**, the oldest in town, built (though not originally on this site) in 1724 for William Ramsay, one of Alexandria's founding merchants and later its first mayor. Ramsay had the house transported upriver from Dumfries in Virginia and placed facing the river, where his ships loaded up with tobacco. The water is now three blocks away: the bluff that the town was built on having been excavated after the Revolution and the earth used to extend the harbor into the shallow bay – which is why Ramsay House stands so high above the street, its foundations exposed.

Ramsay's fellow merchant, John Carlyle, bought two of the most expensive land plots when the town was established and built Alexandria's finest colonial-era house. In the 1750s, when all the town's other buildings were of wood, the white sandstone **Carlyle House**, 121 North Fairfax St (Tues–Sat 10am–4.30pm, Sun noon–4.30pm; $4; ☎ 703/549-2997), made an ostentatious statement about its owner's wealth. Accounts of Carlyle's business dealings – he ran three plantations and traded slaves – inform the half-hour guided tours of the restored house. Contrast the family's draped beds, expensively painted rooms and fine Georgian furniture with the bare servants' hall, which has actually been over-restored – in the eighteenth century it would have had an earthen floor and no glass in the windows. In August 1755, the house was used as General Braddock's headquarters during the planning of the French and Indian War; George Washington was on Braddock's staff and was later a frequent guest in Carlyle's house when visiting from Mount Vernon.

Braddock's troops paraded across the way in **Market Square**, off King Street, the heart of Alexandria since its foundation. The modern brick terrace around the square sounds one of the few discordant notes in the Old Town, and the restored eighteenth-century **City Hall** which faces the square also fails to look its age, though a weekly **farmers' market** still sets up in the City Hall arcades (Sat 5–9am), as it has for over two hundred years.

Follow Cameron Street past City Hall to **Gadsby's Museum Tavern**, 134 North Royal Street (April–Sept Tues–Sat 10am–5pm, Sun 1–5pm; Oct–March Tues–Sat 11am–4pm, Sun 1–4pm; $4; ☎703/838-4242), occupying two (supposedly haunted) Georgian buildings in a prime spot close to the market. Downstairs, *Gadsby's Tavern* is still a working restaurant (complete with "authentic" colonial food and costumed staff). Short tours by a knowledgeable guide lead you through the old tavern rooms upstairs – in the galleried ballroom, George Washington used to cut a rug at parties thrown for his birthday. Three blocks west up Cameron Street, the English-style **Christ Church** (Mon–Sat 9am–4pm, Sun 2–4.30pm; free), set in a beautiful churchyard, retains the Washington family pew.

The Washingtons weren't the only notable family with ties to Alexandria. A descendant of the Lees of Virginia, Phillip Fendall built his splendid clapboard mansion in 1785; in the **Lee-Fendall House**, 614 Oronoco St (Tues–Sat 10am–4pm, Sun noon–4pm; $4; ☎703/548-1789), distinguished Revolutionary War general Henry "Light Horse Harry" Lee composed Washington's funeral oration (in which, famously, he declared him "first in war, first in peace, and first in the hearts of his countrymen"). Henry Lee bought his own house across the road just before the War of 1812 and installed his wife and five children there. This, the **Boyhood Home of Robert E. Lee**, 607 Oronoco St (Mon–Sat 10am–4pm, Sun 1–4pm; $4; ☎703/548-8454), makes much of the early years of Henry's son and future Confederate general, though the enthusiastic tours can't hide the lack of original Lee memorabilia. However, the house itself is a beauty, a red-brick Federal-era property first owned by a Virginia tobacco planter who entertained George Washington at dinner on occasions – his "servants", of whom you'll hear much on the tour, were of course all slaves.

For more on Robert E. Lee, see p.254.

South of King Street, the **Lyceum**, 201 South Washington St
(Mon–Sat 10am–5pm, Sun 1–5pm; free; ☎703/838-4994), houses
the town's history museum in a Greek Revival building of 1839.
The changing displays, film shows and associated art gallery can
put some flesh on the town's history, highlighted in varied exhibits
from old photographs and Civil War documents to locally produced
furniture and silverware (the latter an Alexandrian speciality in the
nineteenth century). Four blocks east you'll find the **Old
Presbyterian Meeting House**, 321 South Fairfax St (Mon–Fri
9am–3pm; free; ☎703/549-6670), in whose quiet graveyard lies
the tomb of John Carlyle. The Scottish town founders met here regularly, most prominently in December 1799 when they gathered in
the cool, white pews for the memorial service for George
Washington, who had recently died on his estate at Mount Vernon.
Patent medicines for Washington were made up at the nearby
Stabler-Leadbeater Apothecary Shop, whose yellow bay windows
jut out at 105–107 South Fairfax St (Mon–Sat 10am–4pm, Sun
1–5pm; $2.50; ☎703/836-3713). The shop was founded in 1792
and still displays its original furnishings, herbs, potions and medical paraphernalia.

The waterfront

Eighteenth century Alexandria wouldn't recognize its twentieth-century **waterfront** beyond North Union Street, not least because the
riverbank is several blocks further east, following centuries of land-
fill. Where there were once wooden warehouses and wharves heaving with barrels of tobacco, there's now a smart marina and boardwalk, framed by the green stretches of **Founders Park** to the north
and **Waterfront Park** to the south. Forty-minute sightseeing **cruises**
depart from in front of the *Food Pavilion* (several daily April–Oct;
$7; information from the Potomac Riverboat Company on
☎703/548-9000); longer trips run to DC or Mount Vernon and back.

Before this whole area was cleaned up, the US government built
a torpedo factory on the river, which operated until the end of World
War II. Restyled as the diverting **Torpedo Factory Arts Center**
(daily 10am–5pm; free; ☎703/838-4565), its three floors contain
the studios of over two hundred artists, all open to the public, displaying sculpture, ceramics, jewelry, glassware and textiles in regu-

larly changing exhibitions. Take a look, too, inside the center's
Alexandria Archeology Museum (Tues–Fri 10am–3pm, Sat
10am–5pm, Sun 1–5pm; free; ☎703/838-4399), where much of the
town's restoration work was carried out.

George Washington Masonic Memorial

In a town bursting with Washington mementos, nothing is more
prominent than the **George Washington Masonic Memorial** (daily
9am–5pm; free; ☎703/683-2007), whose 333-foot tower – built on
top of a Greek temple – looms over town behind the King Street
Metro station. Washington was considered a "deserving brother" by
the Virginian freemasons who built this memorial in his honor in
1932. Inside, there's a tall bronze statue of the man, sundry memorabilia, and dioramas depicting events from his life. To see this, and
– more pertinently – the superb views from the observation platform,
you'll have to wait for a forty-minute **tour**, which leaves from the hall
(on the half-hour in the morning, on the hour in the afternoon, last
tour 4pm). But even from the steps outside, the views are magnificent, across the Potomac to the Washington Monument and Capitol
dome in the distance.

Mount Vernon

George Washington Parkway, Mount Vernon, VA ☎703/780-2000; Huntington
Metro, then Fairfax Connector bus #101. Daily March 9am–5pm; April–Aug
8am–5pm; Sept & Oct 9am–5pm; Nov–Feb 9am–4pm. Admission $8.

*For a life of
George
Washington,
see pp.58–59.*

Set on a shallow bluff overlooking the broad Potomac River, sixteen
miles south of Washington DC, **MOUNT VERNON** is among the
most attractive historic houses in America. The beloved **country
estate of George Washington**, it was his home for forty years, during which he ran it as a thriving and progressive farm, anticipating
the decline in Virginia's tobacco cultivation and planting instead
grains and food crops with great success. When he died, it seemed
only natural that he be buried in the grounds, as his will directed;
America's first president lies next to his wife, Martha, in the simple
family tomb.

His father, Augustine, first built a house on the Washington
estate in 1735. When he died, the house and lands passed first to
George's elder brother Lawrence and, after the death of Lawrence in
1752 and his widow in 1761, to George. Not that he had much early
opportunity to spend time here, since for much of the 1750s he was
away on service with the Virginia militia, later fighting in the French
and Indian War. He married in 1759 and it was during the years
before 1775 – when he was next called away on service, as commander-in-chief of the Continental Army – that Washington came to
know his estate. He tripled its size to eight thousand acres, divided it
into five separate working farms, and landscaped the mansion

grounds – rolling meadows, copses, riverside walks, parks and even vineyards, all laid out for the family's amusement.

Just five hundred acres of the estate remain today, the rest having been split and sold off by the terms of successive wills, but there's more than enough to give an idea of the whole. The lifestyle of an eighteenth-century **gentleman farmer** was an agreeable one, in Washington's case supported by the labor of over two hundred slaves who lived and worked on the outlying farms. The modest house he inherited was enlarged and redecorated with imported materials; formal gardens and a bowling green were added; and the general bred stallions, hunted in his woods, fished in the river and entertained visitors. But it would be unfair to view Washington as a dilettante. Daily at dawn he made a personal tour of inspection on horseback, sometimes riding twenty miles around the grounds. He studied the latest scientific works on farming, corresponded with experts, and, introducing new techniques, expanded the farms' output to include the production of flour, textiles and even whiskey. His experimental methods often cost him financially and, once he was away fighting the Revolutionary War, he was forced to rely on others to run his estate – who were doubtless thrilled to receive his sixteen-page letters from the front directing the latest farm improvements.

Washington spent eight years away from Mount Vernon during the war, but still wasn't allowed to retire there for good, as was his wish, at the end of the fighting. By 1787 he was back at the head of the Constitutional Convention in Philadelphia and two years later was elected to his first term as president – news he heard first at Mount Vernon from a messenger who had ridden all the way from Philadelphia. In the event, he only visited his house another dozen or so times during his presidency, often for just a few days. When he finally moved back in 1797, at the end of his second term in office, he and Martha had just two and a half years together before his death on December 14, 1799. Out on one of his long estate inspections, he got caught in the snow and succumbed to a fever which killed him.

Practicalities

To reach Mount Vernon, go first to **Huntingdon Metro** (Yellow Line) then take Fairfax Connector **bus #101** (hourly, half-hourly after 3pm; call ☎703/339-7200 for schedules) – an easy enough route, though it takes over an hour, or more if you miss the bus. A **cab** from the station costs around $15–20. **Drivers** should follow the George Washington Parkway from DC; there's free parking. The **Mount Vernon Trail** (see p.260) finishes here too.

Spirit **cruises** from Pier 4, 6th and Water streets SW in DC (mid-March to Oct; $26.50 round-trip, reservations recommended; ☎202/554-8000) take ninety minutes to reach Mount Vernon; it's only fifty minutes by water from Old Town Alexandria with the Potomac Riverboat Company (April–Oct; $22; ☎703/548-9000).

*Washington's
birthday
celebration
(around the
3rd weekend
in Feb) sees
free admis-
sion, wreath-
laying and fife
and drum
parades.*

The **Tourmobile** bus (see p.46) also runs out here – a four hour trip. The prices of both cruise and Tourmobile trips include admission to the house and grounds.

Mount Vernon is an extremely popular day-trip, and summer weekends, especially, can be very busy. Come early, or midweek, if you can and allow at least two hours to see the house and grounds. You can't eat or drink on the estate, but just outside the gate – pass-outs allowed – is a snack bar (daily 9.30am–estate closing) and a more refined **restaurant**, the *Mount Vernon Inn* (Mon–Sat 11am–3.30pm & 5–9pm, Sun 11am–4pm; ☎703/780-0011), specializing in colonial food.

The house and grounds

Pick up a map of the grounds at the entrance gate and, if you need historical background, watch a few minutes of the saccharine video, which ends with the treacly entreaty, "Thank you, George Washington, for being there when we needed you."

The path up to the mansion passes various outbuildings, including a renovated set of former **slave quarters**. Ninety slaves lived and worked in the mansion grounds alone, and though there's evidence that Washington was a kinder master than most – refusing to sell children away from their parents, for instance, allowing slaves to raise their own crops, and engaging the services of a doctor – they still lived lives of deprivation and overwork. His overseers were continually enjoined to watch the slaves like hawks and guard against theft and slacking. Washington was quick to realize that the move away from tobacco cultivation to more skilled farming made slavery increasingly unprofitable. He stopped buying slaves in the late 1770s, allowing those he owned to learn occupations such as carpentry, bricklaying and spinning, and to be maintained once they had reached the end of their working lives. His will freed his remaining slaves a year after his death, making provision for them all.

Nearby, a small **museum** traces Washington's ancestry and displays porcelain from the house, medals, weapons, silver and a series of striking miniatures by Charles Willson Peale and his brother James, of Martha and her two children by her first marriage. The clay bust of Washington was produced by French sculptor Jean-Antoine Houdon, who worked on it at Mount Vernon in 1785 prior to completing his famous statue for the Richmond Capitol.

Around the corner, fronting the circular courtyard, stands the **mansion** itself, with the bowling green stretching before it. Join the line and walk through the wings and connecting colonnades into the house, where guides answer questions. It's a handsome, harmonious wooden structure, reasonably modest, but sporting stunning views from the East Lawn. The wooden exterior was painted white, beveled and sand-blasted to resemble stone; inside, the Palladian windows and brightly painted and papered rooms follow the fashion of the day, while the contents are based on an inventory prepared after Washington's death. Fourteen rooms are open to the public: portrait-filled parlors and cramped bedrooms, and the chamber where Washington breathed his last on a four-poster bed still in situ – his body was later laid out downstairs in the striking green dining room. Curiosities in his study give insights into his character – a wooden reading chair with built-in fan, and a globe he ordered from London – while in the central hall hangs a key to the destroyed Bastille, presented by Thomas Paine in 1790 on behalf of Lafayette.

After touring the mansion there's plenty more to see in the **grounds**, including the kitchen (set apart from the house because of the risk of fire), cluttered storehouse, stables, smokehouse, wash-house, overseer's quarters, kitchen garden and shrubberies. There's also a **forest trail** nature walk, and take a stroll down to the **tomb**, where two marble sarcophagi for George and Martha are set behind iron gates, "interred here in a private manner, without parade or funeral oration", as Washington's will stipulated. The will also directed that a new brick vault be erected after his death, since the original family vault on the grounds was in poor shape; the current structure was built in 1831. Nearby lies a slave burial ground, while beyond you may catch one of the occasional demonstrations held on a special site growing crops and displaying farming techniques used by Washington.

Mount Vernon

You can view the third floor (usually closed) on special Christmas tours, which re-create the Washingtons' yuletide celebrations.

Listings

Chapter 12

Accommodation

As you might expect, Washington DC possesses some of the most exclusive hotels in America: Georgetown's *Four Seasons* is top of the scale, while rates at the *Willard Inter-Continental, Omni Shoreham, Hay-Adams* and *Jefferson* reflect their standing as historic landmarks. There's also plenty of reasonably priced, central accommodation, though you'll need to plan ahead if you want to guarantee a certain room at a particular time. For a full list of vacancies contact one of the city information offices listed on p.17 or one of the free **reservation services** listed below. All hotels reviewed here are marked on the **map** on pp.272–73.

There are hotels in all the main downtown **areas**, though those near the White House, on Capitol Hill and in Georgetown tend to be business-oriented and pricey. The occasional budget option exists in Foggy Bottom and Old Downtown (where you'll find the city's youth hostel), while most of the chain hotels and mid-range places are in New Downtown – particularly in the streets around Scott and Thomas circles. Outer neighborhoods tend to have a wider

Unless otherwise stated, all the hotels reviewed in this chapter have the DC-area **telephone code** ☎202, to be used when calling from outside the city.

selection of smaller, cheaper hotels and B&B-style guest houses, and it's no hardship at all to be staying in Dupont Circle, Adams-Morgan or Upper Northwest – you'll probably be eating and drinking in these places anyway. We've also listed a few options in Alexandria, VA, though it's easy to see that city on a day-trip from the capital. You're also more likely to be able to **park** for free in the outer neighborhoods; garage parking is available at most downtown hotels, but you'll be charged $10–20 a night for the privilege. Very occasionally, an inn or hotel we list is on the cusp of a slightly iffy neighborhood; where **safety** is an issue, we've said so, and you're advised to take taxis back to your hotel at night in these areas.

Standard **room rates** throughout the city start at around $100–120 a night,

---

B&B Agencies

Bed & Breakfast Accommodations Ltd ☎202/328-3510, fax 332-3885

Bed & Breakfast League ☎202/363-7767, fax 368-8396

Hotel Reservation Services

Capitol Reservations ☎202/452-1270 or 1-800/847-4832, fax 452-0537

Washington DC Accommodations ☎202/289-2220 or 1-800/554-2220, fax 338-4517

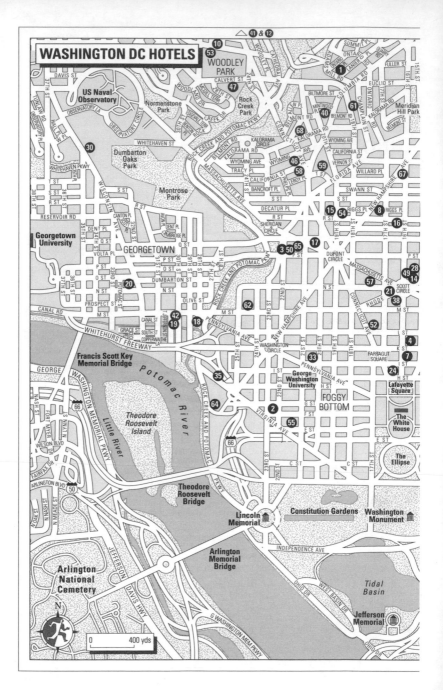

WASHINGTON DC HOTELS

ACCOMMODATION

1 Adams Inn
2 Allen Lee Hotel
3 Brickskeller Inn
4 Capital Hilton
5 Capitol Hill Guest House
6 Capitol Hill Suites
7 Carlton
8 Carlyle Suites
9 Channel Inn Hotel
10 Connecticut-Woodley Guest House
11 Crowne Plaza Washington
12 Days Inn Connecticut Avenue
13 Days Inn Premier
14 Doubletree Hotel Park Terrace
15 Dupont at the Circle
16 Embassy Inn
17 Embassy Row Hilton
18 Four Seasons Hotel
19 Georgetown Dutch Inn
20 Georgetown Inn
21 Governor's House
22 Grand Hyatt
23 Harrington Hotel
24 Hay-Adams Hotel
25 Henley Park Hotel
26 Hereford House
27 Holiday Inn Capitol
28 Holiday Inn Central
29 Holiday Inn Downtown
30 Holiday Inn Georgetown
31 Holiday Inn on the Hill
32 Hotel George
33 Hotel Lombardy
34 Hotel Washington

35 Howard Johnson Premier Hotel
36 Hyatt Regency Washington on Capitol Hill
37 India House Too
38 Jefferson Hotel
39 JW Marriott
40 Kalorama Guest House at Kalorama Park
41 Kalorama Guest House at Woodley Park
42 Latham Hotel
43 Loews L'Enfant Plaza
44 Marriott at Metro Center
45 Morrison-Clark Inn
46 Normandy Inn
47 Omni Shoreham
48 Phoenix Park
49 Quality Hotel Downtown
50 Radisson Barceló
51 Red Roof Inn
52 Renaissance Mayflower
53 Sheraton Washington
54 Simpkins' B&B
55 State Plaza
56 Swiss Inn
57 Tabard Inn
58 Washington Courtyard by Marriott
59 Washington Hilton and Towers
60 Washington International AYH Hostel
61 Washington International Student Center
62 Washington Monarch Hotel
63 Washington Plaza
64 Watergate Hotel
65 Westin Fairfax
66 Willard Inter-Continental
67 Windsor Inn
68 Windsor Park Hotel
69 Wyndham Washington

Accommodation

The Metro stations listed for Adams-Morgan are the nearest, but that doesn't mean they're particularly close; with luggage or at night, you'll want to take a cab.

Airport–hotel Connections

The Washington Flyer Express bus operates **courtesy shuttle services** from the terminal at 1517 K St NW to the following hotels: *Grand Hyatt* (Old Downtown), *Harrington* (Old Downtown), *Omni Shoreham* (Woodley Park), *Sheraton Washington* (Woodley Park), *Renaissance Mayflower* (New Downtown), *Washington Hilton* (Adams-Morgan), and the *JW Marriott* (White House). There's also a direct service from these hotels back to the airports.

but there's plenty of scope for negotiation for canny travelers. Most hotels **discount** their rates on weekends (some by up to fifty percent), while prices are low throughout July and August, when Congress is in recess, and again in December and January. Always ask if the rate you've been quoted is the best available; often, discount information has to be ferreted out of desk clerks. Where places offer particularly good discount deals, we've said so in the review. Also, since hotels charge by the room, three people can often stay in a double for the same (or a slightly higher) price as two. Although **breakfast** usually isn't included in the price at most hotels, it often *is* as part of the special weekend packages.

The **price codes** given in the reviews below reflect the **average price for a standard double room in peak season** (late March to early July); consequently you'll often be paying less. Groups and families should consider the city's **suite hotels**, where you'll get a kitchen and possibly a separate lounge-room, too. One other thing to keep in mind: DC in summer is hot and humid, and **air-conditioning** is essential for getting a good night's rest.

A number of **B&B agencies** offer rooms in small inns, private homes or apartments, starting from around $55–65

per night; luxury B&B, though, can be every bit as pricey as a hotel, reaching as high as $150–250. For rock-bottom alternatives, there's the official international **youth hostel** (which is very central, but at its busiest in July and August) and a couple of similar places, one in Adams-Morgan, the other out in Takoma Park. **Students** can try contacting one of the educational establishments listed in the box below.

Note that all DC hotels add **14.5 percent room tax** to your bill.

Adams-Morgan

Adams Inn, 1744 Lanier Place NW ☎745-3600 or 1-800/578-6807, fax 319-7958. Woodley Park-Zoo Metro. Clean, simple B&B rooms, with and without bath, in three adjoining Victorian townhouses on a quiet residential street (just north of Calvert St). No TVs, but free breakfast, coffee all day, garden patio and laundry facilities. ②–③.

Kalorama Guest House at Kalorama Park, 1854 Mintwood Place NW ☎667-6369, fax 319-1262. Woodley Park-Zoo Metro. Victorian guest house, near Adams-Morgan restaurants. Spacious rooms (31; 12 en-suite) in four spotless houses, filled with period *objets*, plants and handsome furniture (no TVs). Free breakfast, papers, coffee and evening sherry, plus washing machines. Booking essential. ②–③.

Student Accommodation

Georgetown University (☎ 687-4560), George Washington University (☎994-6688), Catholic University (☎319-5277) and American University (☎885-3370) all offer a variety of dorms, doubles and apartments at budget rates in summer (June–Aug). Arrangements must be made well in advance; you may find there's a minimum stay (as much as 30 days), since the service is intended for interns or students in summer educational programs.

Accommodation Price Codes

① Under $50	④ $100–140	⑦ $250–300
② $50–70	⑤ $140–200	⑧ Over $300
③ $70–100	⑥ $200–250	

The price codes given in the reviews below reflect the **average price for a standard double room in peak season** (late March to early July), excluding room tax. Unless otherwise stated all rooms come with bathroom; breakfast is not normally included.

Accommodation

Normandy Inn, 2118 Wyoming Ave NW ☎483-1350 or 1-800/424-3729, fax 387-8241. Woodley Park-Zoo Metro. Quiet hotel in flash neighborhood, with comfortable rooms (each with private bath, fridge and coffee-maker). Continental breakfast is $6, taken in the garden in summer. Coffee and cookies are served daily and there's a weekly wine and cheese reception. ④.

Washington Courtyard by Marriott, 1900 Connecticut Ave NW ☎332-9300 or 1-800/321-3211, fax 328-7039. Dupont Circle Metro. The top-floor rooms have splendid views. Outdoor pool and very keen prices for this area (even better on the weekend). ⑤.

Washington Hilton and Towers, 1919 Connecticut Ave NW ☎483-3000 or 1-800/445 8667, fax 265-8221. Dupont Circle Metro. Massive 1960s convention hotel midway between Dupont Circle (downhill) and Adams-Morgan (uphill). Well-equipped rooms, most with good views. Facilities include pool, health club, tennis courts and bike rental. ⑦.

Washington International Student Center, 2451 18th St NW ☎667-7681. Backpackers' accommodation in plain multi-bedded dorm rooms in the heart of Adams-Morgan. At $15 a night (coffee-and-toast breakfast included) it's downtown DC's cheapest bed, but you may find the surroundings, shared bathrooms and "traveling" crowd tiresome after a while. ①.

Windsor Park Hotel, 2116 Kalorama Rd NW ☎483-7700 or 1-800/247-3064, fax 332-4547. Pleasant little Victorian-style rooms in a quiet neighborhood, just off Connecticut Avenue. Continental breakfast included. ③.

Alexandria, VA

Bed & Breakfast Ltd ☎1-800/470-5588. Call Mon–Fri 10am–6pm for hosted B&B accommodation in historic Old Town homes. All rooms have air-conditioning and private bath, breakfast included; minimum stay two nights at peak times. ③–④.

Holiday Inn Select, 480 King St, Old Town ☎703/549-6080 or 1-800/465-4329. Alexandria's best-situated hotel, just off Market Square, makes a great exploring base – there's an indoor pool, and many rooms have balconies overlooking a quiet internal courtyard. ⑤.

Morrison House, 116 S Alfred St, Old Town ☎703/838-8000 or 1-800/367-0800, fax 703/684-6283. Stunning recreation of a Federal-era townhouse (built 1985, looks like 1795) complete with butlers, parlor, parquet floors and crystal chandeliers, yet with all modern comforts. Rooms are well-appointed, and there's an acclaimed restaurant. ⑤.

Capitol Hill

Capitol Hill Guest House, 101 5th St NE ☎ & fax 547-1050 or 1-800/261-2768. Union Station or Capitol South Metro. Cute Hill townhouse with corner turret and a range of rooms, from sparse singles to doubles with private bath. Continental breakfast included. ③–④.

Capitol Hill Suites, 200 C St SE ☎543-6000 or 1-800/424-9165, fax 547-2608. Capitol South Metro. Popular apartment conversions whose rooms all come with kitchen-diners, free morning coffee, muffins and juice, and daily paper. Busy when Congress is in session – on week-

For details on how to get to Alexandria, see p.260.

Accommodation

ends and in August the price drops a category. ⑤.

Hereford House, 604 South Carolina Ave SE ☎543-0102. Eastern Market Metro. Attractive brick townhouse with hardwood floors, small garden and bright, reasonably sized rooms (no TVs) in residential Capitol Hill (just a block from the Metro), offering B&B in the "true British tradition" – which means a hearty welcome from its English owner and a cooked breakfast. Just four rooms (sharing two bathrooms), and three more in a separate house (no breakfast) five minutes away. ③.

Downtown: New

Capital Hilton, 1001 16th St NW ☎393-1000 or 1-800/445-8667, fax 639-5742. Farragut North, Farragut West or McPherson Square Metro. Art Deco trappings, great location three blocks from the White House, buzzing lobby-bar and spacious rooms. Facilities include health club and a good sports bar-restaurant. Weekend rates are among the lowest for quality downtown rooms. ⑥–⑦.

The Carlton, 923 16th St NW ☎638-2626 or 1-800/562-5661, fax 638-4231. Farragut North, Farragut West or McPherson Square Metro. A 1920s Italian Renaissance palace a couple of blocks north of the White House. Stylish rooms (with great bathrooms), the highly rated *Lespinasse* restaurant and perfect service. ⑦.

Crowne Plaza Washington, 14th and K St NW ☎682-0111 or 1-800/227-6963, fax 682-9525. Metro Center Metro. Resurrected Beaux-Arts style, with fine city views from its sought-after Franklin Square location. Elegant rooms, lobby espresso bar, health club and sauna. ⑥.

Days Inn Premier, 1201 K St NW ☎842-1020 or 1-800/562-3350, fax 289-0336. Metro Center Metro. Handy sightseeing launchpad near Franklin Square, with small rooftop pool. Some rooms have kitchenettes; all have coffee-makers. ④.

Doubletree Hotel Park Terrace, 1515 Rhode Island Ave NW ☎232-7000 or 1-800/222-8733, fax 332-7152. Dupont Circle or Farragut North Metro. Comfortable rooms, marble bathrooms, outdoor terrace for summer dining and good-value buffet breakfasts. You're near the Dupont Circle nightlife, too. ④.

The Governor's House, 1615 Rhode Island Ave NW ☎296-2100 or 1-800/821-4367, fax 331-0227. Dupont Circle or Farragut North Metro. Renovation money's been well spent here, and though the exterior is unpromising, inside it's calm and comfortable. Rooms are decent-sized, some with sofa beds and kitchenettes; there's a popular bar and grill, a pool, and use of the nearby YMCA fitness center. Weekend rates are a good deal. ④.

Hay-Adams Hotel, 1 Lafayette Square NW ☎638-6600 or 1-800/424-5054, fax 638-2716. Farragut West or McPherson Square Metro. One of DC's finest hotels, fashioned from two historic townhouses in 1928 and ever since a byword for indulgence, from the gold-leaf and walnut lobby to the ornate, airy rooms and suites – with fireplaces and original cornicing, marble bathrooms, balconies and high ceilings. Splash out (a lot) for views of St John's Church or (from upper floors) the White House; 8th-floor rooms are best of all. Breakfast in the stylish park-facing restaurant. ⑦–⑧.

Henley Park Hotel, 926 Massachusetts Ave NW ☎638-5200 or 1-800/222-8474, fax 638-6740. Mount Vernon Square-UDC or Metro Center Metro. Former apartment building north of the Convention Center turned into a cozy English country-house-style hotel. It's rather at odds with the borderline neighborhood; take your after-dinner stroll somewhere else. ⑤.

Holiday Inn Central, 1501 Rhode Island Ave NW ☎483-2000 or 1-800/248-0016, fax 797-1078. Dupont Circle or Farragut North Metro. One of downtown's better mid-range options, with pleasant, modern rooms, rooftop pool, bar, and breakfast included. It's at Scott Circle. ⑤.

Holiday Inn Downtown, 1155 14th St NW ☎737-1200 or 1-800/465-4329, fax 783-5733. McPherson Square Metro. At Thomas Circle, a couple of blocks north of Franklin Square, but in a handy enough location. Standard *Holiday Inn* rooms, rooftop pool, and attractive weekend and off-season discounts. ⑤.

Jefferson Hotel, 1200 16th St NW ☎347-2200 or 1-800/365-5966, fax 331-7982. Farragut North Metro. Patrician landmark on 16th Street, a favorite with politicians since the 1920s. Antique-strewn interior, with busts, oils and porcelain at every turn, fine restaurant, personal service and all mod-cons in the superb rooms. Weekend rates can fall to under $200 a night. ⑧.

Morrison-Clark Inn, 1015 L St NW ☎898-1200 or 1-800/332-7898, fax 289-8576. Mount Vernon Square-UDC or Metro Center Metro. Antique-and-lace accommodation in a historic Victorian mansion complete with veranda. Fifty-odd rooms in overblown styles, balconies overlooking a courtyard, a comfortable lounge and a good restaurant. Weekend rates, when available, come down to the $100 mark. Watch your step at night – the neighborhood is a trifle edgy. ⑤.

Quality Hotel Downtown, 1315 16th St NW ☎232-8000 or 1-800/368-5689, fax 667-9827. Dupont Circle or Farragut North Metro. Scott Circle location, spacious rooms, many with sofabed, coffeemakers and kitchenette, plus pub, café and restaurant and free entry to local health club. Buffet breakfasts provided (not included); call for weekend rates. ④.

Renaissance Mayflower, 1127 Connecticut Ave NW ☎347-3000 or 1-800/468-3571, fax 466-9082. Farragut North Metro. Restoration has left the *Mayflower* better than ever, with the Promenade – a vast, imperially decorated hall – one of DC's great public spaces. Rooms, facilities and service are all top-notch, the bars, café and restaurant much in demand by power-diners. ⑧.

Swiss Inn, 1204 Massachusetts Ave NW ☎371-1816 or 1-800/955-7947, fax

371-1138. Metro Center Metro. Friendly townhouse accommodation with eight "efficiencies" (air-con rooms with kitchenettes, TV and bath), multilingual hosts and parking (free at weekends) outside. Book well in advance since prices don't get much better downtown – in winter you may score a small discount for being a Rough Guide reader. ③.

Tabard Inn, 1739 N St NW ☎785-1277, fax 785-6173. Dupont Circle Metro. Three converted Victorian townhouses with forty individually decorated, antique-stocked rooms (some with shared bath), two blocks from Dupont Circle. Laidback staff, comfortable if aging lounges with romantic fireplaces, courtyard and an excellent restaurant. Rates include breakfast. ④–⑤.

Washington International AYH Hostel, 1009 11th St NW ☎737-2333, fax 737-1508. Metro Center Metro. Large (250 beds), clean and very central, just three blocks north of the Metro. Single-sex dorms ($20), some family rooms, kitchen, lounge, laundry, luggage storage, enthusiastic staff and organized activities. Non-members pay $3 more per night (and may be refused in busy spring and summer months). Open 24hr but take care at night around here. Book well in advance, especially in summer; six-night maximum stay. ①.

Washington Plaza, 10 Thomas Circle NW ☎842-1300 or 1-800/424-1140, fax 371-9602. McPherson Square Metro. Convenient location three blocks from the Metro, seasonal outdoor pool and deck and great views across the Circle from the large rooms. Tourists mingle with convention and business guests in the lobby bar. Good weekend discounts. ⑤.

Wyndham Washington, 1400 M St NW ☎429-1700 or 1-800/996-3426, fax 785-0786. McPherson Square Metro. Contemporary comfort near Thomas Circle, with soaring atrium, bars, coffee shop and fitness club. Formerly the notorious *Washington Vista*, where ex-Mayor Marion Barry was arrested in a drugs sting. Weekend rates often include breakfast and parking. ⑥.

Accommodation

Price categories (see p.275 for full details):
① *Under $50*
② *$50–70*
③ *$70–100*
④ *$100–140*
⑤ *$140–200*
⑥ *$200 250*
⑦ *$250–300*
⑧ *Over $300*

Accommodation

Downtown: Old

Grand Hyatt, 1000 H St NW ☎582-1234 or 1-800/233-1234, fax 637-4797. Metro Center Metro. Nearly 900 rooms, but its location opposite the Convention Center keeps it busy. Rooms are fine but not as flash as the 12-storey atrium, lagoon, waterfalls and glass elevators. There's also a deli-café, restaurant and sports bar. ⑥.

Harrington Hotel, 1100 E St NW ☎628-8140 or 1-800/424-8532, fax 347-3924. Metro Center Metro. Large, simple, welcoming, family-owned hotel, off Pennsylvania Ave. Adequate air-con rooms (singles to quads) with TV; cheap parking, too. ③.

JW Marriott, 1331 Pennsylvania Ave NW ☎393-2000 or 1-800/228-9290, fax 626-6915. Metro Center or Federal Triangle Metro. Flagship *Marriott* property in one of the best locations in the city, part of the National Place development and overlooking Freedom Plaza (ask for an avenue-facing room). Weekend rates include breakfast. ⑥.

Marriott at Metro Center, 775 12th St NW ☎737-2200 , fax 347-5886. Metro Center Metro. Revamped downtown hotel with popular bar and grill, and sizable rooms. Weekends can be a real bargain, often including free breakfast and parking. ⑤.

Red Roof Inn, 500 H St NW ☎289-5959 or 1-800/843-7663, fax 682-9152. Gallery Place-Chinatown Metro. Reasonable rates for this location, with Chinatown and the MCI Center on the doorstep. The café serves a buffet breakfast (not included in price) and there's an exercise room with sauna. Good weekend and off-season discounts. ④.

Washington Hotel, 515 15th St NW ☎638-5900 or 1-800/424-9540, fax 638-4275. Metro Center Metro. Historic hotel next to the *Willard* with a popular rooftop bar and heavily decorated Edwardian rooms; some look across to the White House. It rarely needs to offer discount rates, but off-season weekends can see price reductions. ⑤–⑥.

Willard Inter-Continental, 1401 Pennsylvania Ave NW ☎628-9100 or 1-800/327-0200, fax 637-7307. Metro Center Metro. Few hotels have the style of the *Willard* – in business on and off since the 1850s. It's a Beaux-Arts beauty with acres of marble, mosaics and glass, slick service, finely furnished rooms and top-drawer clientele. ⑧.

Dupont Circle

Brickskeller Inn, 1523 22nd St NW ☎293-1885, fax 293-0996. Dupont Circle Metro. Apartment house conversion (the top floor has a view of Rock Creek Park) with clean and simple rooms, most with sinks and a couple with bath and TV – it's above one of the Circle's oldest bars. Good weekly rates. ②–③.

Carlyle Suites, 1731 New Hampshire Ave NW ☎234-3200 or 1-800/964-5377, fax 387-0085. Dupont Circle Metro. Art Deco beauty in a surprisingly tranquil street near Dupont Circle. Furnishings have been upgraded, though the Deco tone prevails throughout the comfortable self-catering suites, which have dining areas and small kitchens; there's also a café, parking, laundry, and weekend discounts. ⑤.

The Dupont at the Circle, 1606 19th St NW ☎332-5251, fax 332-3244. Dupont Circle Metro. Eight beautifully appointed rooms – high ceilings, kitchenette, marble bathrooms – in a non-smoking, Victorian townhouse virtually on the Circle (at Q St), with free continental breakfast and morning paper; parking is available. ④–⑤.

Embassy Inn, 1627 16th St NW ☎234-7800 or 1-800/423-9111, fax 234-3309. Dupont Circle Metro. Welcoming inn, popular with Europeans, on a residential street in northern Dupont Circle, well placed for bars and restaurants. Attractive, good-value rooms, free continental breakfast, coffee and papers available all day, plus an early evening sherry to speed you on your way. ③.

Embassy Row Hilton, 2015 Massachusetts Ave NW ☎265-1600 or 1-800/424-2400, fax 328-7526. Dupont

Circle Metro. Revamped rooms and facilities in this Embassy Row standard have given it a smarter look, with marble bathrooms, cable, complimentary newspaper, lobby bar, rooftop pool and health center. ⑥.

Radisson Barceló, 2121 P St NW ☎293-3100, 1-800/333-3333, fax 857-0134. Dupont Circle Metro. European-style hotel (with great Spanish restaurant, the *Gabriel*) in the heart of the Dupont Circle nightlife scene. Rooms are spacious, and there's a pool and sundeck. ⑤.

Simpkins' B&B, 1601 19th St NW ☎387-1328. Dupont Circle Metro. Victorian townhouse with six rooms just a minute from the Metro – unbeatable rates for such a good location (though prices double if you can't produce a passport, US or foreign). Decor is plain and facilities simple – guests (mostly foreign) share two bathrooms, a small kitchen (and free tea and toast), and the cable TV in the lounge. Call at least two weeks in advance. ①–②.

Westin Fairfax, 2100 Massachusetts Ave NW ☎293-2100 or 1-800/WESTIN-1, fax 466-9867. Dupont Circle Metro. Embassy Row highlight (formerly the *Ritz-Carlton*), once owned by Al Gore's family, and still catering to clubby politicos, media types and business people who frequent its *Jockey Club* restaurant. Anglo-French country-house chic, with impeccable facilities and service. ⑦.

Windsor Inn, 1842 16th St NW ☎667-0300 or 1-800/423-9111, fax 667-4503. Dupont Circle Metro. Under the same welcoming management as the *Embassy Inn*, the *Windsor* is a few blocks further north, its rooms (in twin brick 1920s houses) a shade larger. The spacious suites are a real steal. Ground-floor rooms look onto a terrace; free continental breakfast, coffee and sherry served in the attractive lobby. ③–④.

Foggy Bottom

Allen Lee Hotel, 2224 F St NW ☎331-1224 or 1-800/462-0186. Foggy Bottom-GWU Metro. Misleadingly attractive exterior hides musty rooms (with and without private bath), with clunky air-conditioning – check a couple before checking in. It's seen much better days, but is in a reasonable location and is certainly cheap for DC. ②.

Hotel Lombardy, 2019 Pennsylvania Ave NW ☎828-2600 or 1-800/424-5486, fax 872-0503. Foggy Bottom-GWU Metro. Red-brick apartment-style hotel in favored Pennsylvania Avenue location (it's just as close to Farragut West Metro). Spacious rooms, most with kitchenettes and coffee-makers; the café has outdoor seating and is good for breakfast. ④.

Howard Johnson Premier Hotel, 2601 Virginia Ave NW ☎965-2700 or 1-800/654-2000, fax 965-2700. Foggy Bottom-GWU Metro. Decent high-rise rooms, rooftop pool and free indoor parking. Earned its reputation as the place from where Nixon's "plumbers" supervised the Watergate burglary (see p.170). Good weekend discounts. ④.

State Plaza, 2117 E St NW ☎861-8200 or 1-800/424-2859, fax 659-8601. Foggy Bottom-GWU Metro. Spacious suites with fully equipped kitchens and dining area, plus a rooftop sundeck, health club and good café. Great weekend rates, and there's often room when other places are full. ④–⑤.

Washington Monarch Hotel, 2401 M St NW ☎429-2400 or 1-800/505-9042, fax 457-5010. Foggy Bottom-GWU Metro. High-class West End oasis with extremely comfortable rooms, pool, excellent health club and internal garden courtyard. It's just north of Washington Circle, midway between Foggy Bottom and Georgetown. ⑦.

Watergate Hotel, 2650 Virginia Ave NW ☎965-2300 or 1-800/424-2736, fax 337-7915. Foggy Bottom-GWU Metro. Sniffy hotel with comfortable rooms and suites (some with kitchen, and balconies with river views) in the now notorious complex near the Kennedy Center; it's a bit of a hike from any good bars and restaurants, though there is a small pool, and shops and services in the complex. ⑦.

Accommodation

Price categories (see p.275 for full details):
① *Under $50*
② *$50–70*
③ *$70–100*
④ *$100–140*
⑤ *$140–200*
⑥ *$200–250*
⑦ *$250–300*
⑧ *Over $300*

Accommodation

See p.241 for details of how to get to Georgetown.

Georgetown

Four Seasons Hotel, 2800 Pennsylvania Ave NW ☎342-0444 or 1-800/332-3442, fax 944-2076. DC's most expensive and luxurious hotel – a sympathetic red-brick at the eastern end of Georgetown – is also its most sought after. Stars, royalty and business high-rollers hanker after the lavish rooms and suites with views of Rock Creek Park or the C&O Canal. Service is superb, the *Seasons* restaurant impeccable; there's a pool, fitness center and *Garden Terrace* bar-lounge. ⑧.

Georgetown Dutch Inn, 1075 Thomas Jefferson St NW ☎337-0900 or 1-800/388-2410, fax 333-6526. All-suite hotel nicely located off M Street, near the canal towpath. Some penthouse units are two-level and sleep up to six; all have small kitchens and include free continental breakfast and parking. Summer rates (June–Aug) offer a small saving, as do weekend rates when available. ⑤.

Georgetown Inn, 1310 Wisconsin Ave NW ☎333-8900 or 1-800/424-2979, fax 333-8308. Stylish, hi-tech red-brick hotel in the heart of Georgetown – rooms off the avenue tend to be quieter. ⑥.

Holiday Inn Georgetown, 2101 Wisconsin Ave NW ☎338-4600 or 1-800/465-4329, fax 333-6113. The only relative cheapie in Georgetown – a bit far up Wisconsin Avenue, though buses and cabs get you down to M St pretty quickly. Newish rooms, parking, outdoor pool, fitness room and good discount rates. ⑤.

Latham Hotel, 3000 M St NW ☎726-5000 or 1-800/368-5922, fax 342-1800. Well-sited hotel insulated from the Georgetown noise, with a rooftop pool, sundeck and – in *Citronelle* – one of the city's finest dining experiences; lesser mortals breakfast in *La Madeleine*. Some rooms have canal and river views; there are also some superb split-level carriage suites. Rooms ⑤, suites ⑦.

Southwest

Channel Inn Hotel, 650 Water St SW ☎554-2400 or 1-800/368-5668, fax

863-1164. Waterfront Metro. The city's first (and, thus far, only) waterfront hotel, a 1970s development down at the Washington Channel, with some rooms looking across to East Potomac Park. There's free parking, an outdoor pool and sundeck and a choice of seafood restaurants nearby. ④.

Holiday Inn Capitol, 550 C St SW ☎479-4000 or 1-800/465-4329, fax 488-4267. L'Enfant Plaza or Federal Center SW Metro. Variously sized rooms within walking distance of the Capitol and the Smithsonian museums; there's a bar, restaurant, deli and a rooftop pool. As with all the city's *Holiday Inns*, weekend rates are attractive. ⑤.

Loews L'Enfant Plaza, 480 L'Enfant Plaza SW ☎484-1000 or 1-800/223-0888, fax 646-4456. L'Enfant Plaza Metro. Superbly appointed modern hotel, a couple of blocks south of the Mall and with direct access from the Metro. Spacious rooms in nineteenth-century French style, most with river or city views, plus health club and rooftop pool. Special winter and weekend rates apply, and the hotel is kid- and pet-friendly – ask about special deals. ⑥.

Union Station

Holiday Inn on the Hill, 415 New Jersey Ave NW ☎638-1616 or 1-800/638-1116, fax 638-0707. Union Station Metro. Rooms are nothing special, though you get a coffee-maker, hair-dryer and iron in the pricier ones, and there's a pool, exercise room, and sports bar and grill dedicated to the Washington Senators, DC's one-time pro baseball team. Weekend rates here can be a bargain. ⑤.

Hotel George, 15 E St NW ☎347-4200 or 1-800/576-8331, fax 347-4213. Union Station Metro. A modern makeover for the old *Bellevue*, bringing New York style to DC: sleek lines, contemporary furnishings, hip staff, great marble bathrooms and a very trendy bar-bistro called *Bis*. Weekend rates, when available, typically knock around $50 off the price. ⑥.

Hyatt Regency Washington on Capitol Hill, 400 New Jersey Ave NW ☎737-1234 or 1-800/233-1234, fax 737-5773. Union Station Metro. Monster (800-room) luxury hotel with multistory garden atrium, pool and health club. ⑥.

Phoenix Park, 520 N Capitol St NW ☎638-6900 or 1-800/824-5419, fax 638-4025. Union Station Metro. Pleasing, well-equipped rooms in a conveniently sited, Irish-owned hotel, across from Union Station. Popular with politicos and an after-work crowd who frequent the associated *Dubliner* pub. There's a good restaurant, too, with hearty breakfasts. ⑤.

Upper Northwest

Days Inn Connecticut Avenue, 4400 Connecticut Ave NW ☎244-5600 or 1-800/329-7466, fax 244-6794. Van Ness-UDC Metro. A couple of stops beyond the zoo (and just two blocks from the Metro), in a residential-university neighborhood, with reasonable, if smallish, rooms plus all mod-cons. Call ahead for weekend and special saver rates. ③–④.

Connecticut Woodley Guest House, 2647 Woodley Rd NW ☎667-0218, fax 232-0082. Woodley Park-Zoo Metro. Pleasant guest house opposite the *Sheraton Washington* and near the zoo; rooms (15; some en-suite) are showing their age, but prices are good and there's free parking. Advance reservations essential. ②.

India House Too, 300 Carroll St NW ☎291-1195. Takoma Metro. Rambling Victorian red-brick in a safe neighborhood, ten minutes' from Union Station by Metro – it's on the hill, fifty yards up from the station, on the right. An interna-tional backpacking crowd loves this free-and-easy hostel with bunk-bed dorms (plus two plain doubles) and shared bathrooms. There's a kitchen, cable TV, lockers, parking, rec room, and a deck and garden for summer parties. And at $14 a night, it's the cheapest option in DC. ①.

Kalorama Guest House at Woodley Park, 2700 Cathedral Ave NW ☎328-0860, fax 328-8730. Woodley Park-Zoo Metro. More friendly Victorian charm from the *Kalorama* people, here much nearer the Metro in Woodley Park. Two houses (19 rooms, 12 en-suite), and the same good service and facilities – comfortable brass beds, free continental breakfast, aperitifs, papers and coffee. Book well in advance. ②–③.

Omni Shoreham, 2500 Calvert St NW ☎234-0700 or 1-800/843-6664, fax 756-5145. Woodley Park Zoo Metro. Plush, grand, Washington institution bursting with history. Features include tasteful, comfortable rooms, recently renovated, many overlooking Rock Creek Park, outdoor pool and tennis courts, the foliage-filled *Garden Court* for drinks and, when available, bargain weekend rates. ⑥.

Sheraton Washington, 2660 Woodley Rd NW ☎328-2000 or 1-800/325-3535, fax 387-5436. Woodley Park-Zoo Metro. Second of Woodley Park's historic, celeb-filled hotel-palaces, and the largest hotel in DC, with two pools, health club and restaurants, and bristling with attentive staff. Very good weekend and off-season discounts make this more affordable than you might think, though convention business keeps rooms full most of the year. ⑥–⑦.

Accommodation

Price categories (see p.275 for full details):
① *Under $50*
② *$50–70*
③ *$70–100*
④ *$100–140*
⑤ *$140–200*
⑥ *$200–250*
⑦ *$250–300*
⑧ *Over $300*

Chapter 13

Cafés and Restaurants

Washington's dining scene is thriving at present, fueled in part by the various downtown developments, but also reflecting the amount of disposable income in the country's political and legal capital. The city keeps up with the times (though it's generally a step behind New York and LA), which means that current **trends** are favoring the opening of blockbuster theme restaurants, yuppie bar-and-grills, tortilla wrap and noodle houses, brew-pub-restaurants and cyber cafés. Successful chefs and restaurateurs – Roberto Donna, Gerard Pangaud, the Clyde's group, even Vietnamese families from Arlington – are not above cloning their successes, so you can expect new offshoots of the most popular of DC's eating houses, both in the city and in the suburbs.

As for specific **cuisines**, good southern and southwestern **American** food isn't hard to find, while Georgetown, in particular, has a rash of renowned New-York-style saloon-restaurants serving everything from oysters to strip steaks. **European** restaurants tend to be pricey, but there are some good bistros (Georgetown again), while tapas, tortilla wraps and gourmet pizzas are creeping into restaurants and onto menus everywhere. On the whole, the **Chinese** restaurants in Chinatown don't hold a candle to their counterparts in other cities – you'll do better eating **Thai** or **Vietnamese** (the best of which are across the river, in Arlington). The city's other major treat is the comparatively

large number of **Ethiopian** restaurants (especially in Adams-Morgan); while fans will also be able to track down places serving food from countries as diverse as Argentina, Burma, Greece and El Salvador.

For visitors, it can often prove exasperating to try and find exactly the kind of food you want, when you want it. Certain **neighborhoods** tend to attract similar kinds of restaurants: homey downtown trattorias are as scarce as staid power-dining spots in Adams-Morgan. Perhaps the most annoying discovery is that the areas in which visitors spend much of their time – the Mall, around the White House and Federal Triangle – have a positive dearth of good-value cafés and restaurants.

Happily, the Metro system and the sheer number of taxis means that nowhere is really off-limits when it comes to choosing a restaurant. Downtown, **Chinatown** is the only central ethnic enclave with its own swatch of restaurants, though the **7th Street** corridor, near the MCI Center, is fast emerging as a food street. But it's only really in the outer neighborhoods that you can saunter up and down, checking out the options. There's lots of opportunity to sit

---

All telephone numbers in this chapter are area code ☎ 202, unless otherwise stated.

---

outside too, when the weather's clement: patios, sidewalk tables, and opening front windows are all de rigueur in DC.

Georgetown has the most varied selection of places – rowdy saloons, diners, ethnic restaurants of all shades and some rather more sniffy establishments – most of them in the few blocks on either side of the M Street/Wisconsin Avenue intersection. **Dupont Circle** (chiefly P St and Connecticut Ave) is generally more upmarket: designer Italian restaurants and espresso bars are typical. The most down-to-earth spot is **Adams-Morgan**, a multicultural neighborhood with the city's best bargains – though prices are moving up slowly, 18th Street at Columbia Road is lined with scores of choices, all still pretty good value.

The **listings** in this chapter are split into two sections: "Diners, delis, cafés and coffee shops", for keeping you fueled from breakfast through lunch; and "Restaurants" (starts on p.286). The sections are arranged **geographically** (in alphabetical order), and correspond largely to the city chapters in the Guide. For **listings by cuisine**, turn to the box on pp.286–87.

Diners, delis, cafés and coffee shops

Downtown, it can be surprisingly difficult to find a place to sit and grab a cup of decent coffee or a sandwich. Ubiquitous drinks and pretzel stands aside, the Mall, in particular, is almost utterly devoid of choice except for the occasional, over-subscribed museum café. The lists below pick out the best places, particularly those where you can get more than just a drink. Most will be good for breakfast, snacks, sandwiches, light lunches and, occasionally, full meals. City-wide, all the main **chains** are represented, and you're never very far from a Starbuck's coffee, an Au Bon Pain sandwich or a Burrito Brothers Mexican filler. But quirkier independent coffee shops are spreading like wildfire and there are a couple of smaller businesses with just a few outlets

Food Courts

There are food courts in the following locations, usually open Mon–Sat 10am–9pm, Sun noon–6pm.

Georgetown Park Food Court, Level One, 3222 M St NW, Georgetown.

Old Post Office Pavilion, 1100 Pennsylvania Ave NW, Old Downtown.

Ronald Reagan Building, 1300 Pennsylvania Ave NW, Federal Triangle.

Shops at National Place & Press, 1331 Pennsylvania Ave NW, Old Downtown.

Union Station Food Court, 50 Massachusetts Ave NE.

worth keeping an eye out for, like the great stuffed bagels from Chesapeake Bagel Bakery or Whatsa Bagel, or Italian deli sandwiches and provisions from La Prima/Via Cucina.

Adams-Morgan

Tryst, 2459 18th St NW ☎232-5500. Woodley Park-Zoo Metro. It's not quite Central Perk but it's just as Friendly – no one minds if you hang out all day on the great squishy sofas and tuck into coffee, wine, soup and sandwiches, or just read the paper. Mon–Thurs 7am–2am, Fri & Sat 7am–3am, Sun 8am–2am.

Capitol Hill

Bread and Chocolate, 666 Pennsylvania Ave SE ☎547-2875. Eastern Market Metro. Popular bakery-cum-coffee house with street-view seating and tip-top sandwiches. Mon–Sat 7am–7pm, Sun 8am–6pm.

Le Bon Café, 210 2nd St SE ☎547-7200. Capitol South Metro. Close to the Library of Congress and good for a wholesome lunch of soup, salad or sandwich. Mon–Fri 7.30am–5pm, Sat & Sun 8.30am–3.30pm.

Cafés and Restaurants

Cafés and Restaurants

The Market Lunch, Eastern Market, 7th Ave SE ☎547-8444. Eastern Market Metro. Eat-and-go market-hall counter meals – sandwiches and fries, salads, crab cakes or fish platters – served to a loyal band of local shoppers and suit-and-tie staffers. Tues–Sat 7am–3pm, Sun 11am–3pm.

Misha's Deli, 210 7th St SE ☎547-5858. Eastern Market Metro. Stuffed cabbage rolls, chicken noodle soup, blinis and the like, opposite Eastern Market. Sit inside amid OTT Russian decor, or on the terrace. Mon–Sat 8am–6.30pm, Sun 9am–5pm.

Roasters on the Hill, 666 Pennsylvania Ave SE ☎543-8355. Eastern Market Metro. Coffee in a million guises, and muffin munchies. Mon–Sat 7am–7pm, Sun 8am–5.30pm.

Downtown: New

Café Promenade, *Renaissance Mayflower*, 1127 Connecticut Ave NW ☎347-3000. Farragut North Metro. A serenading harpist and pricey Mediterranean menu set the tone in this elegant hotel coffee shop-restaurant. Daily 6.30am–11pm.

The Mudd House, 1724 M St NW ☎822-8455. Farragut North Metro. Good downtown coffee stop, specializing in organic blends. Mon–Fri 8am–6pm.

Sholl's Colonial Cafeteria, 1990 K St NW ☎296-3065. Farragut West Metro. A DC institution, this remarkably inexpensive self-service café dishes out home-cooked food, cakes and pies – join the lines (enter through the Esplanade Mall), file past the "Patriotism and religion makes this a fine place to work" notice, find a seat and dig in. Mon–Sat 7am–10.30am, 11am–2.30pm & 4–8pm, Sun 8am–3pm.

Downtown: Old

Café Espresso, *Willard Inter-Continental*, 1401 Pennsylvania Ave NW ☎628-9100. Metro Center Metro. Relaxed Art Nouveau hotel café – come for coffee, breakfast, lunch or afternoon tea. Mon–Sat 7am–11pm, Sun 7am–10pm.

Corner Bakery, Shops at National Place & Press, 1331 Pennsylvania Ave NW; entrance on 14th St ☎662-7400. Metro Center Metro. Self-serve bakery-café, handy for the White House and with a full range of ciabatta sandwiches, cookies, salads and pizza slices. Mon–Fri 7am–8pm, Sat 8am–8pm, Sun 11am–6pm.

Dean & Deluca, 1299 Pennsylvania Ave NW 628-8155. Metro Center Metro. Gourmet sandwiches, great homemade soups, hot dishes and an appetizing salad bar in a boiler-room turned café-carryout. Try to avoid the lunchtime crush. Mon–Fri 8am–5pm.

Ebbitt Express, 675 15th St NW ☎347-8881. Metro Center Metro. Carry-out adjunct to the infinitely pricier *Old Ebbitt Grill* (see p.293). Superior salads, sandwiches and snacks to go. Mon–Thurs 7.30am–8pm, Fri 7.30am–6pm.

Harry's, *Harrington Hotel*, 436 11th St NW ☎624-0053. Metro Center Metro. Down-to-earth meals (meatloaf, spaghetti and meatballs); the adjacent self-service *Harrington Café* (Mon–Fri 7am–2.30pm & 5–9pm, Sat & Sun 7–11am & 5–9pm) is even cheaper. Daily 8am–1am, bar open 1hr later.

Patent Pending, National Museum of American Art/National Portrait Gallery, 8th and G St NW ☎357-2700. Gallery Place-Chinatown Metro. Just off the central courtyard in the Patent Building, with good pastries, sandwiches and hot food. Some outdoor seating. Daily 10am–3.30pm.

Reeve's Restaurant and Bakery, 1306 G St NW ☎628-6350. Metro Center Metro. Classic diner, in business since 1886, with an all-you-can-eat breakfast and fruit bar, crisp-coated chicken at lunchtime, and famous pies. Mon–Sat 7am–6pm.

Dupont Circle

Afterwords Café, 1517 Connecticut Ave NW ☎387-1462. Dupont Circle Metro. In the back of Kramerbooks, serving breakfast and brunch, great cappuccino and full meals – salad, pastas, grills and sandwiches, with plenty of vegetarian

choices. Live blues and jazz Wed–Sat.
Mon–Thurs & Sun 7.30am–1am, Fri &
Sat 24hr.

Burro, 1621 Connecticut Ave NW ☎483-
6861. Dupont Circle Metro. Fresh-tasting
Mexican fast food, with big burritos, que-
sadillas, homemade salsas and soups a
specialty. Mon–Thurs & Sun
11am–10pm, Fri & Sat 11am–110pm.

Café Luna, 1633 P St ☎387-4005.
Dupont Circle Metro. Italian coffee, breakfast, weekend brunches and substantial
sandwiches, pasta and pizza in a laid-
back hangout with sunny sidewalk
tables. One of Dupont's best. Mon–Thurs
8am–11pm, Fri 8am–1am, Sat
10am–1am, Sun 10am–11pm.

Firehook Bakery, 1909 Q St NW ☎588-
9296. Dupont Circle Metro. Daily sandwich specials and a huge range of bread
(plus pies, desserts and cookies) from
the renowned bakery-café. Mon–Fri
7am–8pm, Sat & Sun 9am–10pm.

Jolt 'n' Bolt, 1918 18th St NW ☎232-
0077. Dupont Circle Metro. Tucked away
up 18th, this townhouse tea- and cof-
fee-house with side-alley patio is popular with the local gay crowd. Daily
7.30am–midnight.

SoHo Tea & Coffee, 2150 P St NW
☎463-7646. Dupont Circle Metro.
Trendy, late-night hangout for P Street
clubbers refueling on coffee, cakes and
sandwiches. Mon–Wed & Sun
7.30am–3am, Thurs & Fri 7.30am–4am,
Sat 7am–4.30am.

Foggy Bottom

The Breadline, 1751 Pennsylvania Ave
NW ☎822-8900. Farragut West Metro.
DC's best sandwiches made with DC's
best bread – superb open bakery (with
seats inside and out) turning out pizza,
empanadas, flatbreads, salads, smooth-
ies, coffee and tea, using (pricey) organic
ingredients where possible. Mon–Fri
7am–6pm.

Café des Artistes, 500 17th St NW
☎639-1700. Farragut West or Farragut
North Metro. This Corcoran Gallery café
serves coffee, lunches and tea. Book for

the $19 gospel brunch (Sun 11am–2pm).
Mon, Wed & Fri–Sun 11am–4.30pm,
Thurs 11am–8.30pm.

Capitol Grounds, 2100 Pennsylvania Ave
NW ☎293-2057. Foggy Bottom-GWU
Metro. Breakfasts, gourmet sandwiches,
salads and good coffee; handy GWU
location and seats inside and out.
Mon–Fri 7am–6pm, Sat 8.30am–4pm,
Sun 9am–3pm.

World Gourmet, 1917 F St NW ☎371-
9048. Farragut West Metro. Large stuffed
sandwiches served to an office crowd;
grab a hazelnut coffee and sit outside.
Mon–Fri 8.30am–7pm.

Georgetown

Booeymonger, 3265 Prospect St NW
☎333-4180. Crowded deli-coffee shop
at the corner with Potomac St, popular
with students. Daily 8am–midnight.

Dean & Deluca, 3276 M St NW ☎342-
2500. Superior self-service conservatory-
style café (and fantastic attached deli-
market with sushi stand) in one of M
Street's most handsome red-brick buildings. Croissants and cappuccino, designer salads, pasta and sandwiches. Café:
Mon–Thurs & Sun 8am–8pm, Fri & Sat
8am–7pm. Market: Mon–Thurs & Sun
10am–8pm, Fri & Sat 10am–9pm.

Furin's, 2805 M St NW ☎965-1000.
Georgetown's best bet for a home-
cooked eggs-and-fries breakfast, blue-
plate lunch, or soup, salad and sandwich.
Mon–Fri 7.30am–7pm, Sat 8am–5pm.

Patisserie Café Didier, 3206 Grace St
NW ☎342-9083. Outrageously good, if
pricey, French cakes and pastries, specialty teas and coffees, thick hot chocolate and changing daily lunches.
Tues–Sat 8am–6pm, Sun 8am–5pm.

Union Station

Center Café, Union Station, 50
Massachusetts Ave NE ☎682-0143.
Union Station Metro. Split-level café-
restaurant in the main hall. Also breakfast (8–11am) or coffee – served in large
French-style cups – and cake. Daily
8am–10pm.

Cafés and Restaurants

See p.241 for details of how to get to Georgetown.

For bagels, muffins and Starbuck's coffee, the 2nd-floor café in Barnes & Noble, 3040 M St NW, makes a handy break-fast or late-night stop.

Cafés and Restaurants

Restaurants

You can, of course, eat lunch or dinner at many of the diners, cafés and coffee shops listed on pp.283–85; the establishments reviewed below are special enough to make a night of it. It's always worth phoning to check current opening hours; if it's essential to **reserve a table**, we've said so. You'll need to book well in advance to eat at the most renowned restaurants.

We've given each restaurant a **price category** (see box on p.288), which reflects the cost of a three-course meal per person, *excluding drinks, tax and service*. These are only a guideline: most people will be hard pushed to get through three courses in many restaurants and often you'll be able to eat for less than we suggest; on the other hand, don't forget you have to add the price of **drinks** to your bill and (in most places) at least fifteen percent **service**. To keep the price of meals at a minimum, look for **set lunches** (from as little as $5) and **early-bird dinners** (usually

---

Cuisines

Our restaurant reviews are grouped by neighborhood. To track down a particular cuisine, consult the lists below.

African (also see Ethiopian)
Bukom Café p.287
Harambe Café p.288

American
America p.298
Art Gallery Bar & Grille p.295
Ben's Chili Bowl p.297
B. Smith's p.298
Capitol City Brewing Company p.293
Clyde's p.296
District Chophouse & Brewery p.293
Florida Avenue Grill p.297
Fran O'Brien's p.291
Hard Times Café p.289
J. Paul's p.296
Luna Grill & Diner p.294
The Mark p.293
Martin's Tavern p.296
The Monocle p.290
Morton's of Chicago p.296
Mr Henry's p.290
New Heights p.298
Old Ebbitt Grill p.293
Old Glory p.296
Perry's p.288
Peyote Café p.288
Red Hot & Blue p.290
Red Sage p.293
Santa Fe East p.289
Sign of the Whale p.292
Stoney's p.292
Tom Tom p.289

Two Quail p.290
Woodley Café p.298

Burmese
Burma p.291

Caribbean
BET on Jazz p.293
Hibiscus Café p.296

Chinese
City Lights of China p.294
Golden Palace p.291
Go-Lo's p.291
Hunan Chinatown p.291
Mr Yung's p.291
Tony Cheng's p.291

Ethiopian
Fasika's p.297
Meskerem p.288
Red Sea p.288
Zed's p.297

French
Au Pied du Cochon p.295
Bistro Français p.295
Gerard's Place p.292
La Fourchette p.288
Vintage p.297

German
Café Berlin p.290

served before 7pm) – these are not just a feature of budget restaurants, with many fancier establishments maintaining sensible pricing policies in the face of a volatile restaurant market.

Adams-Morgan

Bukom Café, 2442 18th St NW ☎265-4600. Laidback restaurant-bar serving delicious African dishes like *egusi*, a broth of goat meat with ground melon seeds and spinach, and chicken *yassa*, baked with onions and spices, for around $10. All washed down with African beers (try the Ngoma) and African music (live Tues–Sat). Mon, Tues & Sun 4pm–1am, Wed & Thurs 4pm–2am, Fri & Sat 4pm–3am. Moderate.

Fasika's, 2477 18th St NW ☎797-7673. Most upmarket of the local Ethiopian places, with sidewalk seating, live music three nights a week and spicy stews for around $10–12. Mon–Thurs 5pm–midnight, Fri–Sun noon–midnight. Moderate.

Cafés and Restaurants

All the places listed in Adams-Morgan are within a few blocks of the junction of 18th St, Columbia Rd and Calvert St; nearest Metros are Woodley Park-Zoo or Dupont Circle (15min walk from either).

Cafés and Restaurants

The Grill from Ipanema, 1858 Columbia Rd NW ☎986-0757. Worth visiting for the name alone, though the *feijoada* (Brazilian meat stew) and the shrimp dishes are great, and the Sunday brunch sees off most appetites. Try the baked clams to start and watch your *caipirinha* (rum cocktail) intake. Mon–Thurs 5–11pm, Fri 5pm–midnight, Sat noon–midnight, Sun noon–11pm. Moderate.

Harambe Café, 1771 U St NW ☎332-6435 – at Florida Ave and 18th. Simple, family-run African dining room with some of the cheapest food in town – filling chicken, beef and lamb *wot* (spicy stew) served on *injera* bread, plus vegetarian platters, accompanied by some great music. Mon–Thurs & Sun noon–1am, Fri & Sat noon–2am. Budget.

I Matti, 2436 18th St NW ☎462-8844. Roberto Donna's trendy trattoria-pizzeria finds favor with bargain-seekers after accomplished Italian cooking at less-than-stratospheric prices. Classic pastas, gnocchi and pizzas, a great antipasto selection, and grilled meat and fish specials – though dishes like braised rabbit, seared lamb and grilled sea bass push the price up a notch. Daily noon–11pm. Moderate.

La Fourchette, 2429 18th St NW ☎332-3077. The brasserie's been here forever and the food – French classics served at closely packed tables – is reliable. Main bonus is the sidewalk patio. Mon–Fri 11.30am–10.30pm, Sat 4–11pm, Sun 4–10pm. Moderate.

Las Placitas, 1828 Columbia Rd NW ☎745-3751. Not much more sophisticated than shack-dining, but for calorific refueling and friendly service it's hard to beat – all the Mexican standards plus Salvadorean specials like *churrasco a caballo* (basically steak, eggs, rice and beans), *pupusas* (stuffed fried tortillas) and plantains. Mon–Thurs & Sun noon–2am, Fri & Sat noon–3am. Inexpensive.

Meskerem, 2434 18th St NW ☎462-4100. The district's favorite Ethiopian hangout with funky decor and cheery staff. Eat with your hands, scooping food up with the sourdough *injera* bread; the *messob* platter gives you a taste of everything, and there's lots of vegetarian and seafood choice. Daily noon–11pm. Moderate.

Mixtec, 1792 Columbia Rd NW ☎332-1011. You're unlikely to linger but when you want great-tasting, low-priced Mexican food – tacos and tortillas, plus spit-roasted chicken and mussels steamed with chilis – this is where to come. Mon–Thurs & Sun 11am–10pm, Fri & Sat 11am–1am. Inexpensive.

Perry's, 1811 Columbia Rd NW ☎234-6218. The exclusive-o-meter is turned up high in this in-crowd restaurant serving sushi and Asian-influenced American entrées. Rooftop tables are always at a premium. Mon–Thurs & Sun 5–11pm, Fri & Sat 5pm–midnight; bar open 1hr later. Moderate.

Peyote Café/Roxanne's, 2319 18th St NW ☎462-8330. The *Peyote* is a lively basement southwestern bar and grill with above-average food, while *Roxanne's* upstairs has a more adventurous and expensive menu, also southwestern, and a popular roof terrace. Mon–Thurs 5–11pm, Fri 5pm–midnight, Sat noon–midnight, Sun noon–11pm; bar open until 2am, Fri & Sat until 3am. Moderate.

Red Sea, 2463 18th St NW ☎483-5000. Plentiful portions of spicy food (including vegetarian specials) keep diners coming back to the oldest Ethiopian place in the neighborhood – the *yetsom wat* gives a taste of six veggie dishes. There's a good beer list, too. Daily noon–midnight. Moderate.

Saigonnais, 2307 18th St NW ☎232-5300. Gourmet Vietnamese food in a cozy townhouse – splash out on the whole steamed fish. Prices are cheaper at lunch. Daily 11.30am–3pm & 5.30–11pm. Moderate.

Star of Siam, 2446 18th St NW ☎986-4133. Warehouse-style restaurant with a great roof terrace and spot-on Thai food. Mon–Fri 5–11pm, Sat noon–11pm, Sun 10pm. Inexpensive–Moderate.

Tom Tom, 2333 18th St NW ☎588-1300. Big street-facing windows, booths and a buzzy roof terrace draw in a fancy crowd for wood-fired pizza, tapas, salads, mix-and-match pastas, and desserts. Mon–Thurs & Sun 5–11pm, Fri & Sat 5pm–midnight, bar open until 2am, Fri & Sat 3am. Inexpensive–Moderate.

Alexandria, VA

Ecco Café, 220 N Lee St ☎703/684-0321. Gourmet pizza and pasta joint with a neighborhood feel, good lunch specials and jazz brunch on Sunday. Mon–Thurs 11am–11pm, Fri & Sat 11am–midnight, Sun noon–10pm. Inexpensive–Moderate.

Fish Market, 105 King St ☎703/836-5676. Brick-walled restaurant with terrace, serving oysters and chowder at the bar or fried fish platters, pastas and fish entrées. Daily 11am–midnight; bar until 2am. Moderate.

Hard Times Café, 1404 King St ☎703/638-5340. Three styles of chili, wings, rings and fries, country music and microbrews add up to one of Alexandria's better American restaurants; it's up toward the Metro station. Mon–Thurs 11am–10pm, Fri & Sat 11am–11pm, Sun noon–10pm. Inexpensive.

Las Tapas, 710 King St ☎703/836-4000. Best of the local tapas bars with a wide selection, plus paella and regular (free) flamenco sessions. Mon–Thurs &

Sun 11.30am–11.30pm, Fri & Sat 11am–1am. Moderate.

Santa Fe East, 110 S Pitt St ☎703/548-6900. Contemporary Southwestern cooking – lots of exotic chili seasoning, freshly made salsas, hickory-smoked meats and grilled fish – in one of Alexandria's nicest restaurant interiors. Mon–Thurs 11.30am–2pm & 5–10pm, Fri & Sat 11.30am–3pm & 5–11pm, Sun 5–10pm. Moderate.

Seaport Inn, 6 King St ☎703/549-2341. Romantic seafood dinners in a historic eighteenth-century building (once owned by Washington's aide-de camp, Colonel John Fitzgerald) at the bottom of King Street. Pricey but thoroughly nice. Daily noon–11pm. Moderate–Expensive.

Arlington, VA

Café Dalat, 3143 Wilson Blvd, at Highland St ☎703/276-0935. Clarendon Metro. Brisk, formica-tabled Vietnamese joint with a popular lunch buffet and some tasty menu specials like grilled lemon chicken and five-spice pork. Most dishes come with noodles and greens, making for pretty cheap eats. Mon–Thurs & Sun 11am–9.30pm, Fri & Sat 11am–10.30pm. Inexpensive.

Little Viet Garden, 3012 Wilson Blvd, opposite Clarendon Metro ☎703/522-9686. A little smarter than most with a patio out back and authentic food served with gusto. Try the *pho* (noodle soup). Mon–Fri 11am–2.30pm & 5–10pm, Sat & Sun 11am–10pm. Inexpensive.

Queen Bee, 3181 Wilson Blvd, at Highland St ☎703/527-3444. Clarendon Metro. No question – the best Vietnamese food in town, with renowned crunchy spring rolls, seafood over crispy noodles, grilled pork, huge bowls of noodle soup, Saigon pancakes and grilled shrimp. Expect to wait in line. Daily 11am–10pm. Inexpensive.

Il Radicchio, 1801 Clarendon Blvd, at Rhodes St ☎703/276-2627. Court House Metro. The cross-river branch of Roberto Donna's pizza-and-pasta

Cafés and Restaurants

See p.260 for details of how to get to Alexandria.

Cafés and Restaurants

empire is great value: wood-fired pizzas and mix-and-match spaghetti-and-sauce combos. Mon–Sat 11.30am–10pm, Sun 5–10pm. Inexpensive–Moderate.

Red Hot & Blue, 1600 Wilson Blvd, at Pierce St ☎703/276-7427; and 3014 Wilson Blvd, at Highland St ☎703/243-1510. Court House Metro or Clarendon Metro. Memphis barbecue joint that spawned a chain, serving the best ribs in the district – a rack, with coleslaw and beans, costs just ten bucks. Mon–Thurs 11am–10pm, Fri & Sat 11am–11pm, Sun noon–10pm. Inexpensive–Moderate.

Capitol Hill

Café Berlin, 322 Massachusetts Ave NE ☎543-7656. Union Station Metro. Schnitzel, huge *Wurst* platters and German beer. Soup-and-sandwich deals keep prices low at lunch. Mon–Thurs 11am–10pm, Fri & Sat noon–11pm, Sun 4–10pm. Moderate.

The Monocle, 107 D St NE ☎546-4488. Union Station Metro. Elegant saloon-bar-restaurant with a Congress clientele tucking into crab cakes, steaks and the like in between votes. Mon–Fri 11.30am–midnight, Sat 6–11pm. Expensive.

Mr Henry's, 601 Pennsylvania Ave SE ☎546-8412. Eastern Market Metro. Saloon-bar-restaurant, with outside patio, charcoal grill and loyal gay crowd. Even

the most expensive choices – the steak and shrimp plates – don't exceed $10; burgers are half-price on Mon, and jazz trios play weekly. Mon–Thurs & Sun 11am–12.30am, Fri & Sat 11am–2am. Inexpensive.

Taverna The Greek Islands, 307 Pennsylvania Ave SE ☎547-8360. Capitol South Metro. Unsophisticated, rustic, friendly Greek joint. Order something from the grill (all meat) and you won't need appetizers. Also, pricier fish specialties, wine by the carafe and a carry-out section in the basement. Mon–Sat 11am–11pm, Sun 5–11pm. Moderate.

Thai Roma, 313 Pennsylvania Ave SE ☎544-2338. Capitol South Metro. Thai sauces over Italian pasta are not always as successful as you'd hope, but there's a full Thai menu – good on noodles and for vegetarians – in this saloon-style Thai place. You can sink a beer before or after in the cozy attached *Conrad Pub*. Daily 11am–11pm. Moderate.

Two Quail, 320 Massachusetts Ave NE ☎543-8030. Union Station Metro. Romantic little townhouse bistro serving changing menus of modern American food. Set lunches are great value at $10–12, while dinner sees meals like grilled fish or lamb chops over wild rice. Reservations recommended. Mon–Fri 11.30am–2.30pm & 5.30–10pm, Sat & Sun 5.30–10.30pm. Expensive.

Monument, Museum and Gallery Cafés and Restaurants

Most of Washington's major sightseeing attractions have their own cafés and fast-food restaurants and often they're the only local option for lunch, especially on and around the Mall. Those listed below are particularly good; follow the page numbers for more details.

Chinatown

Burma, 740 6th St NW ☎638-1280.
Gallery Place-Chinatown Metro. Plain second-floor dining room with Burmese art,
approachable staff and very filling food.
The noodles are great (try the pork in
black bean sauce), and the beer is Thai
or Chinese. Mon–Thurs 11am–3pm &
6–10pm, Fri 11am–3pm & 6–10.30pm,
Sat 6–10.30pm, Sun 6–10pm.
Inexpensive.

Coco Loco, 810 7th St NW ☎289-2626.
Gallery Place-Chinatown Metro. Large but
relaxed in-crowd restaurant, where you
can choose from new-wave Mexican
tapas or all-you-can-eat Brazilian grills.
The tapas ($5–10 a plate) is the way to
go, a mile away in quality from most
tired Spanish offerings. Mon–Thurs
11.30am–2.30pm & 5.30–10pm, Fri
11.30am–2.30pm & 5.30–11pm, Sat
noon–2pm & 5.30–11pm, Sun
noon–3pm. Moderate–Expensive.

Golden Palace, 720–724 7th St NW
☎783-1225. Gallery Place-Chinatown
Metro. Authentic dim sum restaurant,
hugely popular with Chinese families on
Sundays, when you'll have to wait in
line. Mon & Tues 11am–10pm,
Wed–Sun 11am–11pm. Inexpensive (dim
sum); Moderate (meals)

Go-Lo's, 604 H St NW ☎347-4656.
Gallery Place-Chinatown Metro. Friendly
spot where local office workers are
greeted by name. Rice/noodle lunch
plates are great value, while meals mix
Cantonese and Szechuan influences.
Mon–Thurs & Sun 11am–10.30pm, Fri &
Sat 11am–2am. Inexpensive.

Hunan Chinatown, 624 H St NW ☎783-
5858. Gallery Place-Chinatown Metro.
Sleekly furnished, Western-friendly
restaurant (you'll have to ask for chopsticks), where spiciness replaces taste on
occasion. You probably won't need
appetizers, though the won tun in chili
sauce are good. Mon–Thurs & Sun
11am–11pm, Fri & Sat 11am–midnight.
Moderate.

Mr Yung's, 740 6th St NW ☎628-1098.
Gallery Place-Chinatown Metro. Extremely
amiable Cantonese restaurant, good for
a dim sum or rice-plate lunch, and with
some unusual seasonal dishes – ask for
recommendations. Daily 11am–11pm.
Inexpensive–Moderate.

Tony Cheng's, 619 H St NW,
Mongolian ☎842-8669, Seafood
☎371-8669. Gallery Place-Chinatown
Metro. Good-value DIY all-you-can-eat
Mongolian barbecues downstairs;
upstairs, the Cantonese seafood
restaurant with daily dim sum
(11am–3pm) has been visited by every
president since Carter and sundry
sporting stars besides. Mon–Thurs &
Sun 11am–11pm, Fri & Sat 11am–midnight. Inexpensive (barbecue/dim sum);
Moderate (meals).

Downtown: New

The Bombay Club, 815 Connecticut Ave
NW ☎659-3727. Farragut North or West
Metros. Sleek Indian restaurant a block
from the White House (and a presidential
favorite) – Raj-style surroundings, piano
accompaniment and dishes a little out of
the ordinary. Mon–Sat 11.30am–2.30pm
& 6–11pm. Moderate.

Café Asia, 1134 19th St NW ☎659
2696. Farragut North Metro. Breezy pan-
Asian restaurant in an old townhouse.
This is the place for budget sushi and
sushimi, or try the big plates of lemon-
grass-grilled chicken, seafood bakar (in
banana leaf with spicy prawn sauce),
satay or Thai noodles. Cheap drinks too,
and a sushi happy hour (Mon–Sat
5.30–7.30pm) that's a real bargain.
Mon–Fri 11.30am–10pm, Sat
noon–10pm, Sun 5–10pm.
Inexpensive–Moderate.

Fran O'Brien's, *Capital Hilton*, 1001 16th
St NW ☎783-2599. McPherson Square
Metro. Former Redskins player's steak
house-saloon in the *Hilton* basement:
check out the Hall of Fame, munch on a
bountiful steak or chop and watch the
game on TV. Mon–Fri 11.30am–3pm &
5–10.30pm, Sat & Sun 5–10.30pm.
Moderate–Expensive.

Galileo, 1110 21st St NW ☎293-7191.
Foggy Bottom or Farragut West Metros.

Cafés and Restaurants

Budget:
under $10

Inexpensive:
$10–15

Moderate:
$15–25

Expensive:
$25–40

Very
expensive:
over $40

See p.288 for
more details.

Cafés and Restaurants

Superb Northern Italian cuisine from wonderchef Roberto Donna. Risotto makes a regular appearance on the ever-changing menu. Service is snappy, and the wine list impressive. Book well in advance. Mon–Fri 11.30am–2pm & 5.30–10pm (Fri until 10.30pm), Sat & Sun 5.30–10.30pm. Very expensive.

Gerard's Place, 915 15th St NW ☎737-4445. McPherson Square Metro. Accomplished Michelin-starred French cuisine by Gerard Pangaud. The $60 five-course fixed menu is a good choice; add on $35 if you want a different wine with every course. Reservations essential. Mon–Thurs 11.30am–2pm & 5.30–10pm, Fri until 10.30pm, Sat 5.30–10.30pm. Very expensive.

Grillfish, 1200 New Hampshire Ave NW ☎331-7310. Dupont Circle or Foggy Bottom-GWU Metro. One of the best finds in DC – imperial in size and decor, but offering casual dining and perfectly cooked fish and seafood. The daily catch might include sea bass, tuna, snapper, trout, mahi-mahi, shark or calamari: choose grilled, over pasta or served in a sauté pan – it's all terrific. Mon–Fri noon–2.30pm & 5.30–10.30pm, Sat & Sun 5.30–11pm. Moderate.

McCormick & Schmick's, 1625 K St NW ☎861-2233. McPherson Square Metro. Hugely popular seafood grill and raw bar, complete with booths, Victorian stained glass and lamps, and a buzzing bar. Best food deals are weekdays between 3.30 and 6.30pm, and from 10.30pm–midnight Mon–Sat, when clams, chowders, fajitas and other plate-sized snacks are just a couple of bucks apiece. Mon–Fri 11am–11pm, Sat 5pm–midnight, Sun 5–10pm; bar open until midnight. Moderate–Expensive.

Sign of the Whale, 1825 M St ☎785-1110. Farragut North Metro. Downtown saloon best-known for its supreme burgers (half-price on Mon), grilled to perfection, though there's also famous jerk chicken, pasta, fish and other entrées, most around $10. Daily 11.30am–10.30pm; bar open until 1.30am (Mon–Thurs & Sun), 2.30am (Fri & Sat). Inexpensive–Moderate.

Star of Siam, 1136 19th St NW ☎785-2838. Dupont Circle or Farragut North Metros. Thai townhouse restaurant renowned for its excellently spiced curries, soups and noodles. Mon–Sat 11.30am–11pm, Sun 4–10pm. Inexpensive–Moderate.

Stoney's, 1307 L St NW ☎347-9163. McPherson Square Metro. Down-to-earth saloon and bar, thirty years old and rev-

---

Hotel Restaurants

Some of DC's best power-dining restaurants are in its glitzier hotels. The pick of the bunch are listed below: expect first-rate food and service and high ($60–100 a head) prices. Always call ahead for reservations.

The Carlton (*Lespinasse*), 923 16th St NW ☎879-6900. Contemporary French.

Four Seasons Hotel (*Seasons*), 2800 Pennsylvania Ave NW ☎944-2000. Contemporary American.

Hay-Adams Hotel (*Lafayette*), 1 Lafayette Square NW ☎638-2570. Contemporary American.

Jefferson Hotel (*Jefferson*), 1200 16th St NW ☎833-6206. Contemporary American.

Latham Hotel (*Citronelle*), 3000 M St NW ☎625-2150. Contemporary French-American.

Morrison Clark Inn, 1015 L St NW ☎898-1200. Contemporary American.

Westin Fairfax (*Jockey Club*), 2100 Massachusetts Ave NW ☎659-8000. French-European.

Willard Inter-Continental (*Willard Room*), 1401 Pennsylvania Ave NW ☎637-7440. Contemporary American-European.

eling in its big servings – burgers, fries, chili and country cooking, and two-buck margaritas on Fridays. Daily 9am–1am. Budget–Inexpensive.

Downtown: Old

BET on Jazz, 730 11th St NW ☎393-0975. Metro Center Metro. Art Deco dining from Black Entertainment Television, serving contemporary Caribbean cuisine in seriously cool surroundings. Live jazz completes the picture. Mon–Fri 11.30am–2.30pm & 5.30–11pm & (Fri until midnight), Sat 5.30pm–midnight; bar open later. Expensive.

Capitol City Brewing Company, 1100 New York Ave NW, entrance at 11th & H ☎628-2222. Metro Center Metro. Better known as a brew-pub, but the kitchen serves up burgers, grilled sausages, pasta, salads and other bar standards. Book ahead at weekends, Mon–Thurs & Sun 11am–11pm, Fri & Sat 11am–midnight. Inexpensive–Moderate.

Casa Juanita's, 908 11th St NW ☎737-2520. Metro Center Metro. Family-run Salvadorean-Mexican restaurant with histrionic Latin American music, excellent-value combo dishes and bargain house wine. Mon–Thurs & Sun 11am–10.30pm, Fri & Sat 11am–11pm. Inexpensive.

District Chophouse & Brewery, 509 7th St NW ☎347-3434. Gallery Place-Chinatown Metro. Classy swing-era joint with great music and a grillhouse menu. Portions are huge, which softens the prices a bit, but you could order a burger which comes with the house salad and soak up the atmosphere for just ten bucks. Reservations advised. Mon 11am–10pm, Tues–Thurs 11am–11pm, Fri 11am–midnight, Sat 4pm–midnight, Sun 4–10pm. Expensive.

Haad Thai, 1100 New York Ave NW, entrance on 11th St ☎682-1111. Metro Center Metro. Classy, business-oriented Thai restaurant, featuring coconut-milk curries, tasty steamed fish and shrimp and spicy soups. Mon–Fri 11.30am–2.30pm & 5–10.30pm, Sat

noon–10.30pm, Sun 5–10.30pm. Moderate.

Jaleo, 480 7th St NW ☎628-7949. Gallery Place-Chinatown Metro. Upscale tapas bar-restaurant with fashionable young things draped across the tables. Reserve for lunch or dinner; or call in early for a glass of good house wine and tapas. Mon & Sun 11.30am–10pm, Tues–Thurs 11.30am–11.30pm, Fri & Sat 11.30am–midnight. Moderate (tapas); Expensive (restaurant).

The Mark, 401 7th St NW ☎783-3133. Gallery Place-Chinatown Metro. Fashionable dining on up-and-coming 7th, with seasonally changing, Modern American interpretations of dishes like roast chicken, strip steak, salmon and ravioli; vegetarians should do well too (wild mushrooms are a favorite), and there's a select choice of wines by the glass. Mon 11.30am–3pm & 5–9.30pm, Tues–Thurs 11.30am–3pm & 5–10.30pm, Fri & Sat 11.30am–3pm & 5–11pm, Sun 11am–3pm & 5–9pm. Expensive.

Old Ebbitt Grill, 675 15th St NW ☎347-4801. Metro Center Metro. In business in various locations since 1856, this plush re-creation of a nineteenth-century tavern is a joy, with mahogany bar (serving microbrews), gas chandeliers, leather booths and gilt mirrors. Everything from burgers to oysters, breakfasts to late dinners. Professional/politico clientele. Mon–Fri 7.30am–midnight, Sat 8am–midnight, Sun 9.30am–midnight; bar open Mon–Thurs & Sun until 1.30am, Fri & Sat until 2.30am. Expensive.

Red Sage, 605 14th St NW ☎638-4444. Metro Center Metro. Landmark Southwestern restaurant (reservations essential), owned by Mark Miller and dripping with Santa Fe chic, featuring rotisserie-grilled meats, fish and vegetarian specials. The funkily decorated café-bar is less exclusive, though the menu is more mainstream (but still miles better than any of the other Border pretenders). Café Mon–Sat 11.30am–11.30pm, Sun 5–10pm; restaurant Mon–Sat

Cafés and Restaurants

Budget:
under $10

Inexpensive:
$10–15

Moderate:
$15–25

Expensive:
$25–40

Very expensive:
over $40

See p.288 for more details.

Cafés and Restaurants

11.30am–10pm, Sun 5–10pm. Moderate (café); Very expensive (restaurant).

Dupont Circle

Bua, 1635 P St ☎265-0828. Dupont Circle Metro. Charming Thai restaurant with upstairs terrace overlooking P Street. Filling lunch specials (around $6) and great noodles. Mon–Fri 11.30am–2.30pm & 5–10.30pm (Fri until 11pm), Sat noon–4pm & 5–11pm, Sun until 10.30pm. Moderate.

City Lights of China, 1731 Connecticut Ave NW ☎265-6688. Dupont Circle Metro. Above-average, well-priced Chinese restaurant, with spicy Szechuan and Hunan specialties – try the Hunan shrimp – and a strong emphasis on seafood. Mon–Thurs 11.30am–10.30pm, Fri 11.30am–11pm, Sat noon–11pm, Sun noon–10.30pm. Moderate.

Food for Thought, 1738 Connecticut Ave NW ☎797-1095. Dupont Circle Metro. DC's original arty (mostly) vegetarian café, keeping its mellow clientele happy with live music, salads, sandwiches, rice plates and organic food, all around $7–11, and cheap lunch combos. Mon–Thurs 11.30am–12.30am, Fri & Sat 11.30am–2am, Sun 4pm–12.30am. Inexpensive.

Gabriel, 2121 P St NW ☎956-6690. Dupont Circle Metro. New-wave Spanish restaurant at the *Radisson Barceló* hotel which has gathered plaudits for its inventive tapas and sherry list, great Sunday brunch, and a full range of delicately flavored, lightly spiced, grilled and seared meat and fish entrées. Reservations recommended. Mon–Thurs & Sun 11.30–10pm, Fri & Sat 11.30am–11pm. Moderate (tapas); Expensive (restaurant).

Lauriol Plaza, 1801 18th St NW ☎387-0035. Dupont Circle Metro. Lines form early at this packed, family-run restaurant for the excellent Mexican, Spanish and Latin American food – the fajitas are stunning. Eat on the terrace in summer. Mon–Thurs & Sun 11.30am–11pm, Fri & Sat noon–midnight. Moderate.

Luna Grill and Diner, 1301 Connecticut Ave NW ☎835-2280. Dupont Circle Metro. "Not your usual diner" by virtue of its bright decor, planetary murals and mosaics, and wholesome blue-plate specials, "green plate" (vegetarian) dishes, and organic coffees and teas. Outdoor patio, too. Mon–Fri 11am–10pm, Sat & Sun 10.30am–11pm. Inexpensive.

Pizzeria Paradiso, 2029 P St NW ☎223-1245. Dupont Circle Metro. Arguably DC's best pizzeria, with lines forming nightly on the steps outside. Thunderingly good food and affordable house wine. Mon–Thurs 11am–11pm, Fri & Sat 11am–midnight, Sun noon–10pm. Inexpensive.

Il Radicchio, 1509 17th St NW ☎986-2627. Dupont Circle Metro. Roberto Donna's designer-rustic pizza-and-pasta emporium, tossing out superb wood-fired pizzas (under $10), or all the spaghetti you can eat ($6.50) dressed with one of twenty sauces (up to $4). No reservations: expect a wait. Mon–Thurs 11.30am–11pm, Fri & Sat 11.30am–midnight, Sun 5–11pm. Inexpensive–Moderate.

Skewers, 1633 P St NW ☎387-7400. Dupont Circle Metro. Dupont Circle's funkiest interior doesn't disappoint – the restaurant (above *Café Luna*) is tops for grilled spits of meat or seafood with delicately flavored rice, or put together a meal of Middle Eastern appetizers. Mon–Thurs 11.30am–11pm, Fri 11.30am–midnight, Sat 5pm–midnight, Sun 5–11pm. Moderate.

Straits of Malaya, 1836 18th St NW ☎483-1483. Dupont Circle Metro. Neighborhood Southeast Asian restaurant, popular for its romantic rooftop terrace but also dishing up well-regarded Straits cuisine including great Malaysian noodles, curry puffs and seafood. The attached, candlelit *Larry's Lounge* bar/coffee house serves snacks and appetizers. Mon–Fri noon–2pm & 5.30–11pm, Sat 5.30–11pm, Sun 5.30–10.30pm. Moderate.

Zorba's Café, 1612 20th St NW ☎387-8555. Dupont Circle Metro. Filling Greek

Late-night Eats

At all the places listed below, you'll be able to order a meal after midnight on at least one night of the week (usually Fri & Sat).

America, Union Station, p.298.

Au Pied du Cochon, Georgetown, p.295.

Ben's Chili Bowl, Shaw, p.297.

Bistro Français, Georgetown, p.295.

Bukom Café, Adams-Morgan, p.287.

Clyde's, Georgetown, p.296.

Coppi's, Shaw, p.297.

Fasika's, Adams-Morgan, p.287.

Food for Thought, Dupont Circle, p.294.

Go-Lo's, Chinatown, p.291.

Harambe Café, Adams-Morgan, p.288.

Jaleo, Downtown: Old, p.293.

J. Paul's, Georgetown, p.296.

Martin's Tavern, Georgetown, p.296.

Mr Henry's, Capitol Hill, p.290.

Old Glory, Georgetown, p.296.

Paolo's, Georgetown, p.296.

Peyote Café, Adams-Morgan, p.288.

Las Placitas, Adams-Morgan, p.288.

Stoney's, Downtown: New, p.292.

Cafés and Restaurants

combo platters, kebabs and pitta-bread sandwiches, as well as daily specials and traditional dishes like bean casserole and spinach pie. Everything comes on plastic plates – it's self-service, with hard-to-get sidewalk seating in summer. Mon–Sat 11am–11.30pm, Sun noon–10.30pm. Budget.

Foggy Bottom

Art Gallery Bar & Grille, 1712 I St NW ☎ 298-6661. Farragut West Metro. Play the Wurlitzer jukebox and soak up the Art Deco interior as you tuck into breakfast, salads, burgers, sandwiches, omelets, pizza and grills – or sit on the outdoor patio. Mon–Fri 7.30am–10pm. Moderate.

Kinkead's, 2000 Pennsylvania Ave NW ☎ 296-7700. Foggy Bottom-GWU Metro. One of DC's favorite restaurants, with a contemporary American menu specializing in fish and seafood. You'll need to book ahead – but it's worth every cent. Mon–Wed & Sun 11.30am–2.30pm & 5.30–10pm, Thurs–Sat 11.30am–2.30pm & 5.30–11pm. Very expensive.

Zuki Moon, 824 New Hampshire Ave NW ☎ 333-3312. Foggy Bottom-GWU Metro. Spiffy Japanese-style noodle bar where diners hunker down over big, lip-smacking bowls of soba or udon noodle soups. Before and after, try the tempura appetizer and the green-tea ice cream.

It's all great value. Mon–Fri 11.30am–2.30pm & 5–11pm, Sat & Sun 5–11pm. Inexpensive–Moderate.

Georgetown

Au Pied du Cochon, 1335 Wisconsin Ave NW ☎ 337-6400. So the food isn't the best French you've ever had, but you can't fault the availability or the prices – 24hr bistro-bar with breakfast (until noon), early-bird $10 dinners (3–8pm), and a carte of eggs, fish, coq au vin, steaks and the like. Daily 24hr. Inexpensive–Moderate.

Bangkok Bistro, 3251 Prospect St NW ☎ 337-2424. Pitches some style into Thai dining with a sleek dining room that's often full. The old favorites (tom yum, pad thai, shrimp cakes and satay) sit alongside new takes on mussels (steamed in lemongrass broth), grilled chicken, vegetarian noodles, grilled fish and curries. Mon–Thurs 11.30am–11pm, Fri 11.30am–midnight, Sat noon–midnight, Sun noon–11pm. Moderate.

Bistro Français, 3128 M St NW ☎ 338-3830. Late-opening bistro with renowned French cooking, from a simple steak-frites, rotisserie chicken or roast pigeon to more complex, traditional dishes. There's an early-bird (5–7pm) and late-night (10.30pm–1am) set dinner for under $20, but check the specials board for what the kitchen does best.

Budget:
under $10

Inexpensive:
$10–15

Moderate:
$15–25

Expensive:
$25–40

Very expensive:
over $40

See p.288 for more details.

Cafés and Restaurants

Mon–Thurs & Sun 11am–3am, Fri & Sat 11am–4am. Moderate.

Clyde's, 3236 M St NW ☎333-9180. Classic New York-style saloon-restaurant featuring the obligatory checked tablecloths, Art Deco lampshades and burnished wood interior. It's a Georgetown institution, which makes weekend reservations essential. Book ahead for the great Sunday brunch. Mon–Thurs 11.30am–2am, Fri 11.30am–3pm, Sat 10am–3am, Sun 9am–2am. Moderate.

Enriqueta's, 2811 M St NW ☎338-7772. Perhaps the best genuine Mexican restaurant in DC – not a fancy place, but fine, spiced food with flavorful servings of pork, chicken, beef and shrimp. Be guided by your waiter, but don't miss the mussels appetizer and the excellent margaritas. Mon–Thurs 11.30am–2.30pm & 5–10pm, Fri 11.30am–2.30pm & 5–11pm, Sat 5–11pm, Sun 5–10pm. Inexpensive–Moderate.

Hibiscus Café, 3401 K St NW ☎965-7170. Cool Caribbean restaurant under the freeway at 34th, with hard-to-get outdoor seating, and modish food and style. Reservations recommended. Tues–Thurs 6–11pm, Fri & Sat 6pm–midnight, Sun 5–10pm. Moderate.

Il Radicchio, 1211 Wisconsin Ave NW ☎337-2627. Less frenetically trendy than the Dupont Circle original, but the eager clientele laps up the same great wood-fired pizzas and mix-and-match spaghetti-and-sauce combos. Mon–Thurs 11.30am–11pm, Fri & Sat 11.30am–midnight, Sun 5–11pm. Inexpensive–Moderate.

J. Paul's, 3218 M St NW ☎333-3450. Rivaling *Clyde's* in clientele, style and popularity – distinctive points are a great raw bar and its own-brewed Amber Ale. Otherwise, it's the standard grill/barbecue menu, all of it usually excellent; try the famous crab cakes. Last orders for food are around midnight. Mon–Thurs 11.30am–1.30am, Fri & Sat 11.30am–2.30am, Sun 10.30am–1.30am. Moderate.

Martin's Tavern, 1264 Wisconsin Ave NW ☎333-7370. Four generations of the Martin family (the first a professional baseball player) have run front-of-house here and counted politicos from JFK to Nixon among their regulars. The old-fashioned, clubby saloon serves up famous steaks and chops, great burgers, linguine with clam sauce, and oyster platters – or come for the popular brunch (Sun 10am–3pm). Mon–Thurs 10am–11pm, Fri 10am–1am, Sat 8am–1am, Sun 8am–11pm. Moderate–Expensive.

Morton's of Chicago, 3251 Prospect St NW ☎342-6258. The city's top steak house. Pick your cut – and make sure you've come with a *huge* appetite – or go for entrées ($20 and up) from chicken to swordfish. Mon–Sat 5.30–11pm, Sun 5–10pm. Very expensive.

Old Glory, 3139 M St NW ☎337-3406. Rollicking barbecue restaurant with hickory smoke rising in earnest from the kitchen. Accompany the huge portions of ribs and chicken with one of half-a-dozen sauces on every table and a shot of great bourbon. Live R&B three nights a week. Mon–Thurs & Sun 11.30am–11.30pm, Fri & Sat 11.30am–12.30am. Moderate.

Paolo's, 1303 Wisconsin Ave NW, at M St ☎333-7353. Designer Italian dining with a few, hotly contested, tables open to the sidewalk. Gourmet pizza – feta cheese, grappa-cured salmon, goat's cheese, spinach and sun-dried tomato – and even better pasta: save room for dessert. Mon–Thurs & Sun 11.30am–12.30am, Fri & Sat 11.30am–1.30am. Moderate.

Saigon Inn, 2928 M St NW ☎337-5588. The food served in this eager-to-please Vietnamese restaurant makes a few concessions to Western tastes, but is still eminently enjoyable – and the lunch deal (four dishes for under $5, Mon–Fri 11am–3pm) is a real steal. Mon–Thurs 11am–11pm, Fri & Sat 11am–midnight, Sun noon–11pm. Inexpensive.

Vietnam Georgetown, 2934 M St NW ☎337-4536. The best Vietnamese in

Cafés and Restaurants

Georgetown, with a touch more flair than the adjacent *Saigon Inn* and specials like terrific grilled lemon chicken, stuffed crepes, five-vegetables rice noodle and shrimp curry to warm the heart. Mon–Thurs 11am–11pm, Fri & Sat 11am–11.30pm, Sun noon–11pm. Moderate.

Vintage, 2809 M St NW ☎625-0077. Enjoyable French bistro offering more reasonable prices for Michelin-star-winner Gerard Pangaud's style and menus than those at his downtown base – the twenty-buck steak-frites might just be the best you've ever had. Reservations recommended. Mon–Sat 5.30–11pm. Expensive.

Zed's, 3318 M St NW ☎333-4710. *The* spot for Ethiopian food in Georgetown, and an intimate one at that. The set lunch is a snip but eating from the menu won't ever break the bank – the *doro wot* (chicken stew in a red pepper sauce) is a good spicy choice. Mon–Thurs & Sun 11am–11pm, Fri & Sat 11am–1am. Inexpensive.

Shaw

Ben's Chili Bowl, 1213 U St NW ☎667-0909. U Street-Cardozo Metro. Venerable U Street hangout across from the Metro, serving renowned chili dogs, burgers and fries at booths and counter stools. A scene in *The Pelican Brief* was shot here, as photos on the wall attest. Mon–Thurs

6am–2am, Fri & Sat 6am–4am, Sun noon–8pm. Budget.

Coppi's, 1414 U St NW ☎319-7773. U Street-Cardozo Metro. For an indication of how much the neighborhood has changed, look no further than this trendy little pizza palace with its brick oven, cycling photo fetish and yuppie-collegiate clientele, offering plenty of choice at decent prices. Mon–Thurs 5pm–midnight, Fri & Sat 5pm–1am, Sun 5–11pm. Inexpensive–Moderate.

Florida Avenue Grill, 1100 Florida Ave NW ☎265-1586. U Street-Cardozo Metro. Southern-style diner serving hearty meals for almost half a century to locals and stray celebs. Tues–Sat 6.30am–9pm. Budget.

Southwest

Custis Brown, 12th St and Maine Ave SW ☎484-1068. L'Enfant Plaza Metro. Fish Wharf seafood stand serving humongous fried-fish sandwiches, steamed spiced shrimp, crab and lobster, clam chowder and oyster platters to go – all at giveaway prices. Great for a lunch or sundowner picnic overlooking the Washington Channel. Daily 8am–8pm. Budget.

Hogate's, 800 Water St SW ☎484-6300. L'Enfant Plaza Metro. Marina restaurant with zealous nautical interior, air-con bar and patio. The river view is the main

Budget:
Under $10

Inexpensive:
$10–15

Moderate:
$15–25

Expensive:
$25–40

Very Expensive:
over $40

See p.288 for more details.

Cafés and Restaurants

attraction, for which hundreds pack in to sample the spiced shrimp lunch buffet and full seafood a la carte menu. Mon–Thurs 11am–11pm, Fri 11am–midnight, Sat noon–midnight, Sun 10.30am–10pm. Moderate–Expensive.

Phillips, 900 Water St SW ☎ 488-8515. L'Enfant Plaza Metro. The second major Waterfront seafoodery is firmly on the tour-bus circuit, and only those with a hankering for quantity from the lunch, dinner and weekend brunch buffets are going to get much from the menu. Daily 11am–11pm. Moderate–Expensive.

Upper Northwest

Ivy's Café, 3520 Connecticut Ave NW ☎ 363-7802. Cleveland Park Metro. Neighborhood southeast Asian serving a flavorful mix of Thai and Indonesian dishes. Mon–Wed 5–10.30pm, Thurs 11.30am–10.30pm, Fri & Sat 11.30am–11.30pm, Sun 1–10.30pm. Inexpensive.

Krupin's, 4620 Wisconsin Ave NW ☎ 686-1989. Tenleytown Metro. Jewish deli-diner with attitude – it's a long way from anywhere, though devotees consider the trek worth it for the true tastes of hot corned beef, lox and bagel platters, stuffed cabbage, pastrami and the rest. Daily 8am–10pm. Budget–Inexpensive.

Nam Viet, 3419 Connecticut Ave NW ☎ 237-1015. Cleveland Park Metro. The soups are good, the grilled chicken and fish, the caramel pork, the Vietnamese steak – really, you can't go wrong. Mon–Thurs 11am–3pm & 5–10pm, Fri & Sat 11am–11pm, Sun 11am–10pm. Inexpensive–Moderate.

New Heights, 2317 Calvert St NW ☎ 234-4110. Woodley Park-Zoo Metro. Fashionable, new-wave American restaurant serving an inventive, seasonal menu which culls its influences from many cuisines. Book ahead in summer to sit outside, especially for Sunday brunch. Mon–Thurs & Sun 5.30–10.30pm, Fri &

Sat 5.30–11pm, bar open until 12.30am. Expensive.

Saigon Gourmet, 2635 Connecticut Ave NW ☎ 265-1360. Woodley Park-Zoo Metro. Quality Vietnamese restaurant with lots of surprises, not least that the food isn't overspiced for once – try the roasted quail or a traditional noodle soup. Daily 11.30am–3pm & 5–10.30pm. Inexpensive.

Woodley Café, 2619 Connecticut Ave NW ☎ 332-5773. Woodley Park-Zoo Metro. Roomy neighborhood café-bar attracting a laidback crowd. Breakfast and Sunday brunch are good, there's a full menu for lunch and dinner, and late-night pizza. Daily 9am–10pm, later pizza and bar service. Inexpensive.

Yanni's, 3500 Connecticut Ave NW ☎ 362-8871. Cleveland Park Metro. Popular pit-stop before hitting the Cleveland Park bars. Bargain grilled meat platters, a tasty tzatsiki and pricier house specials like squid and octopus. Daily 11.30am–11.30pm. Inexpensive.

Union Station

America, Union Station, 50 Massachusetts Ave NE ☎ 682-9555. Union Station Metro. Bustling restaurant-bar with a huge menu culled from all corners of the US. Double-decker restaurant inside, concourse or gallery seating outside. Mon–Thurs & Sun 11.30am–11.30pm, Fri & Sat 11.30am–1am. Moderate.

B. Smith's, Union Station, 50 Massachusetts Ave NE ☎ 289-6188. Union Station Metro. Cooking from the American South – pretty rare in DC – brings in punters hankering after fried green tomatoes, Cajun paella, catfish, and red beans n' rice, though just as many come for the glorious restaurant space – this was once the station's presidential waiting room. Mon–Thurs 11.30am–4pm & 5–11pm, Fri & Sat 11.30am–4pm & 5pm–midnight, Sun 11.30am–4pm & 5–9pm. Expensive.

Chapter 14

Bars and Clubs

Bars and pubs congregate in distinct neighborhoods, notably Capitol Hill (near Union Station and along Pennsylvania Ave SE), Georgetown (M and Wisconsin), Dupont Circle (along 17th, Connecticut Ave and P), Adams-Morgan (18th and Columbia) and, latterly, around U Street (near the Metro) in Shaw. The few bars downtown tend to cater to an after-work crowd, though there's a burgeoning bar district along 7th Street, near the MCI Center. There's also a thriving – if relatively small-scale – **gay scene**, with most of the action in Dupont Circle, especially on P Street (between 21st and 22nd) and 17th Street (between P and R).

Most bars **open** daily from around noon until 2am, often later on the weekends. Virtually all have **happy hours** where drinks are two-for-one, or at least heavily discounted; the optimum time for this is weekdays between 4pm and 8pm. Some bars also offer free snacks to happy-hour drinkers.

DC's **club scene** moves at a frenetic pace – *CityPaper*, the *Washington Post's* "Weekend" section, and the gay-oriented *Washington Blade* carry schedules, reviews and ads. The places listed below are some of the better-established venues in a city where clubs open and close with alarming regularity; you're sure to find others that are new or some that have changed hands and style. At many venues the music and clientele may change radically on different nights; call to check if you're aiming for somewhere specific.

Plenty of clubs have low or no **cover charges** – where they exist, they're generally between $5 and $15 (highest on weekends). **Opening hours** vary wildly, though most places don't get going until well after 11pm and stay open until at least 3am, with some continuing (especially on weekends) until 5am. If you're going to be out this late, make sure you have a taxi number with you since some clubs are in dubious parts of town where walking around in the small hours invites trouble. It's also as well to take **photo-ID**, or your passport, with you. You won't get into many places without one, and you need to be over 21 to drink alcohol in DC.

Adams-Morgan

Café Lautrec, 2431 18th St NW ☎765-6436. Eat out on the patio or cozy up inside in the dark old bar-room for a beer or coffee. There's live jazz most nights after 9pm. Mon–Thurs & Sun 4pm–2am, Fri & Sat 4pm–3am.

Chief Ike's Mambo Room, 1725 Columbia Rd NW ☎332-2211. Ramshackle mural-clad bar (featured, briefly, in *Enemy of the State*) with live bands or DJs hosting theme nights. The *Chaos* bar upstairs has indie music and a pool table. Mon–Thurs & Sun 4pm–2am, Fri 4pm–3am, Sat noon–3am.

Cities, 2424 18th St NW ☎328-7194. Periodically changing (cities-of-the-world) decor and menu brings in the high-fashion Eurocrowd. The outdoor terrace over-

Check out the list of music clubs in Chapter 15 for more ideas about where to sink a beer.

All places listed in Adams-Morgan are within a few blocks of the junction of 18th St, Columbia Rd and Calvert St; the closest Metro is Woodley Park-Zoo (a 15min walk away).

Bars and Clubs

See p.260 for details of how to get to Alexandria.

Arlington's music bars, Iota and Galaxy Hut, are good places for a drink too; see p.308.

Beer Talk

Don't want another Bud? **Microbrews** are big business these days and you'll be able to get a decent selection of beers in many bars. For the best choice, hit one of the city's brew-pubs – *Capitol City Brewing Company* (Downtown: Old, & Union Station, p.302 & p.305), *District Chophouse & Brewery* (Downtown: Old, p.302), *John Harvard's* (Downtown: Old, p.302) – or the beer specialist *Brickskeller* (Dupont Circle, p.303). Elsewhere, keep an eye out for the following local brews: Foggy Bottom Ale (from DC), Virginia's Rock Creek, Potomac River or Dominion; and from Maryland, Blue Ridge, Clipper City and Wild Goose.

looks the Adams-Morgan streetlife parade; dance upstairs to world music. Mon–Thurs 5–11pm, Fri & Sat 5pm–3am, Sun 11am–11pm.

Crush, 2323 18th St NW ☎319-1111. Generation-X bar-and-club haunt, hugely busy on weekends when the crowds pour in after 11pm. Wed–Sat 7pm–3am.

Heaven & Hell, 2327 18th St NW ☎667-4355. Grungy *Hell* downstairs and funky *Heaven* up, featuring techno, dance and live indie; no real action until after 10.30pm, when the student/Goth crowd takes the floor. Occasional cover. Mon–Thurs & Sun 6pm–2am, Fri & Sat 6pm–3am.

Kala Kala, 2439 18th St NW ☎232-5433. Basement African bar announced by a large wooden abstract sculpture. African beers and great live bands and DJs. Wed, Thurs & Sun 7pm–2am, Fri & Sat 7pm–3am.

Millie and Al's, 2440 18th St NW ☎387-8131. Crusty neighborhood tavern of a type all too rare in Adams-Morgan – food, beer and shots for local wastrels. Mon–Thurs 4pm–2am, Fri & Sat noon–3am, Sun noon–2am.

Mr Henry's, 1836 Columbia Rd NW ☎797-8882. Grab a seat at this relaxed lounge bar cum cabaret lounge and settle down to one of the regular soul and African gigs, or watch while eating at one of the closely packed tables. Mon–Thurs & Sun 4pm–2am, Fri & Sat 4pm–3am.

Toledo Lounge, 2435 18th St NW ☎986-5416. Barebones café-bar with attitude, featuring windows looking out

on the local streetlife – the patio seats, best spot for hanging out, are like gold-dust in summer. Mon–Thurs 6pm–2am, Fri 6pm–3am, Sat noon–3am, Sun noon–2am.

Alexandria, VA

Union Street Public House, 121 S Union St ☎703/548-1785. Old Town inn that's just as nice for eating as drinking, though it gets chock-full on weekends. Daily 11.30am–1.30am.

Virginia Beverage Company, 607 King St ☎703/684-5397. Brew-pub in the traditional style with copper vats to the fore and half a dozen ales on tap. Mon–Thurs & Sun 11am–midnight, Fri & Sat 11am–1am.

Arlington, VA

Bardo Rodeo, 2000 Wilson Blvd, at Troy St ☎703/527-9399. Court House Metro. Boisterous brew-pub (claiming, believably, to be the largest in the US) housed in a mural-decorated car showroom. Come for a beer, or for the classic movies shown on the big screen. There are stacks of pool tables, and an outdoor café in summer. Mon–Fri 11.30am–2am, Sat 1pm–2am, Sun 5pm–2am.

Ireland's Four Courts, 2051 Wilson Blvd, at N Courthouse Rd ☎703/525-3600. Court House Metro. One of the nicest of the area's Irish bars, drawing a cheery Arlington crowd for the live music (Tues–Sat), dozen tap beers, whiskey selection and filling food. Mon–Sat 11am–2am, Sun 10am–2am.

Whitlow's on Wilson, 2854 Wilson Blvd
☎703/276-9693. Clarendon Metro.
Neighborhood retro bar on Wilson with
something going on most nights −
happy hour drinks and food, live music,
pool, hanging out in the booths or at the
wraparound bar. Daily noon−2am.

Capitol Hill

Capitol Lounge, 229 Pennsylvania Ave
SE ☎547-2098. Capitol South Metro.
More sophisticated than most of the Hill
bars − cigars and martinis are de rigueur
in the downstairs bar − but there's still
plenty of life up in the brick-walled
saloon during happy hour (Wednesdays
are a big hit), with NFL on the TVs and
DJs whipping up the weekend action.
Mon−Thurs & Sun 11am−2am, Fri & Sat
11am−3am.

Hawk 'n' Dove, 329 Pennsylvania Ave SE
☎543-3300. Capitol South Metro.
Famous old pub, a bit tatty at the edges
now, hung with football pennants, bottles and bric-a-brac. The young, loud
crowd come (depending on the night) for
the cheap beer, half-price food or football on TV. Mon−Thurs & Sun
10am−2am, Fri & Sat 10am−3am.

Phase 1, 525 8th St SE ☎544-6831.
Eastern Market Metro. Good-natured lesbian bar and club with dancing, DJs and
videos. Mon−Thurs & Sun 8pm−2am, Fri
& Sat 8pm−3am.

Remington's, 639 Pennsylvania Ave SE
☎543-3113. Eastern Market Metro. Slip
on the cowboy boots and hit the C&W
disco nights, wildly popular with a mostly gay clientele. Small cover on weekends. Mon−Thurs 4pm−2am, Fri & Sat
1pm−3am, Sun 1pm−2am.

Tune Inn, 331 Pennsylvania Ave SE
☎543-2725. Capitol South Metro. Crusty
neighborhood dive bar which − next to
the preppie *Hawk 'n' Dove* − seems in
the wrong neighborhood. Settle down in
a booth, munch on the burgers and feed
the jukebox. Mon−Thurs & Sun
8am−2am, Fri & Sat 8am−3am.

Tunnicliff's, 222 7th St SE ☎546-3663.
Eastern Market Metro. Arty saloon oppo-

Gay and Lesbian Nightlife

The following bars and clubs are all
reviewed in this chapter. The weekly
Washington Blade has news and
listings.

Badlands, Dupont Circle, p.303.
The Circle, Dupont Circle, p.303.
Cobalt, Dupont Circle, p.303.
The Edge, Southeast, p.305.
The Fireplace, Dupont Circle, p.303.
Hung Jury, New Downtown, p.301.
JR's, Dupont Circle, p.303.
Mr P's, Dupont Circle, p.304.
Omega, Dupont Circle, p.304.
Phase 1, Capitol Hill, p.301.
Remington's, Capitol Hill, p.301.
Tracks, Southeast, p.305.

site the market, with a wraparound bar,
a few seats on the terrace outside and
live jazz/blues most Saturday nights.
Mon−Thurs & Sun 11am−midnight, Fri &
Sat 11am−2am.

Downtown: New

Hung Jury, 1819 H St NW ☎785-8181.
Farragut West Metro. Popular women's
bar and disco, tucked away off an alley;
small cover charge. Fri & Sat 9pm−3am.

Lucky's, 1221 Connecticut Ave NW
☎331-3733. Farragut North or Dupont
Circle Metro. Everybody-knows-your-
name kind of place, with plenty of room
and booths at the back to hangout and
shoot pool. Dance nights, swing bands,
cheap drinks and English soccer on TV −
all makes for a home-from-home for
some. Mon−Fri noon−2am, Sat & Sun
4pm−2am.

Lulu's, 1217 22nd St NW ☎861-5858.
Foggy Bottom-GWU Metro. Drinks and
Cajun food in the café-bar, with regular
swing and salsa nights; DJ rock and pop
and a wild party scene at the good-
natured club every night (small cover on
the weekend, when lines form early).
Café-bar: Mon−Thurs 6pm-1.30am,

Bars and Clubs

Fri–Sun 4pm–2.30am; club: Mon–Fri 4pm–3am, Sat & Sun 8pm–3am.

The Madhatter, 1831 M St NW ☎833-1495. Farragut North or West Metro. Homely saloon where the after-office crowd – in for the 4–8pm happy hour – give way later to a free-and-easy student set. DJ music Tues–Fri from 9pm. Mon–Fri 1.30pm–1.30am, Sat 11.30am–2am, Sun 10.30am–midnight.

Quigley's, 1825 I St NW ☎331-0150. Farragut West Metro. College-kid/after-office bar with decent food, drinks specials and a cover (after 9.30pm) when the DJ spins pop/rock. Mon–Wed & Sun noon–midnight, Thurs 11.30am–1.30am, Fri 11.30am–2.30am, Sat 6pm–2.30am.

Tequila Grill, 1990 K St NW ☎833-3640. Farragut West Metro. No one really comes to eat the Tex-Mex food; instead the after-work mob packs in for happy-hour beer, cocktails and dancing. Mon–Thurs & Sun 11.30am–1.30am, Fri & Sat 11.30am–2.30am.

Zei, 1415 Zei Alley NW, 14th St between H and I ☎842-2445. McPherson Square Metro. New York-style warehouse dance club, with emphasis on disco, house, funk and hip-hop – look the part (chic and rich), don't turn up until after midnight, and expect to wait in line. Thurs–Sat 10pm–4am.

Downtown: Old

The Bank, 915 F St NW ☎396-3632. Gallery Place-Chinatown Metro. DJs pump out techno, house, disco, rap and hip-hop on three floors of a converted downtown bank. Call for a schedule; lines form early and Mon night is popular. Mon & Thurs–Sun 10pm–3am.

Capitol City Brewing Company, 1100 New York Ave NW, entrance at 11th and H ☎628-2222. Metro Center Metro. Copper vats, pipes and gantries adorn this techno-microbrewery, serving a changing menu of home-brewed beers to an excitable bunch of drinkers. In September, the Mid-Atlantic Beer and Food Festival kicks off here. Daily 11am–2am.

DC Live, 932 F St NW ☎347-7200. Gallery Place-Chinatown Metro. Huge downtown space (once a department store) for a mainly African-American crowd, though Thursday club nights see more of a mix – reggae, world, salsa, Top 40, hip-hop, jazz depending on the night; call for schedules. Wed & Fri–Sun 9pm–3am.

District Chophouse & Brewery, 509 7th St NW ☎347-3434. Gallery Place-Chinatown Metro. This stunning conversion of an old downtown banking hall lends swing-era class to the emerging neighborhood. Come to eat or just stop by for a drink – the busy bar serves five or six of its own brews. Mon–Thurs & Sun 11am–12.30am, Fri & Sat 11am–1.30am.

Fadó, 808 7th St NW ☎789-0066. Gallery Place-Chinatown Metro. DC's Irish pub scene comes of age with this clever conceit – the usual grocery signs, home-spun quotations and Guinness on tap are all present, but so are expensively designed Victorian, faux-rural and ancient Celtic drinking areas. Mon–Thurs & Sun 11.30am–2am, Fri & Sat 11.30am–3am.

Grand Slam Sports Bar, *Grand Hyatt*, 1000 H St NW ☎637-4781. Metro Center Metro. One of DC's better places to catch the game, with big-screen action, lots of beers and video games, and a DJ most nights. Daily 11am–1am.

John Harvard's, Warner Building, 1299 Pennsylvania Ave NW ☎783-2739. Metro Center Metro. Upscale basement brewhouse and restaurant, with half-a-dozen beers on tap. Mon–Thurs noon–11pm, Fri & Sat noon–midnight, Sun 3–10pm.

Polly Esther's, 605 12th St NW ☎737-1970. Metro Center Metro. The retro craze hits DC with a bang in this enthusiastic 70s, 80s and 90s dance club with theme nights and extended Friday happy hour. No cover before 9pm. Thurs 9pm–2am, Fri 5pm–4am, Sat 8pm–4am.

The Ritz, 919 E St NW ☎638-2582. Gallery Place-Chinatown Metro. Five music bars in one club where fashion-

Restaurant Bars

Some of DC's restaurants have very funky bars in their own right – you'll be welcome for just a drink in any of the following.

America, Union Station, p.298.

BET on Jazz, Old Downtown, p.293.

B. Smith's, Union Station, p.298.

Bukom Café, Adams-Morgan, p.287.

Gabriel, Dupont Circle, p.294.

Grillfish, New Downtown, p.292.

Jaleo, Old Downtown, p.293.

Old Ebbitt Grill, Old Downtown, p.293.

Perry's, Adams-Morgan, p.288.

Peyote Café, Adams-Morgan, p.288.

Red Sage, Old Downtown, p.293.

Tom Tom, Adams-Morgan, p.289.

able power-dressers wallow in everything from pop and reggae to soul, go-go and house. Mainly black crowd, who wait patiently in line after midnight; Friday is the big night. Wed 9pm–2am, Fri 9pm–3.30am, Sat 10pm–3.30am, Sun 10pm–2am.

Sky Terrace, *Washington Hotel*, 515 15th St NW ☎638-5900. Metro Center Metro. Superb rooftop views from the ninth-floor bar-terrace. It's usually very busy – go early or late or expect to wait. Daily 11am–1am (May–Oct only).

Dupont Circle

Badlands, 1415 22nd St NW ☎296-0505. Dupont Circle Metro. Popular, likable gay chart and house disco, at its best on Friday and Saturday nights. Tues, Thurs & Sun 9pm–2am, Fri & Sat 9pm–3am.

The Big Hunt, 1345 Connecticut Ave NW ☎785-2333. Dupont Circle Metro. As well known for its jungle decor – including the tarantula candelabra – as for its beer. Over 25 brews on tap, good juke-box and a groovy crowd. It's always busy during happy hour. Mon–Thurs

4pm–2am, Fri 4pm–3am, Sat noon–3am, Sun 5.30pm–2am.

The Brickskeller, 1523 22nd St NW ☎293-1885. Dupont Circle Metro. Renowned brick-lined basement saloon serving "the world's largest selection of beer" – up to 800 different types, including dozens from US microbreweries. Knowledgeable bar staff can advise. Mon–Thurs 11.30am–2am, Fri 11.30am–3am, Sat 6pm–3am, Sun 6pm–2am.

The Childe Harold, 1610 20th St NW ☎483-6700. Dupont Circle Metro. Friendly old red-brick pub with an out-door patio, which draws in a mixed crew to chew the fat and watch TV sports; there's a good restaurant too. Mon–Thurs 11.30am–2am, Fri & Sat 11.30am–3am, Sun 10.30am–2am.

The Circle, 1629 Connecticut Ave NW ☎462-5575. Dupont Circle Metro. Swish gay bar-club-restaurant, where an upper-income crowd jostles for window stools and space on the summer terrace. Call for theme/club night information. Mon–Thurs & Sun 11am–2am, Fri & Sat 11am–3am.

Cobalt, 1639 R St NW ☎232-6969. Dupont Circle Metro. Newcomer on the Dupont gay scene, with music and dancing for a gay and lesbian crowd. Mon–Thurs & Sun noon–2am, Fri & Sat noon–3am.

The Fireplace, 2161 P St NW ☎293-1293. Dupont Circle Metro. Gay-oriented bar with pool tables, jukebox and a long happy hour. A staging ground for the cruisey P Street scene. Mon–Thurs & Sun 1pm–2am, Fri & Sat 1pm–3am.

Fox and Hounds, 1537 17th St NW ☎232-6307. Dupont Circle Metro. Easygoing bar and grill slap-bang in the middle of the 17th Street action. There's a large sidewalk patio and a good juke-box. Mon–Thurs 11am–2am, Fri 11am–3am, Sat 10am–3am, Sun 10am–2am.

JR's, 1519 17th St NW ☎328-0090. Dupont Circle Metro. Gay saloon-bar with preening clientele; very much the place

Bars and Clubs

to be seen for cocktails. Mon–Thurs
2pm–1.30am, Fri & Sat noon–2.30am,
Sun noon–1.30am.

Mr Eagan's, 1343 Connecticut Ave NW
☎331-9768. Dupont Circle Metro.
Curtained booths, old-time locals and a
narrow bar overseen by Mr E himself –
not very Dupont Circle, and enjoyable for
precisely that reason. Mon–Sat
11am–1am, Sun 7pm–2am.

Mr P's, 2147 P St NW ☎293-1064.
Dupont Circle Metro. Longest-serving gay
bar in the neighborhood, which has
given it time to acquire a bit of character
and attract a mellow, local clientele.
Mon–Thurs 3pm–2am, Fri & Sat
3pm–3am, Sun noon–2am.

Omega, 2122 P St NW, in the rear alley
☎223-4917. Dupont Circle Metro.
Pumping gay bar and disco, mostly
house. Small cover charge. Mon–Wed
4pm–2am, Thurs 4pm–4am, Fri
4pm–5am, Sat 8pm–5am, Sun
8pm–3am.

Foggy Bottom

Red Lion, 2040 I St NW ☎785-2766.
Foggy Bottom-GWU Metro. No gimmicks,
few frills – just a GWU student hangout
doing a roaring trade in cheap food and
drinks. Mon–Thurs 11am–1.30am, Fri &
Sat 11am–2.30am.

Georgetown

*See p.241 for
details of how
to get to
Georgetown.*

Champions, 1206 Wisconsin Ave NW
☎965-4005. Full-on sports bar awash
with memorabilia, with big games on the
TV and high-calorie food to help the
beer down. DJ after 11pm. Mon–Thurs
5pm–2am, Fri 5pm–3am, Sat
11.30am–3am, Sun 11.30am–2am.

Garrett's, 3003 M St NW ☎333-1033.
With the usual brick-and-wood interior
so beloved of DC bars, the *Garrett* stands
out by virtue of the damn big rhino head
by the door, and a pumping jukebox
that keeps the student crowd in party
mood. Mon–Thurs 11.30am–2am, Fri
11.30am–3am, Sat noon–3am, Sun
noon–2am.

Mr Smith's, 3104 M St NW ☎333-3104.
Most welcoming of Georgetown's
saloons, with a splendid garden drink-
ing-and-eating area, cheap beer-and-
burger nights, and live bands on
weekends. Mon–Thurs & Sun
11am–1.30am, Fri & Sat 11am–2.30am.

Music City Roadhouse, 1050 30th St
NW ☎337-4444. Old Foundry building
hangout for pool-shootin', jukebox-
playin', football-watchin', redneck-
wannabees. Cheap beer, live bands on
weekends, full roadhouse restaurant
menu. Tues–Thurs 5pm–midnight, Fri
5pm–2am, Sat 2pm–2am, Sun
11am–midnight.

Sequoia, 3000 K St NW ☎944-4200.
Popular restaurant-bar at the eastern end
of Washington Harbor, with outdoor terrace seating overlooking the river. Get
there early on weekends. Mon–Thurs &
Sun 11.30am–1am, Fri & Sat
11.30am–2am.

Third Edition, 1218 Wisconsin Ave NW,
near M St ☎333-3700. Gung-ho college
bar on several floors. It's a cattle-market
on weekends (when you'll probably
have to wait in line and pay cover after
10pm); arrive early and enjoy the 4–9pm
happy hour. Mon–Thurs 4pm–2am, Fri
4pm–3am, Sat 11.30am–3am, Sun
11.30am–2am.

The Tombs, 1226 36th St NW, at
Prospect St ☎337-6668. Busy, basement student haunt, adorned with rowing blades – Bill Clinton, it's said, used to
drink here in his student days.
Occasional live bands and club nights
(small cover). Mon–Thurs 11.30am–2am,
Fri & Sat 11.30am–3am, Sun
9.30am–2am.

Shaw

*Exercise
caution at
night around
all the places
listed in Shaw
– and take a
cab home.*

Polly's Café, 1342 U St NW ☎265-8385.
U St-Cardozo Metro. Neat little brick-and-
board café-bar with a few outdoor
tables, tap beers and bottled microbrews, good food and acoustic folk
nights. Mon–Thurs 6pm–midnight, Fri
6pm–2am, Sat 10am–2am, Sun
10am–midnight.

Bars and Clubs

Red Room Bar, *Black Cat*, 1831 14th St NW ☎667-7960. U St-Cardozo Metro. Independent, no-cover bar attached to the *Black Cat* music club, with pool, pinball, draft beers and amiable, punky clientele. Mon–Thurs & Sun 8pm–2am, Fri & Sat 8pm–3am.

Republic Gardens, 1355 U St NW ☎323-2730. U St-Cardozo Metro. One of U St's hottest night's out, with DJs spinning hip-hop, soul and jazz in a converted townhouse heavy on the decor. Live music some nights; cover charge. Thurs & Fri 5pm–2am, Sat 5pm–3am, Sun 9pm–3am.

State of the Union, 1357 U St NW ☎588-8810. U St-Cardozo Metro. Long, red, and dimly lit, festooned with hammer-and-sickles and sporting a fearsome vodka list. DJ's music ebbs gently from funk, Latin and jazz to acid jazz and hip-hop; occasional small cover. Mon–Fri 5pm–2am, Sat 6pm–3am, Sun 11am–2am.

Utopia, 1418 U St NW ☎588-7311. U St-Cardozo Metro. Arty, romantic bar-restaurant with regular live blues and jazz, art exhibits and a popular weekend brunch. Mon–Thurs & Sun 11am–2am, Fri & Sat 11am–3am.

Velvet Lounge, 915 U St NW ☎462-3213. U St-Cardozo Metro. Schmooze-and-booze in a relaxed bar, with laid-back live music five nights a week (small cover) and an open-mike session every Tuesday. Mon–Thurs & Sun 11am–2am, Fri & Sat 11am–3am.

Southeast

The Edge, 56 L St SE ☎488-1200. Frenetic gay club with several bars, entertainment and special events. Mon–Thurs 7pm–2am, Fri & Sat 7pm–4am, Sun 4pm–2am.

Tracks, 1111 1st St SE ☎488-3320. Thoroughly enjoyable 70s-style dance club with a large gay and lesbian presence and thumping good vibes. Sat is the big gay night; others (particularly Thursday) are straight or nearly straight. Thurs 9pm–4am, Fri & Sat 8pm–5am, Sun 8pm–4am.

Union Station

Capitol City Brewing Company, 2 Massachusetts Ave NE ☎842-2337. Union Station Metro. Never has a post office looked so inviting. Burnham's beauty has had a brew-pub plonked itside its cavernous interior, making it a stunning place for a beer (though don't bother with the food). Mon & Sun 11am–midnight, Tues–Sat 11am–1.30am; kitchen closes at 11pm.

The Dubliner, *Phoenix Park Hotel*, 520 N Capitol St NW ☎737-3773. Union Station Metro. A wooden-vaulted, good-time Irish pub, with draught Guinness, boisterous conversation and live Irish music. The patio is a popular summer hangout. Mon–Thurs & Sun 11am–1.30am, Fri & Sat 11am–2.30am.

Irish Times, 14 F St NW ☎543-5433. Union Station Metro. Wide range of

Navy Yard Metro is the closest to the Southeast clubs, but it's a risky neighborhood; take a cab there and back.

Bars and Clubs

beers, above-average bar food and live singalong folk from Wednesday to Sunday. Every June there's an overnight read-through of James Joyce's *Ulysses*. Mon–Thurs & Sun 11am–2am, Fri & Sat 11am–3am.

Upper Northwest

Ireland's Four Provinces, 3412 Connecticut Ave NW ☎ 244-0860. Cleveland Park Metro. Rollicking Irish music five nights a week (small cover on weekends) brings in a college crowd. There's a good atmosphere, and outdoor seats in the summer. Mon–Thurs & Sun 5pm–1.30am, Fri & Sat 5pm–2.30am.

Nanny O'Brien's, 3319 Connecticut Ave NW ☎ 686-9189. Cleveland Park Metro. Cleveland Park's other Irish tavern is a smaller, more personable, joint but with the same successful mix of heavy drinking and live music (usually no cover); Monday's jam night is good fun. Mon–Thurs 5pm–2am, Fri 4pm–3am, Sat 11am–3am, Sun 11am–2am.

Oxford Tavern, 3000 Connecticut Ave NW ☎ 232-4225. Woodley Park-Zoo Metro. Timeless suburban saloon known as the "Zoo Bar" (it's across from the zoo), with free live bands three or four nights. Mon–Thurs & Sun 11.30am–2am, Fri & Sat 11.30am–3am.

Chapter 15

Live Music

Washington DC has a pretty good **live music** scene. To find out **what's on**, consult the "Weekend" section in the Friday edition of the *Washington Post,* or the free weekly *CityPaper* (available in cafés, bars and restaurants all over the city). Other sources are the monthly, glossy *Washingtonian* magazine,

---

Major Venues

For details of concerts at the following venues, call the box office numbers, or TicketMaster or Protix.

In the city

Carter Barron Amphitheater, 16th St and Colorado Ave NW, Rock Creek Park ☎ 619-7222 or 426-6837. Outdoor 4250-seat theater for pop, jazz and R&B on summer weekends.

DAR Constitution Hall, 1776 D St NW ☎ 628-4780. Indoor 4000-seat auditorium for major pop, jazz and C&W acts.

Lincoln Theater, 1215 U St NW ☎ 328-6000. 1200-seat theater hosting black pop, jazz, soul and gospel.

Lisner Auditorium, George Washington University, 730 21st St NW ☎ 994-6800. 1500-seat auditorium on the GWU campus for rock, pop and indie acts.

MCI Center, 601 F St NW ☎ 628-3200. Downtown 20,000-seater hosts big-name rock, pop and C&W gigs.

RFK Stadium, 2400 E Capitol St SE ☎ 547-9077. 55,000-seater stadium pulling in the mega-stars.

Warner Theater, 1299 Pennsylvania Ave NW ☎ 783-4000. Jazz, Latin, Broadway and Vegas stars.

Outside the city

Jack Kent Cook Stadium, Raljon, MD ☎ 301/276-6050. The Redskins stadium hosts occasional summer pop and rock concerts.

Merriweather Post Pavilion, off Rte 29, Columbia, MD ☎ 301/982-1800. Pavilion and open-air seating, presenting mid-league and major pop, jazz, country and MOR acts; spring and summer only.

Nissan Pavilion at Stone Ridge, Bristow VA ☎ 1-800/455-8999. The area's newest outdoor summer stadium (25,000-seater) for rock and country gigs.

Patriot Center, George Mason University Campus, Fairfax, VA ☎ 703/993-3000. Big-name concerts and family entertainment.

USAir Arena, 1 Harry S Truman Drive, Landover MD ☎ 301/350-3400; exits 15A or 17A off the Beltway. 20,000-seat stadium for pop, rock, dance and country stars.

Wolf Trap Farm Park, Filene Center and The Barns, 1624 Trap Rd, Vienna, VA ☎ 703/255-1860 (Filene Center) or 703/938-2404 (Barns). Jazz, country, folk, zydeco and pop. See p.315 for details.

Live Music

For classical music and opera performances, see Chapter 16, "Arts and Entertainment".

For a rundown of DC's annual festivals, many of which include live music, see Chapter 18.

and flyers and posters in bookstores and cafés.

Concerts by established stars take place in a variety of **major venues**, in and outside the city: **tickets** tend to be pricey ($20–50) and need to be booked in advance, either direct from the venues (there's a list of the main ones on p.307) or from TicketMaster (☎432-7328 or 1-800/551-7328) or Protix (☎703/218-6500 or 1-800/955-5566), both of which will add on a service charge. Protix also sells tickets at Olsson's Books and Records outlets (see p.318), TicketMaster at Tower Records (see p.321), while some gig tickets are available from TicketPlace at the Old Post Office Pavilion (though not at half-price; see. p.310). The various museums of the **Smithsonian Institution** (☎357-2700) put on jazz and folk events throughout the year, often free and sometimes open-air.

For smaller **gigs** check the music-club schedules, where ticket prices run from $5 to $20. Several of the places listed below are also bars or dance clubs, and are reviewed separately in the previous chapter. We've also listed restaurants where you can catch live bands. Take **ID** with you wherever you go: in many

clubs you have to be 21 to get in, and in those where the age limit is 18, under-21s still won't be able to drink alcohol.

Rock and pop

Asylum in Exile, 1210 U St NW ☎319-9353. U St-Cardozo Metro. U Street grunge and alternative club with live local and national bands several times a week.

The Ballroom, 1015 Half St SE ☎554-1500. Navy Yard Metro. Cutting-edge indie and techno bands, and special club nights, attract a very young, hip crowd to this large warehouse-club. Take a cab home.

The Black Cat, 1831 14th St NW ☎667-7960. U St-Cardozo Metro. Showcase for new bands and veteran alternative acts, with a good mix of music.

Galaxy Hut, 2711 Wilson Blvd, Arlington, VA ☎525-8646. Clarendon Metro. Regular line-up of local talent.

IOTA, 2832 Wilson Blvd, Arlington, VA ☎522-8340. Clarendon Metro. Warehouse-style music club with nightly performances by local and national indie,

---

Live Music in Restaurants and Bars

The following restaurants and bars all feature regular live musicians, from jazz to R&B; there's usually no charge over the price of the meal or drink. See the individual reviews for details of the places themselves.

Afterwords Café (jazz/blues), Dupont Circle, p.284.

BET on Jazz (jazz), Old Downtown, p.293.

Bukom Café (African), Adams-Morgan, p.287.

Café des Artistes at the Corcoran (gospel), Foggy Bottom, p.285.

Café Lautrec (jazz), Adams-Morgan, p.299.

Chief Ike's Mambo Room (R&B/Latin), Adams-Morgan, p.299.

Coco Loco (jazz/Brazilian), Old Downtown, p.291.

Fasika's (African), Adams-Morgan, p.287.

Kinkead's (jazz), Foggy Bottom, p.295.

Lulu's New Orleans Café (jazz), New Downtown, p.301.

Mr Henry's (jazz), Capitol Hill, p.290.

Mr Smith's (R&B), Georgetown, p.304.

Music City Roadhouse (R&B/gospel), Georgetown, p.304.

Old Glory (R&B), Georgetown, p.296.

Utopia (jazz/blues/Brazilian), Shaw, p.305.

folk and blues bands, a great bar and attached restaurant.

Madam's Organ, 2461 18th St NW ☎667-5370. Woodley Park-Zoo Metro. Unsophisticated Adams-Morgan hangout featuring live, raw R&B, blues and funk; usually no cover.

Metro Café, 1422 14th St NW ☎518-7900. Dupont Circle Metro. Friendly little East Dupont rock club with a good mix of touring and local bands. It's an iffy area; take care at night on your way back to the Circle.

New Vegas Lounge, 1415 P St NW ☎483-3971. Dupont Circle Metro. Raunchy Chicago R&B Tues-Sat. Weekends are best for a night out (when there's a cover charge); good jam sessions Tues-Thurs.

9:30 Club, 815 V St NW ☎393-0930. U St-Cardozo Metro. Famous DC venue for indie rock and pop, local, national and foreign. Separate no-cover bar, too. Book in advance for well-known names. It's not in a great part of town – getting there by Metro is OK (two blocks from the Metro; use Vermont Ave exit), but take a cab home.

Jazz, blues and C&W

Birchmere, 3701 Mount Vernon Ave, Alexandria, VA ☎703/549-7500. Longstanding country, blues and folk club with an A-list of current and retro acoustic performers; nightly gigs.

Blues Alley, 1073 Rear Wisconsin Ave NW ☎337-4141. Small, celebrated Georgetown jazz bar, in business for over thirty years, attracting top names. Shows usually at 8pm and 10pm, plus midnight some weekends; cover can run to $40. Book in advance.

Capital City Blues, 2651 Connecticut Ave NW ☎232-2300. Woodley Park-Zoo Metro. Live jazz or blues almost every night in a mural-decorated townhouse. Small cover Thurs-Sat.

Columbia Station, 2325 18th St NW ☎462-6040. Live jazz and blues nightly in a sophisticated Adams-Morgan supper-club setting.

Cowboy Café, 2421 Columbia Pike, Arlington, VA ☎703/486-3467. The region's favorite for C&W, rockabilly and cowboy blues; no cover.

Fort Dupont Summer Theater, Minnesota Ave SE ☎426-7723. Free outdoor jazz on Fri and Sat nights June–Aug under the aegis of the National Park Service, featuring top national and international acts.

The Nest, *Willard Inter-Continental*, 1401 Pennsylvania Ave NW ☎637-7319. Metro Center Metro. Renowned hotel jazz bar attracting quality names, though $10–20 cover and two-drink minimum makes it a pricey night out.

One Step Down, 2517 Pennsylvania Ave NW ☎955-7141. Foggy Bottom-GWU Metro. Intimate neighborhood jazz bar, with live acts most nights and a fine jazz jukebox.

The Saloun, 3239 M St NW ☎965-4900. Cozy Georgetown bar with nightly jazz trios or bands, and 75 bottled beers. Free Mon and before 8pm, otherwise small cover charge.

State of the Union, 1357 U St NW ☎588-8810. U St-Cardozo Metro. Funky bar with progressive and acid jazz bands, and jazz poetry, two or three nights a week.

Takoma Station Tavern, 6914 4th St NW ☎829-1999. Takoma Metro. Laid-back club with jazz Mon-Sat, featuring mostly local acts, decent food, and no cover.

Live Music

Acoustic, Irish and Folk

There are regular Irish, acoustic and folk sessions in the following bars.
The Dubliner, Union Station, p.305.
Food for Thought, Dupont Circle, p.294.
IOTA, Arlington, p.308.
Ireland's Four Courts, Arlington, p.300.
Ireland's Four Provinces, Cleveland Park, p.306.
Irish Times, Union Station, p.305.
Nanny O'Brien's, Cleveland Park, p.306.
Polly's Café, Shaw, p.304.

Chapter 16

The Arts and Entertainment

Many of Washington's annual festivals (see Chapter 18) incorporate arts and music events.

Washington may come a cultural second-best to New York, and a fairly distant one at that, but there's still plenty of choice if you want to take in a play or comedy show, see a movie or attend a concert or recital. The prime mover in cultural and artistic matters is the **John F. Kennedy Center for the Performing Arts**

– hereafter known as the Kennedy Center – encompassing Concert Hall, Opera House, three theaters and the American Film Institute. It's home to the National Symphony Orchestra and stages seasonal productions by the city's top opera and ballet companies, and also has a full program of visiting national

Ticket Agencies

Protix ☎703/218-6500 or 1-800/955-5566. Full-price tickets for performing arts, music and sports events, by phone or at Olsson's Books and Records outlets.

TicketMaster ☎432-7328 or 1-800/551-7328. Full-price tickets for performing arts, music and sports events, by phone or at Tower Records and Hecht's department stores.

TicketPlace, Old Post Office Pavilion, 1100 Pennsylvania Ave NW ☎842-5387; *www. cultural-alliance.org/tickets*. On-the-day (Sun and Mon tickets sold on Sat), **half-price**, cash-only tickets (plus 10 percent surcharge) for theater and music; credit-card bookings for full-price advance tickets. Tues–Sat 11am–6pm.

Important box office/information numbers

American Folklife Center ☎707-6590

Arena Stage ☎488-3300

DAR Constitution Hall ☎628-4780

Kennedy Center ☎467-4600

Lisner Auditorium ☎994-6800

National Theater ☎628-6161

Shakespeare Theater ☎547-1122

Smithsonian Institution ☎357-2700

Warner Theater ☎628-1818

Washington Ballet ☎362-3606

Washington Opera ☎295-2420 or 1-800/876-7372

Wolf Trap Farm ☎703/255-1860 (Filene Center); ☎703/938-2404 (Barns)

Washington Performing Arts Society ☎833-9800

and international artists, companies and ensembles. The other main promoter is the **Washington Performing Arts Society** (WPAS), which sponsors music, ballet and dance productions across the city.

The city also boasts a whole host of **smaller theaters and venues** dedicated to contemporary, experimental, ethnic or left-field productions, where ticket prices (and availability) tend to be more realistic. There's also plenty that you can **see for free**: the **Smithsonian Institution**, in particular, has a year-round program of events and concerts, while the Library of Congress's **American Folklife Center** hosts monthly dance and music performances (May–Oct) in front of the library's Jefferson Building.

To find out **what's on**, consult the Friday edition of the *Washington Post* or the free weekly *CityPaper*. The Washington DC CVA (see p.17) publishes a quarterly *Calendar of Events*.

Tickets

Obviously, ticket prices vary considerably according to the event or production. You can expect to shell out a lot for the high-profile events at the Kennedy Center, National Theater, Arena Stage and the like, and in the case of major opera and ballet productions tickets at any price will be hard to come by unless you book well in advance. But many places, the Kennedy Center included, offer half- or cut-price tickets on the day if there's space. In all instances it's worth a call to the box office: students (with ID), senior citizens, military personnel and people with disabilities qualify for discounts in most theaters and concert halls.

You can also buy many tickets over the phone from various **ticket agencies**, which on the whole sell advance-reserved, full-price tickets (plus surcharge). Usually no changes or refunds are available.

Cinema

The **movie houses** listed below should cover every eventuality; the Cineplex Odeons are the city's main commercial screens, though the Union Station movie house often proves to be the handiest for visitors. The huge stadium-seated megaplexes are all firmly out in the Virginia and Maryland suburbs and inaccessible without your own transportation. Admission everywhere runs around $7–8, with many matinees coming in a couple of dollars cheaper – cheapest of all are the bargain daily rates at Georgetown's Odeon Foundry. Check **listings** in *CityPaper* or the *Washington Post*, which also detail the free films on show in some of the city's **museums and galleries**. Don't forget the IMAX screen at the National Air and Space Museum (see p.78), especially if you've got kids to entertain.

AMC Union Station 9, 50 Massachusetts Ave NE ☎703/998-4262. Union Station Metro. Mainstream nine-screen complex inside Union Station.

American Film Institute, Kennedy Center, 2700 F St NW ☎785-4600. Foggy Bottom-GWU Metro. America's national film theater, showing two to four movies a day in rep: classic, contemporary, national and foreign, often with associated lectures and seminars.

Arlington Cinema 'n Drafthouse, 2903 Columbia Pike, Arlington, VA ☎703/486-2345. Popular suburban venue for cheap movies, great beers and food. You'll need transportation – it's a quarter-mile east of Glebe Rd.

Bethesda Theater Cafe, 7719 Wisconsin Ave NW ☎301/656-3337. Bethesda Metro. Great retro cinema in suburban Maryland serving food and drink at tables while the movie is screened; minimum age 21.

Borders Books & Music, 1801 K St NW ☎466-4999. Farragut North Metro. Independent/avant-garde films and speakers, last Thurs of every month.

Cineplex Odeon. Screenings of mainstream movies. Branches include Dupont Circle (1350 19th St NW), Dupont Circle Janus (1660 Connecticut Ave NW); Georgetown Foundry (M St at Thomas Jefferson St NW); West End (2301 M St NW); Outer Circle (4849 Wisconsin Ave

The Arts and Entertainment

All telephone numbers in this chapter are area code ☎202, unless otherwise stated.

Washington's annual Filmfest DC (April) premieres national and international movies in theaters across the city.

The Arts and
Entertainment

NW, Tenleytown); and Uptown (3426
Connecticut Ave NW) – this last an Art
Deco classic with massive screen and
balcony. For times, reviews and information, call ☎333-3456.

Mary Pickford Theater, Madison
Building, Library of Congress, 1st St and
Independence Ave SE ☎707-5677.
Capitol South Metro. Free classic and for-
eign historic movies from the library's
archives.

Classical music

The Kennedy Center's Concert Hall is the
most prestigious in town for classical
music; it's also the home of the **National
Symphony Orchestra**, tickets to whose
concerts run from $25 to $50 (though the
orchestra also performs free outside the
US Capitol on the West Terrace on
Memorial Day, 4 July and Labor Day). As
well as regular concerts at the venues listed below, check newspaper listings for
events in museums (particularly the
National Gallery of Art and the Corcoran
Gallery of Art), historic houses (like

Dumbarton House), churches (including
the National Cathedral, see p.235) and
embassies. For details of the **Smithsonian
Institution** concerts, call ☎357-2700.

Coolidge Auditorium, Madison Building,
Library of Congress, 1st St and
Independence Ave SE ☎707-5502.
Capitol South Metro. Chamber music
concerts.

DAR Constitution Hall, 1776 D St NW
☎628-4780. Farragut West Metro. Large
(4250-seat) auditorium for major concerts and recitals.

Folger Shakespeare Library, 201 E
Capitol St SE ☎544-7077. Capitol South
Metro. Medieval and Renaissance music
from the Folger Consort ensemble.
Oct–May season.

John Phillips Sousa Band Hall, Marine
Barracks, 8th and I St SE ☎433-4011.
Navy Yard Metro. Free fall and winter
chamber recitals by the marine band
ensemble, and other occasional concerts.

Kennedy Center, 2700 F St NW, at
Virginia and New Hampshire aves

Open-air Concerts

Summer is a good time to catch a free open-air concert in Washington, though certain locations host events all year round – check the following places and see DC's
festival calendar (p.322) for more.

C&O Canal, Georgetown . Varied
Sunday-afternoon summer concerts,
between 30th and Thomas Jefferson St.

Freedom Plaza, Pennsylvania Ave NW.
Year-round venue for folk events and
music festivals.

National Zoological Park,
Connecticut Ave NW. "Sunset sere-
nades" in July, featuring a variety of
musical performances.

Neptune Plaza, Jefferson Building,
Library of Congress, 1st St and
Independence Ave SE. Monthly folk
singing and dancing May–Oct.

Netherlands Carillon, Marine Corps
(Iwo Jima) War Memorial, Arlington, VA.
Carillon concerts every Sat and on
national holidays May–Sept.

Sylvan Theater, Washington
Monument Grounds, the Mall. Army, air
force, navy and marine corps bands perform four nights a week June–Aug
(including annual *1812 Overture* performance in Aug). Other musical events
throughout the year, too.

US Capitol. Armed forces bands four
nights a week (June–Aug) on the East
Terrace; National Symphony Orchestra
on the West Terrace on Memorial Day,
July 4 and Labor Day.

US Navy Memorial, 701 Pennsylvania
Ave NW. Spring and summer concert
series featuring navy, marine corps,
coastguard and high-school bands.
Regular performances June–Aug Tues
8pm.

☎467-4600. Foggy Bottom-GWU Metro. The National Symphony Orchestra performs in the 2800-seat Concert Hall (Sept–June); there are cheaper chamber recitals in the Terrace Theater, and free concerts in the Grand Foyer.

Lisner Auditorium, George Washington University, 730 21st St NW ☎994-6800. Foggy Bottom-GWU Metro. Regular classical and choral concerts, occasionally free.

National Academy of Sciences, 2101 Constitution Ave NW ☎334-2436. Foggy Bottom-GWU Metro. Pleasing 700-seat auditorium with free chamber recitals by various groups, including the Marine Chamber Orchestra.

National Gallery of Art, West Building, West Garden Court, Constitution Ave NW ☎842-6941. Archives-Navy Memorial Metro. Free concerts every Sun at 7pm (Oct–June) in the lovely surroundings of the west garden court; first-come-first-served basis, doors open at 6pm.

The Phillips Collection, 1600 21st St NW ☎387-2151. Dupont Circle Metro. Classical music concerts in the museum's Music Room (Sept–May Sun 5pm,); free with museum admission (see p.218).

Society of the Cincinnati at Anderson House, 2118 Massachusetts Ave NW ☎785-2040. Dupont Circle Metro. Free chamber recitals once or twice a week in fine mansion surroundings (see p.217).

Comedy and cabaret

A couple of central clubs offer the usual mix of big-name **stand-up comedy** acts, **improv**, local/regional circuit appearances and **open-mike** nights. These apart, there are stand-up nights at spots as diverse as Adams-Morgan bars like *Madame's Organ* and *Chief Ike's*, or the Arena Stage and the Kennedy Center; local listings papers have all the latest details. Keep an eye out, too, for comedy troupes which appear in **cabaret** or improv shows at various venues around town, including major hotels like the

Four Seasons, the *Mayflower* and the *Washington Hilton*. Capitol Steps is the best known (and most permanent), but there are also regular shows by ensemble groups like ComedySportz and Gross National Product. Cabaret performances can be expensive, since there's often a drinks-and-food minimum charge on top of the **ticket** price: to see Capitol Steps or a big weekend show can cost as much as $40, though tickets for basic stand-up and improv nights are more like $10–15. **Advance reservations** are essential.

Capitol Steps, *Chelsea's*, 1055 Thomas Jefferson St NW ☎298-8222. Well-established political satire by a group of Capitol Hill staffers. Popular but expensive performances at this Georgetown club (Fri & Sat) and occasionally at other venues.

Improv, 1140 Connecticut Ave NW ☎296-7008. Farragut North Metro. DC's main comedy showcase mixing big names with local and regional acts and open-mike nights.

Dance, ballet and opera

Ballet and **opera** performances are fairly limited in DC, though what there is − provided principally by Washington Ballet and Washington Opera − is of the highest quality. There's more scope to see modern and **contemporary dance**, either at the Kennedy Center, the other main theaters or at a specialist venue like The Dance Place.

The Dance Place, 3225 8th St NE ☎269-1600. Brookland-CUA Metro. Contemporary and modern dance productions, mainstream and experimental. Hosts the Dance Africa festival every June.

Summer Opera Theater Company, Hartke Theater, Catholic University, Michigan Ave and 4th St NE ☎526-1669. Brookland-CUA Metro. Independent company staging two operas each summer, usually July and Aug.

Washington Ballet ☎362-3606 or 467-4600. Classical and contemporary ballet

The Arts and Entertainment

Longest-running show in town is Shear Madness at the Theater Lab in the Kennedy Center, a comedy-crime caper with audience participation; call the Kennedy Center for ticket details.

The Arts and Entertainment

The Kennedy Center Annual Open House (early Sept) offers free concerts, drama and film for all-comers.

performed in rep by the city's major ballet company at the Kennedy Center. Every Dec *The Nutcracker* is performed at the Warner Theater. Tickets $30–45.

Washington Opera ☎295-2420 or 1-800/876-7372. Tickets for one of the country's finest resident opera companies (artistic director: Placido Domingo) sell out well in advance, though you may get standing-room at the box office. Nov–March season; performances are in the Opera House and the other Kennedy Center theaters.

Theater and the performing arts

Most **Broadway productions** either preview or tour in Washington; the city also has an enclave of **alternative venues** in the Shaw (14th St NW) district, where relatively low ticket prices reward the adventurous. Come, or at least leave, by taxi, since the area isn't the most salubrious in town.

African Continuum Theater Company ☎529-5763. Coalition of black theater companies in DC, providing original theatrical productions for African-American audiences. Call for schedules and venues.

Arena Stage, 6th St and Maine Ave SW ☎488-3300. Waterfront Metro. The most respected theatrical institution in the city, with three stages (Arena Stage, Kreeger Theater and Old Vat Room) showing contemporary plays and performance pieces, classics, musicals, comedies and experimental works.

Discovery Theater, Arts and Industries Building, 900 Jefferson Drive SW ☎357-1500. Smithsonian Metro. Year-round, day-time children's theater, musicals and puppet shows at budget prices.

DC Arts Center, 2438 18th St NW ☎462-7833. Woodley Park-Zoo Metro. Performance art, drama, poetry, dance and a whole range of multicultural activities in northern Adams-Morgan; low prices.

Folger Shakespeare Library, 201 E Capitol St SE ☎544-7077. Capitol South

Metro. Full program at the Elizabethan library-theater (Sept–June), not solely Shakespeare.

Ford's Theater, 511 10th St NW ☎347-4833. Metro Center Metro. Site of Lincoln's assassination (see p.204), this restored nineteenth-century theater shows mainstream musicals and dramas.

Gala Hispanic Theater, 1625 Park Rd NW ☎234-7174. Specializes in works by Spanish/Latin American playwrights, performed in Spanish or English, as well as performance art and poetry.

Kennedy Center, 2700 F St NW, at Virginia and New Hampshire Ave ☎467-4600. Foggy Bottom-GWU Metro. Site of the Eisenhower (drama and Broadway productions), the Terrace (experimental/contemporary works) and the Theater Lab (almost permanently home to the long-running *Shear Madness*, a comedy-whodunnit). The Opera House also puts on musicals.

Lincoln Theater, 1215 U St NW ☎328-6000. U St-Cardozo Metro. Renovated movie/vaudeville house hosting touring stage shows, concerts and dance.

National Theater, 1321 Pennsylvania Ave NW ☎628-6161. Metro Center Metro. One of the country's oldest theaters, on this site (if not this building) since 1835. Premieres, pre- and post-Broadway productions and musicals.

Shakespeare Theater, *The Lansburgh*, 450 7th St NW ☎547-1122. Archives-Navy Memorial Metro. Four (often star-studded) plays a year by Shakespeare and his contemporaries. Each June the company puts on free, outdoor Shakespeare at the Carter Barron Amphitheater in Rock Creek Park (see p.307).

Source Theater, 1835 14th St NW ☎462-1073. U St-Cardozo Metro. New and contemporary works and classic re-interpretations. Promotes the Washington Theater Festival, a showcase for new works, every summer.

Studio Theater, 1333 P St NW ☎332-3300. Dupont Circle Metro. Independent

Wolf Trap Farm Park

Wolf Trap Farm Park (1551 Trap Rd, Vienna, VA), about forty minutes' drive from downtown DC, is the country's first national park for the performing arts. Set in 130 acres, the **Filene Center** (☎ 703/255-1860) stages jazz, pop and C&W concerts from June to September with indoor and outdoor seating for seven thousand people; there's also opera, ballet and dance. The **Theatre-in-the-Woods** (☎ 703/255-1827) puts on free performing arts for children during July and August, while the rest of the year the action switches to the indoor **Barns at Wolf Trap** (☎ 703/938-2404), a 350-seat concert hall hosting jazz, blues, folk, world music and zydeco.

The park is outside the Beltway, between Rte 7 and Rte 267 (Dulles Toll Road). For directions on how to get there by public transportation, call ☎ 703/255-1860 – there's a Metro shuttle bus service for most performances. Call the **box office** numbers for details about the program and tickets, which you can buy over the phone. There are concession stands and a restaurant, but it's nicer to bring a **picnic** in summer – you can eat on the grass. **Parking** is free.

The Arts and
Entertainment

theater with two stages presenting classic and contemporary drama and comedy.

Warner Theater, 1299 Pennsylvania Ave NW ☎ 628-1818. Metro Center Metro. Erstwhile movie palace now staging post-Broadway productions and big concerts.

Washington Stage Guild, Carroll Hall, 924 G St NW ☎ 529-2084. Metro Center Metro. Classics and contemporary productions.

Woolly Mammoth Theater, 1401 Church St NW ☎ 393-3939. Dupont Circle Metro. Budget-ticket productions of contemporary, experimental and plain off-the-wall plays.

Visual arts

Quite apart from the public art galleries and museums, DC has a massive range of **commerical art galleries** which often host changing exhibitions (usually free) of paintings, prints, sculpture, photography, applied art and folk art. The galleries listed below are some of the more reliable; call for details of current shows or check *CityPaper* or the *Washington Post's* "Weekend" section. There's also a monthly guide available in bookstores with comprehensive listings of DC's art galleries called, appropriately enough, *Galleries*. The venues themselves are grouped in several distinct city areas: downtown, those along **7th Street NW** specialize in the works of contemporary

DC-area artists, though the major concentration of galleries is in **Dupont Circle** where over thirty congregate in a defined Gallery District (mainly **R Street** between 21st and 22nd). Most are **closed** on Monday and many on Tuesday.

Downtown

Arts Club of Washington, 2017 I St NW ☎ 331 7282. Changing exhibits from local artists.

406 7th St NW: grouping of galleries featuring DC-area artists in mixed-media shows, contemporary sculpture, painting and photography; including Artists' Museum ☎ 638-7001, Baumgartner Galleries ☎ 347-2211, Numark ☎ 628-3810, Touchstone ☎ 347-2787, and Washington Center for Photography ☎ 737-0406.

George Washington University: Colonnade Gallery, Marvin Center, 800 21st St NW ☎ 994-6555; and Dimock Gallery, Lower Lisner Auditorium, 730 21st St NW ☎ 994-1525. Regular changing shows by local, student, national and international artists.

Zenith Gallery, 413 7th St NW ☎ 783-2963. Mainly works by city-based artists.

Dupont Circle

Affrica, 2010 R St NW ☎ 745-7272. African masks, figurines, ceramics, textiles and jewelry.

The Arts and
Entertainment

Fondo del Sol Visual Arts Center, 2112 R St NW ☎483-2777. Pre-Columbian and other art of the Americas, plus lectures, poetry and performance art; also sponsors a summer outdoor Caribbean festival.

Kathleen Ewing Gallery, 1609 Connecticut Ave NW ☎328-0955. Nineteenth- and twentieth-century photography.

Marsha Mateyka Gallery, 2012 R St NW ☎328-0088. Contemporary painting and sculpture.

Tartt Gallery, 2017 Q St NW ☎332-5652. Nineteenth- and twentieth-century photography, plus American folk art.

Troyer Fitzpatrick Lassman Gallery, 1710 Connecticut Ave NW ☎328-7189. Contemporary photography, paintings and sculpture.

Venable Neslage Galleries, 1803 Connecticut Ave NW ☎462-1800. One of the longest-established galleries, showing contemporary impressionist and realist works, and modern sculpture.

Washington Printmakers' Gallery, 2106 R St NW ☎332-7757. Original prints by contemporary artists.

Georgetown

Addison/Ripley Gallery, 1670 Wisconsin Ave NW ☎333-3335. Contemporary fine art.

Atlantic Gallery, The Foundry Building, 1055 Thomas Jefferson St NW ☎337-2299. Traditional paintings and prints of landscapes, hunting scenes and seascapes.

Fine Art & Artists, 2920 M St NW ☎965-0780. Pop and contemporary art.

Spectrum Gallery, 1132 29th St NW ☎333-0954. Local artists' co-op with regular exhibitions.

Chapter 17

Shopping

No one comes to DC to shop, but the city's arty neighborhood stores, fine range of bookstores and incomparable museum and gallery shops – not to mention the profusion of White House, Capitol, Supreme Court and FBI mugs, key-rings, baseball hats, posters and buttons – means no one need go home empty-handed.

The nicest areas for **browsing** are Dupont Circle, Georgetown and around Eastern Market, where art and craft shops coexist with specialist book and music stores and student-oriented clothes-and-accessories hangouts. Adams-Morgan has more ethnic soul, and some good shops to match. Further out in Upper Northwest, the small liberal enclave of Takoma Park also has a range of ethnic design and funky clothes stores along Carroll Avenue.

The shopping heart has been ripped out of downtown, however, as all the major **department stores**, with the honorable exception of Hecht's, have given up the ghost. This may change over the next few years – development plans for the revitalized downtown area around the MCI Center include new retail units – but for the forseeable future you're best off at one of the **mega-malls** on the outskirts of the city for clothing and most other day-to-day items.

Usual store **opening hours** are Monday to Saturday 10am to 7pm; some have extended Thursday night hours. In Georgetown, Adams-Morgan and Dupont Circle many stores open on Sunday too (usually noon–5pm).

Arts, crafts and antiques

The only indigenous local craft is politics, but specialist stores in DC let you take home a piece of the Southwest or American Victoriana if you so wish. Richest pickings are in Dupont Circle, Georgetown (which also has a run of big-ticket antique shops), and Old Town Alexandria, this last positively dripping with antique/bric-a-brac places aimed at the weekend visitor market. For works of art, visit the galleries of Dupont Circle and those downtown in 7th Street – see p.315.

African Eye, 2134 Wisconsin Ave NW, Georgetown ☎625-2552. African-American clothing, crafts, jewelry and textiles.

American Hand, 2906 M St NW, Georgetown ☎965-3273. Decorative hand-crafted ceramics from American artists.

Appalachian Spring, 1415 Wisconsin Ave NW, Georgetown ☎337-5780; Union Station, 50 Massachusetts Ave NE ☎682-0505. Handmade ceramics, jewelry, rugs, glassware, kitchenware, quilts and toys.

Art & Soul, 225 Pennsylvania Ave SE, Capitol Hill ☎548-0105. Handmade clothes and contemporary American ceramics, toys, and crafts by over 200 regional artists.

For Alexandria shopping, stop in first at the Ramsay House Visitor Center (p.260), which has reams of shopping guides, flyers and information.

Shopping

Beadazzled, 1507 Connecticut Ave NW, Dupont Circle ☎265-2323. Antique and new beads from all over the world, plus ethnic jewelry, folk art and related books.

Indian Craft Shop, Department of the Interior, Room 1023, 1849 C St NW, Foggy Bottom ☎208-4056. Quality Native American arts and crafts – Navajo rugs, Hopi jewelry and assorted ceramics. The shop is inside the department; see p.167.

The Old Print Gallery, 1220 31st NW, Georgetown ☎965-1818. Old maps, charts and prints, plus political cartoons, DC scenes and American landscapes.

Bookstores

Washington's bookstores are one of its high points: you'll find a place to suit whether you want discounted new novels or political science books, flagship superstores with coffee bars or cozy local secondhand shops. The weekly *CityPaper* and Friday's *Washington Post* list all bookshop lectures, concerts, readings and events.

General

Barnes & Noble, 3040 M St NW, Georgetown ☎965-9880. Quality chain bookstore on three floors – heavy discounts, one of the best crime/mystery sections in the city, and *Starbuck's* coffee.

Borders Books & Music, 1801 K St NW, New Downtown ☎466-4999. Huge bookstore (entrance on L St) with good selection of magazines, newspapers and discount books, full CD and tape selection, readings, gigs, events and an espresso bar.

Chapters, 1512 K St NW, New Downtown ☎347-5495. Downtown bookstore with a quality range and supporting program of readings and events.

Crown Books, 11 Dupont Circle NW ☎319-1374; 3131 M St NW, Georgetown ☎333-4493; 1275 K St NW, Old Downtown ☎289-7170; 1133 19th St NW, New Downtown ☎659-4172; 1710 G St NW, Foggy Bottom ☎789-

2277; and others. Local chain with substantial discounts on new books. The Dupont Circle branch is the largest.

Kramerbooks, 1517 Connecticut Ave NW, Dupont Circle ☎387-1462. City institution with a good general selection, a great café-restaurant and long opening hours (around-the-clock on the weekend). It's where Monica Lewinsky bought the Pres a copy of Nicholson Baker's *Vox*, hence the store T-shirts ("Subpoenaed for Book Selling").

Olsson's Books and Records, 1239 Wisconsin Ave NW, Georgetown ☎338-6712; 1307 19th St NW, Dupont Circle ☎785-2662; 1200 F St NW, Old Downtown ☎393-1853; 418 7th St NW, Old Downtown ☎638-7613. Massive range in one of the city's nicest places to browse; regular book signings, plus tapes and CDs; there's a café in the 7th St branch.

Politics & Prose, 5015 Connecticut Ave NW, Tenleytown ☎364-1919. Good independent bookstore/coffee shop, plus one of the best programs of author appearances and readings in the city.

Secondhand

Atticus Books, 1508 U St NW, Shaw ☎667-8148. Good used bookstore (with records and CDs), a couple of blocks from U St-Cardozo Metro.

Bryn Mawr Lantern Bookshop, 3160 O St NW, Georgetown ☎333-3222. Great general selection of secondhand books, though only open four or five hours a day.

Idle Time Books, 2410 18th St NW, Adams-Morgan ☎232-4774. Large, late-opening used bookstore with lots of bargains.

Kulturas Books & Records, 1741 Connecticut Ave NW, Dupont Circle ☎462-2541. Not so much a secondhand bookstore as a yard sale: books, records and arty bits-and-bobs.

Logic and Literature, 1223 31st St NW, Georgetown ☎338-8272. Used bookstore with a bent toward the classics, philosophy, science and history.

Food and Drink

Washington isn't exactly known for the quality of its delis, though a few places stand out. Good **coffee**, at least, isn't hard to find – any of the coffee bars listed in Chapter 13 can sell you the beans.

Old-style **markets** are thin on the ground: **Eastern Market** is your best bet (p.131), while the Waterfront **Fish Wharf** (p.141) has a great selection of Chesapeake Bay seafood. There are weekend **farmer's markets** in Adams-Morgan (p.224), Alexandria (p.262), Dupont Circle, Takoma Park and at Arlington Court House.

For bread, you can't beat the **Breadline** (p.285) or **Firehook** bakery/coffee shops (p.285). Best general deli is the splendid **Dean & Deluca** (p.285) in Georgetown. Southwest fanciers should call at the **Red Sage** restaurant's shop (p.293).

Shopping

Second Story Books, 2000 P St NW, Dupont Circle ☎659-8884. Large range of used books and records; a useful spot to find out what's on in the city.

Specialist

Bridge Street Books, 2814 Pennsylvania Ave NW, Georgetown ☎965-5200. Politics, literature, history, philosophy and film.

Lambda Rising, 1625 Connecticut Ave NW, Dupont Circle ☎462-6969. Extensively stocked gay and lesbian bookstore.

Lammas, 1507 17th St NW, Dupont Circle ☎775-8218. Feminist and lesbian bookstore.

The Map Store, 1636 I St NW, New Downtown ☎628-2608. Maps, atlases and travel guides.

Mystery Books, 1715 Connecticut Ave NW, Dupont Circle ☎483-1600. The city's specialist in detective, spy and crime fiction.

Reiter's, 2021 K St NW ☎223-3327. Scientific and professional books – business and computing to finance and engineering.

Travel Books & Language Center, 4437 Wisconsin Ave NW, Tenleytown ☎237-1322. Travel bookstore, featuring guides, maps, atlases, software, international cookbooks, magazines, newspapers and a full program of events and lectures.

US Government Bookstore, 710 North Capitol St NW, Old Downtown ☎512-0132; 1510 H St NW, New Downtown

☎653-5075. All the official facts and figures you ever wanted from the government's own bookstores; open Mon–Fri only.

Vertigo Books, 1337 Connecticut Ave NW, Dupont Circle ☎429-9272. Washington, American and world politics, black and social studies and modern literature. Regular signings and readings.

Yawa, 2206 18th St NW, Adams-Morgan ☎483-6805. African and African-American books, magazines, crafts and cards.

Yes Bookstore, 1035 31st St NW, Georgetown ☎338-7874. Extensive New Age book and music store – Eastern religions and personal development to acupuncture and mythology.

Department stores

Flagship department stores – Neiman Marcus, Nordstrom, Saks Fifth Avenue, Lord & Taylor, Bloomingdale's and Macy's – are all firmly ensconced in the out-of-town malls (see p.320); the two listed below are the only major downtown survivors.

Filene's Basement, 1133 Connecticut Ave NW, New Downtown ☎872-8430; The Shops at National Place, 529 14th St NW, Old Downtown ☎638-2519. Famed Boston-based bargain fashion retailer with good deals on men's and women's clothing, shoes and accessories.

Hecht's, 1201 G St NW, Old Downtown ☎628-6661; and suburban locations. Classic downtown department store with

Shopping

Malls

Although **malls** are flourishing in revitalized downtown areas, they tend to be showy, tourist-oriented collections of gift shops, novelty stores and food courts. Head for the suburbs for the best malls (and, incidentally, slightly lower local sales taxes); there's direct Metro access to those at Friendship Heights, Crystal City and Pentagon City listed below. Opening hours are usually Monday–Saturday 10am–8pm, Sunday noon–6pm.

Downtown

Old Post Office Pavilion, 1100 Pennsylvania Ave NW ☎289-4224; Federal Triangle Metro.

The Shops at National Place, 1331 Pennsylvania Ave NW ☎783-9090; Metro Center Metro.

Union Station Mall, 50 Massachusetts Ave NE ☎371-9441; Union Station Metro.

Georgetown

Georgetown Park, 3222 M St NW ☎298-5577; Foggy Bottom-GWU Metro.

Out of town

Chevy Chase Pavilion, 5345 Wisconsin Ave NW ☎686-5335; Friendship Heights Metro.

Crystal City Shops, Crystal Drive, Arlington, VA ☎703/922-4636; Crystal City Metro.

Fashion Center at Pentagon City, 1100 S Hayes St, Arlington VA ☎703/415-2400; Pentagon City Metro.

Mazza Gallerie, 5300 Wisconsin Ave NW ☎966-6114; Friendship Heights Metro.

Potomac Mills Outlet Mall, 2700 Potomac Mills Circle, Prince William, VA ☎1-800/826-4557; Wed–Sun shuttle from Metro Center, Rosslyn and Pentagon City Metros.

Tysons Galleria, 2001 International Drive, McLean, VA ☎703/827-7700; Capital Beltway exit 11B.

White Flint Mall, 11301 Rockville Pike, Bethesda, MD ☎301/231-7467; shuttle from White Flint Metro.

---

a full range of clothing and home furnishings. The store is a century old, though this stylish building was put up in 1985.

Miscellaneous

Another Universe, 3060 M St, Georgetown ☎333-8651. Sci-fi specialist for games, comics, cards, toys and posters.

Capital Coin and Stamp Company, 1701 L St NW, New Downtown ☎296-0400. Not only rare stamps and coins, but also political campaign buttons, vintage posters, stickers and memorabilia.

Commander Salamander, 1420 Wisconsin Ave NW, Georgetown ☎337-2265. Funky T-shirts, sneakers, sportswear, bags, party gear and gimcrack jewelry – open late.

Discovery Channel Destination Store, 601 F St NW ☎783-5751. Gifts you never knew you wanted, from African art and flying jackets to spaceship models, teapots, games, jewelry and books.

FAO Schwarz, Georgetown Park, 3222 M St NW, Georgetown ☎342-2285. Major toy store with massive stock, modern and traditional, dolls to video games.

Ginza, 1721 Connecticut Ave NW, Dupont Circle ☎331-7991. All things Japanese – chopsticks to clothes.

Khismet, 1800 Belmont Rd NW, Adams-Morgan ☎234-7778. "Wearable art" – meaning hand-crafted jewelry, textiles and clothes.

Movie Madness, 1083 Thomas Jefferson St NW, Georgetown ☎337-7064. Thousands of movie posters, old and new.

Political Americana, Union Station, 50 Massachusetts Ave NE ☎547-1685; 685 15th St NW, Old Downtown ☎547-1871. Everything from historic and topical buttons and bumper stickers to gifts, books and videos on every side of the political divide.

Red River, 641 Pennsylvania Ave SE, Capitol Hill ☎546-5566. DC's only Western-wear store – boots and stetsons to Native American jewelry and Southwestern clothing.

Runes & Relix, 2102 18th St NW, Adams-Morgan ☎265-4460. Retro furniture, vintage clothes and accessories.

Museum and gallery stores

Virtually all DC's museums – in particular the Smithsonians – have well-stocked shops. The list below picks out the best; see the relevant pages for transport and museum details. Note that every other major attraction – US Capitol to Pentagon – has its own store too, selling enough name-emblazoned souvenirs for even the junkiest of collectors.

Arthur M. Sackler Gallery, 1050 Independence Ave SW. Jewelry, prints, waistcoats, fabrics, Asian art, ceramics, rugs, beads and calligraphy.

B'nai B'rith Klutznick National Jewish Museum, 1640 Rhode Island Ave NW. Jewelry, goblets, ceramics, T-shirts, festival arts and crafts, linen and embroidered goods – all with Jewish motifs.

Bureau of Engraving and Printing, 14th and C St SW. Just the place for that presidential engraving, prints of Washington DC, copies of famous texts, and even bags of shredded cash.

National Air and Space Museum, Independence Ave and 7th SW. Fantastic array of air- and space-related goodies, books to ray-guns.

National Gallery of Art, Constitution Ave, between 3rd and 7th St NW. DC's best

art shop – thousands of books, prints, slides, posters and postcards.

National Museum of African Art, 950 Independence Ave SW. Splendid displays of African arts and crafts, including great fabrics and jewelry.

National Museum of American History, 14th St and Constitution Ave NW. The Smithsonian's biggest store is great for souvenirs. Everything about America – music, books, T-shirts, kitchenware, ceramics, posters, toys, crafts, jewelry and repro items from the museum.

Newseum, 1101 Wilson Blvd, Arlington, VA. One of the quirkier giftshops – "Trust Me I'm a Journalist" T-shirts, famous front-page repros, mugs and buttons, caps and newsprint waistcoats.

Textile Museum, 2320 S St NW. Unique T-shirts, ethnic fabrics, textile books, silks, cushion covers, ties, kimonos and jewelry.

Music stores

CD Warehouse, 3001 M St NW, Georgetown ☎625-7101. Good, across-the-board selection of used CDs.

DC CD, 2423 18th St NW, Adams-Morgan ☎588-1810. New and used CDs and vinyl, with late opening hours.

Flying Saucer Discs, 2318 18th St NW, Adams-Morgan ☎265-3427. Basement store with good range of used pop, rock, rap, jazz, world and classical CDs.

Kemp Mill Music, 12th and F St NW, Old Downtown ☎638-7077; 1900 L St NW, New Downtown ☎223-5310. Local chain for mainstream and chart releases, often with good discount offers.

Smash, 3279 M St NW, Georgetown ☎337-6274. Punk, hardcore, new wave and indie music, T-shirts, boots and clothes.

Tower Records, 2000 Pennsylvania Ave NW, Foggy Bottom ☎331-2400. Biggest music store in town, with in-store appearances. Daily until midnight.

Shopping

Check out the used records, tapes and CDs in Atticus Books, Kulturas Books & Records and Second Story Books. Borders Books & Music and Olsson's Books and Records sell new stuff. See "Bookstores" p.318 for locations.

Chapter 18

DC's Festival Calendar

All telephone area codes in this chapter are ☎202 unless otherwise stated.

The best of DC's major **festivals, parades and annual events** are listed below – for a comprehensive list contact the Washington DC Convention and Visitors Association (see p.17). Note that the dates of many festivals vary from year to year, while birthday celebrations for famous people generally take place on the nearest weekend; call the numbers given, check with one of the organizations listed below and watch the local press for exact dates.

Annual music festivals are detailed in chapters 15 ("Live Music") and 16 ("The Arts and Entertainment"); while **open days** at museums, galleries and attractions are covered in the relevant parts of the guide. For a list of **national public holidays**, see Basics, p.23.

January

Dr Martin Luther King Jr's Birthday (15th): wreath-laying at the Lincoln Memorial, reading of the "I have a dream" speech, concerts and speeches. ☎619-7222.

Robert E. Lee's Birthday (19th): celebrations, music and food at Arlington House in Arlington Cemetery; special events in Old Town Alexandria, VA. ☎703/548-1789.

February

Chinese New Year (date varies): dragon-dancers, parades and fireworks on H St NW in Chinatown. ☎724-4093.

Information Lines

National Park Service ☎619-7222
Post-Haste ☎334-9000
Smithsonian ☎357-2700
Washington DC CVA ☎789-7000
Washington DC Events Office ☎619-7222

For more details about these organizations see p.41.

African-American History Month (all month): special events, exhibits and cultural programs. Information from the Smithsonian, National Park Service or Martin Luther King Memorial Library.

Abraham Lincoln's Birthday (12th): wreath-laying and reading of the Gettysburg Address at the Lincoln Memorial. ☎619-7222.

Frederick Douglass' Birthday (14th): wreath-laying and other events at Cedar Hill, Anacostia. ☎619-7222.

George Washington's Birthday Parade (22nd): spectacular parade and events in Old Town Alexandria, VA. ☎703/838-9350. Also, events, concerts and wreath-laying at Mount Vernon. ☎703/780-2000.

March

St Patrick's Day (17th): big parades down Constitution Ave NW, as well as celebrations in Old Town Alexandria and at Arlington House, Arlington Cemetery,

VA. ☎637-2474 for grandstand seats on Constitution Ave. Also an Irish festival of arts, music and dance – ☎347-1450.

Smithsonian Kite Festival (end of the month): kite-flying competitions for all at the Washington Monument. ☎357-2700.

April

National Cherry Blossom Festival (early April): the famous trees around the Tidal Basin (see p.67) bloom in late March/early April; celebrated by a massive parade down Constitution Ave NW, crowning of the festival queen, free concerts, lantern-lighting, dances and races. Parade ticket information ☎728-1137; other events ☎547-1500.

Thomas Jefferson's Birthday (13th): wreath-laying and military drills at the Jefferson Memorial. ☎619-7222.

Blessing of the Fleet (mid-month): nautical celebrations and services at US Navy Memorial. Associated events at Southwest Waterfront marina. ☎737-2300.

Easter Sunrise Service (Easter Sun): sunrise memorial service at Arlington National Cemetery. ☎475-0856.

White House Easter Egg Roll (Easter Mon): entertainment and egg-rolling (eggs provided) on the White House South Lawn. Special garden tours on one weekend after Easter. Call well in advance. ☎456-2200.

Duke Ellington's Birthday (20th): music and events at Freedom Plaza, Pennsylvania Ave NW. ☎331-9404.

Smithsonian Craft Show (late April): craft exhibitions in the National Building Museum. ☎357-2700.

Marvin Gaye/Save the Children Day (end of the month): downtown street festival sponsored by the African-American Music Foundation. ☎678-0503.

May

Flower Mart (first weekend): flowers, booths, children's entertainment and displays at Washington National Cathedral. ☎537-6200.

Asian-Pacific American Heritage Festival (first weekend): cultural displays, food stalls and activities in Freedom Plaza, Pennsylvania Ave NW. ☎659-2311 or 703/354-5036.

Malcom X Day (mid-month): commemorative concerts, films and speeches in Anacostia Park. ☎724-4093.

Bob Marley Commemorative Day Festival (mid-month): reggae concerts and events at Freedom Plaza, Pennsylvania Ave NW. ☎724-9060.

Worldfest (date varies): two-day, outdoor array of ethnic music, food and events on Pennsylvania Ave between 9th and 14th streets. ☎724-5430.

Memorial Day (last Mon): wreath-layings, services and speeches at Arlington Cemetery ☎685-2851; Vietnam Veterans Memorial ☎619-7222; and US Navy Memorial ☎737-2300. The National Symphony Orchestra performs on the Capitol's West Lawn (on the Sun) and there's a jazz festival in Old Town Alexandria. ☎703/883-4686.

June

Philippine Independence Day Parade (3rd): Pennsylvania Ave parade and a fair on Freedom Plaza. ☎724-4093.

Dance Africa (mid-month): festival of African dance, open-air market and concerts at Dance Place, 3225 8th St NE. ☎269-1600.

Marvin Gaye Jr Appreciation Day (mid-month): street events and music on Pennsylvania Ave between 13th and 14th streets. ☎724-4093.

Smithsonian Festival of American Folklife (usually last week of June to first week of July): one of the country's biggest festivals: American music, crafts, food, and folk heritage events on the Mall. ☎357-2700.

July

National Independence Day Celebration (4th): reading of the Declaration of

DC's
Festival
Calendar

DC's Festival Calendar

Independence at National Archives, parade along Constitution Ave NW, free concerts at the Sylvan Theater near the Washington Monument, National Symphony Orchestra performance on west steps of the Capitol, finishing with superb firework display – get there as early as possible for all events. ☎619-7222.

Mary McLeod Bethune Celebration (date varies): wreath-laying, gospel choir and speakers at Bethune statue, Lincoln Park. ☎619-7222.

Caribbean Summer in the Park (mid-month): outdoor music, food and dancing, at RFK Stadium. ☎249-1028.

Hispanic-Latino Festival (end of the month): Constitution Ave parade; food, crafts, music, dance and theater in Adams-Morgan and Mount Pleasant. ☎835-1555 or 454-2464.

August

Arlington County Fair (mid-month): fair with rides, crafts, entertainment, food stalls and concerts at Thomas Jefferson Center, 3501 2nd St, Arlington, VA. ☎703/358-6400.

Georgia Avenue Day (end of the month): parade along Georgia Ave (at Eastern Ave NW), plus carnival rides, music, food and stalls. ☎723-5166.

September

Labor Day Weekend Concert (Sun before Labor Day): National Symphony Orchestra plays on west lawn of the Capitol to mark the end of the summer season. ☎619-7222.

Adams-Morgan Day (first Sun after Labor Day): one of the best of the neighborhood festivals, with live music, crafts and cuisine along 18th St NW – always packed and great fun. ☎332-3292.

Constitution Day Commemoration (17th): Constitution displayed at the National Archives to celebrate the anniversary of its signing; naturalization ceremonies, parade and concerts. ☎501-5215.

National Frisbee Festival (date varies): frisbee-related activities on the Mall, near the Air and Space Museum. ☎301/645-5043.

African Cultural Festival (date varies): ethnic music, dance, cuisine, arts and crafts at Freedom Plaza. ☎667-5775.

Black Family Reunion (date varies): weekend festival on the Mall celebrating the African-American family. ☎383-9104.

German-American Day (end of the month): Teutonic food and entertainment in Freedom Plaza. ☎554-2664.

October

Taste of DC (date varies): restaurant festival mixing tastings with arts and crafts, children's shows, and entertainment on Pennsylvania Ave NW. ☎724-5347.

Columbus Day Ceremonies (second Mon): wreath-laying, speeches and music at the Columbus Memorial in front of Union Station. ☎301/434-2332.

White House Fall Garden Tours (mid-month): garden tours and military band concerts. Call well in advance. ☎456-2200.

Halloween (31st): unoffical block parties, costumed goings-on and fright-nights in Georgetown, Dupont Circle and other middle-class neighborhoods.

November

Annual Seafaring Celebration (date varies): the Navy Museum hosts a family event with maritime activities, food, arts and children's performances. ☎433-4882.

Veteran's Day Ceremonies (11th): solemn services and wreath-laying at 11am at Arlington Cemetery – usually with the President in attendance – Vietnam Veterans Memorial, and US Navy Memorial.

December

Christmas Tree Lightings (beginning of the month): separate ceremonies for the lighting of the Capitol (west side) and National (Ellipse) Christmas trees – the latter lit by the President. The entire month on the Ellipse sees nativity scenes, choral groups, and other seasonal displays. ☎619-7222.

Washington National Cathedral Christmas Services (all month): carols, pageants, choral performances and bell-ringing. ☎537-6200.

Pearl Harbor Day (7th): wreath-laying ceremony at the US Navy Memorial to commemorate the attack on Pearl Harbor. ☎737-2300.

White House Candlelight Tours (usually 26th–28th): extremely popular evening White House tours. Call well in advance. ☎456-2200 or 619-7222.

DC's
Festival
Calendar

Chapter 19

Directory

AIRLINES Air Canada ☎1-800/776-3000; Air France ☎1-800/237-2747; Alitalia ☎1-800/223-5730; American Airlines ☎1-800/433-7300; America West ☎1-800/235-9292; British Airways ☎1-800/247-9297; Continental Airlines ☎1-800/225-0280; Delta ☎1-800/221-1212; Finnair ☎1-800/950-5000; Icelandair ☎1-800/223-5500; Japan Airlines ☎1-800/525-3663; KLM ☎1-800/374-7747; Korean Air ☎1-800/438-5000; Lufthansa ☎1-800/645-3880; Midwest Express ☎1-800/452-2022; Northwest ☎1-800/225-2525; SAS ☎1-800/221-2350; Southwest ☎1-800/435-9792; Swissair ☎1-800/221-4750; TWA ☎1-800/221-2000; United Airlines ☎1-800/241-6522; USAir ☎1-800/428-4322; Virgin Atlantic ☎1-800/862-8621.

BUS DEPARTURES Call Greyhound (☎1-800/231-2222; in DC ☎289-5155) or Peter Pan Trailways (☎1-800/343-9999); departures to Baltimore, Philadelphia, New York, Boston and beyond are from the terminal at 1005 1st St NE.

CITY TAXES DC sales tax is 5.75 percent; restaurant tax 10 percent; hotel tax 14.5 percent.

DOCTORS AND DENTISTS Lists of doctors can be found in the Yellow Pages under "Clinics" or "Physicians and Surgeons". Most large hotels either have a doctor on call or will direct you to a private doctor. For a doctor referral service call ☎362-8677, or contact your embassy (see below). The basic consultation fee is $50–100, payable in advance. Contact the DC Dental Society ☎547-7613 (Mon–Fri 8am–4pm) for dentist referral.

EMBASSIES AND CONSULATES Australia, 1601 Massachusetts Ave NW, 20036 ☎797-3000; Canada, 501 Pennsylvania Ave NW, 20001 ☎682-1740; Ireland, 2234 Massachusetts Ave NW, 20008 ☎462-3939; Netherlands, 4200 Linnean Ave NW, 20008 ☎244-5300; New Zealand, 37 Observatory Circle NW, 20008 ☎328-4800; United Kingdom, 3100 Massachusetts Ave NW, 20008 ☎462-1340.

GAY AND LESBIAN CONTACTS Gay and Lesbian Hotline ☎833-3234, a counseling and referral service; Gay Info and Assistance ☎363-3881; Gay Community Yellow Pages ☎1-800/849-0406. Also visit Lambda Rising, 1625 Connecticut Ave NW, Dupont Circle ☎462-6969, a gay/lesbian bookstore which acts as a clearinghouse for information and events. See p.301 for bar and club details.

HOSPITAL George Washington University Medical Center, 901 23rd St NW ☎994-1000 (general patient information) has a 24hr emergency department (☎994-3211) and travelers' clinic (☎994-5400).

> All telephone numbers are area code ☎202 unless otherwise stated.

Directory

LIBRARIES The general public can use the Library of Congress (see p.127 for details), while the main city library is the Martin Luther King Memorial Library, 901 G St NW (see p.203).

NEWSPAPERS AND MAGAZINES The relatively liberal *Washington Post* is DC's most respected daily newspaper, challenged in news coverage (though not style or balance) only by the conservative, Moonie-published *Washington Times*. Free weeklies include the investigative *CityPaper* – best in the city for news and listings – and the gay *Washington Blade*. Glossy monthlies include the late John F. Kennedy Jr's political mag *George* (whose future is uncertain), the art-and-leisure publications *Washingtonian* and *Where Washington*, plus other local/neighborhood papers and magazines available in bars, restaurants, shops and hotels. Papers from other US cities, as well as foreign newspapers and magazines, can be bought in Union Station and at Newsroom, 1753 Connecticut Ave NW, Dupont Circle ☎332-1489.

PHARMACIES *CVS* has forty different locations throughout DC, with convenient downtown and Georgetown sites and 24-hour stores at 1121 Vermont Ave NW (at Thomas Circle) ☎628-0720, and 7 Dupont Circle ☎785-1466. Foreign visitors should bear in mind that many pills available over the counter at home need a prescription in the US – most codeine-based painkillers, for example – and that local brand names can be confusing; ask if you're unsure.

POLICE In an emergency call ☎911. For non-emergency help, information and location of local stations call ☎727-1010. The Metro Transit Police are on ☎962-2121.

RADIO STATIONS Local AM stations include: WMAL (630) for news, sports and talk; WOL (1450) for African-American music and talk; WPWC (1480) for country and bluegrass; WTOP (1500) for news; and WPGC (1580) for gospel. Local FM stations include: WAMU (88.5)

for news, talk and music; WCSP (90.1) for Congress and public affairs coverage; WETA (90.9) for classical and news; WHFS (99.1) for rock; WGMS (103.5) for classical; WJFK (106.7) for talk (including Howard Stern and ex-Watergate player turned radio-host Gordon Liddy); WRQX (107.3) for 70s–90s pop and rock; and WTOP (107.7) for news.

SPORTS Washington Redskins play at the Jack Kent Cook Stadium, Raljon, MD ☎546-2222, but you'll never get a ticket unless you're prepared to pay ridiculous prices to scalpers, agents and newspaper advertisers (pre-season games are easier). The closest decent baseball team is the Baltimore Orioles, Oriole Park at Camden Yards, 333 Camden St, Baltimore, MD ☎410/685-9800 – Maryland Rail Commuter Service (MARC; ☎1-800/325-7245) trains from Union Station run right there. The most successful local team is the soccer team DC United, which plays Major League games at RFK Stadium, 2400 E Capitol St SE ☎478-6600 (Stadium-Armory Metro). The downtown MCI Center (see p.201) is home to both the NBA's Washington Wizards and the NHL's Washington Capitals – call TicketMaster for tickets on ☎432 7328 or 1-800/551-7328.

TRAIN DEPARTURES Amtrak ☎1-800/872-7245 or 484-7540; buy tickets either at Union Station (ticket office open daily 5.30am–10.30pm); the Amtrak Travel Center, 1721 K St NW; or New Carrollton (MD), Rockville (MD), Silver Spring (MD) or Alexandria (VA) stations. Maryland Rail Commuter Service (MARC; ☎1-800/325-7245) connects DC to Baltimore – tickets from Union Station (from self-service ticket machines).

TRAVEL AGENCIES American Express, 1150 Connecticut Ave NW ☎457-1300; Council Travel, 3300 M St NW ☎337-6464; Hosteling International Travel, 1108 K St NW ☎783-4943; STA Travel, 2401 Pennsylvania Ave NW ☎887-0912.

TRAVELERS AID SOCIETY Useful help,

Directory

emergency and information desks run by a voluntary, non-profit agency. Main office is at Union Station (☎371-1937; Mon–Sat 9.30am–5.30pm, Sun 12.30–5.30pm); other offices at National Airport (☎703/417-3972; Mon–Fri 9am–9pm, Sat & Sun 9am–6pm); Dulles Airport (☎703/572-8296; Mon–Fri 10am–9pm, Sat & Sun 10am–6pm).

TV STATIONS Channel 4 (WRC/NBC); Channel 5 (WTTG/Fox); Channel 7 (WJLA/ABC); Channel 9 (WUSA/CBS); Channel 26 (WETA/PBS); Channel 50 (WBDC/WB).

WEATHER For five-day city weather fore-

Part 4

Contexts

A History of Washington DC

In the two centuries since Washington DC was founded it's been at the heart of American government, a showcase city embodying the ideals and aspirations of the United States of America. However, it's also a city where people live and work, a fact that's easy to forget among the mighty monuments and memorials. The history below provides a brief exposition of the main themes in the city's development. For more detail on specific matters – from biographies of famous people to histories of buildings – follow the pointers at the end of each section.

Early settlers

The first white settlers to clap eyes on the Potomac River region – site of modern DC – were the pioneers under Captain John Smith of the Virginia Company in 1608. Sponsored by the English King James I, they had established the first successful **English colony** in America the previous year at Jamestown on the coast, to the south, and lost little time exploring their surroundings. Despite early setbacks, and conflict with the local native population, the colonists flourished on the back of a thriving tobacco trade. Virginia, and then Maryland (created as a haven for Catholics in 1632), expanded as English, Irish and Scottish settlers poured into the region, displacing the indigenous population and introducing **slaves** from Africa to work the plantations. Not least of these pioneers was one Captain John

Washington, George's great-grandfather, who in 1656 arrived from Essex in England, and immediately set about establishing a plantation on the river. The Potomac remained an important commercial thoroughfare and vibrant new towns sprang up alongside it: notably Alexandria in Virginia (1749) and Georgetown in Maryland (1751).

Establishment of the capital

In 1775, in the context of increasing hostilities with the British, the colonies – now calling themselves states – drafted the Declaration of Independence. Following the ensuing **American War of Independence** (1775–83), during which Virginia's George Washington served as commander-in-chief of the Continental Army, came proposals for the establishment of a permanent **capital city**. There was no obvious site: the exigencies of war and conflicting political interests in the new republic meant that early meetings of Congress had gathered in several different cities. The Constitutional Convention of 1787, which devised a permanent system of government for the nation, was held in Philadelphia, while George Washington was elected as first President of the United States in New York City in 1789. Extended political wrangling between the mercantile North and agrarian South, both of whom wanted the capital, came to an end when a southern site on the Potomac was chosen (near George Washington's beloved estate at Mount Vernon), with land to be donated by Virginia and

Maryland. Washington hired surveyors Andrew Ellicot and the African-American Benjamin Banneker to conduct the preliminary survey.

Building the city

In 1791, French engineer Pierre Charles L'Enfant began work on a grand plan for the new city, and though he was fired the following year, his blueprint was largely followed by his successors. The first stone of the Executive Mansion (later known as the **White House**) was laid in 1792, construction of the **US Capitol** followed in 1793, and in 1800 Congress and second president John Adams moved from Philadelphia to the nascent city. The following year, Thomas Jefferson became the first president to be inaugurated in Washington DC. The population of 3500 was then little more than that of a village, based largely around Capitol Hill and the Executive Mansion, overseen by a mayor and council. Its numbers were boosted by over three thousand slaves who labored on the new buildings, wharves and streets and lived in the swamp-ridden reaches near the river. Progress was interrupted by the **War of 1812** with England; in 1814, English occupying forces burned the White House, Capitol and other public buildings to the ground. President Madison was forced to relocate to a private house, known as the Octagon, while Congress met in a hastily assembled Brick Capitol until the US Capitol was fully restored in 1819.

Mid-nineteenth-century malaise

Between the War of 1812 and the Civil War, the new capital struggled to make its mark. **The Mall** – L'Enfant's showpiece thoroughfare – remained a muddy swamp, and construction was slow and piecemeal. Foreign ambassadors collected hardship pay while stationed in this marshy outpost, and criticism was heaped upon the place, not least by visitors like Charles Dickens (in the 1840s) and Anthony Trollope (1860s). Despite its detractors, however, the city was slowly beginning to look the part. Pennsylvania Avenue was spruced up (and the Treasury Building added in 1836), and work started on the Washington Monument in 1848. British gentleman scientist and philanthropist James Smithson made a huge bequest in 1829, which led to the foundation of the **Smithsonian Institution**; its first home, the Smithsonian Institution Building (or the "Castle") on the Mall, was completed in 1855.

Though the population increased slowly, throughout the first half of the century it rose above 60,000. The balance of the steadily increasing **black population** shifted, however, as the number of runaway slaves and free blacks (migrants from Southern plantations) increased dramatically. Separate black schools and churches were established as debate intensified between abolitionists and pro-slavery adherents – the so-called Snow Riots (1835) saw intimidation and destruction by white mobs intent on maintaining slavery in the capital.

The Civil War

Following the Confederate attack on Fort Sumter, which finally propelled the country into **civil war**, Abraham Lincoln's call to defend the Union in 1861 brought thousands of volunteer soldiers to Washington, virtually doubling the city's population. Others left to join the Confederate cause; not least Robert E. Lee, who abandoned his home at Arlington and his Union Army post to take command of the Virginian military. Washington DC became the epicenter of the Union effort and the North's main supply depot, surrounded by defensive forts, its public buildings turned over to massive makeshift hospitals. Lincoln determined to continue construction in the capital (symbolically, the Capitol dome was added in 1863), despite fear of imminent attack by Southern forces – the city was never overrun, though several of the bloodiest and most decisive battles (including

Bull Run, Antietam and Gettysburg) were fought within ninety miles of it. As Lincoln's war aims became more focused, the Civil War became a war about **slavery**. This was outlawed in DC in 1862, and in 1863 Lincoln signed the Emancipation Act, freeing all slaves in the rebel states. Thus defeated by the North's superior strength and economic muscle, and legally stripped of the right to operate a system crucial to its economic survival, the Confederate South was effectively vanquished. The war ended in April 1865 with Lee's surrender to General Ulysses S. Grant. Five days later, President Lincoln was assassinated in the capital while attending a play at Ford's Theater.

Reconstruction and expansion

The period after the Civil War was an era of tremendous growth in DC as ex-slaves from the South and returned soldiers settled in the city – within thirty years, the population stood at 300,000, and distinct neighborhoods began to emerge. Black residents now comprised forty percent of the population and enjoyed unprecedented rights and privileges in the aftermath of emancipation. Suffrage was extended to all adult men for local DC elections (1866); black public schools became established and the all-black Howard University was founded (1867); segregation was prohibited; and ex-slave, orator and abolitionist Frederick Douglass was appointed marshal (and, later, recorder of deeds) of DC. In 1867, when Congress granted the District of Columbia territorial status, for the first time the city embarked on a coherent public works program under Alexander "Boss" Shepherd – a short-lived exercise in local democracy that ended in 1874, when control of the debt-ridden city passed back to Congress. Washington's cultural profile, however, went from strength to strength, boosted after the 1876 Philadelphia Centennial Exhibition when the Smithsonian

Institution built **America's first National Museum** (now the Arts and Industries Building) on the Mall to provide a permanent home for the exhibition's artifacts. The Renwick and Corcoran galleries – two of the earliest public art galleries in the country – both opened during this period. The **Washington Monument**, first of the city's grand presidential memorials, was finally completed in 1884, as DC began to reshape itself as a national showpiece. As its stock rose, place-seekers and lobbyists (a term first coined during Grant's presidency) flooded into the city, seeking attachment to the administration of the day; in 1881, just four months after his inauguration, president James Garfield became the second president to be assassinated in Washington, shot by a man denied a civil service post.

The turn of the century

By the turn of the century, Washington had established itself as a thriving, modern capital city with civic and federal buildings to match: in a flurry of construction, the Patent Office, Post Office, Pension Building and fine new premises for the Library of Congress (1897) were erected, while Theodore Roosevelt carried out the first full-scale expansion and renovation of the White House (1901). Meanwhile, LeDroit Park, Adams-Morgan and Woodley Park became fashionable suburbs, Georgetown was formally merged with DC, and the Smithsonian branched out again with the establishment of the National Zoo. In 1901, a committee under Senator James McMillan proposed the development and extension of the city's park system, and later the National Commission of Fine Arts was established to coordinate public improvements and new building design: the country's largest train station, Union Station, was completed in the prevailing Beaux-Arts style in 1908 and, in 1910, height restrictions were imposed on downtown buildings to preserve the cityscape. However, after the high hopes of the Reconstruction years, the city's black population suffered from increasing segregation and loss of civil rights. Housing in black neighborhoods like Foggy Bottom and Georgetown was in poor shape, federal jobs became harder to come by, and the black population actually decreased.

World War I and the Depression

The US entered World War I in 1917, despite President Woodrow Wilson's avowed efforts to remain neutral; after the war, Washington's population increased again as soldiers returned home. The post-war years in DC were as troubled as for the rest of the US. Under Wilson (the only president to remain in the city after his term of office), Prohibition was imposed in an attempt to improve the morality of the nation, and a number of strikes were violently broken. **Racial tension** increased in this uneasy climate, which saw segregation entrenched, the Ku Klux Klan parading at the Washington Monument, and race riots, fanned by demobbed white soldiers, breaking out in the city in 1919. Ironically, segregation also worked to boost the fortunes of DC's black neighborhoods: prevented from socializing elsewhere, blacks made Shaw's U Street famous as the "Black Broadway", nurturing stars such as Duke Ellington. Downtown, the Phillips Collection, America's first modern art museum, opened in 1921, while the building of the Lincoln Memorial (1922) and Freer Gallery (1923) represented the last cultural gasps of the McMillan Commission. The capital, with its government agencies and large federal payroll, was not as hard hit as rural or industrial areas by the **Great Depression**; unemployed marchers from the rest of the country descended on the Capitol to register their distress in 1931 and 1932 (the latter march being dispersed by the army). Franklin D. Roosevelt's

New Deal, and, specifically, the **Works Progress Administration** (WPA), put thousands of jobless men to work – in DC, among other projects, building Federal Triangle and the Supreme Court (1935). If proof were needed that racial prejudice was still institutionalized in America's capital it came in 1939 with the banning by the Daughters of the American Revolution (DAR) of black contralto Marian Anderson from singing in their building – she subsequently appeared in front of a huge, desegregated crowd at the Lincoln Memorial.

World War II to 1968

In 1941 the US entered **World War II**. The third great wartime influx boosted the population again; guards were posted at the White House and Capitol, air defences installed in case of Japanese attack, and the **Pentagon** built in 1943 to accommodate the expanding War Department. The war years also saw the opening of the National Gallery of Art (1941), the nation's finest art gallery, and the completion of the Jefferson Memorial (1943). Following the war, under presidents Truman and Eisenhower, Washington grew as the federal government expanded, and by 1960 the population touched 800,000: the White House was completely overhauled, neighboring Foggy Bottom – once a poor, black area – became the seat of various departments and organizations, and new housing proliferated in suburban Maryland and Virginia.

The war had gone some way to changing racial perceptions in America, as black soldiers had again enlisted in their droves to fight for freedom, and in the post-war years the **Civil Rights** movement began to gain strength. Segregation of public facilities was finally declared illegal by the Supreme Court ruling on *Brown vs. Topeka Board of Education*, and schools in DC were desegregated in 1954. In the southern states, however, the ruling was obeyed only in name, leading to an increasingly politicized, nationwide stream of demonstrations, boycotts, sit-ins and marches in the 1950s and early 1960s. A nascent feeling of widespread hope culminated in John F. Kennedy's close election victory in 1961 – the youngest president ever to take office, and the first Catholic – and was epitomized by Rev Dr Martin Luther King Jr's famous "I have a dream" speech during the March on Washington for Jobs and Freedom at the Lincoln Memorial in August 1963. Just three months later, however, JFK was assassinated in Dallas, and buried in Arlington Cemetery. In 1964 DC citizens voted in a presidential election for the first time, following the 23rd Amendment of 1961, which gave them new electoral rights. The contest was won with a huge majority by Lyndon Johnson, who as vice-president had been governing the country since Kennedy's death.

By the late 1960s protest had broadened beyond the realm of Civil Rights, and demonstrations in Washington were called against poverty (notably the Poor People's March, in 1968) and the war in Vietnam. Discrimination against blacks forced itself explosively back onto the agenda with the assassination of Dr Martin Luther King Jr, in Memphis in 1968. His death sparked off nationwide riots, including the worst in DC's history; Shaw and the old downtown neighbourhoods were devastated. The white flight to the suburbs began in earnest and DC became predominantly black.

The 1970s

The 1970s put politics center stage in DC. In 1970, DC got its first non-voting delegate to the House of Representatives; three years later, the Home Rule Act paved the way for the city's first elected mayor – Walter Washington – for more than a century; and the Watergate scandal of 1974 led to the resignation of a president.

Meanwhile, **divisions within the city** became increasingly stark. Downtown areas continued to reshape themselves – the Kennedy Center opened in 1971, the Hirshorn Museum (1974) and East Wing of the National Gallery of Art (1979) were added to the Mall, the K Street business district in New Downtown thrived, the new Southwest Waterfront acquired character, and arty Dupont Circle became one of the city's trendiest neighborhoods – while Shaw and areas of southeast and northeast Washington slipped further into degradation, with a drug-and-crime problem that earned DC the enduring tag as "Murder Capital" of America. Such contradictions were largely ignored, however, and in 1976, Bicentennial year, the city celebrated by opening its Metrorail system and the National Air and Space Museum – still the top museum attraction in Washington.

The 1980s

Under Ronald Reagan, the nation's economy boomed and busted as taxes (and welfare and aid programs) were cut, and the federal budget deficit soared. In DC, the souped-up economy paved the way for drastic **downtown renovation projects**: the building of the Convention Center (1980) signaled the revitalization of Old Downtown; Pennsylvania Avenue and its buildings – an eyesore for three decades – were restored; and the yuppies moved into Adams-Morgan. Reagan survived an assassination attempt in DC in 1981, but his reputation (and that of his successor, George Bush) were put through the mill by the various Iran-Contra proceedings, whose revelations (in an echo of Watergate) were carried live on TV from hearings in the city. As American military spending increased dramatically, major new patriotic memorials were built to the Vietnam veterans (1982) and US Navy (1987). Culturally, the city went from strength to strength. The Smithsonian expanded its collections on the Mall with the addition of the Sackler Gallery and African Art Museum in 1987; the National Postal Museum opened (1986) and Union Station was restored (1988). City politics took a colorful turn with the successive administrations of Mayor **Marion Barry** (first elected in 1978), whose initial success in attracting investment soon gave way to conflict with Congress that was to become the hallmark of the following decade. The city began its slide into insolvency just as Bill Clinton was elected on promises to turn the economy around and restructure welfare.

The city today

On the surface, it was business as usual in the 1990s in DC – now one of the most touristed cities in America, with almost 20 million visitors a year – as new attractions continued to open: the National Law Enforcement Officers Memorial in 1991, Holocaust Memorial Museum in 1993, Korean War Veterans Memorial and White House Visitor Center in 1995, FDR Memorial and MCI Center in 1997. Behind the scenes, though, Washington lurched into crisis in the first half of the 1990s, as the federal budget deficit spiraled. Amazingly, Marion Barry returned from a drug-related prison sentence to be re-elected as mayor in 1994 – only for Congress to revoke Washington's **home rule charter** a year later. A Congressionally appointed control board has responsibility for the city's affairs until 2003, though mayor Anthony A. Williams, elected in the 1998 mayoral elections, is currently negotiating for full executive power to be returned to the city ahead of schedule.

In many ways, 1998 was a watershed year for Washington DC. Not only did a new realism enter local politics, but – with the gradual unfolding of the **Monica Lewinsky** affair – the city was in the national spotlight in a way not seen since the Watergate hearings of the 1970s. President Clinton survived the impeachment hearings of 1999, but at a cost to both the presidency and the city, whose Beltway obsessions came increasingly to be seen as a world apart from the lives of ordinary Americans.

Indeed, presidents, politicians and scandals may come and go, but affairs in the city itself look as bleak as they have ever done. Underfunding, unemployment and service cuts have left the poorer parts of the city – 75 percent of whose population is now black – in dire straits, while the showpiece downtown areas remain targeted at tourists and big business. Arguments over the budget between the Republican-dominated Congress and President Clinton briefly closed DC's museums and federal offices in 1995, and such conflicts are likely to occur again, whichever party has control of Congress. Meanwhile, **security scares** at the White House and the US Capitol (where two police officers were killed in 1998) have led many to question the traditional open-house policy at federal institutions in DC – there are now heightened security measures in place at most major government buildings. Businesses still find downtown DC an attractive investment, as the massive new building around the MCI Center and Chinatown attests, but on a local level the city is in a parlous state. The total population is at its lowest since the 1930s – down to around 600,000 – as the mostly white well-to-do continue to leave in their droves. Away from the Mall, the museums, galleries and memorials, parts of the city look more like the Third World than capital of the First.

The American System of Government

*In a self-governing republic – good govern-
ment in some places, dubious in others –
three thousand miles wide, eighteen hundred miles long, with fifty separate states
which in many important matters have
almost absolute powers – with two hundred
million people drawn from scores of nations,
what is remarkable is not the conflict
between them but the truce.*

Alistair Cooke, *Letter from America*, 1969

The American system of government derives
squarely from the articles of the **Constitution of
the United States**, thrashed out by the original
thirteen states at the Constitutional Convention in
Philadelphia and signed on September 17, 1787.
Deriving its authority from the essential force of
popular sovereignty – "We the People" – this
gave a federal administration certain designated
powers so that it could both resist attack from
abroad and prevent the fragmentation of the
nascent nation. Two centuries and 27 amendments later, the Constitution's provision of
"checks and balances" on the exercise of power
still provides the basis for the fundamental
democratic stability of a country which, often and
awfully, has looked less than united at times.

The idea was simple enough. The earlier
Articles of Confederation (adopted during the
Revolution) had joined a loose grouping of independent states together in Congress under a
weak central legislature, but by the late 1780s it
was clear that the system lacked internal logic –
with no separation of executive powers,
Congress had to request permission from the
states every step of the way; each state retained
the right to refuse consent (whether for money,
permission for new laws or soldiers) and exercised the power in its own interest. What was
needed, according to Federalists like Alexander
Hamilton and James Madison, was a strong central government buttressed by a supreme
Constitution; the Antifederalists who opposed
them, fearing encroachment upon the sovereignty of the individual states, were appeased by the
promise of the ratification of various amendments (adopted in 1791 in the ten-point Bill of
Rights) which would encompass many of their
demands. What was produced at the
Constitutional Convention was nothing less than
a triumph: eighty percent of the original text of
the Constitution remains unchanged today; only
seventeen more amendments have been added
in the two centuries following the Bill of Rights;
and the United States remains, on paper at least,
one of the world's most enduring democracies.

As a **federal republic**, the country splits its
powers between the government and the fifty
individual states, basically protecting the states
from unnecessary intrusions from an overbearing central government while allowing federal
decisions to be made to benefit (or protect) the
whole country: thus the states can police themselves, make local laws and raise taxes, but they
can't issue currency, conclude foreign treaties, or
maintain armed forces; on the other hand, the
Constitution pledges that the federal government
shall protect each of the states against invasion
or "domestic violence". Moreover, those who
framed the Constitution took great pains to
emphasize that individual states should retain all
powers not specifically removed or curtailed by
the Constitution; reinforced by the 10th
Amendment, this notion remains a fundamental
tenet of American democracy, in which local and
national powers are stringently defined within
the framework of a federal, and not centralized,
republic. Thus each state has a significant
amount of autonomy, while their political structures duplicate the federal system, with their
own legislative chambers, state courts and con-
stitutions.

The **federal government** itself comprises three
distinct arms: the **legislative**, **executive** and **judi-**

> The Constitution and the Bill of Rights are on
> display in the National Archives; see p.185.

ciary. Each operates as a check and balance on the other, and each directly affects individual liberties and not just those of the states.

Article 1 of the Constitution vests all **legislative** powers in a bicameral **Congress** made up of a House of Representatives and a Senate, both of which meet in the US Capitol. When established in the eighteenth century, the House of Representatives was conceived of as the body whose directly elected members would represent the people; the addition of a Senate, or upper house, would not only be a check on the House's power, but also a way of balancing the interests of the smaller states against the larger, since each state in the Senate has an equal vote. Moreover, the separation of roles between House and Senate was institutionalized from the start – representatives and senators are elected at different times, from differently sized constituencies for different lengths of office.

The **House of Representatives** (or simply the "House") has 435 members (this size was fixed in 1929), with states allocated a number of representatives based on their population (which is reassessed, or "reapportioned", every ten years; each state is entitled to at least one representative). Members are elected from defined congressional districts (each containing around 500,000 people), serve for two years and receive around $125,000 per annum (plus the support of up to thirty staff members). The House is the more representative of the two chambers: more frequent elections mean a closer convergence with the general public's mood, while the House always has a significantly higher percentage of women and ethnic minority members than the Senate (though neither remotely reflects the demographic make-up of modern America). Apart from the fifty states thus represented, there are also non-voting delegates in the House, representing the territories of Samoa, Guam and the Virgin Islands, and, since 1973, Washington DC itself (see p.188 for more on Washington's peculiar status within the Union). The chief officer of the House is the **Speaker** (chosen from the ranks of the majority party); both parties also elect a leader in the House, known accordingly as the House Majority or House Minority leader, and a whip (to ensure that party members vote).

The **Senate** comprises two senators from each state. At first, in rather aristocratic fashion, senators were chosen by the individual state legislatures, but in 1913, the 17th Amendment allowed for the direct election of senators by state voters. Senators are elected for six years, with one third being elected every two years; they get paid less than representatives, earning a shade over $100,000 a year. Presiding officer in the Senate is the Vice-President (though on a day-to-day basis the Senate Majority Leader takes the chair); the Vice-President doesn't have a vote unless it's to break a tie.

In Congress, the House and the Senate share certain **responsibilities**, like assessing and collecting taxes, borrowing money, overseeing commerce, minting currency, maintaining the armed forces, declaring war and, crucially, making "all Laws which shall be necessary and proper for carrying into Execution" these matters. But each separate chamber also has its own responsibilities: all revenue-raising (ie tax) bills originate in the House of Representatives, though the Senate can propose changes to such bills; only the Senate offers advice to the President on foreign treaties or on nominations to presidential appointments; and while the House has the sole power of impeachment of the President or other federal officer, the Senate is the body which decides whether to remove the person from office or not.

The House and Senate have separate chambers in the US Capitol, in which their debates take place. In practice, however, the **bills** that Congress debates as a prelude to making laws are generally put together and taken apart ("marked up", in the jargon) in over 250 smaller **standing committees** and **subcommittees** (not to mention *ad hoc* committees and joint committees) which meet in rooms in the Capitol building or in the various relevant House or Senate Office Buildings. The committees are made up of members from both parties, in rough accordance with their overall strength, and are usually chaired by senior members of the controlling party.

If a bill survives this process (and many don't), it is "reported" to the full House for consideration, where **amendments** may be added before the particular bill is voted upon. It can be defeated at this stage, and if it passes it's sent to the Senate, which can also make amendments before returning it to the House. Any differences are resolved by wrangles in a joint House-Senate **conference committee** to produce a final bill, acceptable to a majority in Congress. In addition to the standing committees of Congress, on occasion **select committees** are established to deliberate on special Congressional investigations or matters of national importance – most famously, perhaps, the unravelings of the Watergate affair.

Voting in Congress doesn't always divide upon party lines as it usually does in parliamentary democracies. Although the Speaker and the Rules Committee (which arranges the work of the House) can ensure that the majority party influences the make-up of various committees, the order of debates and nature of proposed amendments, strict party discipline is becoming less important. In the House, members often vote along state lines on particular issues, while specific matters are increasingly agreed and voted upon by members grouped into caucuses (or interest groups) which can cut across party loyalties.

Once a bill passes Congress it goes to the **executive** branch of government for approval, whose head is the **President**, or Chief Executive (on a current salary of $200,000; the Vice-President gets $160,000) presidential powers are defined in Article 2 of the Constitution. The President can either sign the bill, when it becomes law, or veto it, in which case the bill goes back to the chamber where it originated; a two-thirds majority in that house, followed by the same in the other, and Congress can override the President to make the bill law. As well as being Chief Executive, the President is also **Commander-in-Chief** of the armed forces; he can make treaties with foreign powers – provided two-thirds of the Senate agrees – and (again if two-thirds of the Senate are in favor) can appoint ambassadors, Supreme Court judges and other federal officers. Lest the Chief Executive get too bold, though, the Constitution provides **parameters** for presidential power: under the terms of the 22nd Amendment, ratified in 1951, the President (and the Vice-President) is elected to office for four years and may only serve two terms. The amendment was a direct result of the presidency of Franklin Delano Roosevelt, who, determined to preserve his New Deal program and wary of impending war, served an unheard-of four consecutive terms. Moreover, the President is not above the law and can be removed from office by Congress "on impeachment for, and conviction of, treason, bribery, or other high crimes and misdemeanors".

This is rarely attempted. The **impeachment** of President Clinton in 1999 was only the second

such attempt in the country's history (the first was against Andrew Johnson; Nixon resigned before he could be impeached) and its failure was due in part to the nebulous nature of the defined standards of impeachment as laid down by the Constitution: "high crimes and misdemeanors" can essentially mean anything the House wants it to – in the eighteenth century, it probably referred to offenses against the state. However, if the President is removed from office by these means, or dies while in office or resigns, the Vice-President gets the job until the next election; the Speaker of the House is third in line in the order of succession, followed by the Senate Majority Leader and then the Secretaries of the various executive departments in order of precedence. For more on the role of the presidency, see the box on p.154.

This entire system is underpinned by the third arm of government, the **judiciary**, whose highest form is manifested in the **Supreme Court**, established by Article 3 of the Constitution. Right from the outset, the Court was designed as the final protector of the Constitution, its task to uphold its articles and the laws made under it – in effect, to maintain what the Constitution calls "the supreme law of the land". Consequently, every Congress member, and all executive and federal officers, are bound by oath to support and uphold the Constitution since they derive their powers from it. Ultimately, this notion of judicial supremacy boils down to the Constitution being what the Supreme Court says it is: the country has an "inferior" federal court system, in which legal decisions are made, and states are empowered to pass their own laws, but the appointed justices of the Supreme Court have the absolute right to throw out any legislation or legal argument which, in their opinion alone, violates the Constitution. Naturally, for this reason, the executive branch in the shape of each president is keen to appoint sympathetic justices to the Supreme Court bench. This, fortunately for the system, is not as easy or as predictable as it might appear. For more on the make-up of the Supreme Court itself, see p.122.

Over the years, constitutional developments have also taken place outside the Constitution – that is, **informal changes** have been introduced to the system of government through custom or historical event. The Constitution makes no mention of political parties, primary elections or the Congressional committee system for example, though each is now firmly entrenched in the system.

That's the theory of American government. In practice, depending on whom you listen to, the entire structure – carefully crafted over two hundred years ago – is in a state somewhere between bare working order and terminal decline. Political historian David McKay puts his finger on the nub when he says that the "federal system, with its myriad governments and what amounts to fifty-one distinct constitutional structures, is the very essence of fragmentation". The most obvious drawback of the system of "checks and balances" is that it can work both for and against political progress. The Constitution forces the President to work with Congress on policy, and some of the wilder presidential excesses are certainly curtailed by Congressional deliberations. But in an entrenched **two-party system** such as exists today, much depends on the prevailing political climate in either House or Senate: stalemate or ineffective compromise tend to be the natural outcome of the checks and balances system.

Real-world Congressional politics, as opposed to the theoretical marvel of American democracy, can be an unedifying spectacle, involving the often squalid trading of political favors, known as "logrolling". Moreover, the people are increasingly isolated from their elected representatives by the simple fact that candidates now need to be very rich to stand in the first place. Partly in response to the Watergate revelations, the 1974 Federal Election Campaign Act limited party and corporate contributions to a candidate's campaign, though failed to place a limit on the candidate's own contributions – a **campaign** for a prospective House seat can now cost $250,000, up to ten times that for a Senate seat, and countless millions for the presidency. Hardly surprisingly, becoming a member of Congress is now seen as a career move: having invested the time and money, incumbent members are less likely to stand down whatever their personal or political failings and, statistically, more likely to be re-elected than a challenger (who doesn't have the same access to the media and to the reflected political glories of Congress colleagues).

As both Democrats and Republicans scramble to occupy the increasingly crowded middle ground, the **electorate** it seems is becoming more sophisticated in its intentions. A reasonably high (though ultimately futile) protest vote went to third-party candidate Ross Perot in 1992 and again in 1996. Moreover, the voters are both becoming less willing to give a president's party control of both houses of Congress at the same time (viz, the 1996 general election and the 1998 House elections) and to give a president an overwhelming popular mandate. Since Richard Nixon's landslide in 1972, the presidential victor's share of the popular vote has bobbed under and around fifty percent – the only one to buck the trend was Ronald Reagan in 1984 (who gained almost 59% of the vote). In the end, though, the general disdain felt for what happens on Capitol Hill is perhaps best indicated by the fact that the **turnout** for presidential and House elections ranges from only thirty to fifty percent – one of the lowest in any democracy in the world.

Presidents of the USA

In our brief national history we have shot four of our presidents, worried five of them to death, impeached one and hounded another out of office. And when all else fails, we hold an election and assassinate their characters.

P.J. O'Rourke, *Parliament of Whores*, 1991

Name	Party	Date	State of birth
George Washington	–	1789–97	Virginia
John Adams	Federalist	1797–1801	Massachusetts
Thomas Jefferson	Democratic-Republican	1801–09	Virginia
James Madison	Democratic-Republican	1809–17	Virginia
James Monroe	Democratic-Republican	1817–25	Virginia
John Quincy Adams	Democratic-Republican	1825–29	Massachusetts
Andrew Jackson	Democrat	1829–37	South Carolina
Martin Van Buren	Democrat	1837–41	New York
William H. Harrison	Whig	1841 (died in office)	Virginia
John Tyler	Whig	1841–45	Virginia
James Polk	Democrat	1845–49	North Carolina
Zachary Taylor	Whig	1849–50 (died in office)	Virginia
Millard Fillmore	Whig	1850–53	New York
Franklin Pierce	Democrat	1853–57	New Hampshire
James Buchanan	Democrat	1857–61	Pennsylvania
Abraham Lincoln	Republican	1861–65 (assassinated)	Kentucky
Andrew Johnson	Union	1865–69	North Carolina
Ulysses S. Grant	Republican	1869–77	Ohio
Rutherford B. Hayes	Republican	1877–81	Ohio
James A. Garfield	Republican	1881 (assassinated)	Ohio
Chester A. Arthur	Republican	1881–85	Vermont
Grover Cleveland	Democrat	1885–89	New Jersey
Benjamin Harrison	Republican	1889–93	Ohio
Grover Cleveland	Democrat	1893–97	New Jersey
William McKinley	Republican	1897–1901	Ohio
Theodore Roosevelt	Republican	1901–09	New York
William H. Taft	Republican	1909–13	Ohio
Woodrow Wilson	Democrat	1913–21	Virginia
Warren G. Harding	Republican	1921–23 (died in office)	Ohio
Calvin Coolidge	Republican	1923–29	Vermont
Herbert Hoover	Republican	1929–33	Iowa
Franklin D. Roosevelt	Democrat	1933–45 (died in office)	New York
Harry S. Truman	Democrat	1945–53	Missouri
Dwight D. Eisenhower	Republican	1953–61	Texas
John F. Kennedy	Democrat	1961–63 (assassinated)	Massachusetts
Lyndon B. Johnson	Democrat	1963–69	Texas
Richard M. Nixon	Republican	1969–74 (resigned)	California
Gerald Ford	Republican	1974–77	Nebraska
James (Jimmy) Carter	Democrat	1977–81	Georgia
Ronald Reagan	Republican	1981–89	Illinois
George Bush	Republican	1989–93	Massachusetts
William (Bill) Clinton	Democrat	1993–	Arkansas

Books

There are plenty of books which touch upon the history, politics and personalities of Washington DC; the problem is in getting an overall picture of the city. There's no one single straightforward and up-to-date history of DC, while visitors through the ages have tended only to include their observations of the capital as part of wider works about America. However, every book on American history contains at least a few pages about the founding of the capital city; Civil War treatises highlight DC as Lincoln's headquarters (and place of assassination), while presidential autobiographies and biographies, from those of George Washington onwards, necessarily recount the daily experience of political and social life in the capital.

In this chapter we've picked out some of the better, and more widely available, books about Washington DC, including novels set in the city. Many are available in good bookshops everywhere, and most in good **bookstores** in DC itself (see p.318 for a list) – where you'll also find local guides to ethnic restaurants, political trivia, cycling in the city, what to do with kids, and the like. Every major museum, gallery and attraction in DC sells related books, too, and these are a good first stop if you're looking for something arcane or specific – say a *History of Cats in the White House* or *101 Things to do with a Beltway Journalist*. The selection in the National Museum of American History is perhaps the finest, while the Smithsonian Institution itself produces a wide range of titles on a variety of city-related topics. Finally, the White House Historical Association (740 Jackson Place, DC 20560 ☎202/737-8292) publishes a series of informative accounts of the

White House, its contents and historical occupants.

In the list below, the US publisher is listed first, followed by the UK publisher. Where the book is published by the same company in both countries, the name of the company appears just once, and where books are published in only one of these countries, UK or US follows the publisher's name.

History

David Brinkley, *Washington Goes to War* (Ballantine/Deutsch). Acclaimed account of the capital during World War II under FDR, charting its emergence onto the international stage.

Francine Curro Cary, *Urban Odyssey: A Multicultural History of Washington DC* (Smithsonian Institution Press, US). A readable historical account of settlement (and racial discrimination) in the city.

Alistair Cooke. Over sixty years as a correspondent has left Cooke with a wealth of American stories, personal histories and snapshots of cities, times and crises that adorn everything he writes and broadcasts. Although the capital appears as a bit player in much of his work, its presidents, politicians and people provide substance.

David Lewis, *District of Columbia: A History* (Norton, US). Useful – if now rather dated (1976) – history of the District.

Lloyd Lewis, *The Assassination of Lincoln: History and Myth* (University of Nebraska Press). Lyrical, minute-by-minute account of the city's most notorious assassination and its aftermath, first published in 1929 (as *Myths After Lincoln*) and still entertaining.

Anthony S. Pitch, *The Burning of Washington: The British Invasion of 1814* (Naval Institute Press, US). Recreation of the dramatic events of the summer of 1814 as the British set fire to the young capital and Francis Scott Key was inspired to write the "Star-Spangled Banner".

Washington Post, *Redskins: A History of Washington's Team* (Washington Post Books, US). An illustrated history of DC's favorite team.

Politics and people

Anonymous, *Primary Colors* (Warner/Random House). Highly readable, barely disguised account of a presidential primary campaign by young, charismatic, calculating, philandering, Southern governor, Jack Stanton. Published amid great controversy in 1996, the book threw into the public domain the more reprehensible antics of press and politicians – its author was eventually unmasked as journalist and Washington insider Joe Klein.

Carl Bernstein and Bob Woodward, *All the President's Men* (Simon & Schuster, US); *The Final Days* (Touchstone, US). America's most famous journalistic sleuths tell the gripping story of the unraveling of the Nixon presidency. *All the President's Men* is a great book, later made into a great film; *The Final Days* saw the duo wrapping up the loose ends. Although both have written investigative books since, none has matched these early classics.

Paul F. Boller, *Presidential Anecdotes; Presidential Campaigns; Presidential Wives; Congressional Anecdotes* (all OUP). Amusing, inconsequential political factoids – who did what, where and when, and with whom.

Ben Bradlee, *A Good Life* (Simon & Schuster). The autobiography of the executive editor of the *Washington Post* between 1968 and 1991. Watergate made him famous and he still lives in DC, offering pertinent political comment.

Nigel Cawthorne, *Sex Lives of the Presidents* (St Martin's/Prion). Cawthorne turns his scurrilous eye to the horizontal pleasures of the world's most powerful men.

Frederick Douglass, *The Life and Times of Frederick Douglass* (Carol/Wordsworth). The third volume (1881) of statesman, orator and ex-slave Frederick Douglass's autobiography sees him finally living in DC as US marshal and recorder of deeds (although the first volume – *Narrative of the Life of Frederick Douglass: An American Slave*, 1845 [Penguin] – covering part of Douglass's early life before he arrived in Washington, is actually more gripping).

Katherine Graham, *Personal History* (Vintage/Phoenix). Acclaimed autobiography of Georgetown society hostess and *Washington Post* owner at the time of Watergate.

Wesley O. Hagood, *Presidential Sex: From the Founding Fathers to Bill Clinton* (Citadel Press). Updated to take Clinton's last misdemeanors into account, Hagood tells you more than you ever wanted to know about illicit presidential nookie.

David McKay, *Politics and Power in the USA* (Penguin). Best general introduction to who does what, why and when in the United States government.

Andrew Morton, *Monica's Story* (St Martin's Press). Bandwagon-climbing biography of DC's most famous intern, telling the warts 'n' all story of Lewinsky and the Pres – by Princess Diana's confidante.

P.J. O'Rourke, *Parliament of Whores* (Random House/Picador). All O'Rourke's demented political insights and raving rightwing prejudices brought together in a scabrous critique of the American political system as practiced in Washington DC. It's also very, very funny.

Kenneth W. Starr, *The Starr Report* (various). Within days of publication, a dozen publishers rushed out various versions of the now infamous Starr Report of 1998 – the findings of independent counsel Ken Starr on Clinton and the Lewinsky affair. Required reading for anyone fascinated by the entire sordid spectacle.

George Stephanopoulos, *All Too Human: A Political Education* (Little, Brown). Political memoir

---

Presidential biographies

Any good bookstore can provide a massive range of presidential biographies and memoirs. It's a growth industry – more books have been written about Bill Clinton than about all the other US presidents put together – which means it's difficult to separate the wheat from the chaff. Well-received biographies have included David Herbert Donald's *Lincoln* (Simon & Schuster/Pimlico), Frank Friedel's *Franklin D. Roosevelt* (Little, Brown) – Theodore Roosevelt, naturally, wrote his own autobiography – Roy Jenkins' *Truman* (Harper Collins/Pan McMillan), David McCullough's Pulitzer-winning *Truman* (Simon & Schuster), Jonathan Aitken's *Nixon: A Life* (Regnery/Wiedenfeld & Nicholson) and Martin Walker's *Clinton: the President We Deserve* (Crown/Vintage).

of arch presidential advisor (under Clinton) and master of spin Stephanopoulos, who knows all there is to know about what makes DC, the White House and the presidency tick.

Hunter S. Thompson. Gonzo's at his best taking sideswipes at corrupt politicians full of cant, and any of his books or collected essays feature a Washington villain or twenty – shot down in flames by a man for whom politics isn't the only drug.

Guides

Alzina Stone Dale, *Mystery Reader's Walking Guide: DC* (Passport, US). Guided walks around the city in the company of the prose of crime and mystery writers.

Claudia D. and George W. Kousoulas, *Contemporary Architecture in Washington DC* (Preservation Press, US). Concentrates on the buildings of contemporary DC which, though no Chicago or New York, has enough to interest architecture buffs.

Christopher Weeks, *AIA Guide to the Architecture of Washington DC* (John Hopkins University Press). Authoritative illustrated guide to the architecture of the city, covering buildings from every period since its founding.

Visitors to DC

David Cutler, *Literary Washington* (Madison, US). The words and wisdom of celebrated writers, past and present, who have visited, worked and lived in DC.

Charles Dickens, *American Notes* (Penguin). One of the most quoted of all visitors, Dickens came in the early 1840s, when it was still, famously, a "City of Magnificent Intentions". Highly enjoyable satirical banter from a British writer at ease with America.

Jan Morris, *Destinations* (OUP). Typically dry observations of Washington high and low life, one of a series of pieces (about international cities) first written in the early 1980s for *Rolling Stone* magazine.

Anthony Trollope, *North America* (Da Capo/Alan Sutton). Two-volume account of Trollope's visit to the US in the early 1860s. Picking up where his pioneering mother, Fanny, had left off in her contentious *Domestic Manners of the Americans* (1832) (Da Capo/Alan Sutton), Trollope lays about him with ire and verve – in Volume II, Capitol building, White House, DC's streets and hotels, the Washington Monument and the Smithsonian all come in for undiluted carping and moaning. Great stuff.

DC in fiction

Henry Adams, *Democracy* (Penguin). A story of electioneering and intrigue set in 1870s DC, written (anonymously) by the historian grandson of John Quincy Adams.

Jeffrey Archer, *Shall We Tell the President?* (Pocket Books/Harper Collins); *The Eleventh Commandment* (Harper Collins). The "master storyteller" serves up the usual offerings – risible characterization, feeble plot development and leaden prose wrapped around tales of assassination plots and Cold War shenanigans set in DC.

William Peter Blatty, *The Exorcist* (Harper Collins/Corgi). Blatty's seminal horror story about

---

Watergate

If Washington has one domestic scandal it can call its own it's **Watergate** (see p.170), whose various aspects have been exhaustively covered since Bernstein and Woodward first set the ball rolling with *All the President's Men*. For the full story you could consult Fred Emery's *Watergate: The Corruption of American Politics and the Fall of Richard Nixon* (Simon & Schuster/Pimlico) or a host of other witnesses, not least Nixon's own *Memoirs* (Simon & Schuster, US), the *Haldeman Diaries: Inside the Nixon White House* (Berkley/Putnam), John Dean's *Blind Ambition* (Simon & Schuster, US) and *Lost Honor* (Stratford Press, US), John Erlichman's *Witness to Power* (Simon & Schuster, US) and Gordon Liddy's *Will: The Autobiography of G. Gordon Liddy* (St Martin's Press) – first-hand (if not completely reliable) testimony from those who were there at the time. Virtually everyone else involved has written about the affair at some time or other, too, from Watergate burglar James McCord to judge John Sirica, while *Nixon: An Oliver Stone Film* (Hyperion/Bloomsbury) presents the original screenplay of said movie alongside transcripts of taped Watergate conversations, previously classified memos and essays by key protagonists.

the possession of a teenage girl, written in 1971, was set around Georgetown University and made into the scariest film ever produced.

Tom Clancy. One of the best of the blockbuster thriller writers, Clancy weaves DC scenes (or at least the White House, Capitol building, FBI and CIA HQ at Langley in Virginia) into nearly every tale of spook and terrorist intrigue – most explosively in *Debt of Honor* (Berkeley/Harper Collins) in which the President, Cabinet and most of Congress perish in an attack on the US Capitol.

Richard Timothy Conroy, *The India Exhibition; Mr Smithson's Bones; Old Ways in the New World* (all St Martin's Press, US). Murder, mystery and labyrinthine goings-on in a series of engaging thrillers set in the Smithsonian Institution.

Allen Drury, *Advise and Consent* (Avon, US). Blackmail and slippery politics in Washington's upper echelons in the late 1950s; the novel was turned into a fine film by Otto Preminger starring Henry Fonda.

John Grisham. DC pops up in most of Grisham's work, notably in *The Pelican Brief* (Dell/Arrow), a renowned legal whodunnit starting with the assassination of two Supreme Court judges and delving into dodgy politics and murky land deals; and in *The Street Lawyer* (Dell/Arrow), a rather good exposé of city homelessness and poverty.

David Ignatius, *A Firing Offense* (Ivy Books). Former *Post* journalist puts his newspaper experience to good use in an intelligent espionage thriller which jumps from DC locations to France and China.

Ward Just, *Echo House* (Mariner Books, US). Elegiac, epic novel of a DC political dynasty, with much to say about the nature of power in the city.

Charles McCarry, *Shelley's Heart* (Ivy Books). Page-turning thriller detailing stolen elections, secret societies and other political jiggery-pokery, notable for its in-depth, highly acute and deeply resonant account of the impeachment process. *Lucky Bastard* (Random House) is the latest of his DC political intrigues.

James Patterson, *Along Came A Spider; Kiss The Girls; Cat and Mouse* (all Warner). High-profile thriller writer whose dreadful prose style and imbecilic characterization do nothing to blunt his success. These three books all feature black DC homicide detective Alex Cross.

William D. Pease, *Playing the Dozens; The Monkey's First; The Rage of Innocence* (all Penguin). Former Assistant US Attorney in DC turned legal-police-thriller writer whose books range across all the usual city locations and power sites.

George P. Pelecanos. DC's hippest chronicler, Pelecanos writes pointedly and beautifully about the city in a series of great thrillers, spanning the years and ethnic divide. *A Firing Offense* (his first), *Nick's Trip*, and *Down By The River Where the Dead Men Go* (all Serpent's Tail) introduce feisty private eye Nick Stefanos; *King Suckerman* (Dell) is a tour-de-force of 70s drugs and racial tension; while *The Sweet Forever* (Little, Brown) updates Suckerman's characters to coke-riddled 1980s DC.

Phyllis Richman, *The Butter Did It* (Harper Collins). The *Washington Post's* longtime restaurant critic turns her hand to mystery, introducing Chas Wheatley, the – surprise, surprise – "Washington Examiner" restaurant reviewer turned detective.

Elliott Roosevelt, *Murder in the . . .* (St Martin's Press & Avon/Severn House). White House murder tales (with the dark deed committed in the Blue Room, West Wing, etc) by FDR's son, with the highly improbable First Lady-turned-sleuth Eleanor riding to the rescue every time.

Margaret Truman, *Murder . . .* (Fawcett/Severn House). Harry's daughter churns out wooden murder-mystery stories set in various neighborhoods and buildings of DC, from Georgetown to the National Cathedral.

Gore Vidal, *Burr; Lincoln; 1876; Empire; Washington DC* (all Ballantine/Abacus). DC's – and America's – most potent, cynical chronicler sustains a terrific burst of form in five hugely enjoyable novels tracing the history of the US from the Revolution to modern times and relying heavily on Washington set-piece scenes. The moving epic *Lincoln* is the real tour-de-force. Vidal's other books include *Palimpsest* (Abacus), a terrific memoir chronicling his life and loves, themes which are developed in his latest work of fiction, *The Smithsonian Institution* (Little, Brown).

Poetry

Walt Whitman, *Leaves of Grass* (OUP/Everyman). The first edition of *Leaves of Grass* appeared in 1855, and Whitman added sections to it for the rest of his life. His war poems, *Drum-Taps* (1865), were directly influenced by his work in DC's Civil War hospitals; later, *Memories of President Lincoln* were added after the assassination – including the famous and affecting *O Captain! My Captain!.*

Index

the perfect getaway vehicle

low-price holiday car rental.

rent a car from holiday autos and you'll give yourself real freedom to explore your holiday destination. with great-value, fully-inclusive rates in over 4,000 locations worldwide, wherever you're escaping to, we're there to make sure you get excellent prices and superb service.

what's more, you can book now with complete confidence. our £5 undercut* ensures that you are guaranteed the best value for money in holiday destinations right around the globe.

drive away with a great deal, call holiday autos now on **0990 300 400** and quote ref RG.

holiday autos miles ahead

*in the unlikely event that you should see a cheaper like for like pre-paid rental rate offered by any other independent uk car rental company before or after booking but prior to departure, holiday autos will undercut that price by a full £5. we truly believe we cannot be beaten on price.

THE METRORAIL SYSTEM

Red Line
Wheaton / Shady Grove

Orange Line
New Carrollton / Vienna

Blue Line
Addison Road / Van Dorn Street

Yellow Line
Mt Vernon Sq-UDC / Huntington

Green Line
U Street-Cardozo / Anacostia
Greenbelt / Fort Totten

Section under construction

MARC Commuter Rail Services

For Metro information
call ☎202/637-7000

N

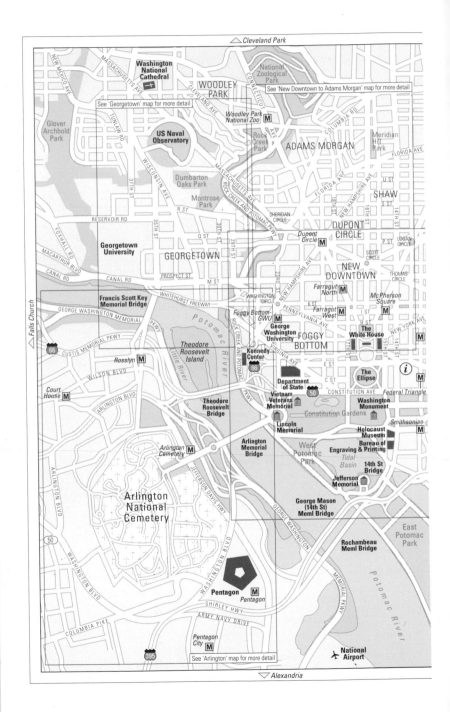

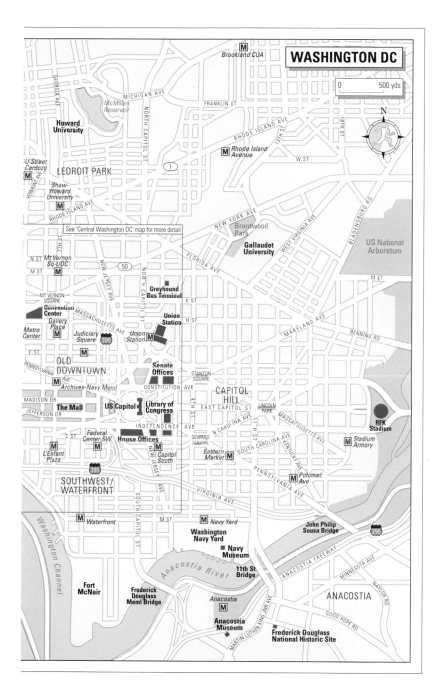

WASHINGTON DC

Brookland CUA

0   500 yds

N

MICHIGAN AVE

FRANKLIN ST

McMillen
Reservoir

RHODE ISLAND AVE

Howard
University

Rhode Island
Avenue

W ST

U Street
Cardozo

LEDROIT PARK

Shaw-
Howard
University

RHODE ISLAND AVE

See 'Central Washington DC' map for more detail

NEW YORK AVE

Brentwood
Park

Gallaudet
University

US National
Arboretum

N ST Mt Vernon
Sq-UDC

M ST

FLORIDA AVE

WEST VIRGINIA AVE

BLADENSBURG RD

M ST

MT VERNON
SQUARE

Greyhound
Bus Terminal

K ST

MARYLAND AVE

BENNING RD

Convention
Center

Gallery
Place

Union
Station

H ST

Metro
Center

Judiciary
Square

Union
Station

F ST

OLD
DOWNTOWN

Senate
Offices

STANTON
SQUARE

CAPITOL
HILL

PENNSYLVANIA

Archives-Navy Meml

CONSTITUTION   AVE

LINCOLN
PARK

RFK
Stadium

MADISON DR

The Mall

US Capitol

Library of
Congress

EAST CAPITOL ST

Stadium
Armory

JEFFERSON DR

INDEPENDENCE   AVE

SEWARD
SQUARE

L'Enfant
Plaza

Federal
Center SW

House Offices

Capitol
South

Eastern
Market

SOUTH CAROLINA AVE

KENTUCKY AVE

Potomac
Ave

SOUTHWEST/
WATERFRONT

VIRGINIA AVE

PENNSYLVANIA AVE

Waterfront

M ST

Navy Yard

John Philip
Sousa Bridge

Washington
Navy Yard

MINNESOTA AVE

Fort
McNair

Navy
Museum

Frederick
Douglass
Meml Bridge

11th St
Bridge

ANACOSTIA FREEWAY

NAYLOR RD

Anacostia River

Anacostia

ANACOSTIA

GOOD HOPE RD

Anacostia
Museum

Frederick Douglass
National Historic Site

MARTIN LUTHER KING JNR AVE

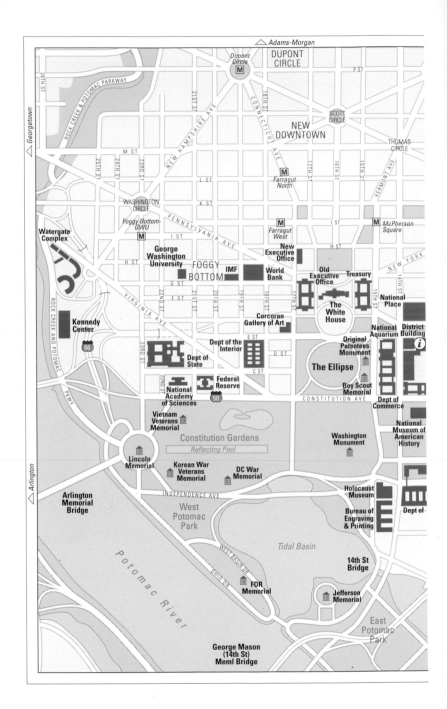

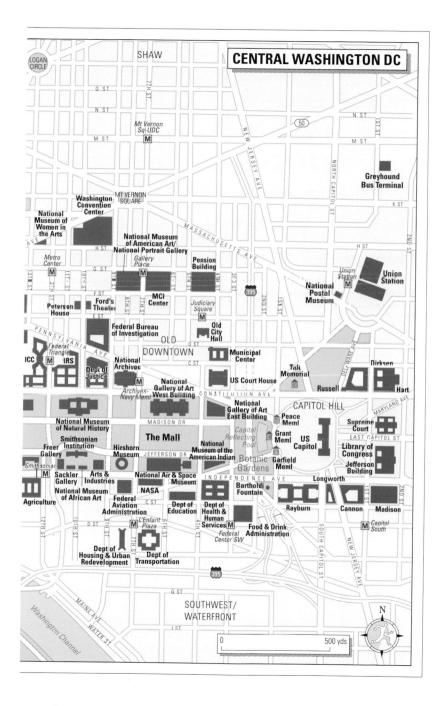

CENTRAL WASHINGTON DC

LOGAN CIRCLE

SHAW

Q ST
N ST
M ST
7TH ST

Mt Vernon Sq-UDC
M

N ST
M ST
1ST ST

50

NORTH CAPITOL ST

Greyhound Bus Terminal

K ST

MT VERNON SQUARE

Washington Convention Center

National Museum of Women in the Arts

National Museum of American Art/ National Portrait Gallery

MASSACHUSETTS AVE

Pension Building

Metro Center
M

Gallery Place
M

H ST

2ND ST

Union Station
M

Union Station

National Postal Museum

G ST
E ST

MCI Center

Judiciary Square
M

Ford's Theater

Peterson House

E ST

Federal Bureau of Investigation

OLD DOWNTOWN

Old City Hall

D ST

Municipal Center

PENNSYLVANIA AVE

Federal Triangle

ICC
M
IRS

Dept of Justice

National Archives

C ST

US Court House

Taft Memorial

DELAWARE AVE

Dirksen

Russell

Hart

Archives-Navy Meml
M

National Gallery of Art West Building

CONSTITUTION AVE

National Gallery of Art East Building

Peace Meml

CAPITOL HILL

MARYLAND AVE

Supreme Court

National Museum of Natural History

MADISON DR

Grant Meml

EAST CAPITOL ST

Smithsonian Institution

The Mall

Hirshorn Museum

JEFFERSON DR

National Museum of the American Indian

Capitol Reflecting Pool

US Capitol

Library of Congress

Jefferson Building

Freer Gallery

Smithsonian
M

Sackler Gallery

Arts & Industries

National Museum of African Art

National Air & Space Museum

INDEPENDENCE AVE

Botanic Gardens

Garfield Meml

Longworth

Agriculture

NASA

Federal Aviation Administration

Dept of Education

Dept of Health & Human Services
M

Bartholdi Fountain

Rayburn

Cannon

Madison

C ST

Food & Drink Administration

Capitol South
M

L'Enfant Plaza
M

Federal Center SW

Dept of Housing & Urban Redevelopment

Dept of Transportation

D ST

SOUTH CAPITOL ST

NEW JERSEY AVE

12TH ST
10TH ST
9TH ST
7TH ST
4TH ST

395

G ST

SOUTHWEST/ WATERFRONT

I ST

MAINE AVE

WATER ST

Washington Channel

0   500 yds

N

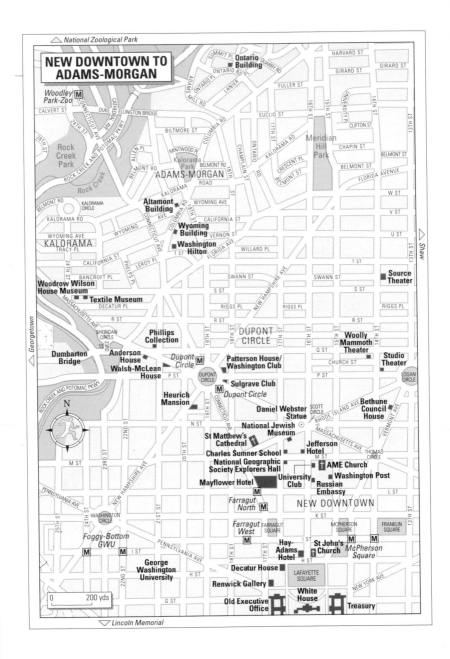

△ National Zoological Park

NEW DOWNTOWN TO ADAMS-MORGAN

HARVARD ST

GIRARD ST GIRARD ST

SUMMIT PL
Ontario
Building
ONTARIO RD PL QUARRY RD

Woodley
Park-Zoo Ⓜ

CALVERT ST

DUKE ELLINGTON BRIDGE

FULLER ST

LANIER

ADAMS MILL RD

ONTARIO RD

UNIVERSITY PL

CLIFTON ST

13TH ST

14TH ST

15TH ST

16TH ST

EUCLID ST

CHAPIN ST

28TH ST

Rock
Creek
Park

ROCK CREEK AND POTOMAC PKWY

BILTMORE ST

COLUMBIA RD

MINTWOOD PL

BELMONT RD

KALORAMA
Park

Kalorama
Park

CHAMPLAIN ST

KALORAMA RD

Meridian
Hill
Park

CHAPIN ST

BELMONT ST

BELMONT ST

Rock Creek

ADAMS-MORGAN

ROAD

KALORAMA

BELMONT RD

FLORIDA AVENUE

W ST

KALORAMA
CIRCLE

Altamont
Building

WYOMING AVE

CALIFORNIA ST

V ST

KALORAMA RD

CONNECTICUT AVE

Wyoming
Building

VERNON ST

U ST

WYOMING AVE

WYOMING

Washington
Hilton

FLORIDA AVE

WILLARD PL

13TH ST

△ Shaw

KALORAMA

TRACY PL

CALIFORNIA ST

T ST

T ST

24TH ST

BANCROFT PL

SWANN ST

SWANN ST

Source
Theater

Woodrow Wilson
House Museum

MASSACHUSETTS AVE

Textile Museum

DECATUR PL

S ST

NEW HAMPSHIRE AVE

S ST

RIGGS PL

RIGGS PL

RIGGS PL

R ST

R ST

R ST

Phillips
Collection

19TH ST

18TH ST

DUPONT
CIRCLE

17TH ST

16TH ST

15TH ST

Woolly
Mammoth
Theater

14TH ST

Dumbarton
Bridge

Anderson
House

Dupont
Circle Ⓜ

Patterson House/
Washington Club

Q ST

CHURCH ST

Studio
Theater

ROCK CREEK AND POTOMAC PKWY

Walsh-McLean
House

P ST

DUPONT
CIRCLE

P ST

LOGAN
CIRCLE

Heurich
Mansion

Sulgrave Club

Dupont Circle

RHODE ISLAND AVE

Bethune
Council
House

VERMONT AVE

Daniel Webster
Statue

SCOTT
CIRCLE

◁ Georgetown

22ND ST

N

N ST

National Jewish
Museum

MASSACHUSETTS AVE

21ST ST

St Matthew's
Cathedral

Jefferson
Hotel

THOMAS
CIRCLE

M ST

M ST

Charles Sumner School

23RD ST

20TH ST

National Geographic
Society Explorers Hall

University
Club

AME Church

Washington Post

Mayflower Hotel

Russian
Embassy

L ST

PENNSYLVANIA AVE

Farragut
North Ⓜ

NEW DOWNTOWN

WASHINGTON
CIRCLE

Farragut
West Ⓜ

FARRAGUT
SQUARE

K ST

MCPHERSON
SQUARE

FRANKLIN
SQUARE

13TH ST

Foggy-Bottom
GWU Ⓜ

Ⓜ

PENNSYLVANIA AVE

Ⓜ I ST

21ST ST

18TH ST

17TH ST

Hay-
Adams
Hotel

St John's
Church

Ⓜ

Ⓜ

McPherson
Square

George
Washington
University

Decatur House

LAFAYETTE
SQUARE

NEW YORK AVE

22ND ST

H ST

Renwick Gallery

White
House

0   200 yds

G ST

Old Executive
Office

Treasury

▽ Lincoln Memorial